SURVEYING THE USER EXPERIENCE

Design and Analysis of Surveys for UX and Customer Research

Jeff Sauro and James R. Lewis

Measuring U
PRESS

CONTENTS

DEDICATION.. XVIII

ACKNOWLEDGMENTS.. XVIII

INTRODUCTION.. XIX

PART I: PLANNING THE SURVEY

CHAPTER I: Introduction to Survey Design 2

CENSUS...3
POLL 3
SURVEY 4
QUESTIONNAIRE..4
SURVEYS IN UX RESEARCH 6
UX QUESTIONNAIRES 7
   Standardization 8
   History of Standardized UX Questionnaires...........................9
     Assessing System Usability.. 10
WHEN A SURVEY IS THE BETTER METHOD 11
PLANNING YOUR SURVEY... 12
CHAPTER SUMMARY 14

CHAPTER 2: Biases & Errors in Survey Design 16

FOUR CORE BIASES IN SURVEY DESIGN 17
   I. Representative Bias... 17
   2. Sponsorship Bias... 18
   3. Social Desirability & Prestige 18
   4. Asking Sensitive Demographic Questions 19
BIAS DOESN'T MEAN ABANDON 20
FOUR TYPES OF POTENTIAL SURVEY ERRORS 20
   I. Coverage Errors.. 20
   2. Sampling Error 22

3. Nonresponse Error...23

4. Measurement Error..24

CHAPTER SUMMARY 25

CHAPTER 3: Defining & Finding Participants 26

DEFINING TARGET PARTICIPANTS 26

Concepts...27

Constructs...27

Defining Subgroups 28

WHERE TO FIND PARTICIPANTS 29

Online Panel Sources...29

1. Participants Belong to Multiple Panels 30

2. Multiple Panel Membership Affects Attitudes..................................30

3. The Length of Panel Membership Also Has an Effect.....................30

4. The Average Online Study Takes Longer..30

5. Population Estimates Can Vary 30

6. UX Metrics Can Vary Too, but Not as Much as Expected.............31

7. Changing Panels Changes Estimates...31

8. Probability Panels Are Probably Better...31

9. Be Wary of Panel Quality 31

Access Existing Customers and Prospects..32

Direct Email 32

Website Intercepts 32

HOW TO INCREASE SURVEY PARTICIPATION RATES....................33

Five Approaches for Increasing Participation 33

1. Provide an Incentive...to a Point...34

2. Appeal to Intrinsic Motivation 34

3. Gamify..34

4. Provide Personalized Feedback 35

5. Share the Findings...35

Some Guidance When Paying Participants 35

1. Incentives Help Response Rates 35

2. Money Is Usually Better Than Gifts...35

3. Paying Can Be Painful 36

4. Lotteries and Raffles May Be Cheaper and Easier...........................36

5. Lotteries/Sweepstakes Are Easier but Probably Not as Effective.................36

6. Lotteries Have Legal Issues...36

7. Consider Other Incentives 36

8. Find the Right Amount 37

9. Budget 37

10. More Legal Issues 37

11. Appeal to the Interest of Your Participants 38

12. Money May Also Hurt Response Rates 38

13. Don't Coerce 38

CHAPTER SUMMARY 38

CHAPTER 4: Sample Strategies 41

PROBABILITY SAMPLING 42

Random Sampling 42

Simple Random Sampling 42

Stratified Random Sampling 42

Proportional Sampling by External Benchmarks 43

NONPROBABILITY SAMPLING 44

Convenience Sampling 44

Snowball Sampling 44

RESEARCH SAMPLING IN PRACTICE 46

Some Level of Unrepresentativeness Is Common 47

Disproportionate Samples Happen 47

Sometimes Controlling Variability is More Important than
Proportional Matching 49

CHAPTER SUMMARY 50

PART 2: WRITING SURVEY QUESTIONS

CHAPTER 5: Survey Question Anatomy and Types 52

THE SIX COMPONENTS OF A SURVEY QUESTION 52

1. Introduction 53

2. Information About the Topic or Definitions 53

3. Instructions 54

4. Opinions of Others 54

5. Requests for an Answer 55

6. Response Options 55

Examples 56

FOUR TYPES OF SURVEY QUESTIONS 57

1. Attributes 58

2. Behaviors (Reported) 59

3. Abilities 60

4. Thoughts, Sentiments, and Judgments 61

CHAPTER SUMMARY 62

CHAPTER 6: How to Write a Survey Question.................................... 64

START WITH THE CONCEPT 64

SEE WHETHER A QUESTION ALREADY EXISTS.............................. 65

DETERMINE THE TYPE OF QUESTION 66

BRAINSTORM IDEAS... 67

INTERVIEW THE TARGET RESPONDENTS 67

CRAFT THE QUESTION 67

SELECT THE RESPONSE OPTIONS 68

CHAPTER SUMMARY 70

CHAPTER 7: Why People Misinterpret Survey Questions 71

SEVEN REASONS WHY SURVEYS ARE MISUNDERSTOOD........................... 71

1. Grammatical and Lexical Ambiguity 71

2. Excessive Complexity... 72

3. Faulty Presuppositions.. 73

4. Vague Concepts.. 74

5. Vague Quantifiers... 75

6. Unfamiliar Terms.. 76

7. False Inferences.. 76

WORDS TO WATCH FOR.. 76

Three Absolutes: *Ever, Always,* and *Never*.................................... 77

Four Modal Verbs: *Could, Should, Might,* and *Would*.................... 78

You 78

Our.. 79

CHAPTER SUMMARY 79

CHAPTER 8: How to Make Survey Questions Clearer 81

KEEP QUESTIONS SHORT 81

USE SIMPLE LANGUAGE 82

PREFER COMMON WORDS... 83

USE THE RESPONDENTS' VOCABULARY... 84

MINIMIZE THE USE OF ACRONYMS 84

AVOID COMPLICATED SYNTAX.. 84

Adjunct Wh-Questions 84

Embedded Clauses 85
Left-Embedded Syntax 85
AVOID PASSIVE VOICE 86
When to Use Active Voice 86
When to Use Passive Voice 86
What About Survey Questions? 86
CHAPTER SUMMARY 87

CHAPTER 9: Why People Forget & How to Improve Recall 89
PEOPLE FORGET 89
1. Retrieval Failure 90
2. Reconstruction Errors 91
3. Memory Distortion 91
4. Mismatches Between Researcher and Respondent Interpretation of Terms 92
HOW TO IMPROVE PARTICIPANT RECALL 92
1. Shorten the Reference Period 92
2. Use Personal Landmarks or Life Events 93
3. Thinking Backward May Help 94
4. Decompose the Question 94
5. Use Introductions to Questions 95
6. Give More Time 95
CHAPTER SUMMARY 95

PART 3: SURVEY RESPONSES

CHAPTER 10: Selecting the Right Response Options 98
DISCOVERY OR MEASUREMENT? 99
Discovery 99
Measurement 101
Categorical 101
Not Categorical: Ranking, Allocation, and Rating 105
USING THE DECISION TREE 112
CHAPTER SUMMARY 113

CHAPTER 11: The Number of Points in a Rating Scale 116
ARE THREE POINTS ENOUGH IN A RATING SCALE? 116
Published Studies on Number of Scale Points 116
Early Research: Two- and Three-Point Scales Are Inadequate 117

Three-Point Scales May Be Good Enough When Using Many Items................ 117

Three-Point Scales Frustrate and Stifle.. 117

Three-Point Scales Contain Less Information 118

More Points Differentiate Better Between Groups 118

Three-Point Scales Can't Identify Extreme Attitudes... 119

Three-Point Scales Rated as Quicker but Five, Seven, and
Ten Points Rated as Easier.. 119

Comparing Five-, Ten-, and Eleven-Point Versions of the
Net Promoter Score 120

Studies of Three vs. Eleven Points for the Net Promoter Score.................... 120

Study Overview... 120

Key Findings 120

Three-Point Scale Summary and Takeaways 123

More Scale Points Increase Reliability.. 123

Three-Point Scales Are Not Reliable.. 123

There's a Loss of Intensity and Validity With Three-Point Scales.................... 123

Two- And Three-Point Scales Are Perceived as Quicker to Complete,
but This Is Largely an Illusion 124

Two and Three Points Are Insufficient to Express Feelings Adequately........... 124

The Claim of a Three-Point Scale Superiority Is a Myth 124

DO TOO MANY RESPONSE OPTIONS CONFUSE PEOPLE?....................... 124

Published Research on Too Many Points... 125

Studies 1 and 2: Number of Response Options and Scale Reliability 125

Study 3: Trouble Distinguishing Between Points.. 126

Too Many Points or Too Many Labels? 128

If More Points Confuse, Do Lots of Points Confuse Even More? 129

Discussion and Summary of Too Many Points.. 129

The Consistently Published Recommendation to Limit
the Number of Scale Points Has Poor Justification... 130

Too Many Labels With Vague Modifiers May Be The Real Issue 130

There Is No Goldilocks Point; More Scale Points Improve Reliability
and Sensitivity 130

Fewer Points Are Less Impactful With Multiple Items 130

More Points Take Up More Space.. 131

Sliders Have 100+ Points... 131

More Than Good Enough Doesn't Mean Bad.. 131

DO PEOPLE REALLY USE ALL POINTS? 131

Not All Response Options Are Used...Does It Matter? 131

Data Point Usage Analysis Study 132

Study Findings: Participants Used All Points.. 133
DOES CHANGING THE NUMBER OF RESPONSE OPTIONS IN
THE SAME SURVEY AFFECT RATING BEHAVIOR?........................... 134
Study Points Experimental Design 134
Study Findings.. 135
No Differences in Response Patterns for Means or Top-Box Scores............. 135
Eighty Percent Didn't Notice the Change in Rating Scales................. 137
Most Have No Preference.. 137
Key Recommendation.. 137
SHOULD YOU INCLUDE A NEUTRAL POINT (ODD OR
EVEN POINTS)?... 137
Neutral Points in UX Surveys... 138
Neutral Point Study: Removing the Neutral Point in the Likelihood-to
-Recommend Item.. 140
Study Results... 141
Neutral Point Study: Removing the Neutral Point from Four
Standard UX Items... 144
Study Details... 144
Study Results... 145
DOES CHANGING THE NUMBER OF POINTS SYSTEMATICALLY
AFFECT SCALE MEANS?.. 147
CHAPTER SUMMARY 148

CHAPTER 12: Labeling Points 152
RESEARCH ON LABELING RESPONSE SCALES............................... 153
EARLY STUDIES FOUND LABELING WAS NOT BETTER 153
Other Studies Did Find Labeling Was Superior................................ 153
Mixed Results of Labeling 155
Labels Aren't Measurably Better... 157
Summary & Discussion of Published Literature on Labeling.............. 158
There Is No Clear Superiority in Labeling.. 158
Context Matters 159
How Do You Judge Which Format Is Better? 159
More Points Likely Increase Scale Reliability, Validity, and Sensitivity 159
Is It a Rubric or a Rating Scale?... 159
STUDY COMPARING FULLY VS. PARTIALLY LABELED FIVE- AND
SEVEN-POINT SCALES.. 160
Study Methodologies Overviews... 160
Studies Summary and Discussion... 161

There Is No Clear Pattern of Labeling on Item Response Behaviors.............. 161
The Claim That Full Labeling Is Always Better Isn't Supported........................ 162
This Study, Like All Studies, Had Some Limitations.. 162
Main Takeaway: Labeling Doesn't Matter Much 162
LABELING THE NEUTRAL RESPONSE... 162
**NEUTRAL LABEL STUDY ON THE LIKELIHOOD-TO
-RECOMMEND ITEM** 163
Summary of Study Findings.. 164
Having a Neutral Label Sometimes Attracts Responses (But Not Always) 164
Neutral Labels May Attract Other Low Scores for Noncustomers.................. 165
Neutral Labels Mostly Affect Noncustomers 165
There's No Clear Pattern on Net Promoter Scores 165
The Means Increased With a Neutral Label... 166
Small Differences Exist, but Be Consistent 167
Higher Scores May Mask Impact.. 168
CHAPTER SUMMARY 168

CHAPTER 13: Item Tone & Left-Side Bias... 170
**SHOULD YOU VARY ITEM TONE WHEN DEVELOPING
A QUESTIONNAIRE?** 170
Most UX Questionnaires Alternate Item Tone.. 170
Advantages to Alternating.. 171
Disadvantages to Alternating... 171
Study on Alternating vs. All-Positive Item Tone... 172
Recent Replication... 172
Another Estimate of the Frequency of Mistakes Due to Mixed Tone 172
Negative Items Distort Factor Structures.. 172
Takeaway: Negatives Outweigh the Positives.. 173
Is There Ever a Good Reason to Alternate Items?.. 174
When There Is a Clear Negative Construct, Use Negatives 174
The Tide May Be Turning 174
IS THERE A LEFT-SIDE BIAS? 174
Wait a Second…Where's the Left-Side Bias? 175
Left-Side Bias in the Personal Distress Scale 175
Evidence Supporting the Left-Side Bias 176
Evidence Against the Left-Side Bias 177
Left-Side Bias in Ratings of Educational Experiences... 178
Evidence Suggesting (but Not Proving) a Weak Left-Side Bias 178

More Evidence Suggesting (But Not Proving) a Weak Left-Side Bias 179

Literature Summary and Takeaways 181

Study Investigating Left-Side Bias in the Single Ease

Question (SEQ) 181

Study Design: SEQ Standard vs. Alternate Formats 182

WHAT ABOUT A TOP-FIRST BIAS? 187

CHAPTER SUMMARY 189

CHAPTER 14: Agreement, End Points, and Cultural Differences .. 191

ARE AGREEMENT ITEMS PRONE TO ACQUIESCENCE? 191

Agreement vs. Item-Specific Study Overview 192

A Check for Acquiescence from a Large SUS Database 193

DO MORE EXTREME ENDPOINTS AFFECT RATINGS? 194

Research on Endpoint Labels 194

Very vs. Extremely Study Overview 195

Study Summary and Discussion 196

CULTURAL/REGIONAL EFFECTS ON RESPONSES TO RATING SCALES .. 197

Published Research on Cultural/Regional Differences 197

Cultural Scale Differences Study 198

Study Summary and Discussion 199

CHAPTER SUMMARY 202

CHAPTER 15: Presentation Effects on Rating Scales 204

GRIDS VERSUS STAND-ALONE ITEMS 204

Published Literature on Grids vs. One at a Time 205

Summary of Published Literature on Grid Studies 207

Three Grid Studies with UX Surveys 207

Study & Literature Summaries 209

YES/NO VERSUS SELECT-ALL-THAT-APPLY 211

Summary of Published Literature 213

National Education Longitudinal Study of 1988 213

Undergraduate Experience at Washington State University 213

NatCen Social Research Omnibus Survey 214

Pew Research American Trends Panel 214

Insights from Previous Research 214

SATA vs. Forced Choice Study Overview 215

Study Results 215

Study Recommendation: We Recommend SATA 216

QUESTION ORDER EFFECTS..217
Published Literature on Order Effects..218
General vs. Specific Order Effect..218
Order Effects on Item-by-Item and Grid Formats................................219
Influence of Culture on Order Effects...219
Order Effects in UX/CX...219
Studies on Order Effects..220
Study Summary and Takeaways...220
HORIZONTAL VERSUS VERTICAL RATING SCALES.....................222
Previous Studies Suggest a Minor and Inconsistent Impact..................223
Study on Horizontal Desktop vs. Vertical Mobile................................224
Study Overview...224
Study Summary and Discussion...225
CHAPTER SUMMARY...227

CHAPTER 16: Response Option Visual Formats....................230
ADDING COLOR TO RESPONSE OPTIONS.....................................230
Research on Scale Colors...231
Study Overview on Colors..232
Summary and Takeaways..233
USING FACE EMOJIS...235
What Are Face Emoji Scales?..235
Literature on Face Emojis..236
Face Emojis vs. Numbers Experiment...237
Study Summary and Takeaways...237
USING STARS INSTEAD OF NUMBERS..238
What Are Star Scales?...238
Stars vs. Numbers Experiment..239
Study Summary and Takeaways...239
USING NEGATIVE NUMBERS IN RATING SCALES..........................241
Published Literature on Neg2Pos Scales...241
Standard Versus Neg2Pos Numeric Scales Experiment........................243
Study Summary and Takeaways...243
USING SLIDERS INSTEAD OF RADIO BUTTONS.............................244
Published Literature on Sliders...246
Sliders Can Be More Sensitive..246
Sliders Take Longer...246
Some People Have Difficulty Using Sliders...246

Nonresponse Rates Are Higher With Sliders 246
Sliders and Numeric Scales Have Comparable Psychometric Properties 246
Sensitivity Advantage of Sliders 246
Sliders vs. Numbers Experiment 248
Study Summary and Takeaways 249
SLIDERS ON MOBILE 250
Slider Versus Numeric Mobile Study 251
Design of the Numeric and Slider Scales 251
Slider Study Summary and Takeaways 253
Click Testing: A Promising Alternative to Sliders 255
CHAPTER SUMMARY 256

PART 4: DATA COLLECTION & ANALYSIS

CHAPTER 17: Sample Size Calculations 260
HOW TO KNOW WHAT SAMPLE SIZE FORMULA TO USE 260
SAMPLE SIZE FOR CONFIDENCE INTERVALS (NO COMPARISONS) 261
Practice Using the Table 264
Sample Size Using Rating Scale Data 265
Converting Rating Scales to 0–100-Point Scales 266
Mapping Margins of Error for 0–100-Point Scales to Five, Seven,
and Eleven-Point Scales 270
SAMPLE SIZE FOR COMPARING AGAINST A BENCHMARK 272
Quick Recap of Power and Tails (Rejection Regions) 272
Sample Size Tables for Comparing Percentages with Benchmarks 273
Sample Sizes for Comparing Means with Benchmarks 274
Standardizing Ratings to a 0–100-Point Scale 274
Comparing a Rating Scale Mean with a Specified Benchmark 274
A Few More Examples 277
SAMPLE SIZE FOR COMPARISONS (WITHIN AND
BETWEEN SUBJECTS) 279
Practice Using the Table 281
Sample Size for Comparing Rating Scale Means 281
Standardizing Ratings to a 0–100-Point Scale 281
Comparing Two Within-Subjects Means 282
Comparing Two Between-Subjects Means 284
A Few More Examples 286
FINITE POPULATION CORRECTIONS 288

CHAPTER SUMMARY AND TAKEAWAYS...291

CHAPTER 18: Planning and Logistics 293
COMMERCIAL SURVEY PLATFORMS...293
PARTICIPANT AND RECRUITING COSTS 294
Survey Recruitment Costs...294
Online Panels 294
Internal Lists...295
Advertising 295
Bulk Mail Costs...295
Professional Services Costs...295
DATA COLLECTION: PRETESTING AND SOFT LAUNCHING TO
PREPARE FOR THE FULL LAUNCH 296
Prepare for Data Collection...296
Check Survey Timing...296
Verify the Logic and Branching 296
Ensure for Randomization...297
EVALUATE REQUIRED QUESTIONS 297
Test With Think-Aloud Participants...297
Prepare to Launch — Softly!...297
What Happens When a Survey Doesn't Fill? 297
Reduce the Survey Length 298
Add more Logic or Branching 298
Increase or Change the Incentive...298
Assess and/or Remove Required Questions 298
Change Panels...298
Use Different Recruiting Methods...298
Send a Reminder 298
CHAPTER SUMMARY AND TAKEAWAYS...299

CHAPTER 19: Preparing for Survey Analysis 300
CLEANING DATA 300
Most Obvious and Easiest Detection Methods 301
Poor Verbatim Responses 301
Irrelevant Responses 301
Cheater Questions 301
Less Obvious and More Difficult Detection Methods 302
Inconsistent Responses...302

Missing Data 302

Pattern Detection 303

Disqualifying Questions 303

DEALING WITH MISSING OR INCOMPLETE DATA 303

PREPARING FOR ANALYSIS 305

CHAPTER SUMMARY 307

CHAPTER 20: Single-Item (Univariate) Analysis 310

CATEGORICAL 310

Mutually Exclusive 311

Non–Mutually Exclusive 312

Frequency Data 313

Confidence Intervals for Categorical Data 315

NOT CATEGORICAL: RATING, RANKING, AND ALLOCATION 316

Rating Scale 316

Measuring the Average: Means and Medians 316

Can You Take the Mean of Ordinal Data? 318

Frequency Distributions 325

Mean or Box Score? 328

Top Box, Top-Two Box, Bottom Box, or Net Box? 328

Scaling to 100 329

Special Item Scoring 329

Ranking 330

Allocation 333

OPEN-ENDED QUESTIONS 334

CHAPTER SUMMARY 336

CHAPTER 21: Two-Item (Bivariate) and Three+ Item Analysis 338

MAKING COMPARISONS (DIFFERENCES) 338

Between-Subjects Comparisons 340

The Two-Sample t-Test 340

The $N-1$ Two-Proportion Test 343

Within-Subjects Comparisons 344

Paired t-Test 345

McNemar Exact Test 346

Additional Two-Way Comparisons 347

Means Over Time 347

Comparing Differences in Net Scores 347

Comparing to a Benchmark 347
Analyzing Preference Data 349
Cross-Tabbing Variables 350
Collapsing Variables 351
Controlling for Prior Experience 353
About the Weighted t-Test 353
Using the Weighted t-Test 353
Measuring Relationships: Correlation and Regression 356
THREE+ (MULTIVARIATE) ITEM ANALYSIS 358
Multiple Regression Analysis 359
ANOVA 360
CHAPTER SUMMARY AND TAKEAWAY 363

CHAPTER 22: Displaying Survey Results 366
WATCH FOR CHART JUNK 367
Y-SCALING 367
ZERO IS NOT ALWAYS A HERO 369
CONSISTENTLY SCALE THE Y-AXIS 371
DIFFERENCE AND RAW SCORES CAN TELL DIFFERENT STORIES 371
BE WARY OF 3D 372
CUMULATIVE GRAPHS ARE EASILY MISUNDERSTOOD 373
A TABLE MIGHT BE BETTER THAN A GRAPH. 374
HEATMAPS: ADD A LITTLE "HEAT" TO THE TABLES 375
INDICATE SAMPLING ERROR 376
Compared to What? 377
DESCRIBING CHANGES 377
WHEN IN DOUBT, TEST 378
CHAPTER SUMMARY 378

APPENDIX A: Statistical Considerations 380
HOW CONFIDENT DO YOU NEED TO BE? 380
WHAT DOES STATISTICALLY SIGNIFICANT MEAN? 381

APPENDIX B: Commonly Used Questionnaires and Questions 384
SYSTEM USABILITY SCALE (SUS) 384
COMPUTER SYSTEM USABILITY QUESTIONNAIRE (CSUQ)
VERSION 3 386
SINGLE EASE QUESTION (SEQ) 388

STANDARDIZED USER EXPERIENCE PERCENTILE RANK
QUESTIONNAIRE (SUPR-Q).. 389
NET PROMOTER SCORE.. 391
USER-EXPERIENCE-LITE (UX-LITE) 392
MICROSOFT NET SATISFACTION (NSAT) 393
PRODUCT-MARKET FIT (PMF) 394
CUSTOMER EFFORT SCORE (CES)... 394

REFERENCES 396

INDEX.. 415

DEDICATION

To my kids and their superpowers:

Nicholas: Your ability to retain and integrate everything you read-- like the details of the 30 Years' War.

Chase: Your steadfast reliability — like still golfing with your Dad even when it's 35 degrees out.

Josephine: Your ability to meet 5 new people and come away with 10 new friends.

—J.S.

To my wonderful wife, Cathy, for her love, patience, encouragement, and support.
—J.L.

ACKNOWLEDGMENTS

We've put this book together over several years and many people played roles in helping make it happen. While we can't acknowledge everyone, we would like to thank our copy editor Adam Waldbrook and Layout editor Jennifer Lam for helping get the manuscript to print. We'd also like to thank Phil Siebler and the MeasuringU research team for contributing to many of the graphics and original research used throughout the book.

INTRODUCTION

Welcome to *Surveying the User Experience*. This is a practical book about how to plan, design and analyze surveys in the user experience (UX) and customer experience (CX) fields.

You might wonder—do we really need another book on surveys?

There are a lot of books on survey design and analysis. While writing this introduction, a search on Amazon for "survey design and analysis" returned 360 results. So, what makes our book different? This book is for UX researchers, CX professionals, designers, product owners, marketers, and anyone else who has a vested interest in collecting data through surveys. In a nutshell:

- **Survey Best Practices Are Constantly Evolving:** Surveys may be an old research method (around for millennia depending on the definition), but the methods and practices are constantly evolving in response to changing styles, new technologies, published opinions, and findings from experiments.

- **Surveys Remain a Popular Method:** Despite criticisms of surveys being a "lazy" research method by some UX research mavens (an unwarranted and overly general criticism, in our opinion), surveys are widely used in UX and CX research (just behind user research and usability testing in popularity according to the User Experience Professionals Association's 2022 survey of its membership).

- **Surveys about Politics are Different from Surveys about Products and Services:** We focus on surveys for UX and CX research. This matters because much of the literature on survey research and design focuses on politics and social issues, which appear to be more prone to response biases such as acquiescence and social desirability.

- **We've Compiled the Largest Collection of Research on Response Options:** Much of our book provides critical literature reviews of research that is often cited to support survey design practices (with a focus on the impact of variations on response options) and data from our own experiments to investigate variations in survey design methods in the context of UX and CX research. In writing this book, we conducted dozens of experiments, using data from over 10,000 respondents to provide up-to-date recommendations (and debunk some lingering misconceptions).

In this book, we use practical examples gleaned through years of experience developing, conducting (and taking) surveys for both Fortune 500 companies and small startups. We use examples of surveys that the team at MeasuringU has performed to give you constructive information for better surveys.

Like most professionals, you have probably taken several surveys and may have created some of your own. Whether you are new to surveys in applied research or you have some experience, the introductory chapters provide a thorough background and overview of developing better survey questions. We've organized the chapters into four sections:

- **Part 1: Planning the Survey (Chapters 1–4):** Guidance on the common "how much," "how long," and "how do we" questions, with practical advice on making the most of your survey.

- **Part 2: Writing Survey Questions (Chapters 5–9):** Methods for choosing and writing survey questions guided by an understanding of the anatomy of survey questions and the effects of human memory and cognition.

- **Part 3: Survey Response Options (Chapters 10–16):** Data-driven guidance on leading practice in survey item formats, starting with a taxonomy of response options and literature reviews then continuing with original experimentation on the effects of the number of scale points, labeling, item tone, primacy bias, acquiescence bias, cultural effects, and numerous presentation effects.

- **Part 4: Data Collection & Analysis (Chapters 17–22):** Several step-by-step guides on gathering raw survey data, graphing survey data, and using leading practices for statistical analysis and reporting.

The book ends with two appendices:

- **Appendix A (Statistical Considerations):** A review of statistical confidence and the meaning of statistical significance.

- **Appendix B (Commonly Used Survey Types and Questions):** Wording, response formats, and additional reading for questionnaires and items commonly used in UX and CX survey research.

Our goal with this book is to help fill in the gaps in conducting and analyzing surveys, differentiating conventions that aren't backed by data from practices where research shows clear pros and cons of response options or techniques. We have also developed a companion online course that covers the bulk of the material in this book, available online at MeasuringUniversity.com.

PART I:
Planning the Survey

CHAPTER 1:
INTRODUCTION TO SURVEY DESIGN

In a typical week, market research companies such as J.D. Power ask us (Jeff and Jim) to complete surveys on our most recent car purchase, our experience with calling the bank's (e.g., U.S. Bank's) customer service department, our experience eating at a restaurant last night (e.g., OpenTable), and much else besides. Surveys seem ubiquitous.

In this chapter, we'll address the following questions:

- How long have surveys been around?
- Are censuses, polls, surveys, and questionnaires the same?
- How many types of survey are there?
- What are the advantages of using standardized questionnaires?
- Where did standardized UX questionnaires come from?
- When is a survey the right research method?
- What are the first steps in planning a survey?

Surveys, in some form, have been around for thousands of years. Figure 1.1 shows a timeline of key dates showing that surveys have a rich and long history (including records from around 3800 BCE of ancient Egyptians using a census for taxing their population). It seems that death, taxes, and maybe even surveys have been certain for at least 5000 years!

Census	"Milles" Questionnaire	US Constitution	1ˢᵗ US Presidential Poll	GE "Mazda" Market Research	Ubiquitous Web Surveys
3800 BC	1753	1787	1824	1910	2000

FIGURE 1.1: A history of key milestones in surveys.

When conducting survey-based research, you'll often encounter the terms words *census, poll,* and *questionnaire* used in conjunction with — and often interchangeably with — the term survey. There are some differences.

CENSUS

A census is the process of gathering information about every member of a population. By definition, the goal is full enumeration, never sampling. Census is the word used when counting all the people in a country or region. The practice occurred in ancient Egypt, Rome, and Babylonia as long as 6000 years ago. In the United States, a census is conducted every ten years as outlined in Article I, Section 2 of the Constitution, which states, "The actual Enumeration shall be made within three years after the first meeting of the Congress of the United States, and within every subsequent term of ten years, in such manner as they shall by law direct." But a census can involve more than just counting people. For example, there's an international census of agriculture (e.g., crop area and livestock numbers).

In applied research, censuses are rarely conducted, but it's common to use existing censuses provided by governments to create census-matching proportional probability samples—samples that are proportionally representative of the population for variables such as geographic location and age.

POLL

In modern usage, poll is strongly associated with elections; for example, you go to a polling station to vote. In thirteenth-century English, *poll* meant "a head." At that time, a common process for local elections was for people to congregate in groups representing their choice as someone counted the heads in each group (this is also the origin of the word *headcount*).

In applied research, polling usually refers to an opinion poll that gauges the attitudes of a population via sampling from that population. The first-known opinion poll was taken of prospective voters in the U.S. presidential election campaign of 1824 (see Figure 1.1). Even today, polls are mostly associated with assessing political attitudes, such as the preference for a presidential candidate. Two of the most famous founders of opinion-polling companies in the twentieth century are George Gallup and Elmo Roper, whose methods are still used today.

Some definitions of a poll specify that its distinguishing characteristic is that it asks just one question. Although modern polls often have a single core question (e.g., voting preference), they can include more than one question (e.g., likelihood to vote), making them increasingly indistinguishable from short surveys (especially when they contain demographic questions). Polls are best thought of as a type of short survey, usually focusing on some preference or choice, and they are often but not always political (Figure 1.2).

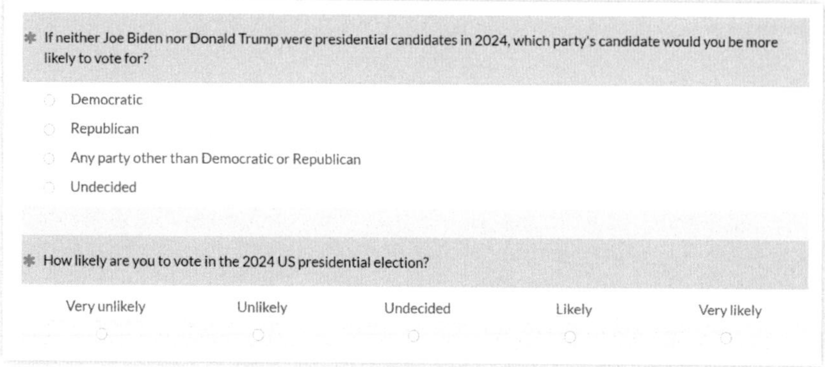

FIGURE 1.2: Example of a two-question opinion poll (created in MUiQ®).

SURVEY

The word *survey* refers to data-collection methods that can include questionnaires or polls. The four primary methods used to conduct surveys are in-person, phone, mail, and online. Researchers use these four survey mechanisms to conduct censuses as well, so it's common to distinguish surveys and censuses based on whether the goal is to fully enumerate a population (census) or to sample from it (survey). There are many different sampling strategies for surveys, each with its strengths and weaknesses.

The terms words *survey* and *questionnaire* are often used interchangeably (perhaps we are guilty). For example, we've heard researchers refer to a System Usability Scale (SUS) survey or a Net Promoter Score (NPS) survey. However, both the SUS and NPS are technically questionnaires that can be included in a survey. Any given survey can include multiple questionnaires and additional questions (such as demographic or open-ended questions).

QUESTIONNAIRE

A questionnaire is a set of questions asked of a participant in surveys and censuses. The first questionnaires appeared in the mid-eighteenth century. For example, the "Milles" questionnaire contained 120 questions about the history of the parishes of the Diocese of Exeter (see Figure 1.1). UX questionnaires often contain groups of items to measure constructs such as satisfaction, usability, loyalty, or brand attitude.

A standardized questionnaire is a set of questions that have gone through the process of psychometric evaluation. This means someone has spent a lot of time going through dozens or hundreds of possible questions and winnowed the set down to the ones that are most reliable, valid, and sensitive. Usually, this process is done by having a representative group of participants answer the candidate questions for a diverse set of interfaces. Examples of standardized UX questionnaires include the SUPR-Q®, SUS (see Figure 1.3), PSSUQ/CSUQ, UX-Lite®, SASSI, and NASA-TLX (and many more).

※ Please rate how well you agree or disagree with the following statements about the website you just visited.

	Strongly Disagree 1	Disagree 2	Neither Agree nor Disagree 3	Agree 4	Strongly Agree 5
I think that I would like to use this system frequently.	O	O	O	O	O
I found the system unnecessarily complex.	O	O	O	O	O
I thought the system was easy to use.	O	O	O	O	O
I think that I would need the support of a technical person to be able to use this system.	O	O	O	O	O
I found the various functions in this system were well integrated.	O	O	O	O	O
I thought there was too much inconsistency in this system.	O	O	O	O	O
I would imagine that most people would learn to use this system very quickly.	O	O	O	O	O
I found the system very cumbersome to use.	O	O	O	O	O
I felt very confident using the system.	O	O	O	O	O
I needed to learn a lot of things before I could get going with this system.	O	O	O	O	O

FIGURE 1.3: Example of a standardized UX questionnaire, the System Usability Scale (SUS) (created in MUiQ).

Some standardized questionnaires from other fields are the Minnesota Multiphasic Personality Inventory (clinical psychology and psychiatry), the Wechsler Intelligence Scale for Children (psychology and education), and the Strong Interest Inventory (career assessment).

SURVEYS IN UX RESEARCH

Surveys are not all created equal. In user and customer research, surveys differ as a function of their primary goal. Figure 1.4 shows a taxonomy of survey types that are common in UX and CX research.

Survey Type Taxonomy

Customer/User Attitudes, Experience, Intention

Loyalty
- Likelihood-to-Recommend and NPS
- Likelihood-to-Buy
- Likelihood-to-Use
- Likelihood-to-Defect
- SUPR-Q Loyalty

Satisfaction
- ASCI
- MS NSAT
- General to specific

Usability/Usefulness (Attitudes towards using)
- SUS
- mTAM
  - Ease
  - Usefulness
- UX-Lite
  - Ease
  - Usefulness
- NASA TLX
- SUPR-Q Usability
- PSSUQ/CSUQ
- AttrakDiff
- UEQ
- CxPi (Forrester)

Delight
- Two-item (joy, surprise)
- Desirability toolkit/index

Trust
- SUPR-Q Trust

Appearance
- SUPR-Q Appearance

Clutter
- Content
- Design

Findability/Navigation
- Tree test
- First click test

Multiple UX attributes
- SUPR-Q (Usability, Trust, Appearance, Loyalty)

Special Purpose Questionnaires

Voice
- MOS-X
- SASSI
- UEQ+

Mobile
- SUPR-Qm

Gaming
- Game User Experience Satisfaction Scale

Individual Differences/Demographics

Product experience
- Tenure
- Frequency
- Depth

Tech-savviness
- Select all that apply (skills)
- Rating-based

Customer Service
- Call Experience
- Post-purchase survey
- ServQual
- SUISQ (experience with IVR applications)
- Customer Effort Score (CES)

Product/Feature Surveys
- MaxDiff/Conjoint
- Kano
- Top-Tasks
- Gap/Needs Analysis (JTBD)
- Benefits/Positioning

Marketing
- Positioning Statements
- Message effectiveness
- Preference testing

Market Surveys
- Characteristics of a Market
- Segmentation
- Salary Surveys (for an industry)

Employee Surveys
- Job Satisfaction/Engagement
- 360 Survey
- Exit Survey

Brand
- Awareness
- Attitudes
- Lift (pre/post)

FIGURE 1.4: Taxonomy of common survey types used in user and customer research.

A more detailed explanation of several common questionnaires/questions used in these surveys is provided in Appendix B. Some of the most common reasons to conduct a survey include measuring customer attitudes by assessing satisfaction, behavioral intention (intent to reuse or recommend), and perceptions of the ease of use and usefulness of a product or feature.

More specialized surveys assess voice quality (such as when using voice assistants), customer service experiences, employee job satisfaction, and awareness and attitudes toward a brand (such as laptop manufacturers). See *Quantifying the User Experience* (Sauro & Lewis, 2016, Chapter 8) for more information about standardized UX questionnaires.

While surveys are a key part of traditional market research, they have been met with some skepticism in UX research. Some practitioners see surveys as a threat to observational research methods like usability testing, ethnographic research, and interviews.

But surveys remain a popular UX research method. We have been tracking method usage in the user experience field since 2011, and most researchers consistently report using surveys. The most recent data from 2022 shows that 63% of respondents reported using surveys (Figure 1.5), up almost 10% over the previous few years (Sauro et al., 2022, Jul 12).

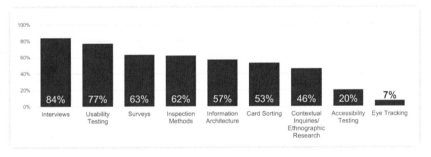

FIGURE 1.5: Reported method usage for UX researchers, with surveys as the 3rd most used method. Adapted from (Sauro et al., 2022, Jul 12).

UX QUESTIONNAIRES

Earlier, we made the distinction between a questionnaire and a survey. Questionnaires are the set of questions given to respondents, and surveys are the method of delivery. Assessing perceptions of a product's experience (ease, usefulness) is one of the first standardized ways user experience was measured. It may also be one of the main reasons UX researchers conduct surveys.

Though you or your product team can cobble together a few questions, many good questions already exist in the form of standardized questionnaires that may work for your research. But first, what do we mean by standardized?

Standardization

A standardized questionnaire has gone through the process of psychometric evaluation. While that sounds like a psycho with a yardstick, it actually means someone spent a lot of time going through dozens or hundreds of possible questions, winnowing the set down to the ones that are most reliable, valid, and sensitive. Usually, this is done by having a representative group of participants answer the candidate questions in response to a diverse set of interfaces. In many cases, the results are published in peer-reviewed journals.

Standardized questionnaires provide these advantages:

Reliability: The repeatability of the questionnaire. It refers to how consistent responses are to the questions. We'd expect the same or similar users to give roughly the same answers when evaluating the same interface. Standardized questionnaires are more reliable than similar homegrown ones (Sauro & Lewis, 2009).

Validity: How well a questionnaire can measure what it is intended to measure. That is, if we hear users complaining about a website or software product being unusable, the questionnaire should be able to distinguish these poor experiences from experiences with websites or software that are acclaimed for their usability. Validity is usually measured by correlating a questionnaire's scores with other established questionnaires or outcome measures, such as task time or completion rates.

Sensitivity: How well the questionnaire can discriminate between good interfaces and bad ones. Even poorly worded questions with a huge sample size can detect differences between horrible and excellent experiences. We're usually dealing with more modest differences and sample sizes, so we want as sensitive an instrument as we can get. Sensitivity can be measured using resampling procedures to see how well the questionnaire can differentiate with different sample sizes.

Objectivity: Standardized questionnaires allow researchers to independently verify the measurement statements of other practitioners. It's harder to stack the deck in favor of or against an application if you use an independent instrument that others have found success with.

Quantification: Standardization allows for a finer grain of reporting and statistical analysis than personal judgment.

Economy: It takes a lot of time to sift through the bad questions to find the good ones. Once this process is complete, we can all take advantage of the process.

Communication: It's easier to communicate results when we have a common standardized questionnaire. For example, if you've used the System Usability Scale (SUS), then just knowing the raw score of an interface is an 80 can be meaningful (that's a good score).

Norms: Some standardized questionnaires have normalized reference databases that allow you to convert raw scores into percentile ranks. Instead of working with just an average, you can see how well your interface stacks up against a large database of comparable products. For example, the SUPR-Q is a standardized questionnaire that measures usability and other factors (such as trust and loyalty) for websites. Scores are compared to a database of hundreds of websites. See Appendix B for more on the SUPR-Q.

More information on standardized questionnaires is available in Chapter 8 of *Quantifying the User Experience* (Sauro & Lewis, 2016).

History of Standardized UX Questionnaires

We'll refer to standardized UX questionnaires frequently in this book. To understand when to use them, it's helpful to understand where they came from.

The early roots of currently used UX questionnaires date back over 100 years, with the most recent evolution of UX questionnaires happening in the 1970s. Using an evolutionary analogy, we can place UX questionnaires on three branches, as shown in Figure 1.6:

1. Management Information Systems (MIS)
2. Assessing System Usability
3. Pragmatic (Classical) and Hedonic (Emotional) Usability

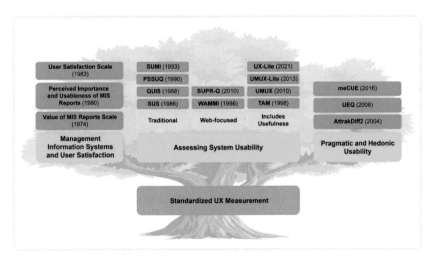

FIGURE 1.6: Three branches of UX measurement.

A detailed discussion of all questionnaires in the tree can be found online (Lewis & Sauro, 2020, Jan 29). In this book, we primarily reference the Assessing System Usability branch. We'll provide more detail on those questionnaires here.

ASSESSING SYSTEM USABILITY

The Assessing System Usability branch started in the late 1980s when, along with the emergence of personal computers and consumer software, there was an uptick in hiring human-factors engineers and experimental psychologists in the computer industry. The questionnaires in this branch were primarily intended for assessing subjective elements in usability testing and included:

- **SUS (1986):** The System Usability Scale was developed at Digital Equipment Corporation (DEC) in the UK. This ten-item questionnaire, published in 1996, is the most widely used standardized measure of perceived usability (Brooke, 2013).

- **PSSUQ (1990):** The Post-Study System Usability Questionnaire was developed at IBM. The current version has 16 agreement items and produces four measures: Overall, System Usefulness, Information Quality, and Interface Quality (Lewis, 2019c).

- **TAM (1998):** The Technology Acceptance Model, although originally developed to predict the likelihood of future use rather than user experience, can be slightly modified for use as a standardized UX questionnaire (Lewis, 2019a). This modification retains the famous factor structure of the TAM so that it measures both perceived ease of use and perceived usefulness.

- **SUPR-Q (2010):** The Standardized User Experience Percentile Rank Questionnaire focuses on the web experience. It is a concise instrument, requiring just eight items to measure four UX attributes: Usability, Trust, Loyalty, and Appearance (Sauro, 2018, Jun 13).

- **UMUX (2010):** The Usability Metric for User Experience was developed to be a short four-item measure of perceived usability whose scores would match SUS scores (Finstad, 2010). Research over the past ten years shows that the UMUX appears to have achieved that goal (Lewis, 2019b).

- **UMUX-Lite (2013):** The UMUX-Lite is an ultrashort two-item questionnaire made up of two items from the UMUX, one addressing perceived usefulness ("This product's capabilities meet my requirements") and the other addressing perceived ease of use ("This product is easy to use"), making it not only a compact measure of perceived usability but also a mini-TAM. Like the full UMUX, its scores correspond closely with concurrently collected SUS scores (Lewis et al., 2013).

- **UX-Lite (2022):** The UX-Lite is an updated and refined version of the UMUX-Lite. It has two changes. The wording of the usefulness item was simplified to "This product's features meet my needs," and this version uses five-point scales to make it easier to add to SUPR-Q and SUS item grids (Lewis & Sauro, 2021, Sep 15).

More details about several of these questionnaires are available in Appendix B.

WHEN A SURVEY IS THE BETTER METHOD

If you're reading this book, chances are you've probably taken a survey that was a horrible experience full of confusing questions. Or perhaps, as a researcher, you've had to deal with interpreting data from a poorly written survey filled with leading questions and poor response options.

While it's become easy to administer surveys electronically and collect results almost immediately, there is no excuse for poorly written or thought-through surveys. There's no doubt that surveys can be overused and abused. Maybe you've even thought about abandoning them altogether as a tool.

But is that abuse greater in surveys than in other research methods? Or is it just that surveys are so common that we're more likely to see a poor survey than another method?

There are times when a survey isn't the right tool for the job. Good qualitative inquiry is often the better approach to inform design changes; it does an amazing job of telling you "why." For example, when you want to understand how people interact with an interface, it's usually best to watch them, not survey them about what they think.

But the same problems that come with surveys can also be applied to qualitative research methods, like customer interviews, usability tests, and focus groups. No method is immune from poor execution.

Surveys are no more a replacement for qualitative research than a hammer is for a drill. We've seen a lot of people misuse drills, but that doesn't mean we throw the drill out of the toolbox! When used properly, the survey is a valuable tool to help inform design decisions. In fact, one of the steps for creating items in a survey (usually part of an instrument or scale) is to do a cognitive walkthrough with your target group—a good mix of qual and quant.

Here are some examples of when a survey (done properly) is an ideal method to answer questions that inform design (Sauro, 2012, Dec 18):

Identifying your users. Personas and segmentation analysis depend on getting a good representative sample of your customers to understand them. It's far more efficient and effective to use website intercepts or surveys emailed to customers rather than individual interviews of dozens or hundreds of customers. Interviews and observation provide rich data and should be included in the process of understanding your users (mixing methods). But some core data points, like age, gender, purchase frequency, and geography are easily discovered with a survey.

Identifying the most important features or content. Running a survey with a top-task analysis question (Sauro, 2013, Sep 10) is one of the most effective ways to differentiate important tasks from trivial ones. No product, website, or app can do everything well. Methods like a top-task analysis provide a prioritized list of customer goals.

Benchmarking attitudes. Attitudes affect behaviors. Knowing what people think about a brand, product, or website is important. How those attitudes (like usability, loyalty, and utility) compare with other products or experiences goes a long way to helping you understand why people do or don't purchase or use a product. Although anyone can write a survey and ask poor questions, there are scientific ways to establish the validity and reliability of attitudinal items and rating scales.

Identifying key drivers of a product or experience. Want to know why customers aren't purchasing or which of the 50 feature requests to include in the next version? Using multiple regression analysis or conjoint analysis allows you to tease out subtle patterns in responses from surveys. This doesn't replace direct observation or negate the need for interviews, but neither of these qualitative approaches can differentiate often subtle yet important differences in attitudes.

Finding the likelihood to repurchase or recommend. People's ability to predict their future behavior is flawed. That doesn't mean you don't ask—it means you don't bet the bank on it. Under many circumstances, attitudes (especially behavioral intentions) can accurately predict future behavior (Sauro, 2019, Jun 12). How likely are you to renew your cellphone service, repurchase the same car brand, or stay at the same hotel again? While the context and time frame affect how accurate customers' answers are to such questions, measuring these attitudes about future behavior is a quick way to get a pulse on what's likely to happen.

It's even better when you're able to validate the attitudes with actual behavior (like seeing what percentage of people eventually did recommend or purchase). To make any measure more meaningful, answer the question, "Compared to what?" Although the actual repurchase rate will differ from the intended repurchase rate, you should pay attention to it when, for example, the intended rate goes down by 30% year over year.

PLANNING YOUR SURVEY

Research efforts should be driven by business questions and good hypotheses. In working through survey details like response options, the original intent of the survey can often get lost. At its worst, survey design can get bogged down by internal politics as multiple stakeholders provide input, so decisions are made that satisfy those stakeholders rather than efficiently address research goals.

To help ensure survey designs address research questions and to guide decision-making, we've found it helpful to use a grid that aligns research questions to study components.

To create a research grid, follow these steps.

1. **List the research goals and hypotheses.** Examples of common survey research questions include:

   - How is our brand perceived by potential customers?
   - Does the advertisement change people's attitudes toward the brand?
   - How likely are customers to recommend our product?
   - What percent of customers are satisfied with our product?
   - Which cloud-hosting features are most important to early-stage start-up founders?
   - How likely are customers to continue using our product?
   - How do we define the different groups of customers using our product?
   - Has employee satisfaction gone up or down in the last six months?
   - Will including ads in our product negatively affect our brand perception?
   - Which new features for our camera matter most to prospective customers?
   - Do people think our website is usable?

2. **Place the research goals, questions, or hypotheses at the top of a grid** (see Figure 1.7). You can use Excel, PowerPoint, Word, or even a whiteboard.

3. **Identify how the research goals or questions will be addressed in the research study.** These are a combination of:

   - Specific questions that are asked, such as in a survey (question numbers can work), and
   - Derived insights, such as from a key driver analysis, factor analysis, or through other combinations of questions or analysis (such as creating variables from verbatim comments).

4. **Look for gaps where you'll have light or no coverage of the research questions.** If a hypothesis or research question has few or no items addressing it, you'll need to modify your study (such as adding questions) or save the research questions for another study. One study can't answer all research questions!

5. **Cut the bloat.** Questions or tasks that don't match up with research questions are candidates for removal (such as excessive demographic questions).

Figure 1.7 shows an example from a customer satisfaction and branding survey. The grid has research questions at the top, and each cell shows how the questions will be addressed using question numbers/names.

	How is our brand received and how loyal is our customer base?	What features are the most important to customers?	How does our brand compare to competitors?
Question numbers	7 {CXI Brand Matrix}	26 {feature importance}	1 {Brand perception}
	8 {NPS}	27 {feature SAT}	12 {CXI brand matrix- non}
	9 {Intent for future use}		13 {NPS for competitors}
	17 {CXI Brand Matrix- SFW}		14 {Intent for future use competitors}
	18 {NPS- SFW}		17 {CXI Brand Matrix- SFW}
	19 {Intent for future use- SFW}		18 {NPS- SFW}
			19 {Intent for future use- SFW}
			21 {Other solution SAT}
			23 {Likelihood to switch}

FIGURE 1.7: Example of a research grid from a customer satisfaction survey.

CHAPTER SUMMARY

This chapter focused on the distinctions between surveys, censuses, polls, and questionnaires, a taxonomy of survey types, a discussion of standardized UX questionnaires, and planning a survey.

How long have surveys been around? …A long time. Depending on the definitions, surveys go back about 250 years and censuses several thousand years.

Are censuses, polls, surveys, and questionnaires the same? …They are similar, but there are important differences. These similarities and differences are evident in their definitions:

- *Census:* The distinguishing characteristic of a census is the gathering of information by a government about an e population rather than a sample, with a historical focus on taxation and allocation of resources.

- *Poll:* Historically, polls are strongly associated with voting (e.g., polling stations), which carries over to the practice of opinion polling of a sample of prospective voters. In current practice, polls are short surveys usually focusing on some preference or choice, and they are often but not always political.

- *Survey:* The distinguishing characteristic of a survey is gathering information from a sample of the target population. The information collected can be, for example, demographic, attitudinal, intentional, and experiential.

- *Questionnaire:* A questionnaire is a set of questions answered by the respondents in a census, poll, or survey. A standardized questionnaire comprises items that have undergone the process of psychometric evaluation.

How many types of surveys are there? ...Too many to list. Just in the fields of UX and CX research, surveys are conducted to assess consumer loyalty/satisfaction, usability, delight, trust, appearance, clutter, findability, quality of voice systems, quality of mobile services, gaming, product experience, tech savviness, customer service, product features, marketing, employee satisfaction, brand awareness/attitude, and this isn't a complete list.

What are the advantages of using standardized questionnaires? ... Scale reliability, validity, and more. Commonly cited advantages of standardized questionnaires include reliability (consistency of measurement), validity (measurement of specific constructs), sensitivity (ability to discriminate good and bad scores), objectivity, quantification, economy, communication, and ideally, normative interpretation.

Where did standardized UX questionnaires come from? ...The early roots date back over 100 years. The most recent evolution of standardized UX questionnaires began in the 1970s with the assessment of management information systems, followed by the assessment of usability and usefulness in the 1980s and 90s, and the distinction between pragmatic and hedonic usability in the 2000s.

When is a survey the right research method? ...When the focus is on quantification. Surveys are not substitutes for good qualitative inquiry, but they can be useful in UX/CX research for identifying your users (e.g., demographics, customer segmentation), identifying the most important product features/content, benchmarking attitudes/intentions, and identifying key drivers of attitudes.

What are the first steps in planning a survey? ...Start with a list of research goals and hypotheses. With that list, you can start constructing a research grid that you can use to identify how each goal/hypothesis will be addressed in the research study. The grid will reveal where to address gaps (missing coverage of goals/hypotheses) and bloat (excessive coverage).

CHAPTER 2:
BIASES & ERRORS IN SURVEY DESIGN

In 1916, a leading periodical called *The Literary Digest* polled its large subscriber base of hundreds of thousands of readers and successfully predicted the winner of that year's presential election. They repeated the poll in 1920 and again correctly predicted the winner. They predicted the winner in 1924, 1928, and 1932, for a total of five elections accurately predicted in a row. In 1936, their poll had candidate Governor Alfred Landon of Kansas as the overwhelming winner ("The Literary Digest," n.d.). But that year, Franklin Roosevelt won overwhelmingly (losing only two states to Landon). The magnitude of the magazine's error (off by almost 20 percentage points!) allegedly destroyed the magazine's credibility, leading to its shutting down 18 months after the election.

What happened? The 1936 poll had over 2 million respondents, a huge sample size! The problem wasn't the size of the sample, but how the characteristics of the sample deviated from the U.S. electorate over the years. The sample became biased as its readers became more educated and wealthier than the general U.S. voting population.

Not all biases are as obvious as that in the *Literary Digest* example, but you've likely heard of similar stories of inaccurate polls and survey results, especially in recent U.S. politics.

For example, consider the following two examples:

> *"We surveyed our **customer base** and found a satisfaction score of 75%."*

> *"How outstanding was your experience with our customer service representative?"*

In the first example, only customers for whom the company had contact information were surveyed. What about those who are no longer customers or those who didn't provide their contact information? In the second example, the wording of the question goads the respondent into giving a positive response.

In this chapter, we'll first cover the most common biases in surveys and some ways to reduce their influence. Then we'll discuss the four errors or "horsemen" of survey design and the ways of addressing them. We'll answer the following questions:

- What are potential sources of bias in survey design, and how might they be controlled?
- What are the four potential survey errors?
- If you can't control for biases, should you even consider running a survey?

FOUR CORE BIASES IN SURVEY DESIGN

Several biases can threaten the integrity of a survey. Here are four of the most common you'll encounter and likely need to address.

1. Representative Bias

The *Literary Digest* survey of its readership had a huge sample size, but its readers were not representative of the U.S. electorate. Other examples of possible representative bias include:

Geographic Bias: Surveying only U.S. customers and generalizing to all markets may not be reflective of noncustomers and non-U.S. customers.

Tech Literacy Bias: Using online panel participants to assess how easy people thought a new feature was to use in a mobile app designed for elderly users. However, people who participate in online panels tend to be tech savvy and younger.

Source Bias: Using a website intercept that assesses satisfaction with the website. It's possible that people who respond to the website pop-up may be less satisfied than those who ignore it. People with a strong negative attitude may be more motivated to respond to the survey.

No amount of statistical manipulation can correct for getting answers to perfectly good questions from the wrong people. Aiming for a representative sample should be one of the top priorities of survey development. We'll cover more on the potential negative impacts of representative bias in our discussion of sampling in Chapter 4.

 TIP:

To minimize representative bias, use a variety of participant sources (and compare sources). Ideally, use random stratified or proportional sampling rather than convenience sampling (covered in Chapter 4).

2. Sponsorship Bias

Knowing where the survey is coming from (the sponsor) will likely influence respondents. If you know that the questions about your online social media experience are coming from Facebook, your thoughts and feelings about Facebook will likely impact your responses.

This can especially be the case for more ethereal measures like brand attitude and awareness, which can be affected by the mere reminder of a brand in the email invitation or a name and logo on the welcome page.

 TIP:

One of the best ways to minimize sponsorship bias is to obfuscate the sponsor as much as possible or use a third-party research firm (shameless self-promotion).

3. Social Desirability & Prestige

If it's socially acceptable (recycling, reading to kids, or caring for your family), respondents are much more likely to endorse and exaggerate.

Don't you agree that recycling is an important initiative for companies to embrace?

Approximately how much time do you spend reading to your children each night?

On average, how much time do you spend planning meals for your family?

How much influence do you have on IT purchase decisions at your company?

What's your income and highest level of education?

 TIP:

To minimize social desirability, prestige, and acquiescence biases, frame participation in the survey as helping the researcher make things better for people like the respondent as long as answers are truthful—for example, improving products, services, or social policies.

4. Asking Sensitive Demographic Questions

Asking certain demographic questions (e.g., income, gender, ethnicity) may prime people to not respond, respond untruthfully, or even drop out of the survey.

 TIP:

Ask these types of questions only if you need the answers. Consider placing them at the end of a survey if you don't need them for screening.

SUMMARY OF BIASES IN SURVEY DESIGN

Table 2.1 has the four biases summarized in a table with some possible corrections.

Bias	Problem	Correction
Representativeness	Restrictions in the sample might affect representativeness (availability, tech savvy).	Consider using a variety of participant sources (and compare sources); use random stratified/proportional sampling, not convenience sampling.
Sponsorship	Knowing where the survey is coming from can influence responses (especially problematic for brand awareness studies).	Obfuscate sponsor and/or use third-party research firm.
Social Desirability, Prestige, and Acquiescence	Participants have a propensity to provide socially acceptable responses and to tell you what they think you want to hear.	Frame participation as helping you improve the product, service, or policy.
Demographic	Asking certain demographic questions may prime people to respond untruthfully, not respond, or even drop out.	Representativeness is important but only ask the questions you need. Ask demographics last (unless needed for screening).

TABLE 2.1: Summary of four biases and corrective strategies.

BIAS DOESN'T MEAN ABANDON

Just because a survey has bias doesn't mean the results are meaningless. It does mean you should be able to understand how each type of bias may impact your results. This is especially important when you're attempting to identify a percentage of a population (e.g., the actual percent that agrees to statements, has certain demographics like higher income, or has an actual influence on purchase decisions).

While there's no magic cure for finding and removing all biases, being aware of them limits their negative impact. We'll cover other types of biases arising from sources like question wording, variation in response options, and potential order effects in Chapter 9 and Part 3.

FOUR TYPES OF POTENTIAL SURVEY ERRORS

Biases are one type of error you need to be mindful of. Even a well-thought-out survey will have to deal with the inevitable challenge these potential errors will pose for the veracity of your data.

Also standing in the way of our dreams of an efficiently collected survey revealing the unvarnished truth about customers or prospects are what we call the *four horsemen of survey errors*.

We've adapted these horsemen from Dillman et al. (2014). Unlike in the Apocalypse, these horsemen don't cause pestilence and war, but they can still wreak mayhem on your results through errors in who answers (coverage, sampling, and nonresponse) and how people respond (measurement error).

1. Coverage Errors

Representativeness is paramount. In our earlier section on biases, representative bias was the first to watch out for because it matters a lot. Asking the right questions to the wrong people is a recipe for misinterpretation. Coverage errors can range from egregious (surveying general U.S. consumers about European corporate financial compliance) to subtle (surveying only current customers about product satisfaction and not recently churned customers).

The more important it is to draw **precise** generalizations about a population from a sample, the more important it is to consider the impact of coverage error. While you might not be trying to predict voter turnout in a presidential election to within 1%, other high-stakes decisions may depend on your coverage. Data on intent to purchase, use, or recommend can impact a product's going to market or affect funding allocations to fix a problem.

For most applied surveys, the question isn't whether there is coverage error, but how much coverage error there is and what it affects.

The first step in having a survey with good coverage is to increase the chance that everyone in your target population has an opportunity to respond. This is often referred to as the *sample frame*. People outside the sample frame have no chance to respond to a survey.

The primary concern with coverage is that the people who are invited and ultimately take the survey may differ in some meaningful way from people who aren't invited to participate because they're not in the frame, resulting in measurements that deviate from the population of interest. This possibility is a primary contributor to the risk of generalizing beyond your sample frame.

Figure 2.1 shows two depictions of sample frames around the same population, one with less coverage and one with more. The dots outside the squares represent people who aren't in the frame and therefore won't be invited to respond. The sample frame may represent a customer list, an online panel, or a database (say, of registered email addresses for a product).

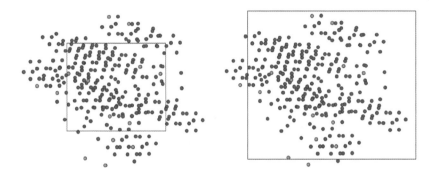

FIGURE 2.1: Examples of two sample frames visualized. The sample frame on the left has less coverage than the one on the right; both have the same target population. The non-blue dots represent respondents with distinctly different characteristics than the larger sample (e.g., different purchase intentions or differences in prior experiences).

Before web surveys were possible, a common strategy to get the right sample frame for a representative set of respondents in the U.S. was to use the phone book and call landlines. In the last 20 years or so, the number of people in the U.S. with landlines has dropped considerably (CEIC, n.d.). This shrinking of the resulting sample frame has disproportionately excluded certain populations and lessened the coverage and representativeness of this approach for gaining a proportionate sample of the U.S. population (with similar patterns in Europe; see Mohorko et al., 2013).

For applied UX research, you're probably not calling participants and are likely relying on emails sent to online panels of paid participants. Not all panels are created equal (Sauro, 2017, Mar 22). Some offer access to probability samples that mirror the broader population of interest on variables such as geography, age, and gender. Most panels, however, collect lists of people and allow them to sign up for individual studies—a process that doesn't necessarily result in a representative population of participants based on the proportions of types of users in a specified general population.

Error Reduction Strategy: Include as much of your target population in your sample frame as possible. Consider using probability samples with known sample frames for high-stakes decisions. Use what you know about your population of interest to define quotas, thus ensuring you collect enough data for each target segment (typically based on experience in certain domains and with specific products).

2. Sampling Error

Unless you have a way of surveying every single person in the population of interest (e.g., all users of a mobile app), you'll have to deal with sampling error. Sample frames that encompass entire populations of interest are exceedingly rare in applied survey research.

But even if you have good (or complete) coverage in your sampling frame, you'll still have to deal with the randomness of sampling error (Figure 2.2).

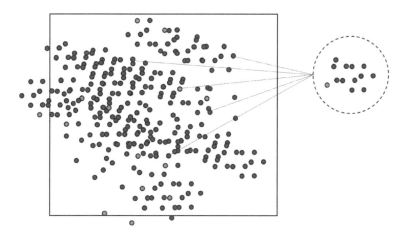

FIGURE 2.2: Visualization of a sample taken from the sample frame.

Fortunately, sampling error can be estimated rather well. Statistical techniques can tell you how precise your estimates are (confidence intervals are covered in Chapter 20) and whether observed differences exceed sampling error (tests of significance are covered in Chapter 21). The greater your sample size, the smaller your sampling error, the more precise your estimates, and the better you can differentiate between subgroups.

While the math behind confidence intervals seems less intuitive than understanding coverage issues, it's straightforward to calculate. In contrast, coverage errors are harder to estimate unless you know something about the people who didn't respond, which we'll cover next.

Error Reduction Strategy: If your measurements aren't precise enough for the decisions you need to make, the best way to reduce sampling error is to increase your sample size. There is, however, a diminishing return as you increase your sample size, especially past a few hundred (Sauro & Lewis, 2020, Jun 24).

3. Nonresponse Error

You can have excellent coverage, a great sampling strategy, and even a large sample size, but some people may not respond. They may drop out before answering any questions, answer only the first few questions, or skip nonrequired questions (see Figure 2.3).

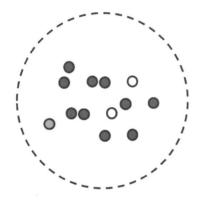

FIGURE 2.3: Visualization of respondents in a survey sample who didn't respond (empty dots).

The response rate is the first place to start when estimating nonresponse error (i.e., the percentage of people who completed compared to those invited). It's better to have a high response rate (e.g., 85%) than a low response rate (e.g., 5%). However, even a high response rate can't fully tell you how much nonresponse error you have. For example, a question asking about income may cause many high- or low-income respondents to abandon the survey.

As in coverage error, the major concern for nonresponse error is that the people who answered the survey may differ meaningfully from people who were invited to respond but chose not to participate.

You can calculate nonresponse error by comparing the characteristics of those who did respond with those who didn't. Ideally, there will be no systematic difference. There are methods to detect whether nonresponses are systematic or random (see Chapter 19).

Error Reduction Strategy: The most common ways of increasing response rates are by offering incentives, re-contacting targeted participants, and keeping surveys as short as possible.

4. Measurement Error

You can have great coverage, a large sample size, and a full response rate, but you'll always have to deal with the final horseman: measurement error. This error encompasses all the things that can go wrong with the presentation of questions and response options and how they might be misinterpreted by respondents. The gap between what we intend to measure and what results we get speaks to the validity of the survey.

Problems that cause measurement errors include:

- Misinterpreting questions (Chapter 7)
- Ambiguous questions and wording (Chapter 7)
- Vague and improper response options (Chapter 7)
- Unclear questions (Chapter 8)
- Forgetting responses (Chapter 9)

These measurement errors can lead to response bias (systematic error) and higher variability (less precision in the response). Both errors are visualized in Figure 2.4.

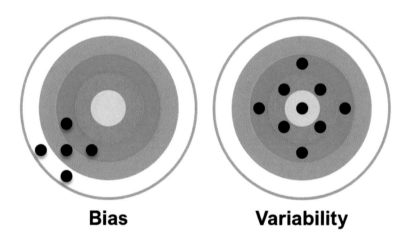

Bias **Variability**

FIGURE 2.4: Visualization of the distinction between bias and variability.

Error Reduction Strategy: When possible, use standardized questions (see Chapter 1) and response scales that have been refined to reduce measurement error, along with other techniques to make questions and response options clearer (see Chapter 8).

CHAPTER SUMMARY

This chapter focused on potential biases and errors in survey design.

What are potential sources of bias in survey design, and how might they be controlled? ...**Four common sources are representativeness, sponsorship, acquiescence, and demographic.** You must be aware of and attempt to control biases in survey design. For example, the Literary Digest poll is a cautionary tale in failing to sample from a representative population. The four common biases discussed in the chapter, and the methods for their control, are:

- *Representativeness of sample:* Use random sampling or consider multiple sources.
- *Sponsorship:* Obfuscate the sponsor or use a third-party firm.
- *Social desirability, prestige, acquiescence:* Frame participation as helping to improve the product or service.
- *Demographic:* Ask only the questions you need to ask, and position demographic questions at the end of the survey.

What are the four potential survey errors? ...**Coverage, sampling, nonresponse, and measurement.** When conducting a survey (or any other method that includes survey-like questions and sampling), watch for these four potential survey errors. Like the Apocalyptic four horsemen, you should strive to avoid them and know how to control or reduce their impact:

- *Coverage errors:* Not targeting the right people.
- *Sampling error:* Inevitable random fluctuations you get when surveying only a part of the sample frame.
- *Nonresponse error:* Systematic differences from those who don't respond to all or some questions.
- *Measurement error:* The gap between what you want to measure and what you get due to bias and variability in responses.

I'm not sure I can control all the sources of bias and errors, so should I never run a survey? ...**You can conduct surveys even when you cannot completely control biases/errors.** The potential for bias and error doesn't mean you should abandon surveys as a UX research method. There's no way to find and remove all biases from a survey, and you can't control all potential sources of error. Just be aware of the sources of bias/error and do what you can to reduce them to limit negative impacts. Results may be more limited (e.g., less broadly generalizable), but they can still be meaningful and useful.

CHAPTER 3:
DEFINING & FINDING PARTICIPANTS

You've decided to conduct a survey. Congratulations. Now it's time to get into the details. To help you, we'll go over some of the logistical details you'll want to sort through before launching your survey to your first participant. We'll answer the following questions: How should I define target participants?

- What variables do you recommend for defining populations and defining subgroups?
- Where can I find participants?
- What should I know about using online panels?
- What are some good ways to get people to participate?
- What do I need to consider for compensating participants?

DEFINING TARGET PARTICIPANTS

In the last chapter, we discussed the potential negative consequences of having a nonrepresentative sample. One of the best ways to avoid those consequences is to know who your target population is and find ways to sample them accordingly. It can be helpful to think of your target participants based on concepts and constructs (see Figure 3.1).

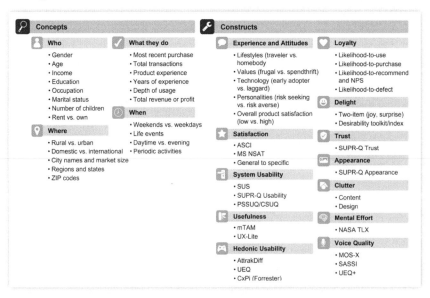

FIGURE 3.1: Concepts and constructs for survey research.

Concepts

Concepts are the demographic variables or "attributes" of your target population. They tend to be concrete rather than abstract (as they are often conceived). They are the typical who (e.g., gender, age, income), where (e.g., country, urban or rural), what they do (e.g., product purchases or usage), and when (e.g., during the day, on weekends, or after life events like purchasing a home).

In UX/CX research, we often see researchers focus too much on respondent attributes like *who* and *where* and too little on *what* people have done (product experience). We have consistently found that prior experience with a product (e.g., QuickBooks) and/or with a domain (bookkeeping) will have a much larger effect on attitudinal metrics like perceived ease, satisfaction, or intent to recommend, than attributes like age or income. It's not that these don't matter, it's that they tend to matter a lot less.

 TIP:

> Minimize relying too much on attributes like demographics (age, gender, education) when defining your target participant profile. These are often not the reasons why people do or don't use a product or service.

Constructs

Constructs tend to be more abstract and multi-faceted than concepts. Concepts include things like tech savviness, travel frequency, or intention to purchase a certain product.

We'll return to the idea of concepts and constructs in Chapter 6 when defining survey questions.

For UX and CX surveys, we recommend considering the following six variables when defining your target population.

1. **Product Experience:** If they have used a specific product (e.g., Salesforce, QuickBooks, United Airlines).
2. **Domain Experience:** If they have experience with specific knowledge and products in an industry (e.g., accountants, IT security admins, lawyers).
3. **Key Tasks:** What people attempt to accomplish with a product (e.g., filing their taxes, posting products for sale).
4. **Attitudes:** Brand attitude, intention to purchase a product.
5. **Demographics:** Age groups (e.g., > 65 or teen).
6. **Accessibility:** People who may need assistive technology (e.g., screen readers) or have conditions that impair their abilities (e.g., vision or hearing impaired).

The following are five examples of defining characteristics of various survey samples:

- People who stream sports (sports watching domain experience).
- DISH subscribers (product experience).
- Sellers on Facebook Marketplace (product experience and task experience).
- People who have recently subscribed to Medicare (government website experience of retirees).
- Smartphone users who have cochlear implants (domain experience and accessibility).

Defining Subgroups

In our experience conducting surveys, the target participant group is rarely homogenous. There are usually distinct subgroups that a stakeholder wants to target. For example, a survey on the attitude of purchasing automobile accessories is the overall target population. But we need to sample participants who have purchased accessories for multiple brands including BMW and General Motors.

If you have different subgroups, this may affect the questions you ask, the tasks you present, and the overall sample size. One of the most common subgroups is based on prior experience with a product or domain, as in the auto-accessory example. Additional examples include:

- Existing online grocery customers vs. those interested in trying the service.
- Owners of a Linksys router vs. owners of other routers.
- Current users of Uber vs. users of Lyft vs. prospective ride-sharing users.

Participants can also be grouped by their amount of experience and frequency of use. For example:

- Purchase from Amazon weekly vs. a few times per year.
- 5+ years using AutoCAD vs. less than 5 years.
- On Facebook multiple times a day vs. a few times per month.

And there are, of course, the more common subgroups by demographics:

- Men vs. women.
- Younger vs. older.
- U.S. vs. international.
- By persona (or predefined customer segment).

Two more examples of surveys where we identified subgroups include:

- People who commute to work daily and who purchase accessories for their car.
- Subscribers to the DISH network who also live in rural areas.

WHERE TO FIND PARTICIPANTS

One of the main advantages of surveys is the ability to collect data from a lot of participants quickly. But this means you'll need access to a lot of participants. The best sources for this are online panels, existing customer lists, and website intercepts.

Online Panel Sources

There are dozens of panel companies with hundreds to thousands of participants willing to take online surveys. Some companies we've worked with include:

- Prodege
- Prolific
- CINT
- Dynata
- Amazon's Mechanical Turk

Prodege, CINT, and Dynata are some of the larger online panels. A typical minimum cost for their service is around $1000, but for that price, they not only provide samples of respondents but also help manage the project for you. They can even find some niche participants beyond general consumers. Amazon's Mechanical Turk is a self-service platform for mostly general consumer profiles that costs less than professional panels. However, watch out for bots and a high number of fraudulent responses, requiring more data cleaning and rejection.

The general process of working with a company that provides participant panels involves the logistics of connecting their participants to your online data-collection tool, ensuring that the right participants take the study and that they are compensated. In general, this involves the following:

- Specifying the profile and sample requirements (e.g., IT decision-makers in small to medium businesses).
- Setting up redirect links to your unmoderated platform (this is how the panel tracks who takes the study and who is screened out or drops out).
- Collecting IDs from participants and confirming with the panel.
- Paying or giving points to participants who complete the study.

For more information on panel and participant costs, see Chapter 18.

Online panels are the go-to method for collecting data quickly for online surveys. Despite their widespread usage, surprisingly little is known about these panels, such as the characteristics of the panel members or the reliability and accuracy of the data collected from them.

While there aren't much published data on the inner workings of panels, we've conducted our own research and compiled findings from the literature to provide insights for you (Sauro, 2017, Mar 22). You can also ask your panel provider for information on their panels.

1. PARTICIPANTS BELONG TO MULTIPLE PANELS

There are a lot of choices in online panel providers. And there's nothing stopping participants from signing up for more than one panel. In fact, one meta-analysis (Callegaro et al., 2014) found that as many as half of all panel participants belong to five or more panels! The implication is that a minority of participants account for a disproportionate amount of participation. Signing up for multiple panels increases panel members' chances that they get access to more studies and earn more rewards.

2. MULTIPLE PANEL MEMBERSHIP AFFECTS ATTITUDES

Belonging to multiple panels isn't necessarily a bad thing, but repeated exposure can influence results. Participants who belong to multiple panels tend to have above-average brand awareness and higher stated intent to purchase products (e.g., soup or paint). Furthermore, participants who belong to multiple panels and take a lot of surveys in a year tend to be inattentive respondents, completing studies much too quickly and providing only terse responses to open-ended questions (Callegaro et al., 2014).

3. THE LENGTH OF PANEL MEMBERSHIP ALSO HAS AN EFFECT.

Callegaro et al., (2014) found that participants who had been with a panel for more than three years were less likely to recommend a product (50% vs. 37%). While there are likely several reasons for this difference, the primary influence has something to do with study exposure and even desensitization. This desensitization may not be bad; generally, participants tend to overestimate their likelihood to do things like purchase or recommend. What is somewhat problematic, though, is not knowing whether your respondents are new to the panel (prone to recommend) or seasoned (somewhat jaded and less likely to recommend).

4. THE AVERAGE ONLINE STUDY TAKES LONGER

Study length is a major contributor to dropout. A meta-analysis of 11 panels (Grey Matter Research & Consulting, 2012) found that the average study time is 17 minutes, with around half of the studies lasting 20 minutes or more, and 13% lasting 30 minutes or more. This is a bit longer than the average completion time in our online studies, but this average duration from the literature can help answer questions about how long is too long relative to the other studies the panel members are taking.

5. POPULATION ESTIMATES CAN VARY

It's common to estimate the attitudes or behaviors of people in the general population. Research has shown that point estimates obtained from different panels varied (in some cases substantially, depending on the panel used) from known external benchmarks (Sauro, 2017, Jan 17). It isn't uncommon for the estimates of metrics, such as intent to purchase and brand awareness, to vary by 15 to 18 percentage points. This discrepancy was seen in a variety of measures, including demographics, stated behaviors (e.g., smoking and newspaper readership), brand awareness, and likelihood to purchase.

6. UX METRICS CAN VARY TOO, BUT NOT AS MUCH AS EXPECTED

The point estimates for common UX benchmark metrics (like the SUPR-Q and NPS—see Appendix B) vary between panels and between general demographic and psychographic variables. On average, the differences were between 3% and 10%, but in some cases, differences exceeded 20%. This variance was less than we expected, given the ethereal nature of UX metrics (Sauro, 2017, Feb 1).

7. CHANGING PANELS CHANGES ESTIMATES

Differences in estimates between panels can, in many cases, exceed real differences in the population. Our recommendation is to not change panels, especially when making comparisons over time, such as likelihood to recommend a product or brand attitudes. Changing panels is, however, often unavoidable. If you make comparisons to historical data and you had to change panels, caution your reader when interpreting the results and provide any known information on the differences in panel characteristics.

8. PROBABILITY PANELS ARE PROBABLY BETTER

Most online panels are called nonprobability panels, as they obtain their members using online ads, snowball sampling, river sampling, and direct enrollments. These panels don't sample proportionally from the general population. In contrast, probability panels, as the name suggests, ensure that every member of a population (often an entire country) has at least some chance of being selected to respond to a study. Probability panel companies have measures in place to ensure some level of representativeness, often for hard-to-reach populations. As expected, probability samples, while rare, tend to (but don't always) perform better than nonprobability samples by more closely matching the external benchmarks.

9. BE WARY OF PANEL QUALITY

It seems that each year there is an increasing demand for people to participate in online research. This pressure on getting samples can increase the likelihood of participants gaming the system, misrepresenting themselves, or providing poor-quality responses.

We have become increasingly critical of online panel sources, as we've seen a slow degradation in the quality of responses. Most concerning is that some participants (especially from some poor-quality panels) will go to great lengths to avoid getting screened out of studies (e.g., by incorrectly stating income and age, which are hard to verify). Consequently, we use multiple panels to fill samples, and we corroborate findings where possible with data from high-quality panels. See Chapter 19 for more on cleaning data to identify and remove poor-quality responses.

Access Existing Customers and Prospects

Existing and prospective customers of a company or its product are an obvious wellspring for testing. However, such respondents aren't a panacea for surveys and have at least two major drawbacks:

- Bias: These participants are more likely to have a favorable attitude toward the company and be familiar with its products and websites. This makes them less than ideal for competitive studies.

- Not new: By definition, most of these participants would be considered experienced users. If you plan to evaluate the new-user experience, these participants wouldn't fit well (unless you are studying a new product).

The two most common ways to reach these existing customers and prospects are by using direct email and website intercepts.

DIRECT EMAIL

Most organizations maintain a customer list, and they usually can communicate with customers using bulk email (for those who have opted in). You can invite customers on these email lists to participate in a survey. Include a short description of what's expected, the honorarium/sweepstakes (if any), and how long the study may take. To email a lot of participants, don't just add them to the cc or bcc line in your email program. You or your organization will need to use a bulk email provider to ensure you don't get blacklisted and your email gets through. See Chapter 18 for some suggestions and costs of sending bulk emails if your company doesn't provide this already.

WEBSITE INTERCEPTS

Visitors to a company website can be invited to participate in a current or upcoming survey. You can use pop-ups (see the MUiQ example in Figure 3.2) or opt-in boxes on websites to solicit volunteers. Using this approach, you'll generally get qualified participants because they were on your website of their own accord. Let participants know the time commitment, honorarium (if any), and the dates of the survey if it's not immediate. You can also use this approach to pre-screen participants based on demographics like age and prior experience, then target them for future studies.

FIGURE 3.2: Website intercept example.

Website intercepts aren't a guaranteed way of finding only qualified participants. The people who respond may only be interested in the incentive (if offered), or users who have had a negative experience may be motivated to express their dissatisfaction.

We worked with one large consumer electronics company that collected participants from an intercept off their home page. The intercept let prospective participants know the honorarium they'd receive for participating in an upcoming study. The company collected thousands of emails from people willing to participate but found that people had posted the survey link to coupon and giveaway websites, which attracted nonqualified participants. To retain only qualified participants, the company had to add additional screening after collecting the names.

HOW TO INCREASE SURVEY PARTICIPATION RATES

A lot of work goes into planning a survey (writing questions, selecting response options), and it can be frustrating if not enough people take the survey. It's like planning a party and no one comes!

Without enough of the right participants agreeing to participate and completing your survey, the generalizability of your findings is limited.

Five Approaches for Increasing Participation

Here are five approaches you can use to get the right people to participate in your surveys. In many cases, you can combine these approaches to achieve higher participation rates.

1. PROVIDE AN INCENTIVE...TO A POINT

Incentives are extrinsic motivators that generally increase response rates in all modes of surveying, including phone, mail, Internet, and panel studies. Monetary incentives tend to increase response rates more than gifts, and prepaid incentives (even as little as $1–2) increase response rates more than lotteries or promised incentives delivered upon survey completion. Unsurprisingly, increasing the amount of the incentive also increases participation rates (Singer & Ye, 2013).

Incentives aren't a panacea, though. Some evidence from social science research suggests that incentives can erode participants' natural motivation to perform well in a study. For example, adults who initially rated a complex task as interesting, and are then paid for their performance based on how well they do, later rate the same activity as less attractive. Interestingly, when participants weren't paid, or paid a flat rate regardless of performance, their interest in the task remained consistent over time (Fessler, 2003).

In most cases, incentives get more people to take your survey but don't seem to affect the quality of the data (positively or negatively). The actual incentive you should offer depends on several variables, including the burden on the respondent and how difficult people are to find. If you're thinking of offering incentives, consider these additional factors.

2. APPEAL TO INTRINSIC MOTIVATION

Some participants can be motivated to take your survey if they feel their responses will make a difference. To attract these participants, be sure to include the benefits or impact participants' responses will have in the survey invitation and welcome screen or script.

A meta-analysis (Cerasoli et al., 2014) looked at 40 years of research on intrinsic motivation and found that intrinsic motivation is a major predictor of performance quality. When people derive natural enjoyment from whatever task they are completing, they will rarely perform poorly. In examining the effects of intrinsic motivation and extrinsic incentives on performance, researchers found that for quality of performance, intrinsic motivation is the most important factor; whereas for quantity of performance, extrinsic incentives are the most impactful.

3. GAMIFY

Gamification attempts to increase user motivation and engagement by using game elements (e.g., points, leaderboards, badges) in non-game contexts. The thought is that by mimicking the hedonic or playful aspects of a game, it's possible to build intrinsic motivation.

While we've seen gamification extensively in UX research, it also extends to traditional survey research. For example, there is some evidence that when market research surveys utilize gamification techniques, participation is improved, and motivation increases (Cechanowicz et al., 2013).

4. PROVIDE PERSONALIZED FEEDBACK

Many people participate in research studies to learn something, whether about themselves or the study being conducted. If you can provide respondents with either immediate or delayed information on their responses, your response rates will likely increase.

For example, when respondents received personalized feedback (Kühne & Kroh, 2016) about their scores on the Big Five personality inventory, they were more likely to rate the survey as interesting and fun. Like providing incentives, however, the quality of the data in this study didn't differ significantly between participants who received personalized feedback and those who didn't.

5. SHARE THE FINDINGS

When possible, if it makes sense, offer to share the results of the findings with respondents. For example, Consumer Reports regularly surveys its millions of members to provide data about their cars' reliability. In return, Consumer Reports provides an aggregated set of responses to participants. Another example is the UXPA salary survey (Sauro et al., 2022, May 31). Practitioners answer scores of questions about themselves and their organization; in turn, respondents get a comprehensive report on industry practices.

Some Guidance When Paying Participants

In the never-ending quest to find participants for survey studies (and any research, for that matter), you'll likely confront the question of whether and how much you should offer to pay participants. Here are 13 things to consider when deciding if an incentive is the way to go for your study.

I. INCENTIVES HELP RESPONSE RATES

Incentives in some form (money, gift cards, iPads, etc.) generally increase response rates to web-based and email surveys (Mercer et al., 2015). If your survey is on the long side, incentives can also encourage participants to finish it, and there's some evidence they help with the quality of open-ended responses (Cole et al., 2015). The good news is that they don't seem to bias the responses systematically (e.g., through satisficing).

2. MONEY IS USUALLY BETTER THAN GIFTS

Monetary incentives generally increase response rates more than gifts. Prepaid incentives help more than promised incentives, though it's difficult to prepay people for web surveys (unlike sending money in the mail with a hard-copy survey). But money doesn't always help; see #12 below.

3. PAYING CAN BE PAINFUL

Mailing out hundreds of $10 checks isn't fun (we've done it) and isn't easy with most banks. Mailing physical gifts is even harder because you need to collect valid physical addresses. You can use the next best thing to cash: Amazon gift cards and PayPal. Both Amazon and PayPal make it easy for you to pay in bulk, but not everyone has a PayPal account, and sometimes you can't use Amazon (e.g., if you're another retailer!). There are bulk payment providers who can distribute cash for you, but the fee is often as much as the honorarium.

4. LOTTERIES AND RAFFLES MAY BE CHEAPER AND EASIER

Instead of paying everyone, you can have a drawing, lottery, or "raffle." The nice thing about a lottery is that you can offer a more substantial incentive (e.g., an iPad or $500) instead of a modest honorarium (e.g., $10). For conducting a lottery or raffle, you'll need to be sure your participants are aware of their true odds of winning (see below on legality issues) and be sure you have a way of sending the prizes (you don't want to offer a new iPad if they're out of stock for months!).

5. LOTTERIES/SWEEPSTAKES ARE EASIER BUT PROBABLY NOT AS EFFECTIVE

Lotteries are easier and probably cheaper than paying everyone, but there's some evidence they aren't as effective (Roberts et al., 2000; Zhang et al., 2017). This is likely a natural consequence of how people view incentives. Which would you have: guaranteed money (even a small amount) or a small chance to win a larger but still modest amount? A professional survey taker put his thoughts succinctly: "Sweepstakes are for people who can't calculate probability properly—scrape a decent budget together and pay people for their time."

6. LOTTERIES HAVE LEGAL ISSUES

You'd think it would be simple: you're giving away things! But it's not that easy, unfortunately. In many U.S. states (and probably most countries), you must be careful about how you conduct your sweepstakes or lottery. You might have to get legal help to ensure you're not breaking the law (e.g., you may have to display the official rules and specify how the winner is determined).

7. CONSIDER OTHER INCENTIVES

You don't have to give away buckets of cash or iPads as an incentive. If you have a product or service people like, store credit or other discounts or coupons (if they're something you can offer) may be an effective incentive. Again, our candid professional survey taker offers his advice: "If you're offering a coupon/gift card, it better be good."

8. FIND THE RIGHT AMOUNT

Higher incentives generally increase response rates (Pedersen & Nielsen, 2016) but with a diminishing return. The good news is that while higher incentives improve responses, they don't seem to negatively affect the nature of the responses or the type of people who respond—you just get more people to respond (Singer, 2017).

The right amount will depend on your audience (higher for higher-paid professions) and the length of the study. You may need to experiment with different amounts to see what works.

 TIP:

You can do a soft launch (sending an invitation to a small sample) to see what the response rate is likely to be based on your planned incentive.

9. BUDGET

Of course, you can only compensate as much as your budget will allow. Even a nominal compensation of $5 adds up quickly if you need more than 1,000 responses. You will also need to budget for the cost (and time) to get the money to these scores of participants. Here are two things to watch for when paying participants directly:

1. Be sure you have a survey quota. Some surveys can fill fast, and you don't want to be on the hook for 2,000 payments if you had budgeted for only 1,000.

2. If you must oversample (because of rejecting poor-quality responses), you will likely have to decide whether to compensate all or just the responses you thought were worth retaining.

If you're running a lottery or raffle, you'll again want to consider the costs of obtaining the incentive and shipping costs if applicable. And if you're using discount codes, be sure that's factored into your actual sales margin.

10. MORE LEGAL ISSUES

Not everyone can receive money or gifts. Physicians, radiologists, and government employees are among the many participant types who are often not allowed to receive money at all or from certain businesses. For example, there are rules against pharmaceutical companies paying doctors even nominal gifts due to the potential conflict of interest.

11. APPEAL TO THE INTEREST OF YOUR PARTICIPANTS

If the participants feel their voice will make a difference, you may not need any incentive. This is especially so if your survey is short (think under 10 minutes). For example, if a customer feels their opinion will help improve a product or service they use, they will be more likely to respond. Or if you have a passionate group of users, they will likely provide their opinions at much higher rates (e.g., nonprofits).

12. MONEY MAY ALSO HURT RESPONSE RATES

Not only does compensating hit the bottom line, but it may also negatively affect your response rate. It may seem like offering an incentive is a no-brainer way to get more people to participate. But money is not just like any other type of incentive; people treat it differently.

If your participants are already intrinsically motivated to provide their feedback (e.g., because they believe in your cause or product), offering money can backfire. There's less research on this effect in survey incentives, but it's a well-documented effect in many contexts ("Overjustification effect," n.d.).

13. DON'T COERCE

While it's generally less of a concern for online surveys or applied research, there is sometimes a concern about incentives being coercive, especially for certain disadvantaged populations (Groth, 2010). If you survey an economically disadvantaged group, be sure your incentive won't coerce people into feeling they NEED to respond.

CHAPTER SUMMARY

This chapter focused on defining target participants, working with panels, and increasing participation.

How should I define target participants? ...Think in terms of concepts and constructs. Concepts include relatively concrete participant attributes such as demographics, answering questions about who the participants are, where they are, what they do, and when they do it. In UX and CX research, what people do and their prior experiences with products tend to be more important to know than standard demographics. In contrast, constructs tend to be more abstract and multi-faceted than concepts (e.g., tech savviness, behavioral intentions).

What variables do you recommend for defining populations and defining subgroups? ...There are six variables we recommend considering. Consider product experience (specific product), domain experience (types of products or industries), key tasks, attitudes, demographics, and accessibility.

Where can I find participants? ...There are three key sources. The best sources are online panels, existing customer lists, and website intercepts.

What should I know about using online panels? ...There are nine things to consider. Online panels are the go-to method for collecting data quickly for online surveys. Here are nine considerations for their use.

- *Participants belong to multiple panels.* People do this to earn more rewards.

- *Multiple panel membership affects attitudes.* Repeated exposure to surveys can lead to inattentive respondents.

- *Length of panel membership also has an effect.* This is another way in which repeated exposure can lead to inattentive responses.

- *The average online study lasts less than 20 minutes.* Avoid studies that are too long. Study length is a major contributor to dropout.

- *Population estimates can vary.* Point estimates obtained from different panels often vary by 15–18 percentage points.

- *UX metrics can vary, too, but not as much as expected.* Point estimates for common UX benchmark metrics vary between panels, on average, between 3–10%.

- *Changing panels changes estimates.* Try to avoid changing panels when you will make comparisons over time.

- *Probability panels are probably better.* Probability panels sample proportionally from the general population. When this is an important research consideration, you should consider such a panel, but they usually come at a higher price.

- *Be wary of panel quality.* Panels can vary in quality from each other and over time, so consider starting the study with participants from multiple panels to fill samples and corroborate findings.

What are some good ways to get people to participate? ...We have five recommendations. Here are five approaches for getting the right people to participate which can often be combined to achieve higher participation rates.

- *Provide an incentive...to a point.* Incentives get more people to take surveys but don't seem to affect the quality of responses.

- *Appeal to intrinsic motivation.* When participants feel their responses will make a difference, they will be more motivated to take the survey, and motivated participants provide higher-quality data.

- *Gamify.* You can use game elements (e.g., points, leaderboards, badges) to increase engagement.

- *Provide personalized feedback.* Providing personalized feedback about someone's responses can increase engagement.

- *Share the findings.* When possible, offer to share the survey findings with participants.

What do I need to consider for compensating participants? ...There are many considerations. Here are 13 things to consider when deciding whether an incentive is the way to go for your study.

- *Incentives help response rates.* They do this without seeming to systematically bias responses.

- *Money is usually better than gifts.* Cash is king.

- *Paying can be painful.* Amazon gift cards and PayPal are easier than mailing hundreds of checks, but they don't always work for every participant.

- *Lotteries may be cheaper and easier.* But it is important to execute them properly.

- *Although they are easier, lotteries are probably not as effective.* This is most likely due to people's beliefs about their odds of winning.

- *Lotteries also have legal issues.* Do not conduct a lottery without getting guidance to ensure you are not putting yourself in legal jeopardy.

- *Consider other incentives.* In some situations, you can offer store credit, discounts, or coupons, but if you do, they need to appeal to the potential participants.

- *Find the right amount.* This depends on your audience and the length of the study.

- *Work within your budget.* And be careful you don't accidentally collect more responses than planned.

- *Know the potential legal issues.* People working in certain occupations (e.g., physicians, government employees) may be legally prohibited from receiving payment for participation.

- *Appeal to the interest of your participants.* When participants care about your research, they may be motivated enough to participate without compensation (especially if the survey is short).

- *Money can sometimes hurt response rates.* This is uncommon, but some participants might be offended by being offered a monetary incentive.

- *Don't coerce.* There can be an ethical concern when offering payment to economically disadvantaged groups such that they feel they must participate even if they don't really want to.

CHAPTER 4:
SAMPLE STRATEGIES

Unless you plan to survey every member of your target population, you'll need to work with only a sample of the population. But even in cases where you *can* survey everyone, you might not want to because of survey fatigue and costs. What's more, most populations are fluid. There may be only a hundred users of a financial product this month, but what about the new users who will join next month or next year?

In this chapter, we'll address the following questions:

- What's the first step in deciding on a sampling strategy?
- What are the different ways to collect a probability sample?
- What are the different types of nonprobability samples?
- Is it OK to use a nonprobability sample?

One of the first concerns practitioners have if they can't survey everyone is that they will be misled by the results from a sample. This includes having too few responses or receiving responses from people who don't represent the population of interest (see Chapter 2).

We'll discuss the mechanics of sample size estimation in Chapter 17, but for now, it's helpful to review the concept of sampling. Survey sampling is like sampling a pot of soup to be sure it tastes right and doesn't need more salt, or it needs to cook longer (Figure 4.1).

FIGURE 4.1: Regardless of the size of the pot, after thorough stirring, you can sample the soup with one tablespoon.

To ensure the soup is ready, you're not going to drink down the whole pot. Instead, you'll sample a small amount. And because you're taking only a small amount, there will always be some uncertainty about the taste of the parts you aren't sampling.

Assuming the soup is reasonably stirred up, it doesn't matter how large the pot is. A sample, even a small one, is a surprisingly reliable way of assessing the entire pot of soup (or population). Yes, there will be uncertainty, and we'll cover how to deal with the uncertainty in upcoming sections. First, let's talk about sampling strategies.

There are different approaches to sampling and ways to categorize them. At a high level, there are two helpful distinctions: probability sampling and nonprobability sampling.

PROBABILITY SAMPLING

Probability sampling means that all members of the population have a chance of participating in the survey.

Random Sampling

Random sampling, as the name suggests, means we randomly select people from the target population to participate in the survey. It can be subdivided into simple and stratified sampling.

SIMPLE RANDOM SAMPLING

This means that once you define your target population, everyone in that population has at least a chance (each person can be selected at random) to participate. In practice, it sounds simple, but it is usually quite challenging, if not impossible, to have the ability to reach out to everyone in your target population. If your target population is all current customers of a product, you could take the list and randomly select a subset and invite them. When the target population is more dynamic, say, prospective users of a new financial service, the target population likely includes millions of people, few of whom you can contact.

There was a time when it was more plausible than now to contact the general population by using listings in phone books, but even then, people could have unlisted numbers. With the shift from landlines to cell phones and people's reluctance to accept cold calls, simple random sampling of the general population has become very difficult.

STRATIFIED RANDOM SAMPLING

It's often the case that your target population isn't completely homogenous, differing on some of the concepts and constructs you've identified. In such cases, you'll want to subdivide the population of users. For example, we conducted a survey for an educational software application. Its core users were teachers and students, who used the software differently (e.g., students were given assignments by the teachers). We used a stratified random-sampling approach to obtain a sufficient sample from both user groups.

You can get carried away with stratification, such as stratifying by age, gender, income, and geography. Sometimes clients request a long wish list of sampling attributes. While each of these can have a major impact on sensitive or political issues, when you ask people to rate their satisfaction with a product experience or their intent to use, usually the major differentiators are product and domain experience.

With the defined subgroup (strata), you then randomly sample each group. Just like with simple random sampling, though, ensuring that every member of each group's population has a chance of participating is challenging unless you have a finite customer list. In the educational software survey, we had access to all current students and teachers using the software.

You can layer the strata to sample from. For example, you can randomly sample by user type and continent, so you sample, for example, teachers and students in North America and Europe. As you add more strata and subpopulations, you'll need to be mindful of the growing sample size you may need to maintain a desired margin of error (see Chapter 17).

 TIP:

Note that there's a type of sampling called *cluster sampling* that can be confused with stratified sampling. Cluster sampling involves sampling all people of a certain group, versus stratified, which involves sampling from the group. For example, in a complex study of medical outcomes, hospitals might be randomly sampled so all patients receiving care at a given hospital are surveyed, then rural and urban patient experiences could be compared. Cluster sampling isn't used as frequently as stratified sampling in surveys.

Proportional Probability Sampling

Even if you can't randomly sample from everyone in the target population, probability sampling helps ensure there's representation from the targeted strata and substrata using external benchmarks and census matching.

PROPORTIONAL SAMPLING BY EXTERNAL BENCHMARKS

If there are known benchmarks about the prevalence of concepts and constructs in the target population, you can use these to achieve proportional sampling. For example, if country/region is a key differentiator for a product, and through product sales data you know 40% of existing customers live in the U.S. and 60% in the European Union, you can use this external benchmark to ensure your sample has 40% from the U.S. and 60% from the EU. Or if you were assessing the sentiment of users of a mobile app, and your usage data showed 80% iOS users and 20% Android, you could proportionally sample to match these criteria. You can also layer subgroups (strata) and sample proportionally (e.g., iOS users in Europe).

CENSUS-MATCHING SAMPLING

If you are surveying prospective users of a product or don't have access to customer lists, a special type of external benchmark to consider is census data. As we mentioned in Chapter 1, the U.S. conducts an official national census every ten years (with interim data published more frequently), and other countries and municipalities conduct censuses regularly. Census data tend to focus on concepts (attributes) like geography, age, education, income, and gender, so its value is limited if your primary target segments are based on product usage. It does, however, work quite well if you're looking for a general consumer population and want to avoid overrepresentation from certain populations that are prevalent in online panels (e.g., younger urban respondents). More information on the data collected in the U.S. Census can be found online at census.gov/data.html.

NONPROBABILITY SAMPLING

Nonprobability means that not everyone in the target population has a chance to be invited or take your survey. This weakens claims of representativeness and generalizability, but it's a lot easier to collect a nonprobability sample (e.g., a convenience or snowball sample) using online panels, social media, or volunteers.

Convenience Sampling

As the name suggests, convenience sampling involves getting just about anyone you can to take your survey. This could be from sending emails to friends and family, posting on social media, or using online panels. You will need to watch out for over- or underrepresented respondents. For example, many online sources tend to skew younger (21 to 25) and more urban than the general population.

Snowball Sampling

Snowball sampling is a type of convenience sample where you ask participants to refer others to take the survey. Some profiles may be so difficult to recruit (e.g., people who trade in NFTs, TikTok accounts with 1,000+ followers) that the only way to get many responses is through a sort of referral campaign.

The major downfall here is that this may introduce dependencies between your responses, as people may invite members of their households or co-workers who share certain attitudes. Having nonindependent responses can complicate statistical interpretation (see Chapter 21). Use snowball sampling as a last resort.

Table 4.1 shows the pros and cons of the sampling methods covered in this section.

Sampling Method	Probability Type	Pros	Cons
Simple random sampling	Probability	Ideal in the abstract	Unrealistic to know all members of a population and have a process for their random selection and participation
Random stratified sampling	Probability	Controlled sampling from defined groups (e.g., product/domain experience)	Potential coverage and participation issues within defined groups and a possibility of not sampling from an important group
Proportional sampling by external standards	Nonprobability	Focused on matching external benchmarks (e.g., frequency of purchase, age groups)	Not a random sample and may not account for all respondents
Census-matching sampling	Nonprobability	A specific type of proportional sampling to match census demographics	Census information is limited to only a few attributes like age, geography, gender

(continued on pg. 46)

Sampling Method	Probability Type	Pros	Cons
Convenience sampling	Nonprobability	Easy nonprobability sampling method	Issues with coverage and representativeness
Snowball sampling	Nonprobability	A special type of convenience sample in which participants (often specialized users) are encouraged to invite others to the survey	Same as general convenience sampling but with clear dependence between participants

TABLE 4.1: Pros and cons of various probability and nonprobability sampling methods.

RESEARCH SAMPLING IN PRACTICE

In principle, it seems like collecting probability-based samples is the better choice. In practice, however, it can be quite challenging or expensive to use a probability-based approach because it is usually quite difficult to reach out to all members of the target population.

Many UX and CX decisions need good-enough input, not perfect input, to help guide decisions about features or marketing. These are not the same high-stakes polls used to predict the outcome of an election, which often has candidates differing by only one percentage point.

Consequently, most surveys we've been involved with use some form of convenience sampling paired with some external benchmarks (e.g., known customer attributes like device type, experience level, and country). In some cases, our surveys start with a random-sampling approach or have quotas that match several external benchmarks like age, gender, and income. As data collection drags on, those quotas may be dropped, and the remaining sample is filled with a convenience sample (see Figure 4.2). In these cases, be careful about generalizing your finding.

| SRS | Proportional | Convenience |
| What Researchers Strive For | What Researchers Plan On | What Researchers Settle On |

FIGURE 4.2: Stages of sampling decisions in the real world.

Some Level of Unrepresentativeness Is Common

You can get hung up worrying about the shortcomings of your sample. In our experience, stakeholders who don't like your findings may be quick to call out weaknesses in both your sample representativeness and your sample size. Although you can't ignore legitimate criticism about representativeness, keep in mind that perfect representation is more of an ideal than a reality, so be appropriately cautious in your generalizations.

We recommend striving for a representative sample by focusing on a small set of key variables, such as prior experience with a product or domain, or a certain base of knowledge. Or focus on some key attributes, like age, if it makes sense. For example, a survey on supplemental insurance for Medicare in the U.S. will skew older. A survey on TikTok usage will skew younger.

Disproportionate Samples Happen

Another reality of using sampling for applied research is that in getting a large enough sample, a disproportionate sample breakdown happens. For example, most online panels tend to skew young (Figure 4.3), so if you aren't properly balancing/adding quotas on age, you may end up with an age distribution that mirrors that panel makeup rather than the target population.

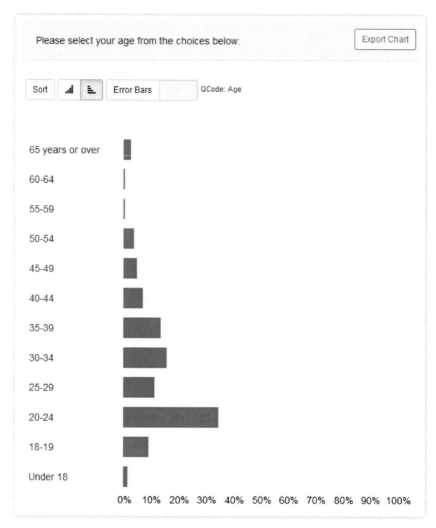

FIGURE 4.3: Most panels skew younger than the population (baby boomers are still a huge %).

This can be a problem. For example, in a survey on the attitude toward a mobile app, women were more likely to take the survey, even though they made up a minority of the target population (Figure 4.4). To improve generalization to the target population, use analytical techniques like weighting (see Chapter 21).

FIGURE 4.4: Example of a mismatch between gender proportions in a sample versus target population.

Sometimes Controlling Variability is More Important than Proportional Matching

Proportional matching matters most when you need to generalize estimates of proportions from a sample to a target population. In the mobile app survey, if the goal of the study was to understand differences in attitudes between female and male users, then the lack of proportionality wouldn't matter much if the sample size in each group was large enough to get sufficiently precise estimates to be able to detect a significant difference.

When conducting surveys about product attitudes and usage, for example, data collected from novices tend to be more variable than data collected from experts (Lewis & Sauro, 2021b). If the goal of a study is to achieve equally precise measurements from each group, then the sample size for each group should be determined by their expected variability rather than their expected proportion (Deming, 1950).

CHAPTER SUMMARY

This chapter focused on sampling strategies.

What's the first step in deciding on a sampling strategy? …Determine if you need a probability sample. Sampling strategies fall into two groups—probability and nonprobability. If you need all members of a population to have a chance of participating in the survey, you'll need a probability sample.

What are the different ways to collect a probability sample? …Simple, stratified, proportional, and census matching. In simple random sampling, each person in the population has been identified for random selection. Stratified random sampling is similar, but the population is subdivided into groups to ensure adequate coverage of each group in the sample. Proportional sampling is similar to stratified sampling with subdivisions of the population defined by external benchmarks (e.g., what an enterprise knows about the percentages of customers in the U.S. and the EU). Census-matching sampling is a special type of proportional sampling where the external benchmarks are based on a government census.

What are the different types of nonprobability samples? …Two of the most common are convenience and snowball. In a convenience sample, you ask anyone you can get to take the survey. In snowball sampling, you start with a group of known participants who fit your profile, then encourage them to not only take the survey but also invite others to take the survey (a strategy that is useful for special profiles that are difficult to recruit).

Is it OK to use a nonprobability sample? …It often is OK in UX/CX research. Most UX and CX decisions need good-enough input, not perfect input. In practice, some level of unrepresentativeness is common, and disproportionate samples happen. When you have these concerns, however, be careful about generalizing your findings.

PART 2:
Writing Survey Questions

CHAPTER 5:
SURVEY QUESTION ANATOMY AND TYPES

As with a book, it can be a challenge to sit down and write a survey. How do you start writing questions? Few professionals we know of have taken a formal course in survey development, and most instead rely on their experiences or on best practices. To help you, we'll answer the following questions:

- What is the anatomy of a survey question?
- What response options should I provide?
- What are the main types of survey questions?

Despite being called questions, survey questions can be both questions and phrases, which is why some researchers refer to them with the broader term item. Other researchers (e.g., Saris & Gallhofer, 2004) have referred to them as assertions, but that seems a bit cumbersome and unfamiliar. In our practice, and throughout this book, we use question and item interchangeably.

When digging into writing, it helps to first think of the "anatomy" of a survey item. Items have two parts: the stem and the response options (e.g., Robinson & Leonard, 2018). Saris and Gallhofer (2007b) break down survey items further into six components. Five describe the stem, and the last is for response options:

1. Introduction
2. Information
3. Instructions
4. Opinions
5. Request
6. Response Options

THE SIX COMPONENTS OF A SURVEY QUESTION

Not all survey questions have all six components, and by understanding the components and their functions, you will know when and how to use them. Figure 5.1 shows more detail on the anatomy of a survey question.

1. Introduction	*e.g.,* This is a survey about online grocery services.
2. Information	*e.g.,* Online grocery services can be offered by a grocery store (e.g., Kroger) or by a delivery company that services multiple stores (e.g., Instacart).
3. Instructions	*e.g.,* We'd like you to think about your most recent food delivery experience.
4. Opinions	*e.g.,* Other users have identified convenience and safety as primary reasons for using this service.
5. Request	*e.g.,* How easy was it to order groceries for your most recent order?
6. Response Options	○ ○ ○ ○ ○

FIGURE 5.1: Anatomy of a survey question overview.

1. Introduction

Surveys are typically on a specific topic, and the introductory statement helps the respondent get into the right frame of mind. For example, "This is a survey about online grocery services." But each question may need its own introduction (for example, "Now we'd like to ask you some questions about your experience ordering groceries online.").

Introductions may be needed when you:

- Shift the topic from prior questions (e.g., you go from asking about the experience of using a desktop website to a mobile app).
- Require more thinking/recall from respondents.

2. Information About the Topic or Definitions

After the introduction, you may need to provide additional information about what you're asking. You won't need this for simple attribute-type questions (age, income, gender), but you may need it for less familiar topics or ambiguous topics that respondents might interpret broadly. For example, when asking about the use of online grocery delivery, information may include something like "Online grocery services can be offered by a grocery store (e.g., Kroger) or by a delivery company that services multiple stores (e.g., Instacart)."

Information about the topic may be needed when presenting:

- New or unfamiliar concepts.
- Complex constructions.
- Response options that may be easily confused.

3. Instructions

While most people don't need instructions on how to indicate their age or select a radio button in a Likert-type question, certain questions require instruction on how to answer. Common question types that benefit from instructions include:

- Ranking questions
- Kano questions
- Task-based questions (pick some)
- MaxDiff questions

For example, when using our MUiQ platform to conduct a Kano study on prioritizing features, we provide instructions on how to answer the functional and dysfunctional questions using a common scenario in which respondents rate features (Figure 5.2).

✳ **Please read the following instructions carefully before beginning this activity.**

For each of the features listed below on the left, consider the following question:

"How would you feel if a general website had this feature?"

Answer this question, using drag and drop to organize the features into the following categories:

- **I like it** (i.e., this feature would be very helpful to me)
- **I expect it** (i.e., this feature is a basic requirement for me)
- **I am neutral** (i.e., this feature would not affect me)
- **I can tolerate it** (i.e., this feature would be a minor inconvenience)
- **I dislike it** (i.e., this feature would be a major problem for me)

FIGURE 5.2: Example instructions for a Kano survey question type.

Instructions may be needed:

- When using uncommon question types (e.g., Kano, pick some, fixed sum).
- To prevent common mistakes (e.g., picking only one instead of all that apply).

4. Opinions of Others

In some cases, you may want to understand how respondents react to the opinions of others, such as politicians, public health officials, or scientists. For example, "Other users have identified convenience and safety as primary reasons for using this service."

Opinions of others may be needed when:

- Reaction to the opinions of others is the primary research focus.
- Including this information provides an appropriate context for asking the question.

This element is especially rare in UX and CX research due to its potentially biasing effects on responses. Don't include it unless there is a clear need to do so.

5. Requests for an Answer

The core part of the question stem is the request for an answer from the respondent. For example, "What was your highest degree obtained?" or "How easy was it to order groceries for your most recent order?"

To create the request, you can use three approaches (Saris & Gallhofer, 2007a):

Direct request: Invert the subject and auxiliary verb of a statement to convert it to a question. For example, "I would need the help of a technical person" becomes "Would you need the help of a technical person?"

Indirect request: Instead of asking a question, use a statement and then have people respond with agree/disagree response options (e.g., "I felt very confident using the software.").

Wh-requests: Use the common interrogatives (e.g., who, what, when, where, why, how much, which) and pose the question directly to the respondent. For example, ask "What is your age?" or "Why did you select the number you did?"

This request for an answer is the last and most important of the stem components. The introduction, information, instructions, and opinions are optional, but without the request for an answer, you don't have a question.

6. Response Options

In addition to crafting the item stem (Steps 1–5), you will have to carefully consider the intent of the question to select the right response options. Researchers can use various response option types, but some types are better suited than others for different research goals. We've identified four key steps to help you get started:

1. **Discovery:** When discovery is the primary goal, use open-ended items.

2. **Measurement:** The key decision when collecting measurements is to determine if the required data are or aren't categorical.

3. **Categorical:** Categorical data can be ordered (e.g., age groups) or unordered (e.g., streaming video services), allowing the selection of multiple items when choices aren't mutually exclusive or restricting selection to one item when choices are mutually exclusive.

4. **Not categorical:** Noncategorical question types can be classified as ranking, allocation, or rating. Of these types, rating scales are the ones most used in UX and CX research.

For more information on selecting the right response options, see Chapter 10 for a detailed discussion and a *decision tree* to guide your choices.

Examples

Example 1: If your goal is to discover the types of problems users have been having with a website, then the response option type should be open-ended (Goal > Discovery > Open-Ended Item—see Chapter 10), with an item stem and response option like those shown in Figure 5.3.

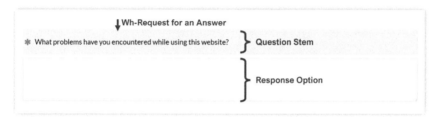

FIGURE 5.3: Stem and response option for a discovery question.

Example 2: If your goal is to measure a respondent's confidence in having correctly completed a task, and you've conceptualized this measure as ranging from no confidence to total confidence, then the response type should be a unipolar rating item (Goal > Measurement > Not Categorical > Rating > None-to-Much > Unipolar Item—see Chapter 10), such as the one illustrated in Figure 5.4.

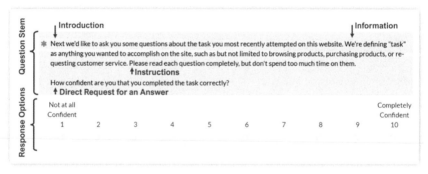

FIGURE 5.4: Stem and response option for a unipolar rating question.

FOUR TYPES OF SURVEY QUESTIONS

With the basic anatomy of a survey question covered, we'll now discuss how the core anatomy can vary across different types of survey questions. In architecture, form follows function. In survey design, question format follows content.

While survey questions are generally distinct in their wording and response options, many share common content characteristics. The contents of the survey questions themselves can be classified. For example, you can think of demographic questions (age and gender) as belonging to one group and satisfaction-type attitude questions as belonging to another group. Both may even use the same question format (closed-ended single response), but they will collect different content. Classification isn't just something for bored librarians (think of the scientific advances driven by biological classification or the periodic table); it can be used to better understand the strengths and weaknesses of similar questions, including possible common response errors.

After over a century of practice with and research on surveys, there's been a lot written about them. The journal Public Opinion Quarterly is one place where researchers have attempted to classify survey questions using various classification schemes.

Schaeffer and Dykema (2011) reviewed studies published in Public Opinion Quarterly and generated a loose classification of seven groups from the types of questions they encountered:

1. Events and behaviors (going to the doctor, purchasing toothpaste)
2. Evaluations or judgments (ratings of ease, satisfaction with products)
3. Internal states or feelings (happiness, anxiety, surprise)
4. Accounts (reasons for taking an action, such as leaving a job or purchasing a product)
5. Classifications (whether you have a 401k, own an electric car)
6. Social characteristics (marital status)
7. Descriptions of the environment (number of employees in a company)

Schaeffer and Dykema didn't intend their list to be an exhaustive taxonomy. While it offers a good start for other researchers, it does have some challenges. For example, how are classification questions differentiated from accounts and social characteristics?

Robinson and Leonard (2018) offered a more compact framework with four types of questions, which contained the groups identified by Schaeffer and Dykema. Their framework works well for the survey questions we typically encounter in CX and UX research. We further built on their classification system to describe four types of questions that should encompass all types of survey questions: attributes, behaviors, abilities, and thoughts/sentiments.

1. Attributes

Typically, demographic-type questions are asked at the beginning of surveys to either screen-out respondents (e.g., include only people 18–44) or characterize them for later analysis and cross tabbing (e.g., high income vs. low income). In addition to standard demographics, questions in this class can also measure attributes of both individuals and groups, such as companies, organizations, or cities (Figure 5.5).

✳ Please select your gender:	✳ How many staff members do you supervise daily?
○ Male	○ None
○ Female	○ 1-5
○ Genderqueer/nonbinary	○ 6-10
○ Prefer not to answer	○ More than 10
○ Other [ ]	

FIGURE 5.5: Examples of attribute questions.

Common attribute questions include:

- Age
- Education
- Location
- Income
- Ethnicity
- Occupation
- Number of employees at your company
- Number of family members you live with

When using these questions to screen, a common question format is multiple choice single response, sometimes with an optional "other" fill-in response. When attributes aren't defined well enough to create a set of likely response options, the appropriate format is an open-ended question. This allows the exploration of unconstrained responses, but it increases the analytical burden.

TIP:

Watch out when using attributes such as income or age (Figure 5.6), where it's easy to create overlapping categories (e.g., 18–21; 21–25) or miss values (e.g., $25,000 to $39,000; $40,000 to $50,000).

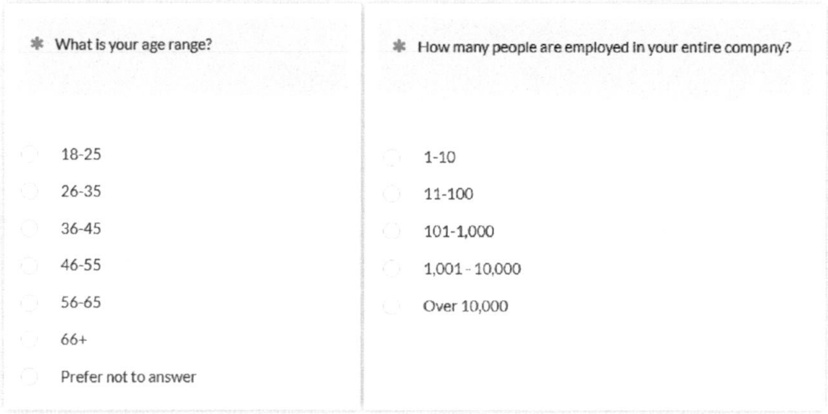

FIGURE 5.6: Additional attribute examples.

Avoid asking too many attribute questions, as some may be sensitive (e.g., income), and you don't want to clutter your survey with questions you don't plan to use (shorter surveys have higher response rates). This is especially the case if the information is available through another source (e.g., from customer records).

2. Behaviors (Reported)

These questions ask for self-reports of past or current actions (Figure 5.7). They should not be confused with actually observing behavior in either moderated or unmoderated UX research (e.g., using a platform like MUiQ to conduct a survey that, in addition to asking questions like those discussed in this article, also has task-based activities that capture actual task behaviors such as completion times, success rates, screen paths, and clicks).

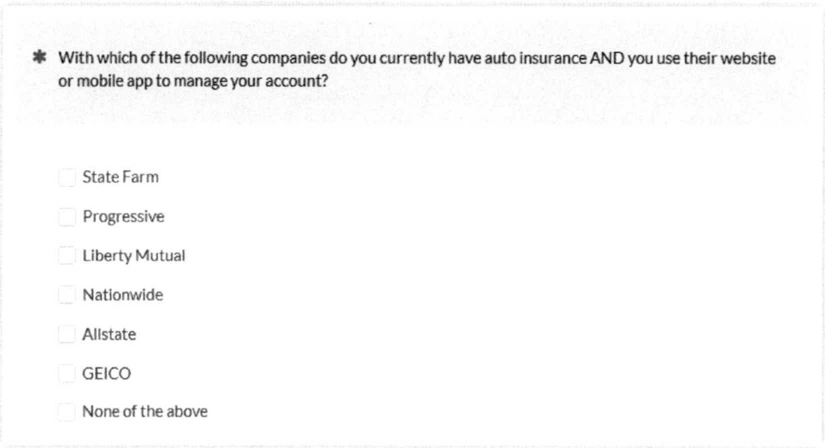

FIGURE 5.7: Example of a self-reported behavioral question.

Examples of self-reported behaviors include:

- Prior experience using a product, app, or service.
- Products purchased online.
- Usage of a food delivery service.
- Frequency of making hotel reservations using Hyatt's mobile app.
- Number of flights booked on Expedia.
- Impact COVID-19 had on job-search behaviors.

Behavioral questions are typically reported as frequency, duration/tenure, and intensity. In UX research, prior experience with a product, website, or app often has a large impact on other metrics. Familiarity breeds content: people who have used the product for a longer time (duration/tenure) use it more often (frequency) and use more of its features (intensity). They're more likely to complete tasks successfully and quickly, and they do so with a generally more positive attitude.

When measuring behavioral questions, watch for vague modifiers ("sometimes," "frequently" — see Chapter 7) that can be interpreted in different ways by different people. Self-reports of prior behavior, when measured correctly, can be a reasonable (but far from perfect) predictor of future behavior (Sauro, 2019, Apr 24).

With behavioral questions, you typically need to have a reference period (e.g., one week, one year, ten years). The longer the reference period, the more likely participants will forget details (see Chapter 9).

3. Abilities

When you want to measure a respondent's knowledge or skills, you ask ability questions (Figure 5.8). These look a lot like a quiz or assessment, either fill-in-the-blank or multiple choice. Ability questions are often used in UX surveys as an indirect way to assess understanding of a design or interface. They can also be used to assess the usability of an interface through task-based questions.

✱ Which number in the following group of numbers represents the smallest amount?

○ .8

○ .33

○ 2

○ 7

○ 31

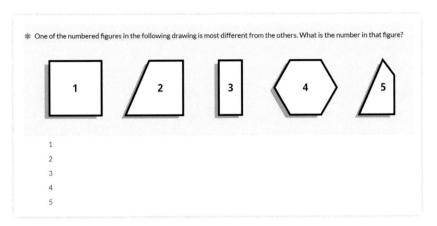

FIGURE 5.8: Examples of ability questions.

Examples of ability questions include:

- What does HDMI stand for?
- Find a blender for under $45 on the Walmart website with an average of at least four stars.
- What is a deductible on a health insurance plan?
- How much is an annual Netflix plan?
- Which of the following does the privacy policy cover?
- Which shipping option will get you the product the fastest?

Asking ability questions is different from asking respondents to assess their abilities, something addressed in thoughts/sentiments questions (covered next). We know some of our UX colleagues may take exception to the idea that a task-based question falls under the category of measuring abilities. To us, however, it seems reasonable to include such questions in this category because task-based questions help gauge the ability of the person to complete tasks, allowing evaluation of users' experiences with an interface.

4. Thoughts, Sentiments, and Judgments

Thoughts, sentiments, and judgment questions are often the heart of CX and UX surveys (Figure 5.9). They encompass a broad range of questions that tap into attitudes, beliefs, feelings, opinions, preferences, awareness, and behavioral intentions.

How would you describe your attitude toward the following companies?

	Very Unfavorable 1	2	3	4	5	6	Very Favorable 7
Hyatt	○	○	○	○	○	○	○
Best Western	○	○	○	○	○	○	○
Holiday Inn	○	○	○	○	○	○	○
Marriott	○	○	○	○	○	○	○
Hilton	○	○	○	○	○	○	○

FIGURE 5.9: Example of sentiment question.

Some common examples include:

- Brand awareness
- Brand favorability
- Satisfaction
- Perceived usability
- Perceived usefulness
- Preference
- Intent to recommend
- Feature ranking
- Self-reported tech savviness

Thoughts and sentiments are often measured using multipoint rating scales which, in many cases, are part of standardized questionnaires, such as the System Usability Scale (SUS), SUPR-Q, or UX-Lite—see Appendix B for details. Even complex survey frameworks, such as the Kano and MaxDiff, use questions that ask about thoughts and judgments (what things are most or least important). See Chapter 10 for more details on these question types.

CHAPTER SUMMARY

This chapter focused on the structure and classification of survey questions.

What is the anatomy of a survey question? … At a high level, a survey question contains a stem and response options. The stem must contain a request for an answer (direct, indirect, or wh-requests). It may also include an introduction, information pertinent to the question, instructions, and information about the opinions of others (rare in UX/CX surveys but more common in social and political surveys).

What response options should I provide? …It depends on the intent of the question. When discovery is the primary goal, use open-ended items. If measurement is the primary goal, then use categorical (e.g., age groups, video streaming services) or noncategorical (e.g., rating, ranking, allocation) response options.

What are the main types of survey questions? ...We classify them into four content types. UX and CX researchers can use these categories when planning surveys to help connect questions to research goals.

- *Attributes:* Typically, demographic-like questions that describe attributes of the respondents (e.g., age, income) or descriptions of other people or groups (e.g., employees at a company).

- *Behaviors:* Self-reports of past or current behavior, which usually include a reference period (e.g., last six months). These should not be confused with observing actual behavior.

- *Abilities:* Assessments of knowledge or skill, including the ability to complete usability tasks (such as finding information).

- *Thoughts, sentiments, and judgments:* Questions that ask for respondents' attitudes, judgments, or preferences, including satisfaction, brand, and ease questions.

CHAPTER 6:
HOW TO WRITE A SURVEY QUESTION

A blank page can lead to writer's block, and writing survey questions can seem like trying to write the Great American Novel. We'll cover the following questions about writing a survey question:

- What's the first step?
- I know what I want to measure—what's next?
- How do I create my own question?

It can be particularly daunting knowing that subtle word changes may lead to unanticipated responses. The good news is that you don't have to start from scratch each time. Instead, you can follow a few steps to help you make decisions, ideally reducing the likelihood of errors (see Chapter 2). Here are seven steps to writing a survey question.

START WITH THE CONCEPT

As we covered in Chapter 3, concepts and constructs are what you intend to measure (Figure 6.1). They can be concrete or abstract. There's a subtle difference between these two terms. Typically, constructs (like satisfaction and delight) are more abstract and multi-faceted than concepts (like age and income).

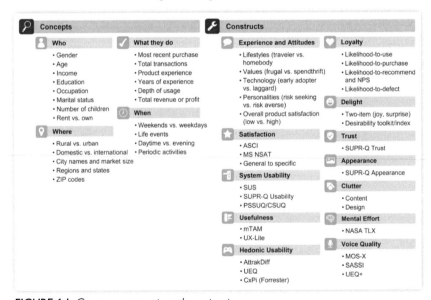

FIGURE 6.1: Common concepts and constructs.

Here are some concepts and constructs that are commonly included in UX/CX surveys:

1. Ease
2. Age
3. Gender
4. Awareness
5. Income
6. Education
7. Current user of product/service
8. Delight
9. Intent to recommend
10. Favorability
11. Priority/rank
12. Intent to use
13. Intent to purchase
14. Satisfaction
15. Understanding
16. Comprehension

Concepts can be simple (e.g., age) or more complex (e.g., gender). In most UX/CX research, concepts measure attributes of people (individual differences), while constructs measure the consequences of interactions between people and systems (e.g., companies, websites).

SEE WHETHER A QUESTION ALREADY EXISTS

Chances are, you're probably not the first researcher to be interested in a particular concept or construct. Others may have already written an appropriate question, which you may find in published research (Figure 6.2). This step is especially important when you're measuring abstract constructs such as usability, appearance, trust, and delight (see Appendix B).

When you can, adopt or adapt an existing question (and its response options), especially if it's both reliable and valid (see Chapter 1). The more you deviate from the original item, the more you risk deviating from what you intend to measure (Sauro, 2016, Aug 30).

Figure 6.2 has some examples of how to convert constructs to items. For example, if you're interested in measuring task-level ease, the SEQ® is a reliable and valid measure. The SUS and UX-Lite also have items that measure broad attitudes toward ease.

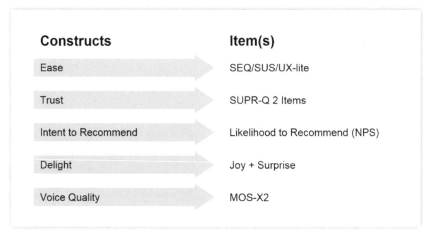

Constructs	Item(s)
Ease	SEQ/SUS/UX-lite
Trust	SUPR-Q 2 Items
Intent to Recommend	Likelihood to Recommend (NPS)
Delight	Joy + Surprise
Voice Quality	MOS-X2

FIGURE 6.2: Examples of constructs converting to item(s).

If you want to measure trust, two items from the SUPR-Q standardized questionnaire tap into trust and credibility (Sauro, 2015). To measure delight, consider using two items to measure the expectation and surprise components of delight (Sauro, 2019, Nov 20). For synthetic voice quality (intelligibility, naturalness, prosody, social impression), consider the MOS-X2 (Lewis & Sauro, 2020, Aug 19). Appendix B has more details for several commonly used UX and CX questionnaires.

If the question you need doesn't exist, continue with the following steps.

DETERMINE THE TYPE OF QUESTION

If you have a concept in mind and you've ruled out using an existing question, first determine what type of question content is most appropriate for measuring the concept/construct. Knowing the type can help with developing typical response options and reveal common pitfalls to avoid. Survey questions fall into four types of content (see Chapter 5):

1. **Attributes:** Typically, demographic-like questions describing attributes of the respondents (e.g., age, income, education) or descriptions of other people or things (e.g., employees at a company).

2. **Behaviors:** Self-reports of past or current behaviors, which usually include a reference period (e.g., last six months) — don't confuse these with observing behavior.

3. **Abilities:** An assessment of a person's knowledge or skill, including the ability to complete usability tasks (e.g., finding information).

4. **Thoughts/Sentiments:** Questions that ask for a respondent's attitudes, judgments, or preferences. Satisfaction, brand, and ease questions are common examples. A lot of concepts fall into this group.

BRAINSTORM IDEAS

To brainstorm ideas, come up with different words, phrases, or ideas to describe the concept or construct you want to measure (by yourself, if necessary, but ideally with a group.) Be concrete and take the perspective of the people who will use the data you collect.

For example, say you're interested in how well people understand a new product. Specific, concrete questions might concern the product's features, its pricing, how well it integrates with other products, its ease of use, the discoverability of its features, how quickly users can complete tasks, or its trustworthiness. If necessary, you can break these concepts down into even more detailed questions. (For example, to what extent is a trust rating due to attitude toward the brand reputation or to an actual positive or negative experience?)

INTERVIEW THE TARGET RESPONDENTS

Conduct a few informal interviews and walkthroughs of the survey with the targeted participants. This step provides an opportunity to validate the words and phrases you might have come up with from brainstorming. For example, do respondents understand the terms you're planning to use? Do they use different terms from what you expected? Are you missing or misrepresenting anything? See Chapter 8 for more details on the importance of using the respondent's language when writing questions.

CRAFT THE QUESTION

With ideas and terms refined about the concept, it's time to craft the questions.

Despite calling them, well, questions, survey questions can be both questions and phrases, so we often refer to them using the broader term item. In Chapter 5, we described the anatomy of a survey question as having a stem and one or more response options. The stem must contain a request for an answer and may include four other parts (introduction, topic information, instructions, and opinions of others), which aren't always used. We also described three ways to write survey questions:

- Use a simple or direct request in the form of a question (e.g., "Are you older than 21?").
- Form an indirect request by presenting one or more statements that people will rate, such as the UX-Lite illustrated in Figure 6.3.
- Use wh-requests (e.g., "What is your age?" or "Who is your cell phone provider?").

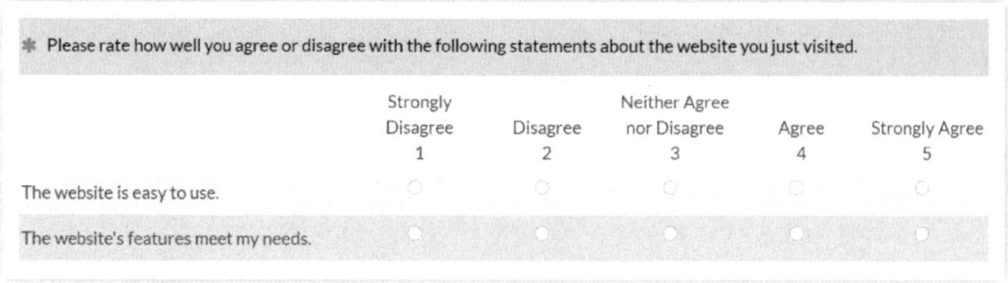

	Strongly Disagree 1	Disagree 2	Neither Agree nor Disagree 3	Agree 4	Strongly Agree 5
✳ Please rate how well you agree or disagree with the following statements about the website you just visited.					
The website is easy to use.	○	○	○	○	○
The website's features meet my needs.	○	○	○	○	○

FIGURE 6.3: The UX-Lite.

SELECT THE RESPONSE OPTIONS

Selecting the best response options requires careful consideration. It's a common stumbling block for survey developers, as there are many options to consider. We recommend starting with the goal of the questions (what you are going to do with the data and how you will present it) to guide the decision. Chapter 10 provides a decision tree to help narrow the choice for response options. But before you start climbing that tree, begin with these four broad categories (branches):

1. **Discovery:** When discovery is the primary goal, use open-ended items.

2. **Measurement:** When collecting measurements, the key distinction is whether the required data are categorical or not.

3. **Categorical:** Categorical data can be ordered (e.g., age groups) or unordered (e.g., streaming video services), allowing the selection of multiple items when choices aren't mutually exclusive, or restricting selection to one item when choices are mutually exclusive.

4. **Not categorical:** Noncategorical question types can be classified as ranking, allocation, or rating. Of these types, rating scales are the ones most used in UX and CX research.

For example, if you want to know how often respondents use a product or service, you'd craft a frequency question (Goal > Measurement > Categorical > Ordered > Frequency > Frequency Item), such as the one shown in Figure 6.4.

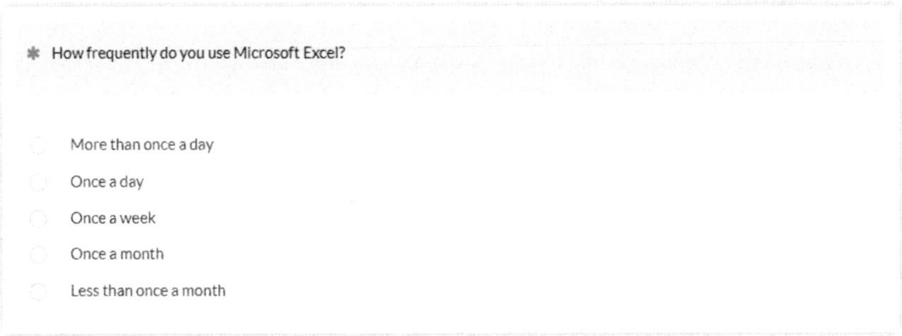

FIGURE 6.4: Example of a frequency question (created with MUiQ).

If your goal is to understand the relative importance of attributes or activities where participants can allocate amounts such as points, dollars, or percentages to attributes or activities, you could use a fixed-sum question (Goal > Measurement > Not Categorical > Allocation > Fixed Sum Item), similar to the example in Figure 6.5.

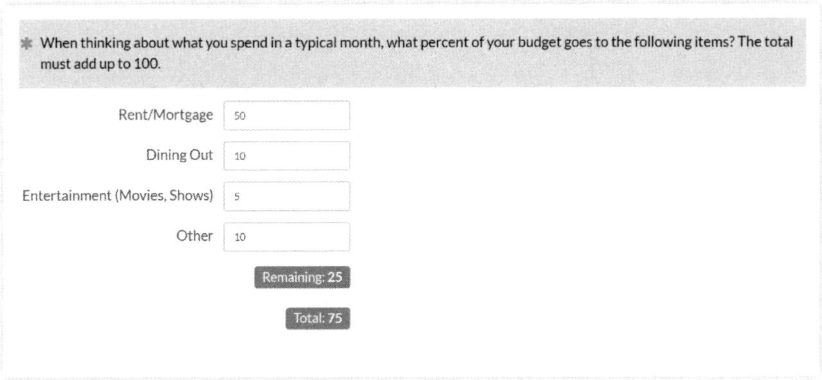

FIGURE 6.5: Example of a fixed-sum question (created with MUiQ).

More examples of using the decision tree are in Chapter 10.

CHAPTER SUMMARY

This chapter focused on how to write a survey question using a process to avoid or overcome writer's block. Writing survey questions isn't always easy, but it can be easier when you have a set of steps to fall back on.

What's the first step? ...Determine the concept or construct you want to measure. Typically, constructs (like satisfaction and delight) are more abstract and multi-faceted than concepts (like age and income).

I know what I want to measure—what's next? ...See whether the question you need already exists. Researchers have been creating and using survey questions for decades, so there's a good chance someone has already created the question you need (and ideally, has assessed its reliability and validity). If the question you need exists, use it. Otherwise, you'll need to create your own. How do I create my own question? ...Determine the question type, brainstorm ideas, interview target respondents, craft the question, and select the response options. To create a survey question:

- *Determine the question type.* Base this on the needed content (e.g., attributes, behaviors, abilities, thoughts/sentiments).

- *Brainstorm ideas.* Come up with different ways to describe the concept/construct you want to measure, ideally with a group.

- *Interview target respondents.* Conduct some walkthroughs with targeted participants to validate the chosen words and phrases.

- *Craft the question.* Decide whether to construct the item stem as a question (direct request or wh-request) or as a statement (indirect request), and make sure it has all the parts it needs (e.g., introduction, topic information, instructions, opinions of others).

- *Select the response options.* Use the decision tree in Chapter 10 to determine the right type of response options based on whether the purpose of the question is discovery (which leads to open-ended items) or measurement (which leads to specific types based on whether the data will be categorical or noncategorical).

CHAPTER 7:
WHY PEOPLE MISINTERPRET SURVEY QUESTIONS

In this chapter, we'll cover the most common reasons people misinterpret survey questions, then we'll dig into possible ways to reduce misinterpretations. We'll address the following questions related to misinterpreting questions:

- What are the different ways people might misinterpret survey questions?
- What can I do to write questions that are easier to understand?
- Are there any specific words I should watch for?

Like in all research methods, many things can go wrong in surveys, from problems with sampling to mistakes in analysis. To draw valid conclusions from your survey, you need accurate responses. But participants may provide inaccurate information. They could forget the answers to questions (see Chapter 9) or just answer questions incorrectly.

SEVEN REASONS WHY SURVEYS ARE MISUNDERSTOOD

One common reason respondents answer survey questions incorrectly is that they misinterpret the question. Understanding the possible reasons for misinterpretation can help you craft better questions. Here are seven common reasons people misinterpret questions, which we adapted from research by Tourangeau et al. (2000).

1. Grammatical and Lexical Ambiguity
Grammar was a pain in elementary school, and it can also be a pain in surveys. In addition to grammatical ambiguity, some words, such as you, have ambiguous meanings (see Chapter 7).

"Do you have a subscription to Amazon Prime?" This you can mean just the respondent or their whole household (you as the second person plural, e.g., all of you living in your house).

A simple question such as "Are you visiting professors?" can mean either 1) "Are you going to visit professors?" or 2) "Are you part of a group of visiting professors?"

In discourse, the prosody of a spoken sentence often provides cues regarding the speaker's intended meaning (Kraljic & Brennan, 2004), but those cues are not available when reading a written sentence. Given the nature of human languages, it can be difficult to avoid ambiguity. Words and phrases can have multiple meanings, sentences (like the example above) have multiple interpretations, and pronouns might have multiple possible antecedents.

As we compose a sentence, we are usually aware, at least implicitly, of how we would say it, so it's hard to predict how others might interpret—or misinterpret—it without prosodic cues. That's why it's important to have other people proofread our survey questions.

2. Excessive Complexity

There's a laudable desire to reduce the number of questions in a survey, but be careful not to pack too much into a single question:

> "During the last 12 months, since January 1, 2020, how many times have you seen or talked to a doctor (or physician assistant) about COVID-19? Do not count any time you might have seen a doctor while you were in the hospital or for planned surgery at an outpatient facility, but count all other times."

Complex questions are hard because they demand that participants keep track of multiple things at the same time, which can lead to misreporting. Complex questions can be simplified by splitting them into shorter ones. We've found that it's the length of the survey rather than the total number of questions that's the biggest detriment to completion (Sauro, 2014, Feb 11). But even short questions can suffer from complex syntax. Watch out for:

- **Adjunct wh-questions: Questions starting with wh-words such as** *who* or *what* often include adjuncts—phrases that can be removed from the sentence without affecting its grammaticality. ("When did [your account representative say] you need[ed] to renew your software license?")

- **Embedded clauses:** Statements that include modifying clauses in the middle of the sentence. ("The task [that I just completed in this study] was easy.")

- **Left-embedded syntax:** Placing many adjectives, adverbs, and/or prepositional phrases before respondents get to the critical part of a question. ("Even if it would cost them some money and might make their code more complex because the 'rules' are a complicated mix of industry regulations and federal, state, and local laws, Twitter, as one of the most influential social media platforms, should comply with industry guidelines.")

See Chapter 8 for strategies for dealing with these kinds of complexities.

3. Faulty Presuppositions

A question that makes assumptions (presupposes something) can present problems for respondents:

How much do you agree or disagree with the following statement?

"Family life has suffered during COVID-19 because parents are having to concentrate too much on their work."

The question presupposes that parents are concentrating too much on their work, but for some respondents, family life might suffer from parents being out of work or having their hours reduced. It's difficult for respondents to work out how to rate the statement.

The presuppositions in leading questions ("Leading Questions: Definitions, Types, and Examples," n.d.) can even plant false memories (Luna, 2019). In a classic psychology experiment (Loftus et al., 1978), participants viewed a slideshow of events that culminated in a traffic accident after a car turned right at a stop sign. After the slideshow, embedded in a battery of twenty questions, half of the participants were asked, "Did another car pass the red Datsun while it was stopped at the stop sign?" and the other half were asked, "Did another car pass the red Datsun while it was stopped at the yield sign?" Later, after a twenty-minute filler activity, the participants had to indicate which of two slides they remembered seeing, where the only difference in the slides was whether the car was stopped at a yield or a stop sign. Even though they had seen a stop sign, 41% of the participants in the yield condition claimed to remember having seen a yield sign.

So, how might we deal with our survey example to make it less leading? It helps to break the statement into multiple parts (Figure 7.1):

> ✳ Do you think COVID-19 has affected family life?
>
> ● Yes
> ○ No
>
> ✳ In your opinion, has the effect of COVID-19 on family life been primarily negative or positive?
>
> Negative   Postive
> 1   2   3   4   5   6   7
> ○   ○   ●   ○   ○   ○   ○
>
> ✳ You indicated that the effect has been primarily negative. Which of these are the main causes for this negative effect? (Pick up to three.)
>
> ☐ Parents are concentrating too much on their work.
> ☐ Families are dealing with job loss.
> ☐ Families are dealing with reduced hours at work.
> ☑ Parents and children are stressed by virtual schooling.
> ☑ There is a fear of infecting older relatives in the family.
> ☑ Other (please describe) [All cramped together]

FIGURE 7.1: Revising a statement with a faulty presupposition by breaking it into parts and eliminating the presupposition (programmed in MUiQ so the second item appears after a Yes response to the first item and the third item appears after a response of 1, 2, or 3 to the second item).

4. Vague Concepts

A concept is vague if it's unclear whether a description applies to a respondent. Consequently, this vagueness can alter respondents' interpretations, leading to ambiguity in responses:

> "How many children are staying at the Airbnb property?" In this question, who counts as a child? Is a child someone who is under 18 years old or someone who is under 16? Does an infant count?

> "How often do you play video games that include violence?" Does it count if you play a racing game that has no violence other than the possibility of crashing a car? Is driving a car that can crash considered violence?

While you want to be clear by spelling out the details of terms, you want to avoid the opposite problem of adding too much complexity (see #2).

The following examples strike a reasonable balance by being unambiguous without adding excessive complexity:

"How many children (aged 0–18) are staying at the Airbnb property?"

"How often do you play first-person shooter video games?"

5. Vague Quantifiers

Vague quantifiers are words (usually adjectives and adverbs) that have different interpretations. They can appear both in question stems and in response options: "Do you consider yourself a frequent Netflix user?"

Peterson (2000) describes the words near, very, quite, much, most, few, often, several, and occasionally as ambiguous. We've seen similar ambiguity with probability words and change verbs (Sauro & Lewis 2020, Dec 1).

Peterson gives an example of how respondents who reported "very frequently" to their reported movie attendance and "very much" to their monthly beer consumption later assigned frequencies ranging from 52–365 as the number of movies per year and beers per month respectively. Using these response options is fine if you want to gauge the perception of a behavior such as online streaming (do respondents think streaming an hour a day is frequent or moderate), but they're not appropriate if you're researching the frequency of a behavior.

There's a misconception that rating scale points all need to be labeled (see Chapter 11). Full labeling becomes a challenge when there are more than five or seven points and may lead researchers to use vague modifiers.

For example, in Figure 7.2, is "quite" truly more than "slightly?" Research has shown that TAM rating scales with only the endpoints labeled (Version B) produce similar ratings to fully labeled scales (Version A) without the potential complication of ambiguous quantifiers.

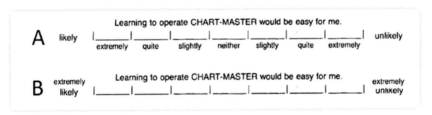

FIGURE 7.2: Two versions of response options for the Technology Acceptance Model (Davis, 1986).

6. Unfamiliar Terms

It's easy to forget how much jargon and novel terminology are in research and industries such as finance, healthcare, and retail, which may be unfamiliar to survey respondents. Such jargon includes initialisms (MPG, IRA, 401K) and terms (assets, deductible, out-of-pocket maximum). The worst combination would be initialisms made from unfamiliar terms (OOPM for out-of-pocket maximum).

Unfamiliar terms are not problematic in surveys only. As we saw in our benchmark study of health insurance websites (Sauro, 2018, Jul 25), UX designs that include unfamiliar terms, whether software or survey, lead to guessing, misinterpretation, confusion, and frustration.

However, when respondents are familiar with industry jargon and initialisms, it's reasonable to use them for more efficient communication, consistent with Nielsen's Heuristic #2 to speak the user's language (Nielsen, 2020, Nov 15).

7. False Inferences

False inferences come from respondents overinterpreting questions, often to infer intent or to get at the spirit of a question:

> "Are there any situations you can imagine in which you would approve of Robinhood removing access to your trading account?"

Some respondents may interpret the question in the spirit of Robinhood promising to provide unbroken access to money and the ability to make timely trades. However, others may interpret the question more literally. In that case, the use of the word any would lead them to agree more strongly with the statement than they otherwise would; "any situations" include acts of fraud, after all. (This issue is similar to the use of absolute modifiers in survey questions, discussed later in this chapter.) Would a high response rate to this question justify locking traders out of their accounts? Probably not…

WORDS TO WATCH FOR

Pew Research Center (2019, Jan 18) asked respondents about the availability of jobs in their area. In that survey, researchers randomly assigned half of the respondents a version of the question that asked about "good" jobs, while the other half were assigned a version that didn't include this positive qualifier.

The experiment found that respondents were more likely to say plenty of "jobs" were available in their community than they were to say plenty of "good jobs" were available (60% vs. 48%).

In UX research, both studies and surveys contain a lot of questions. Getting those questions right can go a long way in improving the clarity and quality of the findings. For example, see Chapter 8 for how to make survey questions clearer.

The example from the Pew survey of how the addition of a single word in a survey led to different results should stick in the mind of the researcher.

We are less sure about the impact of subtle wording changes in typical UX and CX surveys, where questions are less sensitive or politically charged.

Nevertheless, multiple small impacts due to wording can have a cumulative deleterious effect. In this section, we call attention to nine words that may cause trouble. These aren't necessarily problematic words, but before you use one, you should double check that it's the best word to unambiguously capture the concept you intend to measure.

Three Absolutes: *Ever, Always,* and *Never*

When writing survey questions or response options, watch for keywords that make statements absolute. *Ever, always,* and *never* are three such words to watch for.

The problem with questions phrased with absolute words is that respondents will be more likely to agree or disagree with items phrased absolutely than with items phrased in less extreme terms. That may not be helpful.

Would you **ever** consider purchasing a license for accounting software?

Taken literally, most people would find it hard to rule out every point in the future—even the distant future—when they or their organization may consider purchasing accounting software.

Of course, some respondents might read ever to mean just now or in the near future. The challenge is that you don't know how people may interpret it literally without testing it first. Adding a time frame or removing ever may increase clarity and response consistency. If necessary, you can pilot test both versions independently to see if the response distributions differ.

I **always** shop for the lowest price detergent.

There's likely a time when a frugal shopper might need to purchase a specific detergent that's not the lowest in price (perhaps because of an emergency). Using in general or typically instead of *always* may distinguish the typical frugal shopper from the literal question reader.

Customer service **never** responds on time to my requests.

If you get a timely customer service response one out of ten times, technically you need to disagree or even strongly disagree with a statement that may be demonstrably false but doesn't capture the spirit of the concept (unresponsive customer service).

Again, *never* is a strong word that may capture the sentiment of some extreme responders, but it may not reflect the feelings of people less likely to agree with the absolute wording. This effect is similar to research we conducted (Sauro, 2010, Sep 21) on variations of the System Usability Scale (SUS), which found significant changes to response patterns when we rewrote the items to be much more extreme.

Keep in mind that this doesn't mean you can't use the words *ever, always,* and *never.* There may be times when you want to identify the extreme responders to these absolute statements. Researchers use this technique in Item Response Theory when generating difficult items (items few respondents will agree with). For example, the

SUPR-Qm® (Sauro & Zarolia, 2017), contains the item "I would never delete the app," but only because this standardized questionnaire contains numerous items that contribute to its overall score, many of which are less extreme.

A respondent participating in an interview instead of completing a survey might ask for clarification: "You mean like never-ever respond to my requests, or just about never?" In a sense, surveys are standardized conversations with respondents. Avoid these absolutes unless they're associated with a research goal.

Four Modal Verbs: *Could, Should, Might,* and *Would*

In the 3rd grade, if a student asks her English teacher if she can go to the bathroom, the teacher might respond, "I don't know, can you?" There is a difference between can and may (Gunner, 2021, Jun 2), even though we often use these words interchangeably (much to the chagrin of English teachers).

But what gets used loosely in conversation can be interpreted more literally in surveys. Watch for the following modal verbs, which have subtle differences in meaning: *could, should, might,* and *would.*

- *Could* implies something is possible or impossible: Could you recommend the product?

- *Should* implies judgment: Should you recommend the product?

- *Would* implies definite future action: Would you recommend the product?

- *Might* implies permission and possible future action: Might you recommend the product?

These subtle wording differences do not necessarily affect survey question responses. For example, when we tested the difference between *will* and *would* (Sauro, 2019, Nov 13) in different versions of the Likelihood-to-Recommend item used in the Net Promoter Score, we found no statistical (or really any observable) differences. We have not, however, tested all possible variants. To reduce the possibility of misinterpretation when using one of these four words, make sure you've chosen the most appropriate one for your research goal.

You

When using *you*, be clear whether the word *you* refers to just the respondent or includes a whole household.

English has the unfortunate problem of having the same word for the second person singular (just you) and second person plural (all of you). In a spoken conversation, this ambiguity can be cleared up with you guys, you all, or y'all. Harris (2014) emphasizes being clear about who the you is, for example:

Do *you* have a subscription to Amazon Prime?

Respondents may wonder if it counts when they use a parent's or partner's subscription. Depending on the research question, it may be better to ask more inclusively (with appropriate response options):

Do *you or anyone else in your household* have a subscription to Amazon Prime?

If the focus is on the respondent only, then you can clarify that as well:

Do *you* (not including anyone else in your household) have a subscription to Amazon Prime?

Our

Our seems like an innocuous enough word, but Peterson (2000) suggests that its use may subtly influence the respondent due to the sponsorship bias (see Chapter 2), which can occur when respondents know the company they're rating is conducting the survey.

Overall, how likely are you to recommend *our company* to a friend or colleague?

Compare with this:

Overall, how likely are you to recommend *ACME Corp* to a friend or colleague?

The latter comes across as more objective and may remove bias. If you find yourself using *our*, consider replacing it with the company or product name.

CHAPTER SUMMARY

This chapter focused on why people misinterpret survey questions and potentially problematic words.

What are the different ways people might misinterpret survey questions? ...There are a variety of reasons. Here are seven potential contributors to misinterpretation:

- *Grammatical and lexical ambiguity:* This is caused by the inherently ambiguous nature of human language (words, phrases, and sentences with multiple meanings).

- *Excessive complexity:* Sentences that are hard to process, often due to trying to pack too much into a single question.

- *Faulty presuppositions:* Sentences that present assertions as facts when that is not the case.

- *Vague concepts:* Sentences that do not include enough information to clarify their key concepts.

- *Vague quantifiers:* Sentences or response options that include quantifiers that can be interpreted differently, such as near, very, quite, much, most, few, often, several, and occasionally.

- *Unfamiliar terms:* The use of words, phrases, or initialisms that are not part of the respondents' everyday vocabulary.

- *False inferences:* Sentences that may be overinterpreted by some respondents who struggle to infer their underlying intent.

What can I do to write questions that are easier to understand? ...Know the potential causes and review, review, review. If you know the potential causes, you can write first drafts to avoid them, but the best overall strategy is to have other people review your surveys before you launch them. Always run a pilot to allow respondents to identify questions they have difficulty understanding.

Are there any specific words I should watch for? ...Be careful with absolutes, modal verbs, and pronouns. Small changes in wording can subtly change how participants respond to questions, often in unintended ways. This is especially the case with absolute words, modal verbs, and some pronouns.

- *Absolute words:* The three absolute words of *ever*, *always*, and *never* may garner agreement from both extreme responders who interpret the questions literally and respondents who interpret the words more loosely, with no way to determine who is who during analysis. Unless there is a compelling need to use them, avoid absolute words in survey questions.

- *Modal verbs:* The differences between *could*, *should*, *would*, and *might* are slim, but they connote slightly different meanings, so choose your words carefully.

- *Pronouns:* Two words that seem straightforward but can be tricky are *you* and *our*. Clarify the use of *you* (you alone or your household/family), and avoid the potential bias of *our company* by using the name of the company or product.

So, I should never use these words — right? ...Not necessarily. You can use these words when they're appropriate, but don't use them thoughtlessly. If you lack data to help you understand their impact on responses (and their ability to capture the intended concept), you (including everyone in your household) *should* watch out for these nine words.

CHAPTER 8:
HOW TO MAKE SURVEY QUESTIONS CLEARER

As we covered in Chapter 1, the first questionnaires appeared in the mid-eighteenth century (e.g., the "Milles" questionnaire). Scientific surveys have been around for almost a hundred years.

Consequently, there are many sources of advice on how to make surveys better. The heart of each survey is the questions asked of respondents. Writing good survey questions involves many of the principles of good writing in addition to survey-specific guidelines and advice.

We've reviewed recommendations, research, and guidelines for survey and questionnaire design from several sources and reconciled what we learned with our own research and experience conducting surveys.

Many recommendations and guidelines come from social science and political opinion research, which often includes charged and sensitive topics, or educational research, which focuses on assessments of knowledge. These fields are rarely investigated in industrial research surveys, so we've selected and modified the guidance to better fit the domain of the UX or CX researcher.

One of the most important objectives in survey writing is to communicate clearly with respondents. We'll provide seven recommendations to improve the clarity of survey questions, addressing the following questions:

- What are some strategies for writing clear survey questions?
- Which of these strategies is the most important?

KEEP QUESTIONS SHORT

Almost all the sources we reviewed recommend question brevity. Long questions take long to process, which increases the completion time. We and others (Chudoba, n.d.) have found that survey completion time is a strong predictor of dropout (Sauro, 2014, Feb 11), so there is a strong incentive for researchers to ask as few survey questions as possible and to keep questions short. But how short is short enough, and when does a question become too long?

The literature includes some suggested question lengths (Table 8.1). For example, Johnson and Morgan (2016) suggest keeping questions under 25 words, and one of the earliest recommendations (Payne, 1951) suggests questions be fewer than 20 words. Instead of word count, Peterson (2000) recommends using no more than three commas.

Source	Guidance
Johnson and Morgan (2016)	< 25 words
Payne (1951)	< 20 words
Peterson (2000)	< three commas

TABLE 8.1: Recommendations on what constitutes a "short" survey question.

There may be an exception to the shorter-is-better rule in situations when respondents need to recall information that isn't easy to remember. There is some evidence (Laurent, 1972), conducted on in-person administered questionnaires, that some redundancy (and lengthy questions) can help with recall.

While we're not sure how accurate a guideline about the number of words or commas can be at identifying brevity (a topic for future research), we do think it's a good idea to keep questions short by removing superfluous words and connecting phrases. It makes sense to examine questions with more than 25 words to ensure that all the words are necessary.

One way to keep questions short, regardless of the word count, is to remove unnecessary words. Some of the usual culprits suggested by Dillman et al. (2014) include:

- *Due to the fact that:* Replace with Because or *That.*
- *At this point in time:* Replace with Now.
- *If conditions are such that:* Replace with *If.*
- *Take into consideration:* Replace with *Consider.*

When it comes to question writing, strive for Hemingway over Proust.

USE SIMPLE LANGUAGE

While short is good, short and simple is better. If a simple word will do, use it over a multisyllabic, complex word. This principle applies to both question stems and response options.

After all, reducing the number of words is only one way to shorten a sentence. Another is to reduce the number of syllables. The average time required to speak a syllable is about 200 ms (Crystal & House, 1990), so a five-syllable word takes five times as long to say as a one-syllable word. Multisyllabic words are also difficult to read because they're generally less familiar and harder to decode (Heggie & Wade-Woolley, 2017).

Our research on the UMUX-Lite (Lewis & Sauro, 2020, Dec 15) provides a good example of the benefits of using simpler words. The original wording of the Usefulness item was "The system's capabilities meet my requirements" (13 syllables). We found the simpler "The system's features meet my needs" (8 syllables) had nearly identical means and frequency distributions, demonstrating that we could obtain equivalent measurements with a shorter, simpler question.

Several sources recommend assuming a middle school (6th to 7th grade) reading level. Doing so will also help respondents who are answering questions in a language other than their primary language.

PREFER COMMON WORDS

A more specific approach to writing simple questions and response options is to use common words. Words that occur frequently in a language are more familiar and tend to require less mental processing (Rayner & Raney, 1996). Conversely, less common words require more processing time and result in lower comprehension. Examples of infrequently used words and common alternatives are:

- Utilize vs. use
- Discrepancies vs. differences
- Affluent vs. wealthy
- Irate vs. angry
- Be cognizant of vs. know
- Rectify vs. correct
- Top priority vs. most important

While you might not know the actual frequency of a word, a little testing may reveal words that are troublesome to respondents. For example, Item 8 in the System Usability Scale (SUS) has evolved from "I found the system very cumbersome to use" to "I found the system very awkward to use" after research found that some participants struggled with "cumbersome" (Finstad, 2006).

The traditional approach in linguistics to estimate word frequency has been to create and analyze a corpus of text. Few of these formal corpora are available without cost to researchers, but you can use search engines to estimate relative word frequency (Blair et al., 2002).

For example, on January 15, 2021, a Google search of "cumbersome" had 28,000,000 results, while "awkward" had 169,000,000 results (about six times as many). "Utilize" had 627,000,000 results, and "use" had 15,520,000,000 (about 24 times more).

USE THE RESPONDENTS' VOCABULARY

UX researchers often survey specific populations rather than general consumers. For example, in our own research, we have focused on teachers, students, daily users of online streaming, meeting and event planners, IT decision-makers, gamers, automotive fleet managers, and UXPA members.

In general, you'll want to avoid jargon (e.g., value proposition, key driver, delighter) that may be familiar to you as a researcher but not to the respondent. However, if your target respondents are familiar with certain jargon or terms, then you'll want to match their vocabulary. This is consistent with Nielsen's Heuristic #2, which is to "speak the users' language" (2020, Nov 15).

Avoid jargon and technical language unless participants understand it, and it makes questions clearer. If the survey is for IT decision-makers, you can likely use terms such as "identity management" and "infosec." Gamers seem to have their own language, so using terms such as *afk, lul, gg,* and *sus* may be warranted in some situations. UX researchers will, of course, interpret SUS differently from gamers.

MINIMIZE THE USE OF ACRONYMS

Is an MVP a Minimum Viable Product or the Most Valuable Player? Although acronyms shorten questions, there is always a chance that some respondents won't know what an acronym stands for.

This guideline has exceptions, of course. Some acronyms are used so frequently by a set of respondents that they have become acceptable. Some (not many) acronyms are so universally understood that you never need to spell them out (e.g., NATO, SCUBA, RADAR). In general, however, if you find yourself using an acronym, consider spelling it out to improve clarity.

AVOID COMPLICATED SYNTAX

Some surveys try to pack a lot into one question to reduce the number of questions, or they use uncommon syntax to reduce question length. Try to avoid overly complex questions with complicated grammatical structures.

For example, Tourangeau et al. (2000) warn against what they call adjunct wh-questions (grammatically complex questions starting with who, what, when, or where) and constructions with embedded clauses.

Adjunct Wh-Questions

The following wh-question, while grammatically correct and having fewer than 20 words, is hard to process:

> When did you tell your account representative your software license needed to be renewed?

Here's a syntactically simpler version with the same length:

> When did you tell your account representative that you needed to renew your software license?

The first version is complicated for at least two reasons. First, it has characteristics of a garden path sentence: it might appear that "your software license" is a direct object of the verb "tell," but it's actually the subject of a subordinate clause, paired with "needed." Second, the second clause is in passive voice (discussed below): the receiver of the action ("license") appears before the verb that acts on it ("renewed"), requiring additional cognitive processing to understand.

Embedded Clauses

Here are two versions of an item for an agreement (Likert) scale, with and without an embedded clause.

The task that I just completed in this study was easy.

This task was easy.

In the version with the embedded clause, seven words are between the subject and the verb. In the alternate wording, the verb immediately follows the subject (shorter and simpler).

Left-Embedded Syntax

Similarly, Lenzner et al. (2010) recommend avoiding *left-embedded syntactic structures*. These occur when respondents have to read through many adjectives, adverbs, or prepositional phrases before getting to the critical part of a question. Consider the following two agreement items.

With left-embedded syntax:

To what extent do you agree or disagree with the following statement?

Even if it would cost them some money and might make their code more complex because the "rules" are a complicated mix of industry regulations and federal, state, and local laws, Twitter, as one of the most influential social media platforms, should comply with industry guidelines.

Without left-embedded syntax:

To what extent do you agree or disagree with the following statement?

Twitter, as one of the most influential social media platforms, should comply with industry guidelines even if it would cost them some money and might make their code more complex because the "rules" are a complicated mix of industry regulations and federal, state, and local laws.

The advice to avoid left-embedded syntax is similar to the journalistic practice to avoid burying the lead (or lede): Don't take so long to get to the point.

AVOID PASSIVE VOICE

This is one of the best-known writing guidelines. Ever since it appeared in the *Elements of Style*, (Strunk & White, 1959), generations of writing students have struggled to avoid passive sentences. However, passive voice is part of the language for a reason. Although writing in active rather than passive voice is generally good practice, you should understand when active or passive voice is the better choice.

Here's a quick review of passive voice: (1) The object of an active sentence becomes the subject of a passive sentence, and (2) some form of the verb "be" appears before the main verb. If an object appears in a passive sentence, it does so in a "by" prepositional phrase after the verb. For example:

- Active voice: *This system met my needs.*
- Passive voice *with object: My needs were met by this system.*
- Passive voice without object: *My needs were met.*

According to trace theory (Garrett, 1990), a passive sentence requires more effort to parse because a reader or listener must process a trace that is in the passive version of the sentence, co-indexing the passive verb with its active-voice object (which was moved from its normal position following the verb).

When to Use Active Voice

Unless there is a compelling reason to do otherwise, survey writers should use active voice. Passive voice often leads to wordier, weaker writing. Passive sentences rewritten as active can be as much as 40% shorter. Passive voice can be vague. When a sentence lacks an object, the writing can seem evasive, as if the writer is avoiding responsibility. Readers prefer technical documentation with reduced use of passive voice (Lewis, 2006).

When to Use Passive Voice

Passive voice is appropriate in some situations.

- Emphasize the object of the verb when the subject of the verb is unimportant or unknown ("The ball was caught").
- Avoid the use of personal pronouns in scientific writing, although this practice has been changing ("The expected effect was not found").
- Avoid naming a responsible party ("Mistakes were made").
- Politely inform customers of something they must do ("Check-in must be completed 30 minutes before the flight").

What About Survey Questions?

Consider the two versions of the item in Figure 8.1. They both have ten words, but the version in active voice is easier to read.

	Strongly Disagree 1	Disagree 2	Neither Agree nor Disagree 3	Agree 4	Strongly Agree 5
✳ Please rate how well you agree or disagree with the following statements about the website you just visited.					
Most people would learn to use this website very quickly. (Active voice)	○	○	○	○	○
This website would be learned very quickly by most people. (Passive voice)	○	○	○	○	○

FIGURE 8.1: Passive and active versions of an agreement item.

We couldn't invent an example where passive voice was better than active voice in a survey question, probably because the situations in which passive is appropriate are rare when writing survey questions. There might be times when the focus of the question should be on the receiver rather than the performer of an action, but survey question writing is not scientific writing, and using passive voice to obscure responsibility isn't consistent with clear writing.

When writing survey instructions (rather than questions), there may be times when passive voice could soften an otherwise harsh-sounding sentence. For example, here are active (socially direct) and passive (socially indirect) versions of the same message:

> You must answer every required question to receive payment for participation.

> To receive payment for participation, every required question must be answered.

CHAPTER SUMMARY

This chapter focused on additional strategies for making survey questions clearer.

What are some strategies for writing clear survey questions? ...We listed seven. To improve the clarity of your survey questions:

- *Keep questions short.* Look for opportunities to replace wordy phrases with shorter versions (e.g., replace "at this point in time" with "now"). When a sentence has more than 25 words, check to make sure all the words are necessary.

- *Use simple language.* Stri ve to replace multisyllabic words with shorter words (e.g., prefer "The system's features meet my needs" to "The system's capabilities meet my requirements").

- *Prefer common over rare words.* Words that occur frequently in a language are more familiar and tend to require less mental processing than less common words (e.g., use "angry" instead of "irate").

- *Use the respondents' vocabulary.* For surveys of the general population, avoid jargon, but for surveys of specific populations, match their vocabularies including their jargon.

- *Minimize the use of acronyms.* Avoid acronyms except those so common that spelling them out would require more mental processing (e.g., NATO, SCUBA).

- *Avoid complicated syntax.* In particular, be careful with adjunct wh-questions, embedded clauses, and left-embedded syntax.

- *Avoid passive voice.* Passive voice is appropriate in some situations, but survey writers should use active voice unless there is a compelling reason to do otherwise.

Which of these strategies is the most important? ...That's hard to determine. As applied researchers, one of our goals is to achieve ease of use for the artifacts we design and evaluate, including the surveys we design and administer. It might be hard to measure the effect of any one of these guidelines on the respondent experience, but there is likely a cumulative positive effect across many survey questions.

CHAPTER 9:
WHY PEOPLE FORGET & HOW TO IMPROVE RECALL

Surveys often rely on participants recalling prior events or behaviors. For example, survey questions could be about purchasing a product or service or the frequency of its use.

How much did you spend last month on clothing?

What grocery stores have you visited in the last three months?

How helpful were your recommendations last time you were viewing Netflix?

Here, we'll review the reasons why people forget and some methods for helping improve recall. We'll address the following questions:

- Why do people forget when answering survey questions?
- How can we write survey questions to help people remember?

PEOPLE FORGET

The usefulness of people's recollections of events and experiences rests on the accuracy of their memories. Memory is, of course, fallible (*where did I put my phone again?*).

While direct observation and usability testing are great for understanding and preventing problems, they aren't always feasible. You can't always observe or collect data while important events are happening. Even contemporaneous records might provide only a partial picture, failing to fully represent the user experience.

You will then need to leverage customers' recollections of events. Understanding what causes participants to forget the details needed to answer interview and survey questions correctly is the first step in preventing memory errors and getting more accurate information. We'll first cover why we forget and provide guidance for helping your survey participants recall the details you're looking for.

Groves et al. (2009) describe four types of memory problems that can affect the accuracy of answers to questions.

1. Retrieval Failure

You can't forget what you didn't notice. Forgetting something means details were encoded into memory in the first place. When trying to recall these details, you either remember (memory retrieval) or forget (retrieval failure).

It's hard enough to remember details about significant life events, but details about routine events are even harder to remember. Did the problem with finding your premium amount happen on your auto-insurance website, or was it your health insurance website? An in-store shopping experience from six weeks ago can be hard to recall, as can the call to customer support last week.

Time may heal all wounds, but time also wounds all recall. There's a rich history of published work on memory (Mcleod, 2023, June 15), and one clear finding is that the more time has passed, the less likely you'll be able to remember things.

Forgetting isn't a steady, linear decay. Instead, we tend to forget much soon after, and then the rate of forgetting tapers off in a reverse exponential function. Interestingly, a significant number of people remember personally salient facts and events (teacher names, grades, classmates), even after decades. Figure 9.1 shows the inverse exponential decay of memory for four different types of personal facts.

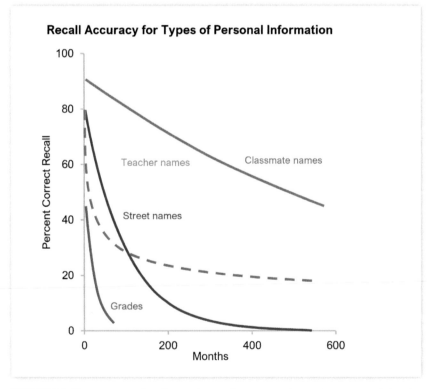

FIGURE 9.1: Memory over time for grades, teacher names, classmate names, and street names (source is Tourangeau et al., 2000).

2. Reconstruction Errors

Similar events may blend to create a sort of generic memory. Were you transferring money, checking your balance, or paying your mortgage when you last used your banking app? Gaps in our memory are often filled in with guesses of what we probably did ("Reliability of Memory," n.d.). There is also evidence that we project our current thinking onto the past, even the recent past (Pearson et al., 1992). For example, answer the following question that appeared in a recent survey:

How many prescriptions have you ordered online in the last two years?

What are the steps you go through to come up with your best answer? How confident are you that your answer is accurate?

Other than the dates of significant events such as birthdays, anniversaries, or holidays, it can be hard to remember the date on which an activity occurred or, as is often the case with surveys, whether something happened in a time period (for example, within the last two years).

People tend to misplace into the reference period events that really happened earlier or later (technically referred to as *forward and backward telescoping errors*). This leads to respondents overreporting activities such as the frequency of home repairs (Neter & Waksberg, 1964) and underreporting how much money they've spent (Fricker et al., 2015). This likely also affects the accuracy of responses to consumer survey questions about general product purchasing and usage.

3. Memory Distortion

Our memory of significant events such as weddings, graduations, and hospital visits can be affected by contemporary details gathered from photos, videos, or stories from others. This distortion almost certainly happens to some extent for the routine tasks asked about in customer and UX surveys. Was the problem you remember having with your banking app something you encountered? Or might others commenting on Twitter about the bad experience distort your recall?

Psychologist Elizabeth Loftus is famous for showing how easily memories can be created, changed, or manipulated, even for significant events. This has implications for the reliability of memories recovered during talk therapy and for the use of eyewitness testimony in courtrooms (Loftus, 2005).

Loftus herself has experienced the formation of a false memory, which she recounted in an NPR interview (Raz, 2017):

> Well, personally, I had a kind of an amazing experience. I have to preface this with the fact that when I was 14 years old, my mother drowned in a swimming pool. And, you know, jump ahead decades later. I went to a 90th birthday party of one of my uncles. And one of my relatives told me that I was the one who found my mother's body. And I said, no. No, it didn't happen. And this relative was so positive that I went back from that family reunion and I started thinking about it. And I started maybe visualizing.

And I started to think maybe it really did happen. I started to make sense of other facts that I did remember in light of this news. And then my relative called me up a week later and said, I made a mistake, it wasn't you. And so I thought, oh, my gosh, I just had the experience of my subjects, where someone convincingly tells you and you start to visualize and you start to feel it. And then it wasn't true.

4. Mismatches Between Researcher and Respondent Interpretation of Terms

The terms we use to ask respondents about prior events might not trigger recall. Does ordering food from Grubhub count as online shopping? How about ordering a prescription online for pickup at the drugstore? Maybe the researcher is interested in capturing these activities, but the term online shopping might not cause the participant to recall them.

HOW TO IMPROVE PARTICIPANT RECALL

With an understanding of why people forget, researchers have come up with some techniques to reduce forgetfulness and improve the accuracy of self-reported events.

The following techniques, summarized from the influential books *The Psychology of Survey Response* (Tourangeau et al., 2000) and *Survey Methodology* (Groves et al., 2009), may improve recall, but keep in mind that the evidence for their effectiveness is stronger for some techniques than for others.

1. Shorten the Reference Period

People forget things. In general, it's easier to recall what you did yesterday, last week, or the last month compared to six months or a year ago.

Events that happened a long time ago are harder to remember. As more time passes, we make more errors in dating events (Baddeley, 1992).

Cognitive psychologists have identified a phenomenon called the *telescoping effect* that describes the tendency of people to incorrectly remember the time frame in which something has happened. *Backward telescoping* occurs when people recall recent events as having happened more distantly. *Forward telescoping* occurs when they recall older events as having happened more recently. Telescoping errors, therefore, result in respondents reporting more events during a reference window than actually happened in that period.

Some studies have shown a decrease in the number of reported events as the length of the reference period increases. For example, Neter and Waksberg (1964) reported a study where some participants recalled the number of home repairs in the last six months, and others recalled only one month. Participants in the six-month condition reported 32% fewer repairs than participants who had to recall only one month. The longer the reference period, the more likely respondents are to use current behavior to estimate prior events. It's unclear from these studies, however, how many "real" events there are, as it's challenging to validate many of the events.

Based on these findings, one way to reduce telescoping errors (and incorrect recall in general) is to use the shortest reference period that is consistent with the research goals (e.g., Figure 9.2).

a. 6-month reference period	b. 1-month reference period
☀ Over the past six months, how many times have you made a purchase at BuyNow.com?	☀ Over the past month, how many times have you made a purchase at BuyNow.com?
0	0
1-2	1-2
3-4	3-4
5-6	5-6
7-8	7-8
9-10	9-10
If more than 10 times, how often?	If more than 10 times, how often?

FIGURE 9.2: Example of frequency of purchase items with six- and one-month reference periods.

2. Use Personal Landmarks or Life Events

Though people tend to be forgetful, some things are easy to recall even after decades, such as names of teachers, where you were on 9/11, and spells of unemployment (Mathiowetz & Duncan, 1988).

It's easy for people to remember events associated with strong emotions (Thompson et al., 1996). These events typically include personal landmarks such as birthdays, anniversaries, weddings, the birth of a child, and graduations.

There's also some evidence that referencing notable events can reduce telescoping. Loftus and Marburger (1983) decreased forward telescoping by framing the response period in terms of meaningful events (e.g., the 1980 eruption of Mount St. Helens for people living in Washington State). Kurbat et al. (1998) found that college students recalled more events at school/vacation boundaries than at other times of the year, suggesting that calendar events can help memory organization and retrieval. Figure 9.3 has examples of questions that use these kinds of landmarks.

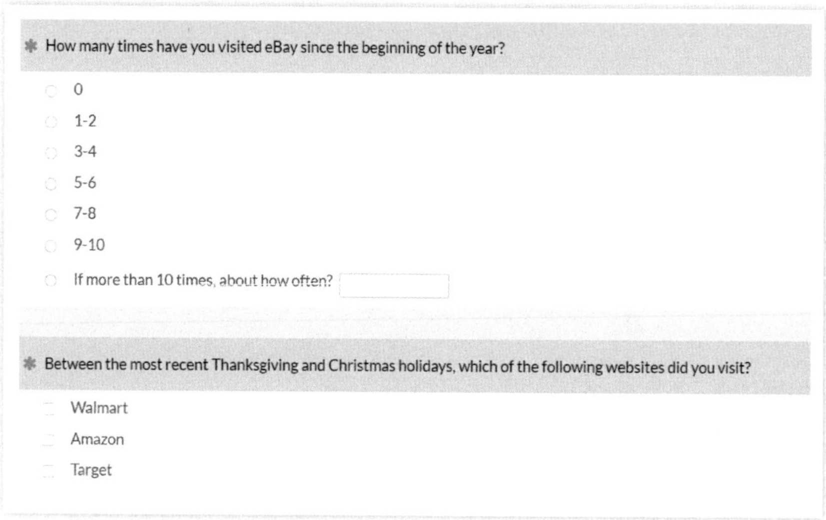
* How many times have you visited eBay since the beginning of the year?

- 0
- 1-2
- 3-4
- 5-6
- 7-8
- 9-10
- If more than 10 times, about how often?

* Between the most recent Thanksgiving and Christmas holidays, which of the following websites did you visit?

- Walmart
- Amazon
- Target

FIGURE 9.3: Examples of questions using personal landmarks for reference periods.

3. Thinking Backward May Help

Some evidence suggests that respondents recall information better in reverse chronological order (e.g., the names of teachers, Whitten & Leonard, 1981; the contents of psychology exams, Loftus & Fathi, 1985).

People who are asked to recall visits to a hardware store may follow the progress of a home improvement project, with each visit impacted by what was purchased earlier in the project. Visits to health insurance websites may also follow the course of an illness or surgery, with reverse order aiding recall about the reason for prior visits.

The effectiveness of this strategy likely depends on what you ask, but if you're studying events such as multiple doctor visits or multiple visits to a store, especially in interviews, consider asking about the most recent occurrences first and working backward.

4. Decompose the Question

When asking respondents to recall events, there's some evidence that decomposing broader categories (e.g., shopping; visiting a doctor) into smaller events (e.g., shopping for clothing, groceries, or furniture; visiting a dermatologist) can help with recall (Means et al., 1994).

Conceptually, this reduction in the scope of the event of interest is similar to reducing the chronological reference period.

5. Use Introductions to Questions

As shown in Figure 9.4, you can add a twist to the decomposed question by providing concrete cues in an introduction to the question—another way to constrain the scope that the respondent considers when answering.

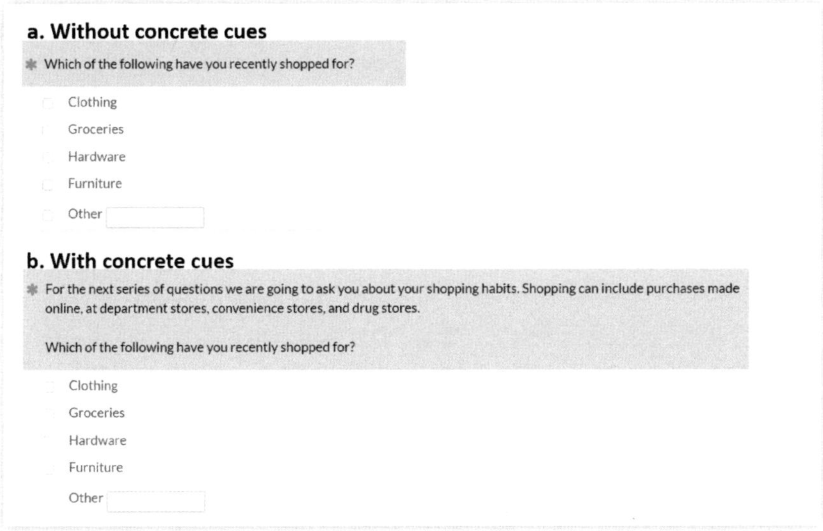

a. Without concrete cues

Which of the following have you recently shopped for?

- Clothing
- Groceries
- Hardware
- Furniture
- Other

b. With concrete cues

For the next series of questions we are going to ask you about your shopping habits. Shopping can include purchases made online, at department stores, convenience stores, and drug stores.

Which of the following have you recently shopped for?

- Clothing
- Groceries
- Hardware
- Furniture
- Other

FIGURE 9.4: Examples of questions with and without concrete cues in the introduction

6. Give More Time

Finally, there's some mixed evidence that giving respondents more time can improve recall (Burton & Blair, 1991). If you're conducting an interview or administering a survey over the phone or in person, allow plenty of time for respondents to recall. In an online survey, encourage respondents to spend as much time as they need to answer questions if you have noticed recall problems.

CHAPTER SUMMARY

This chapter focused on why people forget and how to improve recall.

Why do people forget? …Retrieval failure, reconstruction errors, distortion, and mismatches. Using surveys and interviews to ask participants about their past experiences can help you understand what does and doesn't work for developing better products or services. People, of course, forget details. We forget things for many reasons. Four primary culprits are:

- *Retrieval failure:* The more time has passed and the less salient the detail, the more imperfect the recollection.

- *Reconstruction:* People fill in gaps with generic memories.

- *Distortion:* People's memories are influenced by contemporary details such as photos and videos of an event.

- *Mismatching terms:* People might not associate memories with the terms used by interviewers or in surveys.

How can we write survey questions to help people remember? ...There are several strategies. People forget. Some of the following techniques, especially when used in combination, may help to improve participant recall in surveys and interviews (they are particularly useful for controlling "telescoping" errors—the tendency of people to incorrectly remember the time frame in which something has happened).

- *Shorten the reference period.* To control telescoping errors, prefer short over long reference periods.

- *Provide personal landmarks.* It's easier for people to remember events associated with strong emotions, so framing response periods in terms of meaningful events can decrease telescoping errors.

- *Ask people to think backward.* This can be especially effective when studying events that have happened more than once.

- *Decompose the question into small, concrete questions.* When appropriate, decompose broad categories (e.g., shopping) into more specific events (e.g., shopping for clothes).

- *Use introductions to questions.* Survey question writers strive to keep questions as short as possible, but it may sometimes be helpful to constrain a broad scope with specific instructions.

- *Give more time.* Encourage participants to take the time they need to remember the details of the events of interest.

PART 3:
Survey Response Options

CHAPTER 10:
SELECTING THE RIGHT RESPONSE OPTIONS

Should you use a rating scale, checkboxes, or an open-text field? The number of choices can seem daunting, and researchers want to avoid the pitfalls of bias and error covered in Chapter 2. We'll answer the following questions about selecting the right response option:

- When should I just use an open-ended response option?
- What are the key considerations for the response options of measurement questions?
- What are the main types of noncategorical measurement questions?
- How should I decide which question type to use?

In Chapter 5, we introduced the idea of different types of response options for discovery vs. measurement and subdividing measurement into categorical and noncategorical. Those are the tip of a daunting iceberg of response options that we'll cover in depth.

Crafting survey questions involves thinking first about the content (e.g., attribute, behavior, ability, or sentiment) and then about the format (form follows function, e.g., open- or closed-ended).

As with any taxonomy, there are several ways to categorize response options (e.g., open- vs. closed-ended). We recommend starting with the goal of the question and then picking the response option that best achieves that goal while minimizing the burden on the respondent.

Often, more than one kind of response option will meet a goal, but we've put together a decision tree that should help you narrow your choices.

As shown in Figure 10.1, the tree shows the flow from the research goal to the recommended type of question and response option. The rest of this article describes the decision points in the tree and guides each decision.

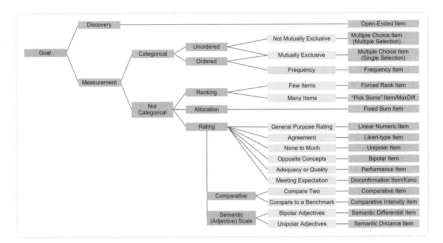

FIGURE 10.1: Decision tree for types of survey questions.

DISCOVERY OR MEASUREMENT?

The first decision is whether the goal of the question is to discover something or to measure something.

Discovery

Discovery is a key aspect of qualitative inquiry. Open-ended questions are well suited for discovering things with minimal response bias. For example, Figure 10.2 shows an open-ended question designed to discover problems respondents experienced on their last visit to a website. The resulting data require significant effort to categorize and count, but they aren't constrained by a specific set of options.

FIGURE 10.2: Open-ended question to explore self-reported tasks and associated usability problems (created with MUiQ).

FIVE REASONS FOR OPEN-ENDED QUESTIONS

There are five good reasons to use open-ended questions (for details and examples, see Sauro & Lewis, 2021, Jan 12).

Conduct exploratory research. A common reason to use open-ended questions is to learn more about a phenomenon or topic. Sometimes the responses to the open-ended questions tell you all you need to know. Other times, they can be a first step toward developing closed-ended questions.

Reduce bias or other unintended influences. As a check on potential bias, you can include one or more open-ended questions before presenting rating scales. Be sure that the wording of the open-ended question is as neutral as possible.

Assess unaided recall or awareness. A common strategy used in branding studies known as aided awareness is to present a list of brands for each category. A weakness of this strategy is that the list can influence which brands come to mind because all that respondents need to do is recognize the brands. An alternative strategy is unaided awareness, which uses open-ended questions to require respondents to recall rather than just recognize brands. This method reveals which brands are foremost in respondents' minds, reducing the importance of brands they have heard of but not experienced.

Ask follow-up questions. An important use of open-ended questions is to get follow-up clarification to close-ended questions. We use this strategy frequently, even in surveys that have dozens of closed-ended questions (e.g., asking respondents to give reasons for their Net Promoter Score (NPS) or Single Ease Question (SEQ) ratings).

Reveal unanticipated events or unexpected attitudes. Sometimes you need to give respondents a chance to tell you whatever is on their minds. In those times, open-ended questions are the only option, and those questions need to be completely nondirective. For example, at the end of a survey, you should include a final question so respondents can tell you anything that they think the survey failed to ask, or if they noticed anything, negative or positive, that happened during the survey.

Measurement

The second and dominant path down the decision tree is through the Measurement branch, which includes Categorical or Not Categorical items.

CATEGORICAL

When focusing on measurement, the next question to consider is whether the responses contain categories. For example, many attribute questions tend to be categorical (gender, education, age, location). Some categorical questions have a natural order (e.g., age, income), while others do not (e.g., gender, problem lists).

With categorical data identified, your next decision is whether participants can select only one response (mutually exclusive) or multiple responses (not mutually exclusive).

Not mutually exclusive

When the categorical question doesn't have a natural order and respondents could reasonably select more than one response option, the appropriate question type is Multiple Choice with Multiple Selection, also known as "Select-all-that-apply" questions (Figure 10.3).

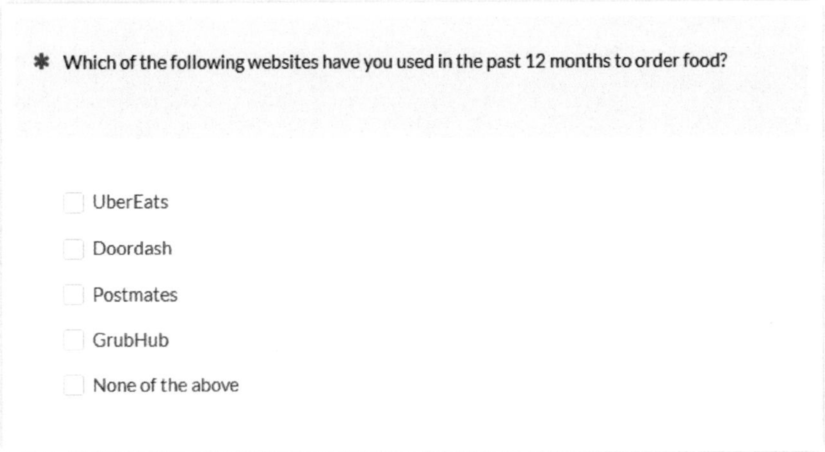

---

* Which of the following websites have you used in the past 12 months to order food?

☐ UberEats

☐ Doordash

☐ Postmates

☐ GrubHub

☐ None of the above

FIGURE 10.3: Example of response options that are not mutually exclusive.

Examples of categories that aren't mutually exclusive include:

- Universities attended
- Places lived
- Food delivery services used in the last six months
- Activities performed in a job
- List of problems encountered

On a practical note, when the primary purpose is measurement, you can design hybrid questions that allow for some discovery by making one of the responses an open-ended "Other" option (see Figure 10.4). Also, any primarily measurement-focused question can be dynamically followed by an open-ended question designed to get at the why behind the measurement. Take care not to do this too much because it can fatigue respondents, and a key driver of survey dropout is excessive survey length.

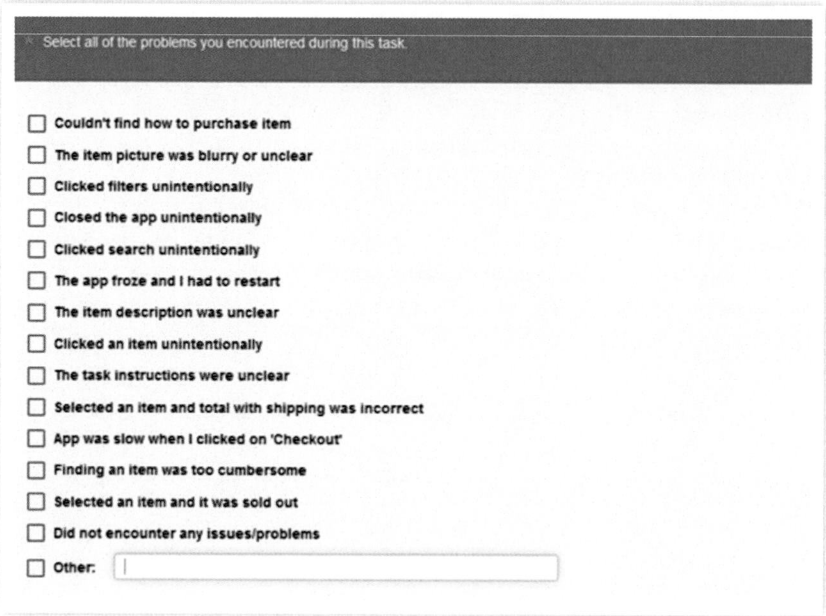

FIGURE 10.4: Sample problem list with open-ended "Other" option (created with MUiQ).

Mutually exclusive

When a set of categories has a natural order and the options are mutually exclusive, it isn't reasonable to select more than one (Figure 10.5). (Some unordered options, such as choosing a preferred design from a set, may also be mutually exclusive.)

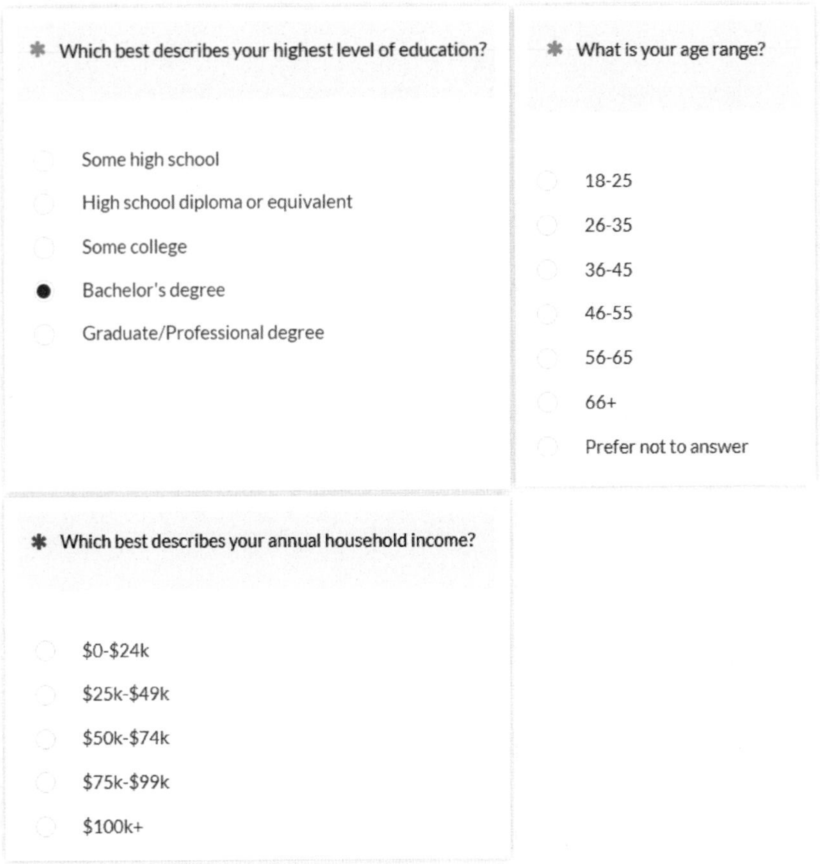

Which best describes your highest level of education?

○ Some high school

○ High school diploma or equivalent

○ Some college

● Bachelor's degree

○ Graduate/Professional degree

What is your age range?

○ 18-25

○ 26-35

○ 36-45

○ 46-55

○ 56-65

○ 66+

○ Prefer not to answer

Which best describes your annual household income?

○ $0-$24k

○ $25k-$49k

○ $50k-$74k

○ $75k-$99k

○ $100k+

FIGURE 10.5: Examples of mutually exclusive response options.

For example, mutually exclusive categorical options would be appropriate for:

- Highest degree obtained
- Current geographic location
- Age
- Income
- Number of children
- Frequency of use

TIP:

One of the most common mistakes we see in surveys is response options presented as mutually exclusive when they really aren't—a mistake that prevents respondents from giving accurate answers. Other common mistakes with ordered categories are incomplete lists of options and overlapping ranges. For example, what are the issues with these response options for age ranges: 10–20, 20–30, 30–40, 40–50, and 60+? Which option would you select if you were 20? Which would you select if you were 55?

Frequency

Frequency items are special types of mutually exclusive questions. Figure 10.6 shows two examples. We generally recommend using specific response options (e.g., more than once a day) rather than nonspecific (vague) options (e.g., rarely).

When purchasing electronic products, how often do you do each of the following?	Never	Rarely	Sometimes	Often	Always
Read customer reviews	○	○	○	○	○
Read expert reviews and comments	○	○	○	○	○
Look at technical specs (e.g., dimensions and adapters)	○	○	○	○	○
Watch a video demonstration	○	○	○	○	○
Watch a video submitted from another customer	○	○	○	○	○

How frequently do you use Microsoft Excel?

- ○ More than once a day
- ○ Once a day
- ○ Once a week
- ○ Once a month

FIGURE 10.6: Two examples of frequency questions (created with MUiQ).

NOT CATEGORICAL: RANKING, ALLOCATION, AND RATING

The remaining (and the majority of) question types in the decision tree are not primarily categorical. One consequence of collecting categorical data is that the appropriate descriptive and inferential statistical analyses are limited to counts and proportions. It's possible (and sometimes advisable) to analyze noncategorical data with counts and proportions, but these data aren't limited to those methods. By assigning numbers to response options, either explicitly or after data collection, you can use sophisticated univariate and multivariate methods to analyze data collected with ranking, allocation, and rating questions.

Ranking

It's common to ask participants to rank features or content that may appear in a product or website. The primary benefit of ranking is that it forces participants to make tradeoffs and identify what's important. This helps prevent the "everything is important" problem when having participants rate features (see below on rating).

Forced ranking

If you have only a few items for participants to rank (fewer than ten or so), then requiring participants to rank each item is probably not too much of a burden (see Figure 10.7).

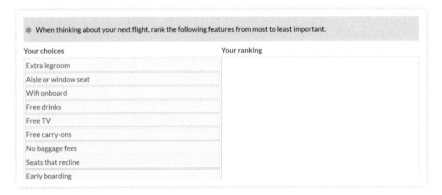

FIGURE 10.7: Example of forced ranking question (created with MUiQ).

Pick some

If you have a lot of items (more than twenty or so), you'll want to minimize the burden on the participants by using a pick-some option. We use this option in top-task studies where we often present 50–100 pieces of content or features and ask participants to select their top five (see Figure 10.8).

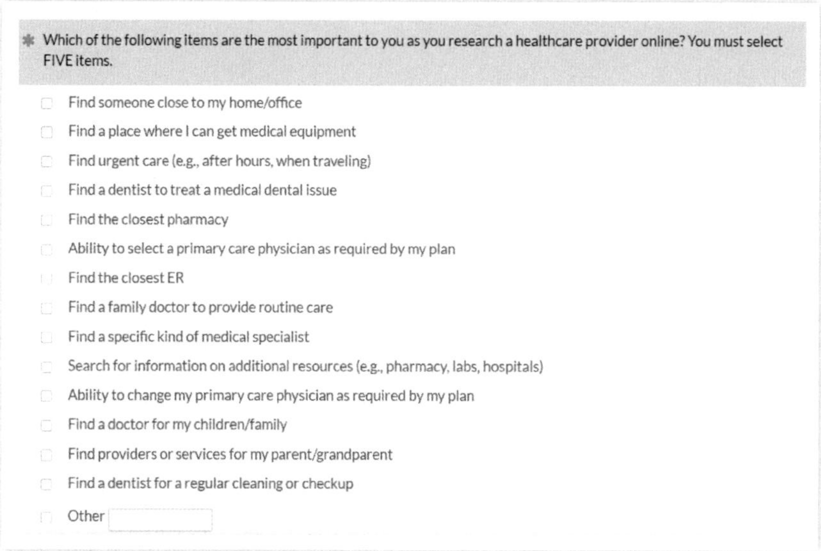

* Which of the following items are the most important to you as you research a healthcare provider online? You must select FIVE items.

☐ Find someone close to my home/office
☐ Find a place where I can get medical equipment
☐ Find urgent care (e.g., after hours, when traveling)
☐ Find a dentist to treat a medical dental issue
☐ Find the closest pharmacy
☐ Ability to select a primary care physician as required by my plan
☐ Find the closest ER
☐ Find a family doctor to provide routine care
☐ Find a specific kind of medical specialist
☐ Search for information on additional resources (e.g., pharmacy, labs, hospitals)
☐ Ability to change my primary care physician as required by my plan
☐ Find a doctor for my children/family
☐ Find providers or services for my parent/grandparent
☐ Find a dentist for a regular cleaning or checkup
☐ Other

FIGURE 10.8: Example of pick-some ranking question (created with MUiQ).

MaxDiff

When there are many features to rank, an alternative to pick some is the MaxDiff question, which iteratively presents a subset of the features. This presentation allows participants to select the options that are most and least important. MaxDiff requires specialized software, such as our MUiQ platform, to present the combinations and calculate ranks and scores (see Figure 10.9).

From the options presented, please select the feature that would be the most important and the one that would be the least important as you decide on the right hotel for your upcoming vacation.

Is LEAST important to my decision		Is MOST important to my decision
○	Airport Shuttle	○
○	Location	○
○	Pet Friendly	○
○	Star Rating	○
○	WIFI	○

FIGURE 10.9: Example of MaxDiff question (created with MUiQ).

Allocation

A specialized type of forced-choice method has participants allocate points, dollars, percentages, or other amounts to indicate relative importance. Ideally, the software will sum the number to minimize mental math for participants! Figure 10.10 shows an example.

When thinking about what you spend in a a typical month, what percent of your budget goes to the following items. The total must add up to 100.

Rent/Mortgage	50
Dining Out	10
Entertainment (Movies, Shows)	5
Other	10

Remaining: 25
Total: 75

FIGURE 10.10: Example of a fixed-sum question for allocation of a budget (created with MUiQ).

Rating

This category encompasses the remainder and bulk of question types. We divide rating items into three categories: Comparative, Semantic, and Other (general purpose, agreement, none-to-much, opposite concepts, adequacy or quality, and meeting expectation).

Comparative questions

Items that ask participants to compare items or compare to a benchmark have a distinct format. Figure 10.11 shows examples of comparative and comparative intensity questions.

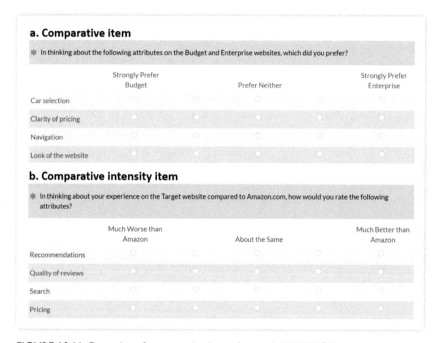

FIGURE 10.11: Examples of comparative items (created with MUiQ).

Semantic adjective items

Semantic adjective items have participants rate either one (unipolar semantic distance) or two putatively opposite (bipolar semantic differential) adjectives such as "easy" and "difficult." See Figure 10.12 for examples.

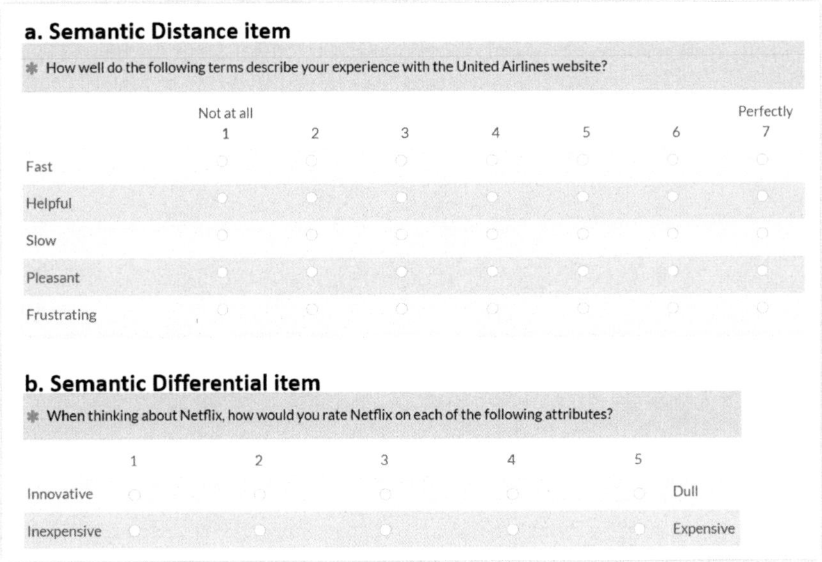

a. Semantic Distance item

✳ How well do the following terms describe your experience with the United Airlines website?

	Not at all 1	2	3	4	5	6	Perfectly 7
Fast	○	○	○	○	○	○	○
Helpful	○	○	○	○	○	○	○
Slow	○	○	○	○	○	○	○
Pleasant	○	○	○	○	○	○	○
Frustrating	○	○	○	○	○	○	○

b. Semantic Differential item

✳ When thinking about Netflix, how would you rate Netflix on each of the following attributes?

	1	2	3	4	5	
Innovative	○	○	○	○	○	Dull
Inexpensive	○	○	○	○	○	Expensive

FIGURE 10.12: Examples of semantic scales (created with MUiQ).

Linear numeric (general purpose) items

Most rating items are linear numeric (Figure 10.13), with numbers assigned to each response option (visibly or invisibly), endpoint labels, and optionally, one or more labels between the endpoints. When sample sizes are reasonably large, these responses can be treated as continuous data. If tied scores would be problematic when making comparisons, use a ranking item instead of a rating item.

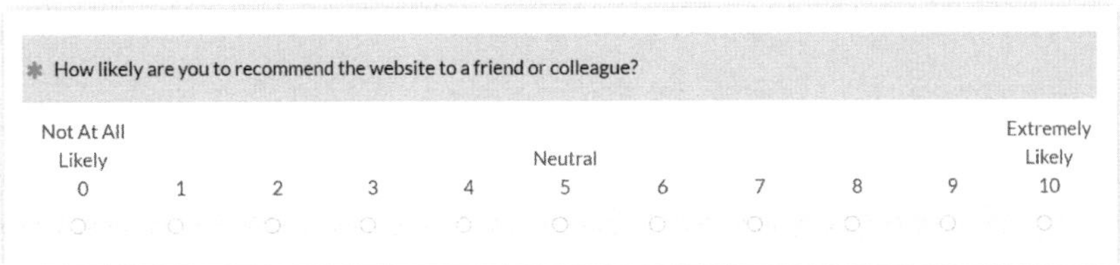

✳ How likely are you to recommend the website to a friend or colleague?

Not At All Likely 0	1	2	3	4	Neutral 5	6	7	8	9	Extremely Likely 10
○	○	○	○	○	○	○	○	○	○	○

FIGURE 10.13: Example of linear numeric scale (the Likelihood-to-Recommend item used to compute NPS).

Likert-type (agreement) items

Agreement scales are very common in UX and CX surveys, almost as common as disagreements on what they should be called. We loosely refer to them as Likert-type, Likert, or agreement scales, but there are subtle differences that some people make a point to call out (hopefully not on you).

The Likert scale was developed and named after psychologist Rensis Likert. A Likert scale consists of an average or sum of *multiple* Likert-type items labeled from Strongly Disagree to Strongly Agree (Figure 10.14). Many of Likert's original response options (Likert, 1932) used "approve" instead of "agree," but many of the measurement establishment consider "agree" to be the purest Likert response format.

✳ Please rate how well you agree or disagree with the following statements.	Strongly Disagree 1	2	3	4	Strongly Agree 5
I think that I would like to use this system frequently.	○	○	○	○	○
I found the system unnecessarily complex.	●	●	●	●	●
I thought the system was easy to use.	○	○	○	○	○

FIGURE 10.14: Example of Likert-type agreement items (from the SUS).

A Likert response format *usually* has only five, fully labeled, response options, and most measurement experts (and some journal reviewers) consider calling anything else a Likert item, like a seven-point agreement item with only endpoints labeled, a mistake. While a bit silly, to avoid the discussion, call any variations on labels or the number of response options a Likert-type scale. You don't need to stick with just five points in an agreement scale — that is just what's most strongly associated with a Likert scale. But whatever you do, don't call a single Likert item a Likert scale — that will get everyone mad. The scale is technically the average or sum of a set of related items. See Chapter 20 for a discussion (and the controversy) on taking the mean of ordinal data.

 TIP:

It's pronounced **LICK-ert.** But we, like most others we know, mispronounce it as LIKE-ert, because, well, it sounds better and makes so much sense — a scale about something you like! So, we're sticking with LIKE-ert. Don't you strongly agree?

Unipolar (none-to-much) items

This is a specific type of linear numeric scale that is appropriate when you can conceptualize the measured attribute as having levels from low to high (Figure 10.15).

Not at All Satisfied 0%	10%	20%	30%	40%	50%	60%	70%	80%	90%	Completely Satisfied 100%
○	○	○	○	○	○	○	○	○	○	○

FIGURE 10.15: Example of a unipolar item (a feeling thermometer for measurement of satisfaction).

Bipolar (opposite concept) items

In contrast to unipolar items, this is a linear numeric scale in which the measured attribute is conceptualized as having opposing endpoints (Figure 10.16).

a. Task Ease item (SEQ)

Very Difficult						Very Easy
1	2	3	4	5	6	7

b. Delight item

Delighted	Pleased	Mostly Satisfied	Mixed (about equally satisfied as dis-satisfied)	Mostly Dissatisfied	Unhappy	Terrible
7	6	5	4	3	2	1

FIGURE 10.16: Examples of bipolar items (SEQ and delight).

Performance (adequacy or quality) items

This is another linear numeric scale appropriate for gauging the quality of experiences (Figure 10.17).

Very Inferior						Very Superior
1	2	3	4	5	6	7

FIGURE 10.17: Example of a performance item (superiority).

Disconfirmation (meeting expectation) items

This type of linear numeric scale assesses if a product/experience was better or worse than expected. A common way to assign numbers to these response options is to set "About What I Expected" to 0, "Much worse..." to –1, and "Much better ..."" to +1. It is possible to have more than three response options to increase the scale's sensitivity, but the number of response options should always be odd so the center point will be "About What I Expected" (Figure 10.18).

Much worse than I expected		About what I expected		Much better than I expected

FIGURE 10.18: Example of a disconfirmation item.

USING THE DECISION TREE

Table 10.1 shows some example goals, which question types achieve the goal, and the path through the decision tree (Figure 10.1).

Goal	Question Type	Path Through Decision Tree
Discover potential uses of a new feature	Open-Ended Item	Discovery
Assess the extent to which the experience of attempting a task matched participants' expectations	Disconfirmation Item	Measurement > Not Categorical > Rating > Meeting Expectation
Determine the relative importance of five product features	Forced Rank Item	Measurement > Not Categorical > Ranking > Few Items
Assess the extent to which respondents agree or disagree that they are confident in having completed a task successfully	Likert Item	Measurement > Not Categorical > Rating > Agreement
Find out which of five video content streaming services respondents have used in the past year	Multiple Choice Item (Multiple Selection)	Measurement > Categorical > Unordered > Not Mutually Exclusive

TABLE 10.1: Examples of using the decision tree to match goals with question types.

CHAPTER SUMMARY

This chapter focused on how to select the right response options for survey questions.

When should I just use an open-ended response option? ...When the purpose of the question is discovery rather than measurement. At a high level, the purpose of asking open-ended questions is discovery, but there are finer-grained reasons to ask open-ended questions (differing in their specific research contexts and how directive they are), including:

- Conducting exploratory research.
- Reducing bias or other unintended influence.
- Assessing unaided recall/awareness.
- Asking follow-up questions after closed-ended ratings.
- Revealing unanticipated events or unexpected attitudes.

What are the key considerations for response options for measurement questions? ...Start by determining if the data you need are categorical. Many attribute questions tend to have categorical response options, some of which do not have an implied order (e.g., gender) and some that do (e.g., age range). You also need to determine if the response options are mutually exclusive (e.g., age range) or are select-all-that-apply (e.g., which streaming services someone uses).

What are the main types of noncategorical measurement questions? ...Ranking, allocation, and rating. Ranking questions ask participants to arrange response options in order (e.g., preference, importance). Allocation questions have participants allocate a fixed quantity (e.g., points, dollars, percentages) to response options to indicate relative importance. Rating scales are the best-known and most frequently used noncategorical survey questions, where participants select a point on a scale to indicate their response to the question (usually an attitude or behavioral intention).

There are so many types of questions—how should I decide which to use? ... Use the decision guide. The number of question types available for use in surveys can seem overwhelming. Having a decision tree as a decision guide can simplify connecting a research goal to an appropriate type of question (starting with discovery vs. measurement, then categorical vs noncategorical). As an additional aid, Table 10.2 summarizes the question types covered in this chapter.

Type		Pros	Cons
📝	Open-Ended	Unconstrained verbatim data	Requires coding before analysis; limited analytical options
⊙— ○— ○—	Multiple Choice (Single)	Easy collection of mutually exclusive categorical options	Not appropriate when options not mutually exclusive; limited analytical options
☒— ☐— ☒—	Multiple Choice (Multiple)	Easy collection of categorical options that are not mutually exclusive	Not appropriate when options are mutually exclusive; limited analytical options
1 5 ○○○○◉	Rating and Ranking Scales	Easy ordered data measurement of sentiments and attitudes; many analytical options	Extensive variation in formats, most of which don't matter much in UX research, but some that do (see next tables)
⊙—○ ○—○ ○—◉	Adaptive Conjoint/MaxDiff	Dynamic presentation of features rated for preference or interest	Requires custom advanced statistical analysis

Type		Pros	Cons
Not At All Extremely Likely Likely 0 ••• 10	Linear Numeric Scale	Most common type of rating scale; familiar to participants; with reasonably large n can be treated as continuous data	Possible for scores to tie, so not suitable when the research question requires ranking
Strongly Strongly Disagree Agree 1 ••• 5	Likert (Agreement)	Type of linear numeric scale (same pros); research shows that they are not overly influenced by acquiescence bias; widely used in standardized UX questionnaires	Type of linear numeric scale (same cons)
Never ••• Often	Frequency Scale	Appropriate for tracking effect of frequency of use on other UX metrics	Can be tricky to get the response options right for given research questions

Type		Pros	Cons
Not At All Completely Satisfied Satisfied 1 ••• 7	CSAT: Unipolar	Type of linear numeric scale (same pros); appropriate when conceptualizing level of satisfaction from none to high; feeling thermometer seems to work well	Not appropriate when conceptualizing satisfaction as bipolar construct
Very Very Dissatisfied Satisfied 1 ••• 7	CSAT: Bipolar	Type of linear numeric scale (same pros); appropriate when conceptualizing level of satisfaction from negative to positive	Not appropriate when conceptualizing satisfaction as unipolar construct; some evidence that standard endpoints might not have equal pull on responses
Terrible Excellent 1 ••• 5	CSAT: Performance	Type of linear numeric scale (same pros); appropriate for guaging quality of experiences (e.g., Terrible to Excellent)	Type of linear numeric scale (same cons)
Much Much worse than better than I expected I expected 1 ••• 5	CSAT: Disconfirmation	Type of linear numeric scale (same pros); assesses if a product/experience was better or worse than expected	Type of linear numeric scale (same cons)

		Type	Pros	Cons
Strongly Prefer A	Strongly Prefer B	**Comparative Scale**	Type of linear numeric scale (same pros); useful for compact comparison of two products/services for list of attributes	Limited to comparison of two products/services in a grid
Much Worse than A	Much Better than A	**Comparative Intensity Scale**	Type of linear numeric scale (same pros); useful for compact comparison of one product with a known external benchmark product	Limited to comparison of one product/service with benchmark in a grid
Boring ••• Exciting		**Semantic Differential Scale**	Type of linear numeric scale (same pros); popular format for standardized questionnaires; familiar to participants	Difficult to develop pairs of adjectives that are polar opposites
Not At All Fun ••• Extremely Fun		**Semantic Distance Scale**	Type of linear numeric scale (same pros); avoids need for pairs of polar opposites by using unipolar scales	Limited to list of adjectives for items

Type		Pros	Cons
	Forced Ranking Scale	Good for prioritizing small number of product features	Becomes unwieldy with more than ten items to rank
	Pick Some (Top Task) Ranking	Good for prioritizing large number of product features; results are similar to forced ranking	Must randomize order of presentation of features; some information lost relative to forced ranking
A: 60 B: 40 100	**Fixed Sum Scale**	Good for prioritizing features	More cognitively demanding than other prioritization methods, even with running totals

TABLE 10.2: Summary of survey item types with usage pros and cons.v

CHAPTER 11:
THE NUMBER OF POINTS IN A RATING SCALE

In this chapter, we'll (1) get into some of the folklore and controversies concerning rating scales and (2) provide a summary of the published research and our primary research on the number of points to use in rating scales. We'll go over these key topics:

1. Are three points enough in a rating scale?
2. Do too many points confuse people?
3. Will people really use all the points?
4. Does changing the number of points in a survey confuse people?
5. Should you have a neutral point (i.e., an odd or even number of points)?
6. Does changing the number of points systematically affect scale means?

ARE THREE POINTS ENOUGH IN A RATING SCALE?

Few things seem to elicit more opinions (and misinformation) in measurement than the "right" number of scale points to use in rating scale response options.

While it's good to hypothesize why one response scale is better than another (for example, the theory that shorter scales are easier and better), it's important to verify or falsify those claims with data. A good place to start is with the wealth of research in the published literature.

Published Studies on Number of Scale Points

For as long as researchers have used rating scales, there have been questions (and concerns) about the "optimal" number of scale steps (e.g., Boyce, 1915).

When questionnaire scores are computed from multiple items, the number of scale points in individual items matters less (although it still has an effect). For example, the SUMI questionnaire, with its 50 items, uses three-point response options (see Chapter 11). Although a response to one of its items is rather coarse (agree, undecided, disagree), averaging responses across 50 items increases the fidelity of the overall score.

As a general rule, when using a single item to measure a construct that falls on a continuum from low to high (such as satisfaction, ease, and Likelihood-to-Recommend), the more points you have in your rating scale, the greater its reliability (consistent responses) and validity (reflects true attitudes), up to about 11 points (Nunnally, 1978).

EARLY RESEARCH: TWO- AND THREE-POINT SCALES ARE INADEQUATE

For the last 100 years, there has been a lot published on the different numbers of scale points in general, but there has also been specific research on the use of two- and three-point scales versus scales with more points.

In one of the earliest studies, Ghiselli (1939) found that four-point scales performed better than two-point scales. The author had 200 undergraduate students rate the sincerity of advertising pieces for 41 different brands across 12 commodity types. Half the respondents were given two options (Yes or No), while the other half were given a four-point scale: very sincere, fairly sincere, fairly insincere, and very insincere. In both conditions, respondents had the choice of selecting "uncertain." They found more people responded favorably (top-two box) with the four-point compared to the two-point scale, and fewer people selected the "uncertain" response when given four points.

In the ensuing decades, the debate continued. In 1970, Green and Rao summarized the debate on scale points and described two factions. One advocated for using fine-grained scales (11 or 21 points), while another, based on opinions about respondents' ability to differentiate between many points, advocated for only two or three response options. The loss of fidelity by having only two or three points, they argued, is made up for by asking more questions. Green and Rao conducted a simulation study and found that adding more questions did NOT make up for the loss in fidelity from using two or three points (at least in their specific study type). So, this scored one point for the more-than-three-point-scale faction.

THREE-POINT SCALES MAY BE GOOD ENOUGH WHEN USING MANY ITEMS

In response to Green and Rao, Jacoby and Mattell, in the article rather bluntly titled "Three-Point Likert Scales Are Good Enough" (1971), argued that three points are good enough in some cases. They had 360 undergraduate psych students answer one of eighteen versions of a 60-item questionnaire, varying the number of scale points between two and nineteen (so there were twenty respondents for each condition).

Respondents were then given the same questionnaire three weeks later. The authors found little difference in reliability and their measure of validity, concluding that as few as two response options may be adequate in practice. They suggested that both reliability and validity are independent of the number of response options, and their results implied that collapsing data from longer scales into two- or three-point scales would not diminish the reliability or validity of the resulting scores. This scored one point for the two–three-points-are-good-enough faction.

THREE-POINT SCALES FRUSTRATE AND STIFLE

In another paper, Lehmann and Hulbert (1972) argued that the main problem with two- and three-point scales is that they force respondents to choose options that do not accurately reflect their attitudes, which introduces rounding errors. In their also aptly named "Are Three-Point Scales Always Good Enough?" article, they conducted a simulation study with items with three, five, seven, and nine points.

They concluded that two or three points are probably fine when averaging across people and many items. But **if the research is focused on individual scales, using a minimum of five scale points is probably necessary to accurately measure the variable**. They found, for example, that even when 30 items are summed, using six or seven points instead of three cuts the error approximately in half.

Cox (1980) offered one of the more comprehensive reviews of the topic, spanning 80 years. His analysis concluded that "scales with two or three response alternatives are generally inadequate and ...tend to frustrate and stifle respondents," and that the return from using more than nine response alternatives is minimal.

THREE-POINT SCALES CONTAIN LESS INFORMATION

Researchers often use rating scales as dependent variables in multiple regression analysis to understand what drives brand attitude or satisfaction. Morrison (1972) showed that using discrete points for an underlying continuous variable (like satisfaction) will reduce information. Little is lost at eleven points, where 99% of the information is transmitted, but only 87.5% is transmitted with a three-point scale (illustrating loss of discriminating ability with a coarser measure).

Morrison is building on information theory (Shannon & Weaver, 1949), where the "bits" of information transmitted are the log of the number of response options. A two-point scale communicates only one piece of information (yes/no, agree/disagree). Three-point scales communicate two pieces of information (neutrality and direction). Four-point scales communicate intensity and direction, but no neutral opinion. Five-point scales are, then, better theoretically because they provide three pieces of information: direction (positive/negative), intensity of opinion, and a neutral point.

MORE POINTS DIFFERENTIATE BETTER BETWEEN GROUPS

In another study, Loken et al. (1987) examined the criterion validity of various telephone-administered scales through their ability to differentiate between different population groups and **found eleven-point scales to be superior to three-point or four-point scales**.

Lozano et al. (2008), using a simulation study, analyzed scales with between two and nine response options and concluded, "the optimum number of alternatives is between four and seven. With fewer than four alternatives the reliability and validity decrease, and from seven alternatives onwards psychometric properties of the scale scarcely increase further" (p. 73). The authors didn't test ten- or eleven-point scales, however.

Alwin (1997) compared seven- and eleven-point scales from a 1978 life satisfaction survey and found that **eleven points were superior to seven points**. He used a large probability sample of 3,692 U.S. respondents, who rated 17 domains of satisfaction (e.g., residence, living, and life satisfaction) and used three scales in the same order: a seven-point satisfied to dissatisfied (endpoints and midpoint labeled); a seven-point delighted-terrible (fully labeled); and an eleven-point feeling thermometer (only endpoints labeled). He found that eleven-point scales had higher reliability than seven-point scales and, in many cases, higher validity coefficients. He recommended eleven-point scales when measuring life satisfaction and rejected the idea that the eleven-point scale is more vulnerable to measurement errors.

In a study using a UX questionnaire, Lewis (2021) found little difference between scales with five, seven, and eleven points but found that **three-point scales were inadequate**. He had 242 participants randomly assigned to a three, five, seven, or eleven-point version of the UMUX-Lite. He found little difference in reliability or correlations with other measures except for the three-point version, which had the poorest coefficient alpha (an unacceptably low value of .61).

THREE-POINT SCALES CAN'T IDENTIFY EXTREME ATTITUDES

In our analysis of top-box scoring (Sauro, 2018, May 2), we reviewed studies that showed that extreme responders (those making the most favorable and least favorable responses) tend to be better predictors of behavior. With three-point scales, as other studies have shown, there is no way to differentiate between extreme and tepid responses.

THREE-POINT SCALES RATED AS QUICKER BUT FIVE, SEVEN, AND TEN POINTS RATED AS EASIER

One of the more compelling studies comes from Preston and Colman (2000). In the study, 149 (mostly) students responded to their experiences at a store or restaurant using a 101-point scale and five questions rating their experiences (e.g., promptness of service) repeated 11 times, where the only thing changing was the number of points, ranging from 2 to 11.

All scales were anchored with "very poor" on the left to "very good" on the right. Participants also rated the scale formats on ease of use, quickness of use, and allowing them to express feelings adequately. They then had respondents answer the same questionnaire again one to three weeks later to assess test-retest reliability; 129 participants (86%) completed the second one. The authors found:

- **Ease:** Five, seven, and ten-point scales were rated as easiest to use, and eleven- and 101-point scales were the least easy to use. Note that it is unclear whether the eleven-point scale was numbered from 0–10 (which seems as if it should be reasonably easy to interpret) or 1–11 (which might require more effort to interpret).

- **Quickness:** Two, three, and four-point scales were rated as the quickest to use, and scales with eleven and 101 points were rated the least "quick."

- **Express feelings adequately:** Two- and three-point scales were rated "extremely" low on "allowed you to express your feelings adequately," whereas scales with nine, ten, eleven, and 101 points were rated the highest.

- **Reliability:** Two, three, and four-point scales were least reliable (test-retest and internal consistency), while scales with five or more points were more reliable (all test-retest reliabilities at least .90).

The authors concluded that scales with small numbers of response categories yield scores that are generally less valid and less discriminating than those with six or more response categories. They concluded that rating scales with seven, nine, or ten response categories are generally to be preferred.

COMPARING FIVE-, TEN-, AND ELEVEN-POINT VERSIONS OF THE NET PROMOTER SCORE

The Net Promoter Score (NPS) is widely used in UX and CX research. Based on responses to an eleven-point Likelihood-to-Recommend (LTR) item, respondents are classified into one of three groups (0–6: detractors; 7–8: passives; 9–10: promoters). The NPS is the percentage of promoters minus the percentage of detractors.

Sauro (2017, Nov 29) compared five, ten, and eleven-point versions of the LTR item, finding comparable results when computing Net Promoter Scores (an average absolute difference of around four percentage points).

Studies of Three vs. Eleven Points for the Net Promoter Score

Around 2019, some UX practitioners began arguing that if you're going to convert NPS ratings to three categories, why not just use a three-point scale (e.g., "Will you recommend — No, Maybe, Yes")? Some claimed that simplifying the rating scale would be easier and faster, with no loss of fidelity.

In response to this claim, Sauro (2019, Aug 21) conducted three studies using the Net Promoter Score item to corroborate or clarify earlier research findings that three-point scales would be less valid and reliable. Modifying the method used in Preston and Colman (2000), the studies focused specifically on the LTR item, tested only eleven- and three-point scale variations, and used larger and more diverse (non-student) sample sizes.

STUDY OVERVIEW

Three studies (*n* = 824; *n* = 634; *n* = 113) were conducted using U.S.-based online panel participants between November 2018 and July 2019 to compare the differences and preferences between three-point ("No, Maybe, Yes") and standard eleven-point LTR items across dozens of brands.

KEY FINDINGS

The key findings from these three studies were:

Three points are perceived as quicker and easier but stifling
Participants in these three studies rated three-point scales as easier and quicker, but they rated eleven-point scales as better at allowing them to express their feelings adequately, consistent with the Preston and Colman (2000) findings.

The results of the scale preferences from Study 1 are shown in Table 11.1.

	Three-Point Preference	Eleven-Point Preference
Easier	63%	37%
Quicker	72%	28%
Express feelings more adequately	19%	81%

TABLE 11.1: Preference for three- vs. eleven-point response options for the LTR item (*n* = 824). All differences are statistically significant.

Scores are not interchangeable

Net Promoter Scores derived from three-point scales differed substantially from those derived from eleven-point scales. Using the aggregated data to create Net Promoter Scores across multiple brands resulted in much higher net scores for the three-point version. The three-point NPS and eleven-point NPS differed by 17 points in Study 1, 26 points in Study 2 (see Table 11.2), and in Study 3, by 42 points (recent restaurant) and 67 points (cellphone carriers).

Aggregated	Count	Percent	Aggregated	Count	Percent
Yes	780	41%	Promoters	634	33%
Maybe	506	27%	Passives	309	16%
No	616	32%	Detractors	959	50%
NPS (Yes–No)	1902	9%	NPS	1902	-17%

TABLE 11.2: Correspondence between Yes/Maybe/No and Promoters/Passives/Detractors, and corresponding "Net" scores, which differed by 26 points (9% vs. −17%) in Study 2.

Not all yeses are created equal

One attractive aspect of the three-point scale is the seemingly universal understanding of the labels applied. After all, doesn't everyone know what Yes, No, and Maybe mean compared to numbers from 0 to 10? However, our analysis showed a lot of ambiguity in those words. One person's "Yes" might be better read as a "YES!" compared to another person's more tepid "Yes, I guess." In contrast, a 10 is greater than a 9, which is greater than an 8, and these quantities are universally understood as being greater. Providing eleven response options on this scale can better reflect the underlying attitude continuum that is only coarsely measured with three-point scales. The distribution of responses in Figure 11.1 shows that on the eleven-point scale, roughly half of the yeses selected a 10 (YES!!!), 70% selected a 9 or 10 (YES! or YES!!!), and almost a third (30%) selected less intense responses (Yes, I guess).

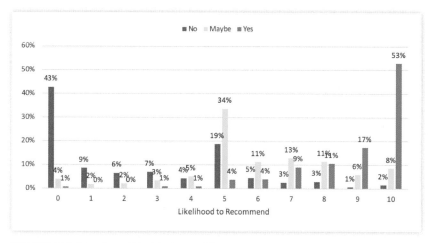

FIGURE 11.1: Mapping of No, Maybe, and Yes to the eleven-point LTR item.

Maybe probably means no

One of the main differences between the three-point and the eleven-point version was how the maybes were treated. Many respondents who said "Maybe" had corresponding eleven-point scores near the neutral point (5). The NPS computation treats these responses as detractors—that is, people who won't recommend and are more likely to discourage others from a brand. One criticism of the NPS designations is that while respondents classified as detractors are less likely to recommend, it doesn't necessarily mean these respondents will always discourage others from a company. Our research demonstrates that promoters tend to promote (Sauro, 2019, May 29) and detractors tend to detract (Sauro, 2018, Nov 28), but in general, MOST people don't recommend or detract, especially those with more tepid responses (between 5 and 7). This lends credence to the practice of treating these mediocre responses as people who are not likely to recommend.

Three points are nominally but not statistically faster than eleven

It took about five and a half seconds on average for respondents to answer both forms of the questions. The eleven-point scales nominally take longer, but the difference in time is barely perceptible, **at an average difference of between one-tenth to three-tenths of a second**. That's about the same amount of time it takes to blink!

A slight gain in speed is more than offset by a substantial loss in validity
Whatever little is gained in the reduction of time to answer an eleven-point scale is more than lost by both the frustration you are giving respondents in limiting their response options and the subsequent loss of reliability and validity of the scale. Using only three points loses information about the extreme responders, who tend to be better predictors of behavior. As in all research, there are tradeoffs. What's worse: asking respondents to spend a fraction of a second more to respond, or forcing them to pick a response option that doesn't reflect how they feel? Then is that error made worse by thinking that a response of Yes/Maybe/No truly reflects their feelings?

Three-point scales permanently lose information
Why not just have a three-point scale if you are going to collapse eleven points to three points? This analysis shows that eleven points allow you to better differentiate intensities, and therefore likely recommenders, whereas showing only three points puts mediocre responses with the most intense. Although converting an eleven-point scale to three points loses information, the loss isn't permanent as you can still examine the distribution of responses and, if you wish, track the mean LTR along with the NPS. However, if you start with a three-point question, you give up any ability to capture the intensity of response needed to accurately map to standard Net Promoter Scores.

Three-Point Scale Summary and Takeaways
In summary, a literature review of several studies conducted on the quality of three-point scales and our own research on a three-point version of the NPS found:

MORE SCALE POINTS INCREASE RELIABILITY
The literature overwhelmingly shows that as you increase the number of scale points, you increase reliability. Reliability increases most when increasing from three to five points; less is gained as you exceed seven or eleven points.

THREE-POINT SCALES ARE NOT RELIABLE
Across multiple studies, using only three points was shown to have not just low, but inadequate reliability, and in some studies, even when averaging across items, too much is lost. The low reliability is a consequence of using a coarse scale to represent a continuum. Forcing respondents to choose from too few categories introduces more error in responding and thus makes responses less consistent in the same study (internal reliability) and over time (test-retest reliability).

THERE'S A LOSS OF INTENSITY AND VALIDITY WITH THREE-POINT SCALES
Using only three points loses important information about the intensity, or the strength, of people's opinions. Not everyone feels equally favorably or unfavorably toward a brand, interface, or experience. All but one of the studies we examined recommended using more than three points in a rating scale. In the one study that

did suggest three-point scales were enough, results were averaged across multiple items (no analysis of single items). Our analysis of NPS computed from three- versus eleven-point scales found that using three points led to a substantial loss of validity through failure to identify extreme responders.

TWO- AND THREE-POINT SCALES ARE PERCEIVED AS QUICKER TO COMPLETE, BUT THIS IS LARGELY AN ILLUSION

Participants generally rate two- and three-point scales as quicker and easier to use, lending credence to the idea that shorter scales require less mental effort. Our analysis of completion times for three- and eleven-point versions of NPS found, however, that the difference, if any, is no more than the blink of an eye. If speed and the perception of ease are paramount (especially when using multiple items), a researcher may decide that two or three points are good enough. But this must always be balanced against the knowledge that these rating scales stifle respondents' ability to accurately express their opinions.

TWO AND THREE POINTS ARE INSUFFICIENT TO EXPRESS FEELINGS ADEQUATELY

Although participants may perceive two- and three-point scales as faster and easier, they consistently report feeling that those scales are inadequate for the expression of their feelings.

THE CLAIM OF A THREE-POINT SCALE SUPERIORITY IS A MYTH

Our literature review and experimentation with a three-point version of the NPS provided convincing evidence against the use of three-point scales for most UX or CX research. The literature is inconsistent regarding their perceived ease, the perception that they are quicker to complete appears to be illusory, and their reliability and validity are much lower than scales with more points. Along with the discredited idea that all website content should be reachable within three clicks, (Porter, 2003, Apr 16), the idea that three-point scales are always (or even sometimes) better than scales with more points needs to go into the UX myth dust bin.

However, if three points are too few, is there a point where there are too many? It's a topic we will cover in the next section.

DO TOO MANY RESPONSE OPTIONS CONFUSE PEOPLE?

One concern we've read is that people may have a hard time differentiating between too many response options in rating scales. If true, this would lead to a recommendation to avoid response options with more than, say, seven points.

For example, on an eleven-point satisfaction scale such as the one shown in Figure 11.2, what is the difference between 6 and 7 in terms of satisfaction? Does having so many points increase the cognitive burden of responding, leading to measurement problems?

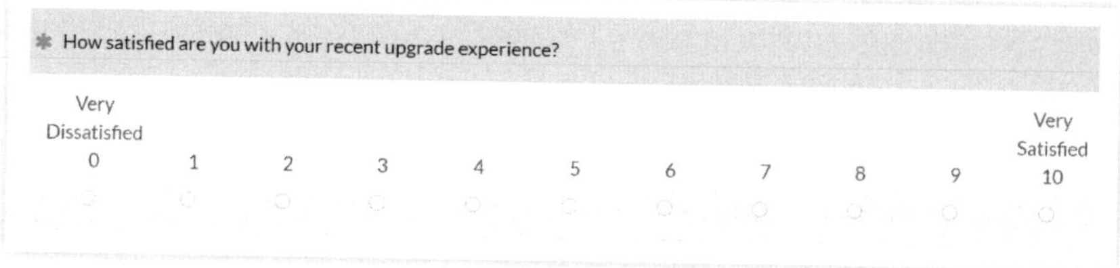

How satisfied are you with your recent upgrade experience?

Very
Dissatisfied
0   1   2   3   4   5   6   7   8   9   Very Satisfied 10

FIGURE 11.2: A sample eleven-point satisfaction item.

Earlier in this chapter, we showed that having too few response options (three or fewer) leads to a significant reduction in both reliability and validity as respondents could not accurately express the intensity of their feelings (Sauro, 2019, Aug 14). But what about the opposite: do too many points cause problems? Is the optimal number of response options driven by a Goldilocks effect, where too few is a problem, and too many is also a problem? In this section, we dive deep into many sources to understand the evidence for or against many points.

Published Research on Too Many Points

We first looked to some commonly referenced survey books for any rationales and data on why more points might add problems. We saw see guidelines in some survey books on not using too many points.

For example, Dillman et al. (2014) generally recommend limiting scales to four or five response options because "respondents can only hold a limited number of categories in their head at once, so offering fewer categories can help reduce the cognitive complexity involved in providing a response, especially over the telephone" (p. 153). The authors don't provide a study to support the guideline, but the caveat about phone administration may be warranted when the response options are words or phrases rather than a numeric scale. The guideline is probably not applicable to electronically administered surveys where respondents can see all options, changing the mental processing from memorization-plus-selection to simple selection.

In *Survey Scales*, Johnson and Morgan (2016) also warn against using too many scale points, which "might result in respondents experiencing problems discriminating the scale points" (p. 75). They argue this will contribute to measurement error — one of the four horsemen of survey errors (see Chapter 2). They cited three studies to support this warning against too many points, which we summarize below.

STUDIES 1 AND 2: NUMBER OF RESPONSE OPTIONS AND SCALE RELIABILITY

Consistent with the foundational work of Nunnally (1978), the first study (Lozano et al., 2008) concluded that beyond "seven alternatives onwards psychometric properties of the scale scarcely increase further" (p. 73). They used simulations to explore the effect of varying both the correlations among items and the number of response categories per item from two to nine. Their main finding was that increasing the number of response options increased the reliability of the associated scales (monotonically increasing with diminishing returns from three to nine options).

The second study Johnson and Morgan cited is Weng (2004), which replicated the finding that too few categories decreased reliability and also reported that fully labeled scales increase reliability:

> The results indicated that the scales with few response categories tended to result in lower reliability, especially lower test-retest reliability. The scales with all the response options clearly labeled were likely to yield higher test-retest reliability than those with only the end points labeled. (p. 956)

Carefully reading Weng's methods and results paints a more nuanced picture regarding the comparison of full versus endpoint labeling: "The hypothesis that the full specification of response options improves reliability was only partially supported in the present study" (p. 969). Weng put forth several hypotheses as potential explanations for why one set of data showed increased test-retest reliability for the fully labeled format with no difference for a second set of data, but the bottom line is that the findings were inconsistent. This is an example of statements made in the abstract of a peer-reviewed paper making broader claims than the data support, which is why we recommend against taking these statements at face value when reviewing research.

STUDY 3: TROUBLE DISTINGUISHING BETWEEN POINTS

The third citation (Frary, 2002) includes the following warning against using too many points under the heading of "Scale Point Proliferation":

> Psychometric research has shown that most subjects cannot reliably distinguish more than six or seven levels of response, and that for most scales a very large proportion of total score variance is due to direction of choice rather than intensity of choice. Offering four to five scale points is usually quite sufficient to stimulate a reasonably reliable indication of response direction. (pp. 4–5)

This quote may have been the inspiration for the similar recommendation in Dillman et al. (2014). Unfortunately, Frary didn't provide a reference for the "psychometric research," but he did provide a frequency item scale from Never to Always as an example (see Figure 11.3).

| ✳ How often do you use a streaming video service? |

| Never | Rarely | Occasionally | Fairly Often | Often | Very Often | Almost Always | Always |

FIGURE 11.3: Example of frequency item scale response options derived from Frary (2002, p. 4).

Frary presented these response options as an example of what NOT to do: "Such stimuli run the risk of annoying or confusing the responder with hairsplitting differences between the response levels" (p. 4). Frary suggested just a bit later that more response options would probably be acceptable for numeric scales, as long as they had only the endpoints labeled: "Questionnaire items that ask the responder to indicate strength of reaction on scales labeled only at the endpoints are not so likely to cause responder antipathy if the scale has six or seven points" (p. 5).

Johnson and Morgan also cited a survey from Kouzes and Posner (2003) that used a ten-point frequency scale with similar labels: Almost never, Rarely, Seldom, Once in a while, Occasionally, Sometimes, Fairly often, Usually, Very frequently, and Almost always.

In addition to splitting hairs, both of these sets of frequency response options use vague modifiers (Sauro & Lewis, 2021, Mar 23) that can have wide variations in interpretation. For example, in Figure 11.3, what's the difference between "fairly often" and "often"? Indeed, it may be quite challenging to differentiate between these categories. However, the problem shown here is more about the use of vague modifiers rather than the number of them. A five-point version drawn from these sets of vague modifiers may present similar challenges (although the problem is probably exacerbated as the number of response options increases and would be especially severe when conducting research over the phone).

One strategy for avoiding this problem is to use specific options (e.g., 0–2 times per day, 3–4 times per month, etc.) rather than vague modifiers (see Chapter 7 for more on vague modifiers).

The preceding examples are about the frequency of behavior, but what about sentiment? Johnson and Morgan also referenced a study by Dawes (2008). In the study, each participant answered a five, seven, or ten-point scale for the same eight purchasing items. The study was conducted over the phone with participants instructed to "please answer using the scale from 1 to X where 1 equals strongly disagree and X equals strongly agree'. X was either 5, 7, or 10 depending on the treatment group" (p. 65).

Despite being conducted over the phone, the surveys had comparable results when Dawes rescaled all scores to ten points (p. 62). The study also found that if a scale with more response options was administered, respondents made use of those additional response options, a finding that Dawes interpreted as favoring scales with more points.

Johnson and Morgan, however, noted that while the number of points used increased for the longer scales, the *percentage* of the available points used decreased. On average, respondents used 58% of the options for five-point scales (2.9/5), 51% for seven-point scales (3.6/7), and 40% for ten-point scales (4.0/10). Johnson and Morgan used this outcome to argue against using scales with more points.

While the percentage of available points used did indeed decrease by 18 percent-age points in the Dawes study (a 31% relative reduction), it's unclear how this metric indicates respondents had trouble differentiating between the number of points. If we reduce a scale from five to two response options, the percentage used would likely be close to 100%. At the other extreme, if respondents used slider scales with a hundred points of discrimination, then across eight items, they would likely land on eight different values, using only 8% of the available points. The percentage of points used seems like a poor metric for assessing discriminating ability.

TOO MANY POINTS OR TOO MANY LABELS?

In another survey book, Harris (2014) echoed the guidance from Johnson and Morgan and warned against scales with too many points. One example he cited is a ten-point bipolar scale used for assessing soap. Figure 11.4 is a recreation illustrating two example items in the scale:

✳ Please rate this soap on the following characteristics. You may click any number from 1 to 10 to represent your opinion.									
Bar was too small									Bar was too big
1	2	3	4	5	6	7	8	9	10
○	○	○	○	○	○	○	○	○	○
Bar was too soft									Bar was too hard
1	2	3	4	5	6	7	8	9	10
○	○	○	○	○	○	○	○	○	○

FIGURE 11.4: Example multipoint items from Harris (2014).

Harris argued that respondents probably don't have five levels of positive ratings and five levels of negative ratings for soap. He recommended using a six-point scale, claiming that that would be easier for respondents to understand, but he provided no data showing six points was easier than ten points.

Harris advised that if you have trouble adding labels to all scale points (e.g., on a ten-point scale), then you probably have too many points. For example, consider the ten hypothetical desirability options in Figure 11.5:

✳ Please rate how desirable you find this service to be.									
Not at all desirable	Very slightly desirable	Slightly desirable	A little bit desirable	Somewhat desirable	Moderately desirable	Desirable	Very desirable	Extremely desirable	Completely desirable
1	2	3	4	5	6	7	8	9	10
○	○	○	○	○	○	○	○	○	○

FIGURE 11.5: Example of an excessive number of response option labels from Harris (2014).

Based on our literature review of 17 studies (Sauro & Lewis, 2020, Jan 8) and our own experimentation (Sauro & Lewis, 2020, Jan 22), we'd argue that this isn't an example of having too many points, but too many labels. You don't need to label all points all the time.

If More Points Confuse, Do Lots of Points Confuse Even More?

Consider Figure 11.6, which shows the arrangement of response options for 3, 5, 7, 11, and 101 points on a 0–100-point grid. We've used linear interpolation to place the options in the grid because (1) it's simple and (2) it works well in practice.

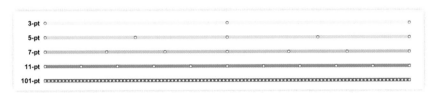

FIGURE 11.6: Depiction of 3, 5, 7, 11, and 101 points on a common scale.

Imagine working with the three-point scale. With those three points, you can indicate the direction of your feeling—negative, neutral, or positive, but you can't express the intensity of your feeling. When you move to the five-point scale, you can provide at least some indication of intensity, but only two points worth in a positive or negative direction. With a seven-point scale, you now have three points of intensity in either direction; with eleven points, you have five.

Moving now to the 101-point scale, you have 50 points of intensity on either side of the neutral point in the center. If there is some limit on the human capacity for engaging with this many points of discrimination, then why do some researchers prefer slider scales, which are, for all practical purposes, linear numeric scales with lots of points of discrimination? For example, if you set up a slider scale to measure from 0 to 100 in 1/10th point increments, you would have 1,001 points of discrimination, 500 on either side of the neutral point. But we know of no books on survey design that disparage sliders due to some hypothesized inability of humans to work with so many points of discrimination. Although the devil is in the design details when crafting usable sliders (Lewis & Sauro, 2020, Jul 15), we have found that 101-point sliders are indeed slightly more sensitive than five-point scales (Sauro & Lewis, 2020, Nov 10).

Discussion and Summary of Too Many Points

In this section, we've examined the claims made in three books about survey design regarding the best number of response options to use in rating items (Dillman et al., 2014; Harris, 2014; Johnson & Morgan, 2016). The key findings from this review are:

THE CONSISTENTLY PUBLISHED RECOMMENDATION TO LIMIT
THE NUMBER OF SCALE POINTS HAS POOR JUSTIFICATION

All three books recommend against providing too many response options based on the rationale that people can't reliably distinguish among more than a small number of choices (usually no more than seven). The specific cognitive limitation responsible for this inability, however, is never clearly spelled out. We suspect it might be due to a vague memory from psychology classes of Miller's (1956) article on the magic number seven (plus or minus two). This paper was a landmark in the genesis of cognitive psychology, but attempts to apply it to the design of artifacts such as visual menus and auditory menus have resulted less in effective design guidelines and more in misguidelines (Commarford et al., 2008; Paap & Roske-Hofstrand, 1986).

TOO MANY LABELS WITH VAGUE MODIFIERS MAY BE THE REAL ISSUE

The data cited in these survey books to justify using fewer points say more about labeling too many points with vague modifiers than about the number of points themselves. The need to label each response option clearly can restrict the number of options you can easily present. For numeric scales, consider setting aside the "requirement" to label all response options in favor of simply labeling endpoints. People are perfectly capable of using numeric linear scales with numerous response options, even when those options come as slider scales with as many as a thousand underlying points.

THERE IS NO GOLDILOCKS POINT; MORE SCALE POINTS IMPROVE RELIABILITY AND SENSITIVITY

There is strong evidence from psychometric research that scales with more points tend to have better reliability and sensitivity (and, in some cases, validity). The increase in reliability does taper off, but importantly, we're not aware of any evidence that reliability decreases as the number of points increases. In other words, we have not seen compelling evidence for a Goldilocks effect for the number of points in linear numeric scales. Guidelines that recommend using no more than five or seven response options should be interpreted with care, as they probably apply only to questions that require labels for each response option (and many questions don't have this requirement).

FEWER POINTS ARE LESS IMPACTFUL WITH MULTIPLE ITEMS

It's often the case that five or seven response options are sufficient for much UX research, especially when using standardized metrics such as the System Usability Scale, which have scores based on responses to multiple items. An exception to this is when there is a need to identify extreme responders, in which case eleven response options often appear to be sufficient.

MORE POINTS TAKE UP MORE SPACE

For numeric linear scales with only endpoints labeled, there does not appear to be an upper limit on the number of response options to provide due to some sort of human cognitive limitation. As a practical consideration, scales with more options take up more screen real estate, especially on mobile devices. This problem also applies to slider scales, which become difficult to manipulate when presented in a small space. (This practical issue has nothing to do with the claims we've been exploring in this section.)

SLIDERS HAVE 100+ POINTS

The survey books we reviewed did not discuss slider scales, but they can have hundreds to thousands of points of discrimination. Yet we know of no book on survey design that recommends against sliders due to some hypothesized cognitive inability of humans to work with so many points. Some researchers argue against the use of sliders, but those arguments are based on the increased physical demands of manipulating sliders to the desired point relative to the ease of clicking on a response option.

MORE THAN GOOD ENOUGH DOESN'T MEAN BAD

There is a big difference between claiming that five- or seven-point scales are good enough for certain types of measurement — they clearly are — and claiming that there is a cognitive limitation that prevents people from effectively using numeric scales with more response options. Despite the extent to which books on survey design make the second claim, the evidence simply doesn't support it. Finally, as Nunnally (1978) pointed out over four decades ago, any increase in overall measurement variation due to presenting more response options in numeric scales appears to be more than made up for by an increase in reliability and sensitivity.

DO PEOPLE REALLY USE ALL POINTS?

A related argument to the potential confusion caused by having too many points is that too many points may be unnecessary because people don't use them. This is a plausible argument in making a case for fewer options, and it is supported by some published data. In this section, we review that data and discuss it before presenting findings from our own analysis, which demonstrate the usage of all available response options — even for eleven-point items.

Not All Response Options Are Used...Does It Matter?

In their book *Survey Scales*, Johnson and Morgan (2016) advised against using too many scale points, which "might result in respondents experiencing problems discriminating the scale points" (p. 75). In the previous section, we argued it's less about the number of points but potentially about the number of labels, especially those using vague modifiers.

But we were intrigued by Johnson and Morgan's reinterpretation of findings published by Dawes (2008). In the Dawes study, participants in a phone survey were presented with either a five, seven, or ten-point scale for the same eight purchasing items. After rescaling all the items to ten points, Dawes found comparable means across the eight items for all three item formats. The study also found that if a scale with more response options was administered, respondents used more response options, a finding that Dawes interpreted as *favoring* scales with more points.

Johnson and Morgan, however, noted that while the number of points used increased for the longer scales, the percentage of the available points used by individual respondents *decreased* from 58% to 40% (see Table 11.3). They used this outcome to argue *against* scales with more points.

Points	# Used	% Used
5	2.9	58%
7	3.6	51%
10	4.0	40%

TABLE 11.3: Average number of points used by respondents across eight items using five, seven, or ten-point variations (phone administered, *n* = 185).

We don't find this argument compelling for two reasons. First, while the *percentage* of points used certainly decreased for items with more points (from 58% to 40%), the *average number* of points used *did* increase (from 2.9 to 4.0). That suggests that if you provide more points, participants will use them, albeit at a rapidly diminishing rate (imagine if there were a hundred points).

The second reason we don't see this as a compelling argument is that respondents were presented with eight related items in the scale (e.g., "When I am in a shop I will always check prices on alternatives before I buy" and "When I buy or shop, I really look for specials"). Dawes did not report the correlations among the items, but such similar items would likely be highly correlated, so it's not surprising that individual respondents did not use the full range of response options. A more interesting research question is the extent to which manipulating the number of options affects the response distributions of diverse samples of respondents, so we conducted our own analysis to find out.

Data Point Usage Analysis Study

We analyzed two datasets of previously collected survey data. The first set was collected in three surveys from U.S.-based online panel participants participating in studies of the auto-insurance, food delivery, and mass-merchant industries (Lewis & Sauro, 2021, Jan 26, Mar 30, Aug 3). The data contained five-point (SUPR-Q, eight items), seven-point (brand attitude, one item), and eleven-point (LTR, one item) scales from 975 respondents. The second dataset (n = 245) came from a published study (Lewis, 2021) that compared ratings collected with four different versions of the UX-Lite (three, five, seven, and eleven-point versions).

STUDY FINDINGS: PARTICIPANTS USED ALL POINTS

We found that respondents used all scale points for response scales with three, five, seven, and eleven points. Table 11.4 shows the distribution of response results from the eleven-point LTR item analyzed in the first dataset. Across the three surveys, each scale point was selected at least once, with 1 being the least selected. Even though the sample size was smaller, we saw similar results for the second dataset (Sauro & Lewis, 2021, Oct 5).

LTR	0	1	2	3	4	5	6	7	8	9	10	n
Auto Insurance	3	0	4	4	9	14	31	46	73	51	66	301
Food Delivery	3	1	5	10	7	20	29	35	37	31	34	212
Mass Merchants	9	1	6	5	8	40	32	57	88	86	130	462
Total	15	2	15	19	24	74	92	138	198	168	230	975

TABLE 11.4: Response distributions for the eleven-point LTR item.

These results add to the growing body of evidence that respondents are not confused by large numbers of response options and, across samples, tend to use all available response options for agreement scales with as many as eleven points.

DOES CHANGING THE NUMBER OF RESPONSE OPTIONS IN THE SAME SURVEY AFFECT RATING BEHAVIOR?

Surveys commonly contain a mix of five, seven, and eleven-point scales. That mixture of scales of differing lengths causes some to express concern. Why are there different numbers of points? Why not just make them all, say, all five-point scales? Won't this confuse respondents and lead to error?

A recommended practice in UX research is to use standardized items, such as the Single Ease Question (SEQ), UX-Lite (which has two items, one for rating perceived ease of use and one for rating perceived usefulness), and Likelihood-to-Recommend (LTR).

That makes sense. Once an item is widely used, and its measurement properties are well understood, researchers should be reluctant to modify them in any way, other than the most cosmetic (e.g., simple word changes such as "system" to "product").

A consequence of maintaining item standardization is that research participants will often be confronted by a sequence of rating scale items that have different numbers of response options. For example, the standard version of the SEQ has seven response options, the UX-Lite has five, and LTR has eleven.

We've researched many aspects of rating scale formats over several decades and do our best to stay on top of the literature. As far as we know, no one has specifically studied this potential effect on rating behavior. Consequently, we've had little to point people to when this concern has come up.

So, experimented to see whether changing scale points within a study affected scores, whether people even noticed, and if so, whether they were bothered by the changes (Lewis & Sauro, 2022, Aug 16).

Study Points Experimental Design

To understand whether varying the number of points in a scale causes confusion or errors, we conducted a Greco-Latin experiment that presented participants with a task (easy or hard) and questions with only five-point scales, and we compared it to a task with five, seven, and eleven-point scales. Data were collected from 279 U.S.-based online panel participants. We also asked participants if they noticed any differences in the number of points being used.

In this study, we were particularly interested in what, if anything, happens when the scales change. What would we expect if item sequence made a difference? Figure 11.7 illustrates two possibilities. Maybe the transition from more to fewer response options tends to increase ratings while a transition from fewer to more response options tends to decrease ratings (Panel A), or maybe the effect is in the opposite direction (Panel B).

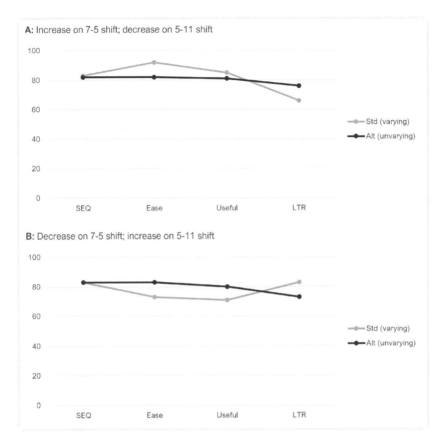

FIGURE 11.7: Two possible outcomes if there is an effect of item sequence.

So, when interpreting the results, our primary focus was on what happened in the transitions from SEQ to Ease and from Useful to LTR. Interactions (nonparallel lines) at those transitions would be evidence that the item sequence affected response behaviors. The absence of interaction indicates that item sequence has no effect.

Study Findings

The key findings were that changes in the number of scale points did not affect response patterns, most participants didn't notice the changes, and most of those who noticed didn't care.

NO DIFFERENCES IN RESPONSE PATTERNS FOR MEANS OR TOP-BOX SCORES

We found no compelling evidence for differences in response means or top-box scores based on varying the number of points. Although we had anticipated the possibility of a difference, especially when the number of points changed from seven to five and from five to eleven, there was no noticeable difference in the response patterns at those transitions.

Figure 11.8 shows the within and between-subjects differences in top-box scores for the two item sequences for each level of task difficulty. Both panels clearly show the significant main effect of task difficulty (manipulation check). The between-subjects analyses (Panel B) show no differences for the two item sequences in their transitions from SEQ to Ease or from Useful to LTR.

The within-subjects analyses also showed no differences for the two item sequences in their transitions from Useful to LTR. Consistent with the overall analyses of top-box scores, even though there were nominal differences in SEQ and ease top-box scores for the two item sequences, there were no large differences in the transitions from SEQ to Ease.

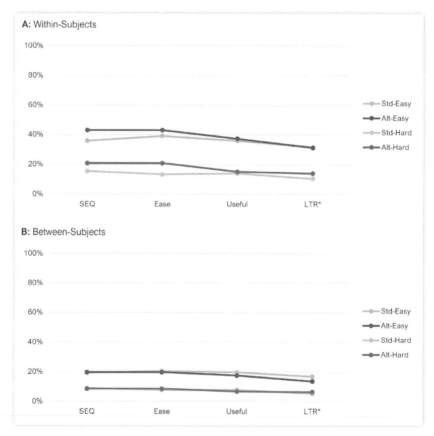

FIGURE 11.8: Within and between-subjects differences in top-box scores as a function of item sequence by task difficulty (Std: varying; Alt: unvarying; * = top-two-box score for the eleven-point LTR item).

EIGHTY PERCENT DIDN'T NOTICE THE CHANGE IN RATING SCALES

Not only were response behaviors similar in the two item sequences, but also, over 80% of respondents reported not noticing any difference in formats. This suggests that most respondents did not experience additional cognitive effort or confusion when presented with varying numbers of response options.

MOST HAVE NO PREFERENCE

Of the 20% (36 participants) who noticed the differing numbers of response options, most (38.9%) had no preference for one sequence over the other. Among those who did express a preference, 13 (36.1%) preferred the alternate (unvarying) sequence due to its perceived ease, while 9 (25.0%) preferred the standard (varying) sequence because they felt they were able to provide more precise ratings (no statistically significant difference in these preferences).

Key Recommendation

In general, we recommend using the standard versions of well-known items like the SEQ, UX-Lite, and LTR, which use seven, five, and eleven points, respectively. When crafting custom items, we recommend using five-point scales when items will be combined into multi-item scores (such as the UX-Lite), seven-point (or more) scales for stand-alone ratings of attitudes and experiences (such as the SEQ), and eleven-point scales for behavioral intentions (such as LTR), which are often used as dependent variables in regression/key driver analyses (see Chapter 21).

SHOULD YOU INCLUDE A NEUTRAL POINT (ODD OR EVEN POINTS)?

As for topics with strong opinions and heated debates, close behind the number of points to use in a rating scale is whether a rating scale should offer a neutral response.

Unlike rating scales with an even number of points, rating scales with an odd number of points contain a middle, "neutral" point.

Researchers who avoid providing a neutral response option are concerned that having a neutral point attracts respondents who slightly lean toward a favorable or unfavorable response but don't want to commit. Having a neutral response would mask those sentiments.

With an even number of options, respondents are forced to decide whether they think favorably or negatively toward an item.

Some early research by Presser and Schuman (1980) found that typically between 10–20% of respondents chose the neutral option when it was provided, compared to a survey where it wasn't. Their research was conducted using politically sensitive questions:

- Tendencies on political issues: liberal to conservative
- Federal funding for schools
- Penalties for marijuana use

In fact, Presser and Schuman did find that the biggest shifts happened for the political tendency scale (liberal to conservative). Then, as now, there was a certain social acceptability to being "middle-of-the-road" politically.

Such neutral options provide an easy out for respondents who are disinclined to express their opinion, but that potentially means a large proportion who slightly favor or oppose a topic aren't counted.

Despite the major shifts seen when including or excluding neutral options, Presser and Schuman found that the distribution of responses for the items didn't change significantly.

In other words, if 20% chose somewhat-liberal without the neutral option, then approximately 20% still chose somewhat-liberal with the neutral option. The total numbers would be less, but when reporting the proportions, they found that researchers would essentially draw the same conclusion — even on the sensitive topics they studied.

However, results reported by Bishop (1987) would lead researchers to draw different conclusions about the proportion of respondents who favor or oppose an issue based on the inclusion of a neutral response. His research also included politically sensitive topics:

- Social Security benefits
- Defense spending
- Nuclear power

Bishop concluded that the type of question (and the type of opinion it elicits) does matter, so one should carefully consider the context and the consequences of neutral options.

If you find yourself summarizing the proportion of respondents who favor or oppose an item exploring a sensitive topic, having a neutral response *may* matter. But what about neutral points for UX and CX topics?

Neutral Points in UX Surveys

Many standardized questionnaires measure attitudes toward the satisfaction and usability of applications (e.g., software, hardware, and websites), as we covered in Chapter 1. Table 11.5 shows some of the most popular toward product or interface experiences.

Questionnaire	# of Points in Response Options
SUS	5
PSSUQ	7
SUMI	3
QUIS	9
SUPR-Q	5
UMUX/UMUX-Lite	7
UX-Lite	5
SEQ	7
LTR/NPS	11
Microsoft NSAT	4

TABLE 11.5: Commonly used questionnaires used in UX research. Almost all use neutral points.

All but one of the questionnaires in Table 11.5 have an odd number of response options, implying that the authors of these questionnaires believed that a neutral response is legitimate. The exception is the Microsoft NSAT which, as far as we know, hasn't undergone any psychometric validation (Sauro, 2019, Sep 25).

It seems reasonable that people could genuinely have a neutral attitude about some items that ask about usability or general satisfaction with a system, where there's little incentive to hide sensitive beliefs in the neutral zone). But having data from a UX research context would be helpful, so we explored what happens if the neutral point is removed from the standard LTR item used to compute Net Promoter Scores.

Neutral Point Study: Removing the Neutral Point in the Likelihood-to-Recommend Item

The published literature on neutral points tends to be focused on politically sensitive topics. To investigate the impacts of an odd or even number of points (including a neutral point), we conducted a study manipulating the eleven-point Likelihood-to-Recommend item used to compute the NPS (Sauro, 2017, Nov 29).

To understand what effect changing the number of response options would have on the NPS, we examined the difference in scores using three response option variations: an eleven-point original and ten and five-point variations (Figure 11.9).

FIGURE 11.9: Eleven, ten, and five-point versions of the LTR item.

We collected data from 520 U.S.-based participants, with a mix of ages, genders, and occupations, using an online panel in November 2017. There were two studies: a retrospective analysis and an unmoderated UX benchmark study.

Our goal was to include brands and products with a range of NPSs (high to low performers). In the retrospective study, we recruited participants who had used a product or service from three U.S. airlines, three entertainment/media providers, and three cable/satellite providers. Between 49 and 53 responses were collected per company/product.

In the UX benchmark study, participants were randomly assigned to one of two online learning platforms (Lynda.com — part of LinkedIn — or Udemy) and asked to complete two tasks on the website using the MUiQ research platform.

In both studies, participants were assigned all three variations of the Likelihood-to-Recommend (LTR) question in a randomized order to avoid sequence effects. The questions were not presented on a single page, and in the retrospective study, an additional experience question was placed between each variation of the item.

We used the scoring rubrics shown in Table 11.6 to convert all raw LTR responses to a Net Promoter Score with promoters, passives, and detractors by company/product.

Variation	Promoters	Passives	Detractors
11 Point	9–10s	7–8s	0–6s
10 Point	9–10s	7–8s	1–6s
5 Point	5s	4s	1–3s

TABLE 11.6: NPS scoring for eleven, ten, and five-point versions of the LTR item.

STUDY RESULTS

This analysis provided the following insights from changing the scales used in computing the Net Promoter Score.

Changing the scales affects the scores, but only a little

As shown in Table 11.7, the average absolute difference in NPS when changing the number of response options was around 4 percentage points (for sample sizes of around 50) but fluctuated as high as 14 points (for Delta Airlines NPS 10). The more continuous measure of mean LTR (all three versions rescaled to 0–100 points) was even more stable across versions (Table 11.8), with no absolute difference greater than 3.5 points.

Company	NPS 11 (Neutral)	NPS 10 (No Neutral)	NPS 5 (Neutral)
American	−8%	−6%	−8%
Comcast	−55%	−53%	−63%
Delta	−10%	4%	−8%

(continued on pg. 142)

Company	NPS 11 (Neutral)	NPS 10 (No Neutral)	NPS 5 (Neutral)
DirecTV	−14%	−12%	−20%
DISH	−16%	-8%	−16%
Facebook	29%	31%	21%
iTunes	8%	2%	2%
Lynda	−15%	−15%	−21%
Netflix	63%	63%	61%
Udemy	0%	3%	6%
United	−15%	−8%	−13%
Mean	−3%	0%	−5%

TABLE 11.7: NPS for eleven, ten, and five-point versions of the LTR item.

Company	NPS 11 (Neutral)	NPS 10 (No Neutral)	NPS 5 (Neutral)
American	70.4	68.7	68.9
Comcast	40.8	38.5	39.3
Delta	68.4	67.8	69.4
DirecTV	64.3	61.9	60.8
DISH	60.2	60.8	61.2
Facebook	79.4	78.9	78.6
iTunes	73.4	70.9	71.5

(continued on pg. 143)

Company	NPS 11 (Neutral)	NPS 10 (No Neutral)	NPS 5 (Neutral)
Lynda	64.8	62.3	63.6
Netflix	89.2	88.0	88.8
Udemy	73.4	71.7	72.9
United	64.6	64.3	66.8
Mean	68.1	66.7	67.4

TABLE 11.8: Mean Likelihood-to-Recommend for eleven, ten, and five-point versions of the Likelihood-to-Recommend item (all rescaled to 0–100 points).

Five vs. ten-point scales have about the same overall error
Interestingly, there wasn't a notable difference in the average NPS difference between the ten and five-point versions—both had average absolute errors of around 4 percentage points despite the ten-point version having no midpoint.

The changes in LTR format affected the distributions of detractors and promoters
McNemar tests revealed significant differences in distributions of detractors and promoters between the standard eleven-point version and the two alternate versions. The effect on detractors was about the same for five- and ten-point versions, with respective drops of 3.3 and 2.9% relative to the eleven-point version. The effects on promoters, however, were different, with a significant 6.1% drop for the five-point version and a nonsignificant increase of 0.8% for the ten-point version.

The ten-point scale is a slightly poorer substitute than the five-point scale
To some extent, the changes in distributions of detractors and promoters for the five-point scale canceled out, which maintained its NPS relative to the eleven-point version. This was not the case for the ten-point version, making it a slightly poorer substitute for the standard version despite having almost the same number of scale points (possibly a consequence of the loss of the neutral position).

Net Promoter Scores stayed within a range
For the most part, regardless of the scale used (five, ten, or eleven points), the different Net Promoter Scores stayed in a similar range. For example, Netflix consistently had a high score (in the 60s), Facebook, an average score (20s to 30s), and Comcast, a very low score (–50s to –60s).

Nonstandard versions lose correspondence with external benchmarks
The main disadvantage of using five or ten-point versions is external benchmarks will differ. This analysis suggests the typical difference could be around 4% between your scores and published benchmarks but in some cases could be more.

Differences in NPS may be more noticeable due to the range of the scale
The observed differences (some statistically significant) can seem large, but even the most extreme difference (the 14-point shift) represents only a 7% change over the 200-point range of the Net Promoter Score (−100 to +100).

Participants' responses can vary
Some differences between scales may come from the inevitable variation in participant responses. For example, participants may vacillate between 6 and 7 when posed with the LTR item. This one-point shift will have a more noticeable effect on the NPS (passives to detractors) when there are fewer response options associated with detractors.

Keep consistent unless there's a strong reason to change
This analysis suggests if you have historical data using a ten or five-point version, stick with what you're using if your comparisons are with only your own data. If, however, you need to improve the accuracy of your comparisons with external benchmarks, consider using the standard eleven-point version.

Neutral Point Study: Removing the Neutral Point from Four Standard UX Items

To further explore the effect of removing the neutral point, we conducted a follow-up study to replicate our "study points" experimental design findings (Lewis & Sauro, 2023, Aug 8).

STUDY DETAILS

In March 2023, 200 U.S.-based panel participants rated the experience of attempting two tasks (an easy task about an Amazon purchase and a hard task about a mobile phone plan cost) and then rated their attitude toward the overall website.

Participants were presented with both standard SEQ (seven points), UX-Lite Ease and Usefulness (five points), and LTR (eleven points) items and alternate versions with no neutral response option (with, respectively, six, four, and ten points) in a Greco-Latin experiment. Scales with an odd number of response options had an unlabeled neutral point; those with an even number did not.

Because participants completed scales with and without neutral points, we also asked if they noticed any difference in the number of points being used throughout the study.

STUDY RESULTS

Figure 11.10 shows the within- and between-subjects differences in mean ratings for the two item formats for each level of task difficulty.

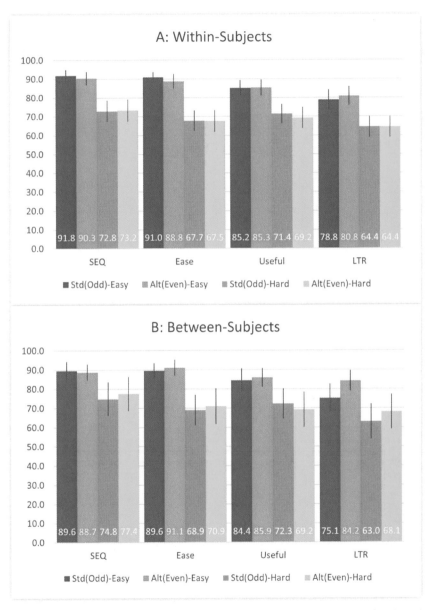

FIGURE 11.10: Within- and between-subjects differences in mean ratings as a function of item format by task difficulty (with 95% confidence intervals).

Analyses of both the within- and between-subjects results shown in Figure 11.10 indicated highly significant main effects of task difficulty. The outcomes for SEQ, Ease, and Useful ratings were almost identical for both analyses, and for LTR in the within-subjects analysis. The pattern of means for LTR in the between-subjects analysis was different. When the task was easy, the difference in formats was statistically significant (alternate format 9.1 points higher than the standard format, $t(122) = 2.025$, $p = .045$). The pattern in means was similar when the task was hard, but the difference was not statistically significant (alternate format 5.1 points higher than the standard format, $t(74) = .81$, $p = .423$).

Figure 11.11 shows the within- and between-subjects differences in top-box scores for the two item formats for each level of task difficulty. The only statistically significant difference between standard (odd) and alternate (even) formats was the between-subjects comparison of Ease (N-1 two-proportion test, $z = 2.0$, $p = .04$).

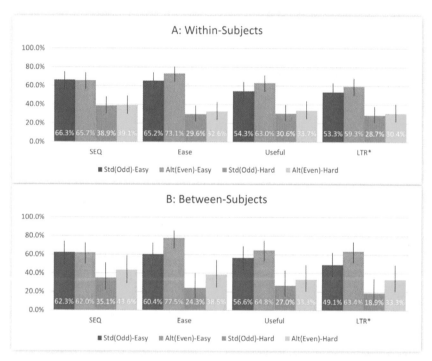

FIGURE 11.11: Within- and between-subjects differences in top-box scores as a function of item format by task difficulty with 95% confidence intervals (* = top-two-box score for the 11-point LTR item).

After attempting both tasks, participants were asked whether they had noticed a difference in the rating scale formats they had used and, if so, what it was. Over 90% of participants indicated they had not noticed any difference. Only 9 participants (4.5%) indicated they had noticed the difference and selected the correct choice from a list of plausible differences. Ten participants (5.0%) selected one of the two distractors (5-7-11 point vs all 3-point items; numbers shown or not shown).

In summary, we found some evidence suggesting that absence of a middle option in rating scales tends to increase the magnitude of ratings by a small amount, at last when scale means are greater than the midpoint. Our best estimate is that this effect size for means is about 1.5% of the range of the scales and for top-box scores is about 3.0%. When responding to both formats, most people don't notice the difference.

DOES CHANGING THE NUMBER OF POINTS SYSTEMATICALLY AFFECT SCALE MEANS?

A key design decision for rating scales is the number of response options (i.e., points) to include. This is an obvious difference in format that researchers have vigorously debated for over 100 years (Cox, 1980, citing Boyce, 1915). In their literature review, Lewis and Erdinç (2017) found that many researchers have studied the effect of different numbers of scale points in different contexts with different optimization criteria, including reliability, validity, sensitivity, ease of use, preference, structural recovery, and information processing.

One of the fundamental questions in UX research is the extent to which changes in the number of points affect means. We compiled 12 datasets from five of our studies that compared the effects of using different numbers of points within the same study, such as comparing five vs. seven-point or ten vs. eleven-point scales. One challenge to comparing rating scales with different points is that the means will look different even when the relative position of the mean, given the scale boundaries, is comparable. For example, an "average" score on a five-point scale may hover around 3.8, but an average on a seven-point scale will be closer to 5. One technique to make the differing points comparable is to rescale raw scores to 0–100 points.

Table 11.9 shows unstandardized effect sizes (differences in means expressed as percentages after rescaling to 0–100 points) for 12 comparisons of means collected in UX research since 2017 (Lewis, 2021; Lewis & Erdinç, 2017; Lewis & Sauro, 2023, Aug 8; Sauro, 2017, Nov 29; Sauro & Lewis, 2022, Aug 16).

The overall mean effect is –1.2% (95% confidence interval from –2.6% to 0.2%), showing a slight but nonsignificant tendency for higher means when there are fewer points, possibly due to a smaller ceiling effect when there are more points.

Source	% Effect
Sauro (2017, Nov 29) 11 v 10	1.4%
Sauro (2017, Nov 29) 11 v 5	0.7%
Erdinç & Lewis (2017) 11 v 7	−0.4%
Lewis (2021) 11 v 7	1.6%
Lewis (2021) 7 v 5	−6.0%

(continued on pg. 148)

Source	% Effect
Lewis (2021) 7 v 3	−2.3%
Sauro & Lewis (2022, Aug 16) 7 v 5	−3.9%
Sauro & Lewis (2022, Aug 16) 11 v 5	−0.9%
Sauro & Lewis (2023, Aug 8) 7 v 6	−0.8%
Sauro & Lewis (2023, Aug 8) 5 v 4	−1.0%
Sauro & Lewis (2023, Aug 8) 5 v 4	−0.5%
Sauro & Lewis (2023, Aug 8) 11 v 10	−2.6%
Mean	−1.2%

TABLE 11.9: Comparisons of means for items with different numbers of response options after rescaling to 0–100 points (positive values indicate a higher mean with more points).

These results show that overall, and in most individual cases, the number of scale points has little effect on the means of rating scales, at least in UX research.

CHAPTER SUMMARY

We tackled six questions related to the number of points in rating scales.

Are three points enough? …No, they aren't. We never recommend using just three points in rating scales. Three points are the minimum number needed to measure negative, neutral, and positive attitudes. For individual items, this limits the sensitivity of measurement (no way to measure extreme attitudes) and reduces scale reliability. For multi-item questionnaires, these limitations aren't as damaging, but people are familiar enough with rating scales that have five or more points that the purported ease of responding to three-point items isn't compelling given their disadvantages. Using the NPS as an example, you can always reduce the number of response categories by combining groups of points, but if you start with three points, you can't extrapolate to more than three.

Do too many response options confuse people? …No, they don't. The argument that too many response options (scale points) will confuse people appears to be based on a misapplication of the well-known limits of human short-term memory to item design—misapplied because people don't need to memorize visually-presented response options. Researchers who want to provide verbal labels for each point begin running into problems when there are more than four or five points, but this is more of an issue with having too many labels than with having too many points. After all, people don't seem to find it conceptually difficult to use a slider to select from 0 to 100 points. The claim that cognitive limitations prevent people from effectively using numeric scales with many points doesn't seem to hold up. For most applied UX research, scales with five to eleven points are good enough, but that doesn't mean that providing more points would somehow be problematic.

Do people really use all points? ...Yes, they (usually) do but it doesn't matter much. Some authors of influential books on survey research have suggested that it isn't necessary to have many points because people don't use them all. However, examination of the usage of rating scales with five, seven, and eleven-point scales shows that across studies (but not necessarily within each study), all response options were selected at least once. We wouldn't expect this to happen for scales with very large numbers of response options (e.g., sliders that record responses from 0 to 100), but we definitely expect the usage of each response option for scales with eleven or fewer points.

Does changing the number of response options in the same survey affect rating behavior? ...No, it doesn't. It seems plausible that mixing rating scales with different numbers of scale points might affect how people make their ratings, either due to confusion or perhaps some kind of priming effect. However, when we conducted a carefully designed experiment to see if this happens, we found that changes in the number of scale points did not affect response patterns, most participants didn't even notice the changes, and most of those who did notice didn't care.

Should you include a neutral point? ...It doesn't seem to matter much in UX research. Most standardized UX questionnaires use scales that have an odd number of points, with the (usually unlabeled) center point interpreted as the neutral point between the endpoints. We found little difference in LTR ratings made with eleven-point (0–10 with center point at 5) and ten-point (1–10 with no center point) versions, UX-Lite items with five-point (1–5 with 3 at the center) and four-point (1–4 with no center point) versions, or SEQ items with seven-point (1–7 with 4 at the center) and six-point (1–6 with no center point) versions. We recommend including neutral points in UX rating scales unless there is a compelling reason not to do so.

Does changing the number of points systematically affect scale means? ... This doesn't seem to make much difference in UX research. This is one of the most-studied attributes of rating scales, with literature going back over 100 years, assessed with many different optimization criteria. Our examination of mean differences for comparisons from four to eleven points from five UX experiments that manipulated the number of points found similar means after rescaling results to a common 0–100-point scale. Our current rule-of-thumb is to use five points for items that will be combined into a composite score (e.g., SUS), seven points for most stand-alone UX rating scales (e.g., SEQ), and eleven points for most behavioral intentions (e.g., Likelihood-to-Recommend).

Table 11.10 summarizes the studies associated with the estimated effect sizes for the four scale manipulations discussed in this chapter.

Topic/ Studies	n	Study Description	Scales
3-pt LTR*	1737[a]	Ratings of common brands across three studies	LTR (11-pt), LTR (3-pt)
Neutral Point	720[b]	One retrospective and one task-based study varying number of scale points	LTR (10/11-pt), SEQ (7/6-pt), Ease (5/4-pt), Useful (5/4-pt)
Number of Points	1302[c]	Multiple studies with variation in number of scale points	LTR (11/10-pt), CSUQ (7-, 11-, 101-pt), UX-Lite (3-, 5-, 7-, 11-pt), SEQ (7/6-pt), Ease (5/4-pt), Useful (5/4-pt)
Point Shifting	279[d]	Respondents rated a sequence of SEQ, UX-Lite, and LTR items with standard numbers of response options or unvarying 5-pt scales (alternate)	LTR (11/5-pt), SEQ (7/5-pt), Ease (5/5-pt), Useful (5/5-pt)

TABLE 11.10: Summary of effect size estimates for Chapter 11 presented in descending order of effect size. These unstandardized effect sizes are mean differences divided by the range of the scale. * = statistically significant. Respondents are from panels unless otherwise indicated. The sources for this table are:

a: Sauro (2019, Aug 21), $n = 1737$

b: Sauro (2017, Nov 29), $n = 520$; Lewis & Sauro (2023, Aug 8), $n = 200$

c: Sauro (2017, Nov 29), $n = 520$; Erdinç & Lewis (2017), $n = 58$; Lewis (2021), $n = 245$; Sauro & Lewis (2022, Aug 16), $n = 279$; Sauro & Lewis (2023, Aug 8), $n = 200$

d: Sauro & Lewis (2022, Aug 16), $n = 279$

Effect Size	Takeaway	Design Notes
22.0%	3 points not enough to measure extreme responses required to compute NPS	Within Subjects
3.0%	Top box slightly higher w/o neutral point (effect on means is 1.5%)	Within subjects (counterbalanced)
1.2%	Slightly lower number with more points	Mixed between/ within subjects
0.5%	Slightly higher means overall for unvarying 5-pt scales	Within Subjects, Greco-Latin counterbalancing

CHAPTER 12:
LABELING POINTS

Much has been written on the subject of labeling scales, with mixed findings and some studies contaminated with confounding effects. We'll address the following two questions:

- Do you need to label each response option in rating scales?
- Is it good practice to label the neutral response in rating scales?

In Chapter 11, we covered the impacts of having a neutral point (typically little effect), and in this chapter, we'll review the data on the effects of labeling the neutral point.

One core question about multipoint rating scales is whether to label all points (Figure 12.1) or just the endpoints (Figure 12.2). Proponents of labeling all points argue that it makes it clear what people are responding to. Adding labels adds clarity for the respondent. After all, what exactly does 5 mean on the following agreement scale?

1	2	3	4	5	6	7
Extremely Dissatisfied	Mostly Dissatisfied	Somewhat Dissatisfied	Neutral	Somewhat Satisfied	Mostly Satisfied	Extremely Satisfied

FIGURE 12.1: Rating scale with all points labeled.

1	2	3	4	5	6	7
Strongly Disagree						Strongly Agree

FIGURE 12.2: Rating scale with only endpoints labeled.

While labeling points does provide more information to respondents, it may also introduce error due to interpretation and ambiguity (discussed in Chapter 11). What exactly does "Somewhat Satisfied" mean?

What's more, there's also the practical problem of coming up with the right labels for scales with more than five or seven points. For example, coming up with labels for each of the points on the eleven-point Likelihood-to-Recommend (LTR) item would be impractical; endpoints and a neutral label may be all that can be done. On the other hand, labeling each response option for five- and seven-point scales is practical and a fairly common practice. But even when it's easy to do, should you do it?

There has been a fair amount of research on the effect of labeling scales. Much of it comes from the context of public opinion polling, which can result in outcomes that are both high-stakes and controversial.

RESEARCH ON LABELING RESPONSE SCALES

One of the more comprehensive discussions of assessing the impacts of full versus partial labeling of response scales comes from Krosnick and Fabrigar (1997), focusing on scale reliability and validity, which we summarize here.

EARLY STUDIES FOUND LABELING WAS NOT BETTER

The first studies Krosnick and Fabrigar cited are relatively old and found no impact on reliability for full versus partially labeled scales (e.g., Finn, 1972; Madden & Bourdon, 1964). Finn (1972) varied the number of response options and labeling strategies for scales to rate different types of jobs, finding no significant difference in scale reliability for labeled versus unlabeled response options. Madden and Bourdon (1964) studied nine different configurations of scales with nine response options, also in the context of rating different types of jobs, but the configurations they studied and their method of assessing reliability were unusual, making their results difficult to integrate into this literature review.

A study by Andrews (1984), contrary to the author's expectation, found that **data quality was actually below average when all category scales were labeled** compared to only partially (including just the endpoints) labeled. Andrews used data from six North American surveys, totaling 7,706 respondents. The surveys were administered over the phone and in person, asking about a variety of topics, including quality of life, business activities, and lifestyle behaviors.

However, these three studies seem to be the exception with Krosnick and Fabrigar (1997), who cited more studies showing higher reliability and validity when all points were labeled, especially for respondents with low to moderate education. They cited a few studies supporting full labeling that we will summarize in more detail.

Other Studies Did Find Labeling Was Superior

A study by Dickinson and Zellinger (1980) had 86 veterinary students rate faculty performance on six dimensions using three scale variations. The scales had five points fully labeled: Always, Very Often, About As Often As Not, Very Seldom, and Never; two scales contained behavioral examples to help the students judge the faculty's performance. The scales with examples were generally preferred and performed better than the less-labeled version. This study didn't compare a partially labeled (or numeric-only scale), so the context was more akin to a rubric, suggesting that more information for each scale point led to improved measurement quality.

Another study by Wallsten et al. (1993) had 442 college students (including statistics and MBA students) answer questions about preferred communication using verbal or numerical information regarding judgments of uncertainty. For example, when asked, "Which mode do you usually prefer to use when communicating your opinion to others?" 65% of respondents indicated "Verbal" over the "Numerical" choice. However, when asked whether there were times when they'd prefer the opposite, 93% indicated so, suggesting the context of the question may dictate preference. It's unclear how this stated preference translates into the sort of rating scales administered in web surveys.

Krosnick and Berent (1993) examined political party identification and ratings of governmental policies across eight experiments that compared endpoint-labeled scales to fully labeled scales. Surveys were administered over the phone, in person, or on paper (self-administered). Several studies had confounding effects related to an additional independent variable of branching (whether the direction and intensity for a question were collected in one item — nonbranching — or separated into two items — branching), making it hard to isolate the effects of labeling.

For example, in one study, they compared response scales by asking respondents over the phone to judge the right amount of U.S. defense spending. The fully labeled version of this policy question appears in Figure 12.3.

1	2	3	4	5	6	7
A Lot Less	Somewhat Less	A Little Less	The Same	A Little More	Somewhat More	A Lot More

FIGURE 12.3: Fully labeled version of an opinion scale about the right amount of U.S. defense spending.

In another study, they examined U.S. political orientation using the scale in Figure 12.4, compared to a scale with just the endpoints labeled.

1	2	3	4	5	6	7
Extremely Liberal	Liberal	Slightly Liberal	Middle of the Road, Moderate	Slightly Conservative	Conservative	Extremely Conservative

FIGURE 12.4: Fully labeled version for U.S. political orientation.

In only two of the studies in the Krosnick and Berent (1993) paper (Study 5, face-to-face interview; Study 6, telephone interview) were there any attempts to separate the effects of labeling and branching. In those studies, the experimental designs were fractional rather than fully factorial, so the results were confounded. Specifically, the conditions were partially labeled nonbranching, fully labeled nonbranching, and fully labeled branching. Study 6 suffered from a different methodological issue because participants were initially exposed to a partially labeled nonbranching format, then divided into three groups exposed to the three different formats.

In this review, we focus on Study 5, which was the only one where there was a longitudinal comparison of partially labeled and fully labeled nonbranching conditions. The primary conclusion of Study 5 was "To our surprise, the combined reliability of the five partially labeled nonbranching items (58.9%) was not significantly different from the combined reliability of the fully labeled nonbranching items (57.8%)" (p. 957).

In another study, Alwin and Krosnick (1991) used data from five U.S. national surveys for 13 items assessing political attitudes. They reported higher reliability when seven-point scales were fully labeled (mean reliability of .783) versus partially labeled (mean reliability of .570).

Wedell et al. (1990) conducted two experiments with UCLA undergrads using different scales to gauge clinical judgment. Across two studies, they had students read 36 case histories of psychiatric patients using different scales with anchors including "Very, Very Mild Disturbance" to "Very, Very Severe Disturbance" and from "Superior" to "Very Poor." They found that fully labeled scales performed better. Their findings suggest that including clear and calibrated categories improves the reliability of judgments. But the use of the rating scale categories in this context also may be considered more of a rubric and less like a rating scale of attitudes.

Mixed Results of Labeling

More recent research on this topic has shown mixed results.

Weijters et al. (2010) found that fully labeled scales evoked more acquiescence response bias and less extreme-response bias than scales with only endpoint labeling. They hypothesized that in the case of a fully labeled scale, the center categories become more salient to respondents than they are in scales with only endpoint labeling. Based on a set of complex outcome metrics, they concluded that endpoint labeling was better for studies that had the primary purpose of any sort of general linear modeling, and full labeling was better for opinion measurement (see their Figure 3, p. 246).

In a study by Lau (2007), there was no significant effect of endpoint labeling versus full labeling on the incidence of extreme responding. He found that more-absolute descriptors (e.g., Completely Disagree/Completely Agree) yielded more extreme responses than did less-absolute descriptors. Ultimately, however, he concluded that the extreme-response style's effect on substantive findings was negligible, with no differences in estimates of effect sizes in a study of the relationship between individualism/collectivism on satisfaction.

Tourangeau et al. (2009) conducted two studies that varied the style of rating scales in a web-based survey. Over 5,000 U.S.-based panel respondents answered 16 seven-point items, including seven dietary habits items with endpoints of "Strongly Oppose" and "Strongly Favor" and nine mood-related items with frequency endpoints of "None of the Time" to "All of the Time." They manipulated color, labels, and the type of numeric label (e.g., negative numbers vs. positive numbers). They found that fully labeling the scale increased mean scores in some conditions (as was first reported by Schwarz et al., 1991), and this effect was larger than the effect of changing colors.

They also found that respondents took longer to answer the items with fully labeled scales than items with endpoints labeled only (approximately seven-tenths of a second longer per item). The authors hypothesized that there may be a hierarchy of features that respondents attend to, with verbal labels taking precedence over numerical labels, and numerical labels taking precedence over purely visual cues such as color. Referring to Krosnick and Fabrigar's recommendation to label every point in a scale, Tourangeau et al. speculated it may partly reflect the added time respondents give to the question.

Moors et al. (2014) conducted a study with 3,266 U.S.-based panel respondents to examine the effects of extreme-response styles (picking the highest and lowest options) and acquiescent response styles (agreeing). Participants were randomly assigned to one of five formats that asked about the environment and attitudes toward risky driving, each consisting of four items for each construct, two positively worded and two negatively worded. All used seven-point scales. The five formats were:

1. Full labeling with numerical values
2. Full labeling without numerical values
3. End labeling with numerical values
4. End labeling without numerical values
5. End labeling with bipolar numerical values

The authors found that all scale formats exhibited extreme-response bias, but end labeling evoked more ERS than full labeling. However, they felt that ERS, similar to what they found in an earlier study they conducted, is a stable trait that holds across different questionnaires and times (Kieruj & Moors, 2013).

Hjermstad et al. (2011) conducted a meta-analysis of self-reported pain scales that varied in scale points and the use of labels (and included visual analog scales). They concluded it was unclear to what extent and in which direction the actual scores were influenced by labeling.

A study by van Beuningen et al. (2014) involved three experiments comparing five-point fully labeled scales with ten- and eleven-point scales with only endpoints labeled. They collected over 10,000 respondents on life happiness and satisfaction measures. They didn't disentangle the effects of labels and number of points but ultimately recommended that Statistics Netherlands use a ten-point scale with only the endpoints labeled for both international comparability and the increased ability to discriminate between happiness and unhappiness gained from adding more points.

Coromina and Coenders (2006) had 383 PhD students from three cities in Spain, Slovenia, and Belgium rate how frequently they were able to accomplish tasks such as asking colleagues for information and engaging in social activities outside of work with their colleagues in the past year (Figure 12.5).

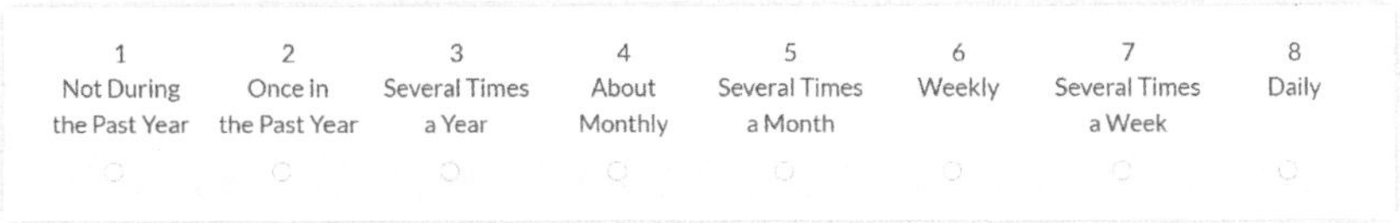

1	2	3	4	5	6	7	8
Not During the Past Year	Once In the Past Year	Several Times a Year	About Monthly	Several Times a Month	Weekly	Several Times a Week	Daily

FIGURE 12.5: Frequency scale from Coromina and Coenders (2006).

They found that the fully labeled variation generated higher validity scores than one with only endpoints labeled. The type of labeling used here (specific frequencies) differs from other scales that measure more abstract concepts such as agreement. Regarding full labeling versus endpoints only, they concluded: "Our results for factor 2 (all categories or only endpoints of the scale labeled) show that a higher validity is obtained when all labels are used. The reason why extra labels are helpful may be that in our questionnaire, labels indicate precise social contact frequencies and not vague or unclear quantifiers like "agree," "not much agree," "undecided' and so on. This is typical of any frequency-of-contact question (a most common type of question in social network research), and we hypothesize that it may generalize to any data collection mode" (pp. 227–228). It does seem reasonable that this would be the case for frequency-of-contact questions in general, but it's not clear whether it would be the case for the measure of sentiments (e.g., perceived usability).

Labels Aren't Measurably Better

Schneider et al. (2008), including Krosnick as a co-author, conducted two studies using intent-to-recommend scales such as those used to compute the Net Promoter Score (NPS), varying the number of response options from five to seven to eleven. Contrary to their expectations, they concluded that assigning full labels did not improve scale validity; instead, it produced weaker relationships between the scales and the validity criteria (stated historical recommendations). The partially labeled eleven- and seven-point scales were almost identical and better predictors of stated historical recommendations than the fully labeled scales for customers and noncustomers.

Lewis (2019a) investigated the effect of manipulating item formats for a revised version of the Technology Acceptance Model (TAM) questionnaire, originally designed to assess likelihood of use with fully labeled seven-point items (from left to right: Extremely Likely, Quite Likely, Slightly Likely, Neither, Slightly Unlikely, Quite Unlikely, Extremely Unlikely). To modify the items for the assessment of user experience for full labeling, the word "Likely" was changed to "Agree" and "Unlikely" was changed to "Disagree."

The experimental design of the study was fully factorial based on crossing two independent variables: response format (full labeling with no numbers or numbers only) and response order (increasing in level of agreement from right to left or from left to right), illustrated in Figure 12.6.

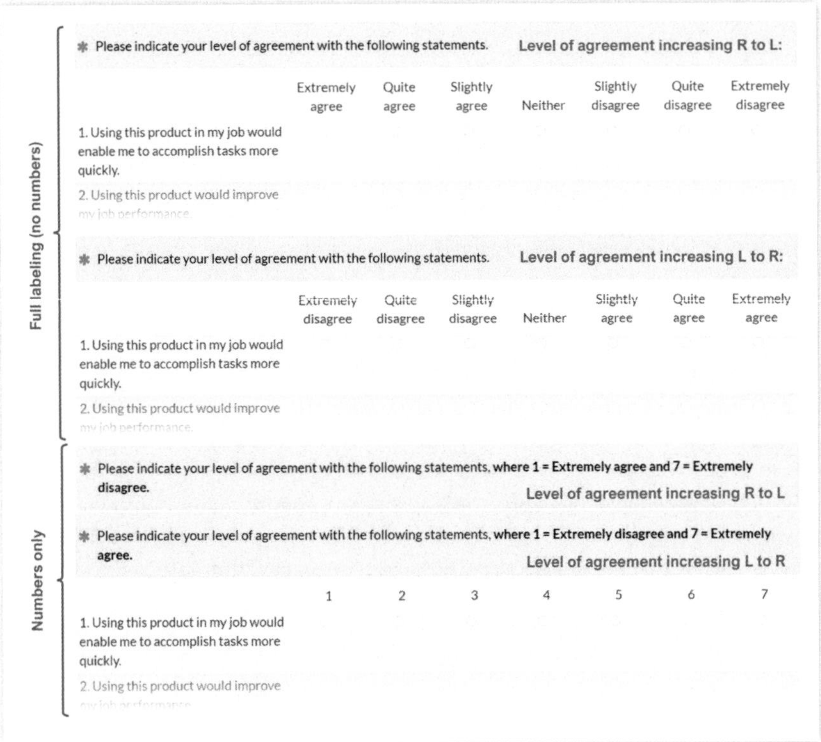

FIGURE 12.6: Rating scales used in Lewis (2019a).

Respondents used the items to rate their experience with their company's email application. With n = 546 and roughly equal numbers of participants in each of the four conditions, there was no significant effect of either format or order on mean ratings. The results indicated that the item-format differences didn't lead to any important differences in the magnitude or structure of measurement, but there were significantly more response errors when the magnitude of agreement increased from right to left.

Summary & Discussion of Published Literature on Labeling
Our comprehensive (although not exhaustive) review of research on scale labeling found:

THERE IS NO CLEAR SUPERIORITY IN LABELING
Despite some recommendations and "best" wisdom, we didn't find a clear pattern of fully labeled scales being measurably superior. When comparisons were well controlled (no confounding), labeling differences didn't matter much. The most direct

and unconfounded comparisons of full and endpoint-only labeling were reported by Lewis (2019a) and Krosnick and Berent (1993, Study 6 only), which reported no significant effects due to differences in labeling formats.

CONTEXT MATTERS

As is often the case with survey research, knowing the topic, how the survey was administered (e.g., over the phone, in-person, or via web survey), and other contextual variables is important to understand the generalizability of the findings. We found significant variation in methods and conclusions across the literature. Scales with specific frequencies (e.g., daily vs. monthly) have objective meanings, whereas user experience measurement is usually focused on measuring sentiments (e.g., subjective concepts such as agreement or satisfaction). Full labeling of objective items seems like it should lead to better data quality than endpoint-only labeling, but it's not clear whether this is the case for subjective items.

HOW DO YOU JUDGE WHICH FORMAT IS BETTER?

Response scales have been evaluated in the published literature in many ways: comparing differences in scores, different distributions, reliability, correlations to other measures (validity), measures of extreme-response bias, participant response time, and preference. The strongest arguments for or against a response format would be its validity (is it predicting or measuring what it's intended better) and reliability (consistent responses). The literature has been mixed.

MORE POINTS LIKELY INCREASE SCALE RELIABILITY, VALIDITY, AND SENSITIVITY

Furthermore, there is good evidence that scales with seven, ten, or eleven points increase the sensitivity, reliability, and in some cases, the validity of the measure (e.g., Lewis & Erdinç, 2017), especially when there is a known relationship between extreme responses and behavior. It's impractical to label all points when there are more than seven response options. The mixed results we found from the literature suggest that keeping the number of points low merely to enable full labeling will usually not be worth it.

IS IT A RUBRIC OR A RATING SCALE?

Krosnick and Fabrigar wrote their chapter before the proliferation of web-based surveys. After examining the studies cited by Krosnick and Fabrigar, some of the scales evaluated are more like grading rubrics rather than attitudes (e.g., Wallsten et al., 1993)—like the distinction between measurement of objective and subjective items. When comparisons were well controlled (no confounding), labeling differences weren't statistically significant. In cases where there were effects of labeling, the scales used were more like rubrics (e.g., rating faculty performance or clinical judgments) rather than measures of sentiment such as satisfaction or agreement.

STUDY COMPARING FULLY VS. PARTIALLY LABELED FIVE- AND SEVEN-POINT SCALES

Seeing the mixed findings and shortcomings in some studies on labeling, we embarked on an endeavor to isolate the effects of labeling from other scale variations. We conducted two studies that better isolated the effects of labeling on commonly used scales of sentiment in UX and customer research.

Study Methodologies Overviews

We conducted two studies between September and October 2019 with U.S.-based online panel participants (Sauro & Lewis, 2020, Jan 22). In Study 1, 202 participants rated their satisfaction with their smartphone on a five-point scale, along with other questions about brand attitude and intent to recommend. They were presented with three variants randomly shown at different points in the middle of the survey.

The first version of the satisfaction item had only the endpoints labeled (Figure 12.7); the second version was labeled at the endpoints and midpoint (Figure 12.8); and the third version was fully labeled (Figure 12.9). All variations included numbers.

FIGURE 12.7: The endpoint version of the five-point satisfaction scale.

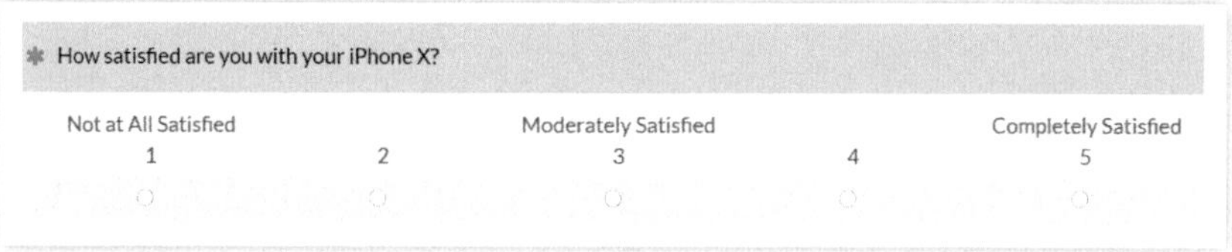

FIGURE 12.8: The endpoints and midpoint version of the five-point satisfaction scale.

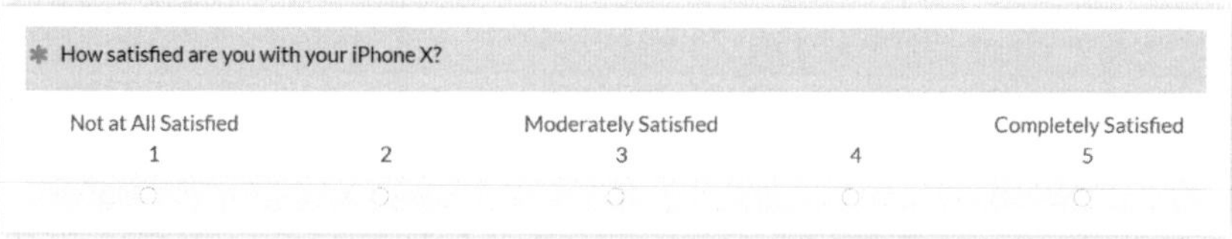

FIGURE 12.9: The fully labeled version of the five-point satisfaction scale.

In Study 2, 213 participants were also presented with three versions of a rating scale, but this time they were shown seven-point satisfaction items. Like Study 1, the first version of the satisfaction item had the endpoints labeled (Figure 12.10); the second version was labeled at the endpoints and midpoint (Figure 12.11); and the third version was fully labeled (Figure 12.12).

FIGURE 12.10: The endpoint version of the seven-point satisfaction scale.

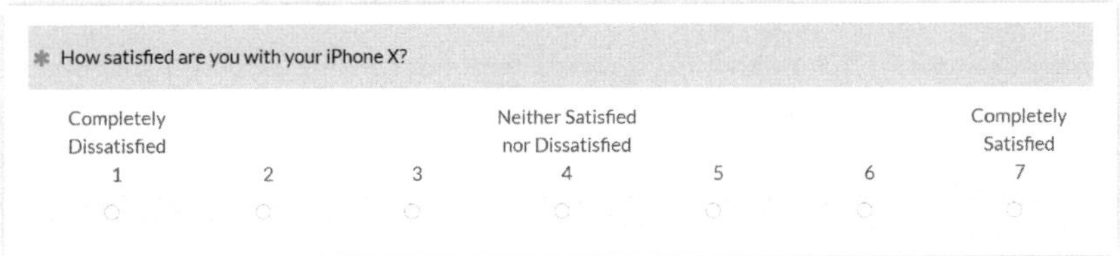

FIGURE 12.11: The endpoints and midpoint version of the seven-point satisfaction scale.

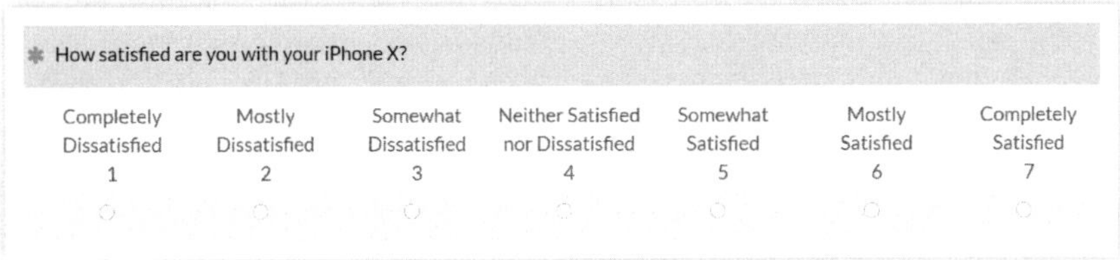

FIGURE 12.12: The fully labeled version of the seven-point satisfaction scale.

Studies Summary and Discussion

Across the two studies measuring the impact of labeling on responses from 415 respondents to different versions of five-point and seven-point satisfaction items, we found:

THERE IS NO CLEAR PATTERN OF LABELING ON ITEM RESPONSE BEHAVIORS

In our first study with the five-point satisfaction scale, we found a small but statistically significant (~2%) decrease in mean scores when the scale was fully labeled compared to the endpoint-only scale, and a 1% difference compared to a scale with endpoints and neutral point labeled. However, this pattern was not replicated when we used a seven-point variation. The fully labeled seven-point scale in the second study had the opposite effect—slightly but not significantly increasing scores compared to the endpoint-only version.

As discussed by Krosnick and Presser (2010) regarding neutral labels, when participants have low interest in a topic they may be more likely to respond to neutral labels and endpoints (see the next section on labeling neutral points). This may explain the slightly higher number of respondents selecting points with labels in Study 1, but if this strongly affects how participants select response options, we would have expected replication in Study 2.

THE CLAIM THAT FULL LABELING IS ALWAYS BETTER ISN'T SUPPORTED

Both our literature review and this study showed that labeling every response option isn't necessarily better. Some studies found negligible results, but in at least some cases, partial labeling offered superior results in both predictive validity and reliability. Fully labeled scales will likely be superior when the scale is being used more as a rubric than a rating scale of simple (and noncontroversial) attitudes.

THIS STUDY, LIKE ALL STUDIES, HAD SOME LIMITATIONS

It isn't possible in this area of research to run one study that answers all possible questions—there are just too many potential independent variables. Our two studies had some limitations: there was no assessment of validity, we tested only two versions, we always included numbers, and there were possible carry-over effects due to the within-subjects design.

MAIN TAKEAWAY: LABELING DOESN'T MATTER MUCH

This research adds to the growing list of item-format differences that people love to argue about, but, at least in UX research, don't seem to matter that much. When planning research, spend your time on substantive research issues rather than engaging in extensive discussion about item-format differences that have trivial effects on measurement. Then be consistent with your scale choice.

LABELING THE NEUTRAL RESPONSE

In Chapter 11, we discussed including a neutral point and noted that most UX questionnaires contain a neutral point. Given the prevalence of neutral points, a corollary question is whether to label the neutral point. As with labels in general, there's a bit of a debate around whether you should label the middle neutral point, especially when used on a long eleven-point item (e.g., the LTR item used for the NPS).

The original Harvard Business Review article (Reichheld, 2003) that introduced the NPS stated that "five means neutral." However, a neutral label didn't appear on the scale in the article or the first edition of *The Ultimate Question* (2006, p. 31).

An extensive analysis was conducted by Schneider et al. (2008). They posited that placing the neutral label on the midpoint would be problematic because neutral "represents a lack of evaluation, rather than a 50% chance of recommending a company."

In their analysis, across two studies and thousands of participants, they found that a labeled neutral point attracted responses. However, the eleven-point and seven-point versions of the LTR question with the endpoints **and neutral point labeled** tended to perform as well as or better than fully labeled seven- and five-point versions in predicting stated past recommendations and historical growth in the airline and car industries.

Their research suggests that while the neutral label may attract responses, it may not necessarily have a deleterious effect on the concurrent or predictive validity of the NPS. They didn't explore how including the label affects the NPS, nor did they look at an endpoint-only version.

NEUTRAL LABEL STUDY ON THE LIKELIHOOD-TO-RECOMMEND ITEM

To further understand the effects of labeling a neutral midpoint, we conducted three studies that varied the presentation of a neutral label on the eleven-point LTR item used to compute the NPS (Sauro, 2019, Mar 6).

Study 1 was conducted between November and December 2018 using 2,104 online U.S.-based panel participants spread across ten surveys. Participants were randomly assigned either an LTR item with or without a midpoint in a grid, as shown in Figure 12.13. They were asked to rate nine well-known brands (including airlines, retail stores, and online services) and their most recent purchase or most recently recommended product.

Participants were asked to rate all the brands they were shown even if they hadn't purchased from them. Many of the brands were presented together on the same page but randomized from survey to survey. This means that response patterns were not independent. This setup is similar to Schneider et al. (2008) but keep this nonindependence in mind when interpreting the results (and see Chapter 15 for more on presenting items in grids).

Study 2 was conducted in February 2019 using 600 U.S.-based online panel participants. Participants were asked to rate how likely they'd recommend common consumer software products (e.g., Photoshop, Dropbox, Excel) that they had used at least once in the last year. Half of the respondents saw a labeled neutral point and half did not.

Study 3 was also conducted between January and February 2019, using 501 respondents who rated their LTR using a ten-point item for several well-known brands, including retailers, airlines, and car rental agencies. Because the item had an even number of points, there wasn't a true midpoint, but the 5 was labeled as neutral or left without a label. Participants responded to all brands, even if they had no relationship with them. The brands were randomized but presented together in a grid (e.g., all retail sites were shown together). Therefore, again, the responses were not independent, meaning there were potential carry-over effects from one response to the next.

✳ How likely are you to recommend each of the following products or services to a friend, colleague, or family member?

	Not at all likely 0	1	2	3	4	Neutral 5	6	7	8	9	Extremely likely 10
Whole Foods	○	○	○	○	○	○	○	○	○	○	○
Microsoft	○	○	○	○	○	○	○	○	○	○	○
United Airlines	○	○	○	○	○	○	○	○	○	○	○
Facebook	○	○	○	○	○	○	○	○	○	○	○
Delta Airlines	○	○	○	○	○	○	○	○	○	○	○
7-Eleven	○	○	○	○	○	○	○	○	○	○	○
Southwest Airlines	○	○	○	○	○	○	○	○	○	○	○
Target	○	○	○	○	○	○	○	○	○	○	○
Netflix	○	○	○	○	○	○	○	○	○	○	○

✳ How likely are you to recommend each of the following products or services to a friend, colleague, or family member?

	Not at all likely 0	1	2	3	4	5	6	7	8	9	Extremely likely 10
Whole Foods	○	○	○	○	○	○	○	○	○	○	○
Microsoft	○	○	○	○	○	○	○	○	○	○	○
United Airlines	○	○	○	○	○	○	○	○	○	○	○
Facebook	○	○	○	○	○	○	○	○	○	○	○
Delta Airlines	○	○	○	○	○	○	○	○	○	○	○
7-Eleven	○	○	○	○	○	○	○	○	○	○	○
Southwest Airlines	○	○	○	○	○	○	○	○	○	○	○
Target	○	○	○	○	○	○	○	○	○	○	○
Netflix	○	○	○	○	○	○	○	○	○	○	○

FIGURE 12.13: Example of NPS items with and without a labeled neutral midpoint.

Summary of Study Findings

Across the three studies examining the effects of labeling the neutral midpoint of the LTR item, we found the following:

HAVING A NEUTRAL LABEL SOMETIMES ATTRACTS RESPONSES (BUT NOT ALWAYS)

As suggested in earlier studies, adding a neutral label will attract more respondents to the midpoint option. This happened for both the eleven-point and ten-point versions of the LTR item. However, the differences (when they occurred) were generally small and often not statistically significant, even with large sample sizes for recent purchases or recommendations.

NEUTRAL LABELS MAY ATTRACT OTHER LOW SCORES FOR NONCUSTOMERS

Adding the neutral point label appears to attract other "detractor" responses from the 0 to 4 range when considering *noncustomers only* (Figure 12.14). When a neutral label was included, the percentage of people choosing 5 increased from 10% to 16% for respondents who didn't have a recent purchase history with the brand. Interestingly though, this didn't significantly impact Net Promoter Scores (most remained detractors), but it did tend to increase the mean scores.

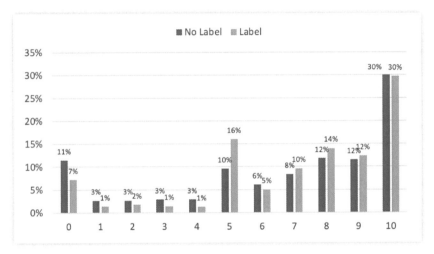

FIGURE 12.14: Change in distribution when the neutral label is present for aggregated (nonindependent) responses across all nine brands for the eleven-point version used in Study 1.

NEUTRAL LABELS MOSTLY AFFECT NONCUSTOMERS

Though we saw a change in response patterns, the difference was most pronounced when we included noncustomers and generally disappeared for respondents with a recent experience with the brand. When people don't have a relationship with a brand, it's hard for them to recommend it. A neutral label provides a logical choice for people who have no opinion. If you're collecting NPS data from noncustomers, consider NOT having a neutral label, having an N/A option, or allowing participants to skip the question. It may reduce the noise (albeit only a small amount) in your analysis by separating true detractors from those who just don't have any experience with the brand.

THERE'S NO CLEAR PATTERN ON NET PROMOTER SCORES

Across nine brands that included both customers and noncustomers, we found nominal differences in Net Promoter Scores. However, none was statistically significant (with sample sizes of 250–500 per condition), and there wasn't a clear pattern of increasing or decreasing scores. This was especially the case when looking at frequent users of software products: none of the differences was statistically significant, and there was no clear pattern of an increase in neutral responses or decreasing scores nor of a consistent pattern in shifts in promoters, passives, and detractors (see Table 12.1 below).

Product	No Label	Neutral Label	Diff	Sample Size
Photoshop	49%	22%	27%	80
Dropbox	21%	35%	-14%	83
Google Calendar	22%	49%	−27%	137
Excel	−33%	−12%	−21%	87
iTunes	9%	4%	5%	97
McAfee	0%	−33%	33%	24

TABLE 12.1: Differences in Net Promoter Scores based on the presence of the neutral label for participants who reported using the software product the most in the last year.

When we limited the analysis to the most recent purchase and recommendation (by definition, this only includes customers), there was only a 1% difference in the aggregated Net Promoter Scores (see Table 12.2).

Most Recent Actions	Label	No Label
Most Recent Purchase	36%	37%
Most Recently Recommended Product	60%	61%

TABLE 12.2: Difference in NPS when using a neutral or no label for respondents' most recently purchased product and most recently recommended product.

THE MEANS INCREASED WITH A NEUTRAL LABEL

While the NPS wasn't systematically affected, we did find a clear pattern of the mean LTR score increasing when using a neutral label (See Table 12.3) from Study 1. This was again most pronounced when including noncustomers. All nine brands saw increases in scores (which included a substantial number of noncustomers).

When examining frequent users of software, the effects were again smaller, with only one of six products having a statistical increase in mean LTR scores and two having means scores decreasing.

All brands saw a mean increase, ranging between .05 and .96 with an average increase of .43 on the eleven-point scale (see Table 5). Only the increase in Target's mean score was statistically significant ($p < .01$).

Product	Label	No Label	Diff
Netflix	4.34	4.29	0.05
United	5.89	5.50	0.38
Southwest	4.32	4.17	0.16
Facebook	7.37	7.09	0.28
Delta	4.59	4.31	0.28
Microsoft	6.37	6.09	0.28
Target*	4.30	3.34	0.96
Whole Foods	5.23	4.69	0.54
7 Eleven	4.69	3.77	0.92
Average	5.23	4.80	0.43

TABLE 12.3: Difference in mean LTR scores when including a neutral label. The mean increased by .43 points (on the eleven-point scale). * Statistically significant at $p < .01$.

SMALL DIFFERENCES EXIST, BUT BE CONSISTENT

This analysis suggests that including a neutral label will have a negligible impact on Net Promoter Scores and means when collecting data from existing customers (on average, about an increase of 1% in the selection of the center point when labeled "Neutral"). Even when using noncustomers to collect NPS data, the differences were modest. As is often the case with changes in scale points or labels, differences are generally small, and it's more important to be consistent over time. If you're starting with data collection, it's probably best to leave off the neutral label when asking about Likelihood-to-Recommend.

HIGHER SCORES MAY MASK IMPACT

We generally see that the neutral label mainly affects people with little or no experience with a brand. For current customers or users of software, there is little effect. One possible explanation is that people with experience with a product are generally more likely to recommend it, and so don't consider the lower end of the scale (below 7) as much as those who have little experience (consequently the neutral label doesn't have as much impact).

CHAPTER SUMMARY

The focus of this chapter was a review of research and recommendations for labeling response options in multipoint scales. The literature and our studies addressed the following three questions:

Do you need to label each response option in rating scales? …No, you don't. Some researchers have strongly held opinions that it's important to label each response option in a rating scale. However, research on how the presence or absence of labels affects rating behaviors doesn't conclusively support this practice. To estimate how much labeling matters in a UX context, a study of satisfaction ratings for smartphones found nonsignificant differences for five-point and seven-point scales, averaging to less than half a percent.

Should you label each response option in rubric scales? …Yes, you should. A caveat to the fully labeling response is for when the response option is more a rubric than a rating scale. The most common rubric scales in UX research are frequency scales. Unlike measures of attitudes, which can be represented with numbers, response options for frequency scales need to be labeled to guide accurate selection (e.g., daily, weekly, monthly, annually).

Is it good practice to label the neutral response in rating scales? …It doesn't seem to matter much. There is substantial variation in reports on the effect of labeling neutral responses in rating scales. Our research on this labeling decision suggests that labeling the neutral point on standard eleven-point LTR scales increased the selection of that point by about 1%, having very little effect on means or Net Promoter Scores computed from those ratings.

Table 12.4 summarizes the studies associated with the estimated effect sizes for the two scale manipulations discussed in this chapter.

Topic/Studies	n	Study Description	Scales	Effect Size	Takeaway	Design Notes
Neutral Point Labeling	2704[a]	Ratings of common brands across two studies	LTR (11-pt)	1.0%	Slight increase in selection of center point when labeled "Neutral"	Mixed between/ within subjects
Endpoint v Partial v Full Labeling	415[b]	Ratings of satisfaction with smartphone across two studies	Sat (5-pt), Sat (7-pt)	0.4%	Different outcomes: slightly higher means for 5-pt endpoint-only; slightly higher means for 7-pt all labeled	Within Subjects

TABLE 12.4: Summary of effect size estimates for Chapter 12 presented in descending order of effect size. These unstandardized effect sizes are mean differences divided by the range of the scale. * = statistically significant. Respondents are from panels unless otherwise indicated. The sources for this table are:

a: Sauro (2019, Mar 6), n = 2704
b: Sauro & Lewis (2020, Jan 22), n = 415

CHAPTER 13:
ITEM TONE & LEFT-SIDE BIAS

Here, we'll discuss two related presentation topics that some researchers hypothesize affect how people respond to surveys. The first topic is about whether items in a questionnaire should alternate their tone (including both positively and negatively worded items). The second is about whether respondents, especially those in Western cultures, are more likely to select response options on the left side of a scale. We'll address two core questions:

- Should you vary item tone when developing multi-item UX questionnaires?
- Is there a left-side bias?

SHOULD YOU VARY ITEM TONE WHEN DEVELOPING A QUESTIONNAIRE?

There is a long tradition of including items in questionnaires that vary their tone. That is, the items are phrased both positively and negatively. For example, the SUS (see Appendix B) uses alternating items such as:

- I thought this website was easy to use (positive tone).
- I found this website unnecessarily complex (negative tone).

Most UX Questionnaires Alternate Item Tone

The SUS isn't unique in alternating item tone. Of the most frequently used questionnaires to measure attitudes about usability, all but the CSUQ and UX-Lite use a mix of positive and negative items.

- System Scale (SUS): 10 items, mix of positive and negative tone.
- Computer System Usability Questionnaire (CSUQ): 16 items, all-positive tone.
- Software Usability Measurement Inventory (SUMI): 50 items, mix of positive and negative tone.
- Questionnaire for User Interaction Satisfaction (QUIS): 27 items, mix of positive and negative tone.
- Usability Metric for User Experience (UMUX): 4 items, mix of positive and negative tone.
- UX-Lite: 2 items, all-positive tone.

Advantages to Alternating

There are two major reasons for alternating item wording:

1. **Reducing acquiescence bias:** This is what happens when respondents go on autopilot and agree to all the statements. In a five-point scale, these would be all 4s and 5s.

2. **Reducing extreme-response bias:** Participants who select the maximum high or all low ratings (select only 5s or 1s on a five-point scale).

Since at least the 1940s, it's been advised to watch out for these biases: "…the fact that people are more likely to agree with a statement than disagree with it" (Cronbach, 1946).

By including a mix of both positive and negative items, respondents are (in theory) forced to consider the question, and they (hopefully) provide a more meaningful response that reduces these biases.

But how prevalent are acquiescence and extreme-response biases? And does alternating tone actually help? Despite the clear concerns about these biases, there is surprisingly little evidence that the common wisdom of including both positive and negatively worded items solves the problem. To our knowledge, there is no research documenting the magnitude of acquiescence bias in general or its effect on the measurement of attitudes toward usability.

Disadvantages to Alternating

There are some downsides to alternating items. We are aware of at least three that we call the 3Ms:

1. **Misinterpret:** Users may respond differently to negatively worded items in a way that reversing responses from negative to positive doesn't account for the difference. There is evidence that this lowers internal reliability, distorts the factor structure, and is problematic in cross-cultural settings.

2. **Mistake:** Users might not intend to respond differently, but may forget to reverse their score, accidentally agreeing with a negative statement when they meant to disagree. We have been with participants who have acknowledged either forgetting to reverse their score or commented that they had to make a correction because they forgot to adjust their score.

3. **Miscode:** Researchers might forget to reverse the scales when scoring and would consequently report incorrect data. Despite the ease of using software to record user input, researchers still must remember to reverse the scales. Forgetting to reverse the scales is not an obvious error, as the aggregated store is still plausible. We found in three of 27 "donated" SUS datasets (11%) that the scales were not reverse coded correctly.

Study on Alternating vs. All-Positive Item Tone

We don't want the "cure" to be worse than the putative problem. Does alternating item wording outweigh the negatives of misinterpreting, mistaking, and miscoding? To find out, we created an entirely positively worded version of the SUS and tested it against the original alternating SUS (Sauro & Lewis, 2011).

In the study, 213 U.S. panel-based participants answered either the standard alternating SUS or an all-positive SUS after attempting tasks on one of seven websites (e.g., Autotrader.com, Fidelity.com).

The results of the study found little evidence that the purported advantages of the alternating items outweighed the disadvantages. There were no significant differences in means between the alternating and all-positive versions. The average number of agreeing responses (a measure of acquiescence bias) was also almost identical between the two versions. There was no statistical difference in the mean number of extreme responses selected — there were actually slightly more for the original SUS.

RECENT REPLICATION

Kortum et al. (2021) replicated our research on the positive version of the SUS. They had 268 participants rate a variety of products with the standard SUS and 698 rate the products with the positive version. Across 20 products, the mean for the standard SUS was 78.8 and for the positive version was 78.1 (a difference of 0.7). They concluded that either version could be used with confidence and that the scores could be directly compared.

Another Estimate of the Frequency of Mistakes Due to Mixed Tone

Using our large dataset of SUS questionnaires, we focused on the two items of opposing tone that have the strongest correlation — Item 3 ("I thought the system was easy to use") and Item 8 ("I found the system very awkward to use") ($r = -.64$). Out of 18,353 cases, we found only 93 (0.5%) in which respondents selected 5 for both items. We suspect that many of these cases may have been due to respondents who forgot to alternate their responses in accordance with the changes in item tone. For more information about this unpublished study, see the discussion of acquiescence in Chapter 14.

Negative Items Distort Factor Structures

Our study on the all-positive SUS showed no measurable benefit to using alternately toned items, but unfortunately, we have encountered an additional negative consequence, which we explored in another study.

While the SUS was designed to be unidimensional (measuring only the construct of perceived usability), there was some evidence it was multidimensional (it measured more than one thing). In 2009, we published a paper using independent datasets that showed the SUS had a second factor based on items 4 and 10 (Lewis & Sauro, 2009). Based on the wording of those items, we called it the learnability factor:

- I think that I would need the support of a technical person to be able to use this system.
- I would imagine that most people would learn to use this system very quickly.

However, other papers since 2009 consistently found more than one factor (good), but there wasn't consistency in which items loaded on the two factors (not good). More troubling, several papers found that, in fact, the two factors were based on the positively and negatively worded items. That is, items that were phrased positively clumped together (e.g., The system is easy to use) and negative items clumped together (e.g., I found the system very awkward to use). In light of these findings, we conducted another study, reviewing over 9,000 completed SUS questionnaires using confirmatory factor analysis, to see whether the learnability factor should stay or go (Lewis & Sauro, 2017).

We compared three versions (models) of the factor structure of the SUS:

Single Factor: Original SUS.

1. Two Factor: Learnability and usability factors.
2. Two Factor: Positive and negative item factors.

The best-fitting model was #3, the positive and negative two-factor version. Because a distinction based on item tone is of little practical or theoretical interest, we recommended that practitioners treat the SUS as a unidimensional measure of perceived usability. Additionally, we discouraged others from using a mix of negative and positive items in the same questionnaire unless they have a good reason other than avoiding acquiescence or extreme-response biases.

TAKEAWAY: NEGATIVES OUTWEIGH THE POSITIVES
Both our 2009 study and a 2021 replication study comparing the original SUS to an all-positive SUS found little evidence for any differences in acquiescence or extreme responses. We did see 11% of datasets miscoded because of the negatively worded items. More troubling, in another study we found that the negative items distorted the factor structure.

Is There Ever a Good Reason to Alternate Items?

We primarily examine questionnaires that measure usability, usefulness, or product satisfaction. These analyses are done at the group level (we're not testing people, but rather applications that people use), so we care about differences between groups. It could be that in other areas of behavioral research where the emphasis is on the individual (e.g., clinical or counseling psychology), alternating item wording provides benefits that outweigh the problems. Otherwise, it's best to stay positive.

WHEN THERE IS A CLEAR NEGATIVE CONSTRUCT, USE NEGATIVES

We recommend sticking with positively worded items when measuring constructs, except when the construct you are measuring is itself negative (e.g., measuring design clutter, anxiety, or depression). Although it is uncommon in UX and CX, we have employed negative wording in ongoing research on how to measure attitudes toward design clutter.

THE TIDE MAY BE TURNING

In our experience, we feel that the tendency to reflexively include alternating tone items as is conventional and recommended in questionnaire design books may be waning. For example, Dalal and Carter (2015) recommend that researchers avoid using negative items unless they are measuring negative attitudes. And as we look back in the literature, we see more evidence of the problems with negative items. For example, when developing the Technology Acceptance Model (TAM), Davis originally used mixed tone items but switched to all positive after obtaining better measurement results (Davis, 1989).

IS THERE A LEFT-SIDE BIAS?

A related concern to acquiescence and extreme-response bias is the so-called left-side bias. That is, are people more likely to select response options on the left side of a rating scale (closer to the item stem)?

In 2010, we provided a brief literature review of the published evidence (Sauro, 2010, Sep 14), which suggested that this hypothesized left-side bias not only existed but also was detected almost 100 years ago in some of the earliest rating scales.

Across the publications we reviewed, the effect size seemed to be about 7.5% of the total possible range of the items used to measure the bias, leading to the claim that "an unethical researcher interested in manipulating results could place the desired response on the left side of the scale" (Friedman & Amoo, 1999, p. 117).

This didn't seem unreasonable, given theories on participant motivation, reading habits, and education level, which operated in conjunction with a primacy effect consistent with the observed bias. For ten years this was our understanding of the left-side bias.

But after a study conducted by Lewis (2019a) found little evidence for a left-side bias, we wondered how robust the purported bias really was.

Could other variables account for the lack of effect in the new study? Was it the study design or something about the UX measures? Or was there more (or less) to the earlier papers than their titles and abstracts suggested?

The only way to find out was to revisit the published papers from the original literature review and check the quality of their data and citations. This took us on a journey through six studies published over the course of 90 years.

Wait a Second...Where's the Left-Side Bias?

In Lewis' 2019 study, 546 IBM employees rated IBM Notes using a modified version of the Technology Acceptance Model (mTAM). Participants were randomly assigned to complete the mTAM questionnaire with item scales oriented from either left to right (Figure 13.1, top) or right to left (Figure 13.1, bottom).

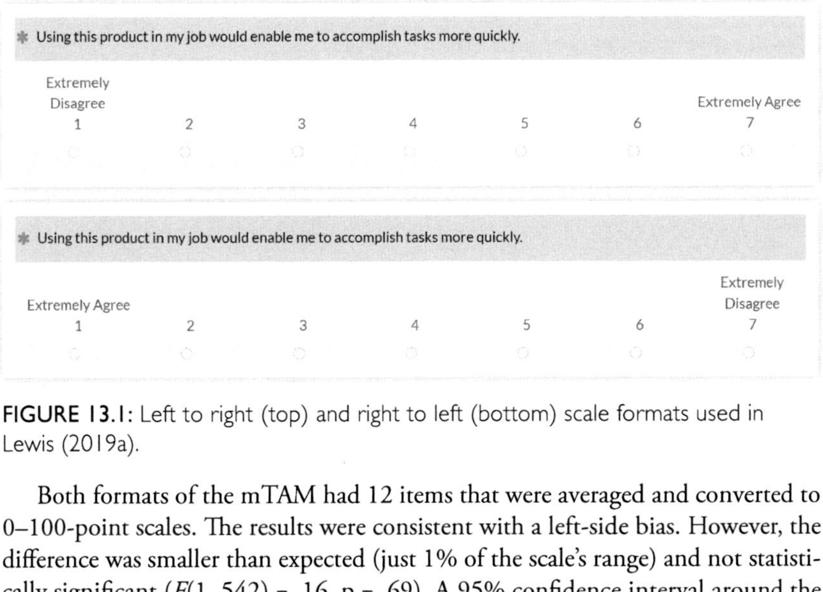

FIGURE 13.1: Left to right (top) and right to left (bottom) scale formats used in Lewis (2019a).

Both formats of the mTAM had 12 items that were averaged and converted to 0–100-point scales. The results were consistent with a left-side bias. However, the difference was smaller than expected (just 1% of the scale's range) and not statistically significant ($F(1, 542) = .16$, $p = .69$). A 95% confidence interval around the mean difference of 1 ranged from –3.9 to 5.8, so if the nominal difference of 1 is real, it would take a sample size much larger than 546 to prove it.

Left-Side Bias in the Personal Distress Scale

With this result in mind, we revisited the literature and tracked down earlier papers on this topic. The papers we reviewed follow two research threads:

- Personal Distress Scale
- Rating of educational experiences

EVIDENCE SUPPORTING THE LEFT-SIDE BIAS

Chan (1991) conducted a study using five items from the Personal Distress Scale of the Interpersonal Reactivity Index, translated into Mandarin, with 102 students from two senior high schools in Taipei participating. The items used five-point Likert-type response scales, as shown in Figure 13.2. There were two versions of the items. Version 1 (top of Figure 13.2) had response labels from positive on the left to negative on the right. Version 2 (bottom of Figure 13.2) had response labels from negative on the left to positive on the right. In the first administration of the survey, all participants completed Version 1. Five weeks later, they completed Version 2. In the abstract, he reported, "It was proposed that subjects tended to choose the first alternative acceptable to them from among the ordered response categories so that a primary effect was predicted. Findings supported the hypothesis." In reviewing this paper, we wanted to know the magnitude of the reported effect and whether any aspects of the experimental design might have contributed to the effect.

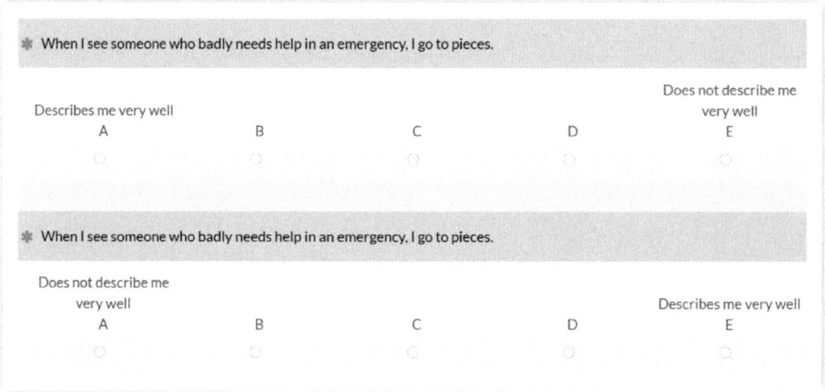

FIGURE 13.2: Sample item from the Personal Distress Scale (top: Version 1; bottom: Version 2).

Chan reported higher means for four of the five items for Version 1, the positive-first response order. A multivariate test of all five items indicated a significant difference between the versions. Of four univariate tests, two were significant, one was marginal, and one was not significant. He did not publish the mean differences, either by item or overall, so we can't assess the effect size.

There were several alternative explanations for the apparent left-side bias. Because the study was conducted with teenage students in Taipei, there were potential cultural effects.

Bottom Line: The biggest problem is that this was a within-subjects study without counterbalancing, so the differences could be due to scale format, order of presentation, or some combination of the two.

Almost ten years later, Weng and Cheng (2000) replicated Chan's study, but with experimental protocols in place to control the order of presentation. The total sample was 858 students: 490 from a university in Taipei and 368 from a junior high school in Taitung. Participants completed the same surveys as those administered by Chan (1991). Two five-item surveys were given one week apart, but the order of presentation was completely balanced, with the results shown in Table 13.1. The means ranged from 6.59 to 8.69; the scores were the sums of five-item ratings (0–4) for a combined score that could range from 0 to 20.

Education	Order	n	Mean 1	Mean 2	d	% Range	SD 1	SD 2
University	Neg–Neg	93	8.58	7.24	1.34	6.7%	3.58	3.48
	Neg–Pos	184	8.09	7.36	0.73	3.6%	3.72	3.57
	Pos–Neg	104	8.31	7.67	0.64	3.2%	3.01	4.31
	Pos–Pos	109	7.84	6.66	1.17	5.9%	3.76	3.96
Jr. High	Neg–Neg	78	8.26	8.69	−0.44	−2.2%	3.85	4.42
	Neg–Pos	105	7.85	6.95	0.90	4.5%	3.65	3.70
	Pos–Neg	83	7.30	7.31	−0.01	−0.1%	3.57	3.91
	Pos–Pos	102	7.48	6.59	0.89	4.5%	3.33	3.65

TABLE 13.1: Results from Weng and Cheng (2000), d = mean difference, % Range = $d/20$.

Surprisingly, the largest effect sizes were when university students received the same version on both administrations (6.7% and 5.9%).

When replicating Chan's conditions (Pos–Neg), Weng and Cheng reported similar results for university students (a higher mean on first administration). However, the means were nearly identical for the junior high students.

Collapsing over all eight conditions, the mean effect size (% Range) was 3.3%, apparently due to a tendency for **most groups to provide lower scores on the second administration** regardless of the manipulation of item format.

Table 13.2 shows the results for the conditions where students completed two different forms, showing the mean difference (d) for the two Pos–Neg groups and the two Neg–Pos groups. If there was a left-side bias, the effect size for Pos–Neg should be larger than the one for Neg–Pos, but it clearly isn't.

Condition	d	% Range
Pos–Neg	0.31	1.6%
Neg–Pos	0.81	4.1%

TABLE 13.2: Overall results from Weng and Cheng (2000).

Bottom Line: If anything, these data suggest (but don't prove) a right-side bias of 2.5% (4.1%–1.6%).

Left-Side Bias in Ratings of Educational Experiences

In their review article "Rating the Rating Scales," Friedman and Amoo (1999) included a section on order effects in rating scales in which they concluded that the left-side bias was real and strong enough for unethical researchers to use it to manipulate results. Two of the papers they cited as evidence for this claim were Mathews (1929) and Friedman et al. (1993).

EVIDENCE SUGGESTING (BUT NOT PROVING) A WEAK LEFT-SIDE BIAS

In Friedman et al. (1993), college students ($n = 208$) provided ten ratings of their school, evenly split between two response formats, in a between-subjects study; 104 with Strongly Agree on the left (SA/SD) and 104 with Strongly Agree on the right (SD/SA). They scored Strongly Agree as a 1 and Strongly Disagree as a 5, so if there was a left-side bias, you'd expect higher scores when Strongly Disagree was on the left. Table 13.3 shows the results.

Item	SA/ SD	SD/ SA	d	% Range	sd SA/ SD	sd SD/ SA
1	3.57	3.64	0.07	1.8%	0.90	0.94
2*	2.10	2.31	0.21	5.3%	0.60	0.75
3*	2.14	2.42	0.28	7.0%	0.78	0.95
4	2.50	2.55	0.05	1.3%	0.78	0.70
5	3.72	3.58	−0.14	−3.5%	0.91	0.88
6	3.69	3.78	0.09	2.3%	0.88	0.89
7*	2.20	2.54	0.34	8.5%	0.82	1.00
8	2.70	2.87	0.17	4.3%	0.92	1.12
9	3.47	3.36	−0.11	−2.8%	0.91	0.98
10	4.28	4.13	−0.15	−3.8%	0.63	0.78

TABLE 13.3: Results from Friedman et al. (1993), * = significant $p < .05$.

The three items with asterisks are those for which the mean differences were statistically significant. Friedman et al. (1993) focused on these items in their discussion to support a claim of a left-side bias. But what about the other seven items? If you average across items to use all the available data, the average difference is .08 on a five-point scale. After rescaling to 0–4, this translates to 2% of the range of the scale (0.8/4, nonsignificant across items; t(9) = 1.5, p = .17).

Bottom Line: Considering all ten items, these results suggest a small left-side bias, but it's not proven.

MORE EVIDENCE SUGGESTING (BUT NOT PROVING) A WEAK LEFT-SIDE BIAS

Mathews (1929) is particularly interesting because it's the oldest investigation of the left-side bias, cited by Chan (1991), Friedman et al. (1993), and Weng and Cheng (2000). Mathews reported two studies, both of which had students complete a 50-item Likert-type questionnaire.

In Study 1, Mathews used a counterbalanced experimental design (n = 184) in which half of the students in the sample got Form A (strong positive on left) and the other half got Form B (strong negative on left). Later in the same class session, he had them complete the questionnaire again, but with the other form.

In Study 2 (n = 130) he used the same questionnaire but gave all students Form A first. Then, a week later, gave them all Form B—the same confounded experimental design as in Chan (1991).

The data in Tables 1 and 2 of his paper show the total number of responses for each response option, summed over items and students. It looks like Mathews conducted something like a z-test to compare the percentages for each response option in each study, claiming some significant differences, but it seems he used the sum of all the responses (50 items times the number of students—almost 9,200 in Study 1 and almost 6,500 in Study 2) as the denominator rather than restricting the denominator to the number of students and adjusting the numerator accordingly.

From the data presented, it's possible to reconstruct how many students tended to give each response option by dividing the numbers in the response option columns by 50 (the number of items). It's not possible, however, to set up a within-in-subjects analysis of the mean difference because the paper doesn't show which student gave which responses, a limitation to keep in mind. Figure 13.3 shows a graph of the mean scores for both studies (transformed to a 101-point scale), so we can see the overall mean differences equivalent to percentages. For these data, a larger mean for Form A is consistent with a left-side bias.

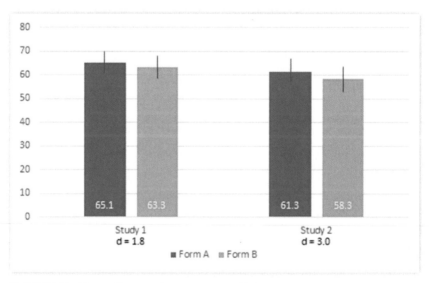

FIGURE 13.3: Mean differences from Mathews (1929).

For Study 1, the difference was 1.8%; for Study 2, it was 3.0%. Due to the confounding in Study 2, however, we can't take that difference at face value, since it's similar to the pattern in other studies where the mean is lower on the second administration regardless of item manipulation (e.g., Weng & Cheng, 2000). The results of Study 1 are consistent with a left-side bias, but a small one that doesn't appear to be statistically significant (note the substantial overlap of the 95% confidence intervals).

Bottom Line: These results suggest a small left-side bias, but it's not proven.

Literature Summary and Takeaways

Of the six studies we reviewed, four reported credible effect sizes for a bias. Three were consistent with a left-side bias (Lewis, 2019a, 1%; Friedman et al., 1993, 2%; Mathews, 1929, 1.8%), and one was consistent with a right-side bias (Weng & Cheng, 2000, 2.5%), averaging just 0.6%. This modest effect (even if it is consistent) makes it unlikely unethical researchers could use a left-side bias to manipulate results. It's also possible that much of this effect is just the unwanted side effect of improper counterbalancing in within-subjects experiments. Scores tended to be lower on the second administration of a questionnaire and were confounded with the presentation of left-side versus right-side formats.

Finally, given the variation in participants in the various studies (adults and teenagers, U.S. and Taiwanese), it doesn't seem likely that results were driven by maturation or cultural effects.

Study Investigating Left-Side Bias in the Single Ease Question (SEQ)

Given the weak and inconsistent effects from the literature and the problems with confounding, we conducted a study using the popular Single Ease Question (SEQ).

We developed the seven-point SEQ in 2009, and it has since become a standard in assessing post-task perceptions of ease. Although there has been variation in this aspect of rating scale design over the years, the most common format is to have lower scores (poorer experiences) on the left and higher scores (superior experiences) on the right.

The rationale for using the standard format includes pragmatic and theoretical elements. Pragmatically, it's generally easier to interpret results when larger numbers indicate a better outcome. Theoretically, putting the negative-tone endpoint on the left has been hypothesized to strike some balance between two potential response biases: left-side bias (tendency to select the leftmost response option) and acquiescence bias (tendency to be agreeable or positive).

So, the hypothesis is that putting Very Difficult on the left and Very Easy on the right splits the biases between the endpoints. On the other hand, putting Very Easy on the left might artificially increase the likelihood of its selection because it would attract both types of bias, manipulating the response distribution to an apparently more favorable outcome.

Based on this reading of the literature, it is plausible that data collected with the two SEQ formats illustrated in Figure 13.4 would be very similar. To test this possibility, we conducted an experiment. The only difference is in the polarity of the endpoints. The standard version has Very Difficult on the left, and the alternate version has Very Easy on the left.

STUDY DESIGN: SEQ STANDARD VS. ALTERNATE FORMATS

We collected data from 301 participants (sampled in February and March 2022 from a U.S. panel provider) using a Greco-Latin square experimental design (Lewis & Sauro, 2022, Apr 19, May 17). After attempting each task, participants completed either the standard or alternate version of the SEQ (Figure 13.4), following the experimental design. After completing both tasks, they indicated whether they preferred the standard or alternate format.

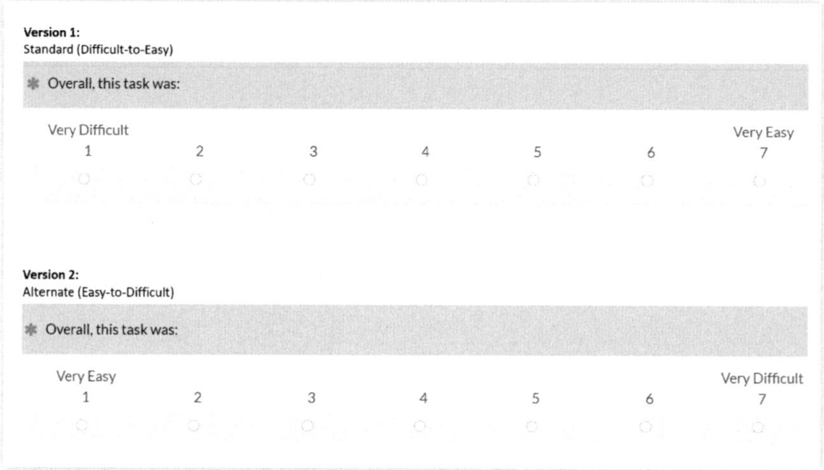

FIGURE 13.4: Two SEQ item formats differing in the polarity of the endpoints.

In this experimental design, there were three independent variables:

- **Item Format:** standard or alternate, as shown in Figure 13.4

- **Rating Context:** easy or difficult task

- **Order of Presentation:** Greco-Latin design with four orders of presentation (standard/easy then alternate/difficult; standard/difficult then alternate/easy; alternate/easy then standard/difficult; alternate/difficult then standard/easy)

Participants were randomly assigned to one of the four orders of presentation. Across the experiment, this controls for the "nuisance" variables of Rating Context and Order of Presentation, although, in this experiment, we were also interested in the interaction between item format and task difficulty.

If the biases were present and of reasonable magnitude, we would expect them to inflate the alternate format means relative to those collected with the standard format.

Study summary and takeaways
Bottom Line: There was little evidence of a left-side bias.

No overall difference in means
When separately analyzed for easy and difficult tasks, the alternate was slightly higher for the easy task and slightly lower for the difficult task, as shown in Figure 13.5, but the differences due to format were not significant for either level of task difficulty.

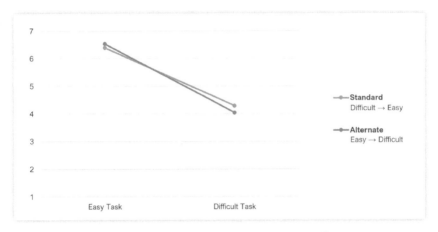

FIGURE 13.5: Overall interaction between item format and task difficulty.

Small (nonsignificant) interaction effect on means
The Greco-Latin design allowed us to examine the effects of the first task experience, eliminating any possible carry-over effects from participants rating the same item multiple times. When we look at just the first task attempt, there was a slightly higher mean score on the standard SEQ (Very Difficult on Left) than on the alternate (Very Easy on Left), but the difference was not statistically significant ($p = .15$).

Small (statistically significant) interaction effect on top-box scores
We also examined the top-box and top-two-box scores for the initial ratings by each participant and found strong visual evidence of an interaction effect (see Figure 13.6). Notice the separation of the points on the hard task.

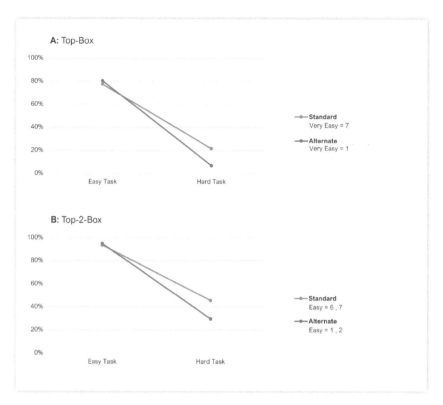

FIGURE 13.6: Top-box and top-two-box percentages for initial ratings ($n = 150$ for standard and 151 for alternate in each panel).

Table 13.4 confirms the interaction effect was statistically significant for top-box and top-two-box scores for the hard task.

Task Type	Box Type	z	p	d	lower	upper
Easy Task	Top Box	0.44	0.66	2.9%	−10.2%	15.9%
Hard Task	Top Box	2.58	0.01	14.7%	3.3%	25.3%
Easy Task	Top-2 Box	0.36	0.72	1.4%	−6.7%	9.5%
Hard Task	Top-2 Box	2.02	0.04	16.0%	0.5%	30.7%

TABLE 13.4: Standard vs. alternate comparisons of extreme Easy response percentages for easy and hard tasks (initial ratings).

Figure 13.7 shows the response distributions for the between-subjects (initial ratings) portion of the data. Again, notice the large separation in ratings between the standard and alternate for the Very Easy rating in Panel B for the hard task—a substantial 16-point difference.

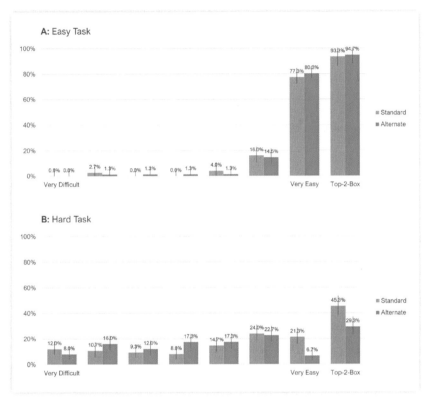

FIGURE 13.7: Full response distributions for SEQ initial ratings collected in easy and hard tasks (*n* = 150 for standard and 151 for alternate in each panel).

These analyses demonstrated an interaction between SEQ format and task difficulty. Top-box and top-two-box percentages were almost the same for both formats in the easy task but were significantly different in the hard task. But why?

Is the interaction effect evidence of a left-side bias?

We have evidence of differences in extreme SEQ ratings of ease when a task is difficult, but is there any evidence that this might be due to, or at least influenced by, a left-side bias? The short answer is no.

Because the experimental design for this study was balanced, one way to check for a left-side bias is to ignore everything about SEQ format and task context, and just count the number of selections of 1 and 7 across all the data. If there's a consistent left-side bias, more participants should select 1 than 7.

Because each participant in the study provided two SEQ ratings, there were a total of 602 SEQ ratings. Of those 602 ratings, there were 152 selections of 1 (25.25%) and 151 selections of 7 (25.08%), a difference of about 0.2%.

Focusing on just the 301 initial ratings, we found 75 selections of 1 (24.92%) and 80 selections of 7 (26.58%). Not only is this difference not statistically significant (N–1 two-proportion test: $z = 0.47$, $p = .64$, observed difference = 1.66% with 95% confidence interval from –5.3 to 8.6%), there were more selections of 7 than 1 — the opposite of what you would expect if a robust left-side bias was present.

This pattern is also evident in Figure 13.7, which showed no difference in initial selection frequency for 1 and 7 for the easy task, but significantly more selection of 7 than 1 for the hard task. In other words, there's no evidence of left-side bias.

If not a left-side bias, what's causing the interaction effect?
If left-side or right-side (acquiescence) biases aren't good explanations, what could be causing the interaction effect between versions? We're not quite sure, but we do see something happening.

When tasks are hard, participants appear to be more repelled by the Very Easy (1) option on the left side and/or attracted by the Very Difficult (7) option on the right side.

If there's no left-side bias in play, then how might we account for this difference in response distributions of Very Easy between the SEQ formats when tasks are hard? There's no compelling justification for hypothesizing a right-side bias. Any acquiescence bias should also be evenly distributed across this experimental design, so that's not an answer. There is always the possibility that despite its statistical significance in this experiment, it was a fluke (Type I error), which can only be investigated through replication. Whether or not we can explain it, the effect was consistent in this data.

Preference
Because participants in the experiment used both formats during the task sessions, we asked them which they preferred. To our surprise, participants preferred the alternate to the standard SEQ format.

Takeaway 1: Regardless of format, we found no significant difference in mean SEQ scores.

Takeaway 2: We did find a difference in top-box scoring. If your key dependent measure will be a top-box or top-two-box score based on SEQ ratings, then you can't count on getting the same result with the different formats, especially if your tasks tend to be difficult.

Takeaway 3: Even though most participants preferred the alternate format, unless there is a compelling reason to do otherwise (e.g., comparison with historical data), we recommend using the standard format for SEQ response options (Difficult–Easy). This will improve the consistency of UX measurement, and we know from experience that communicating with stakeholders is easier when higher numbers represent a better outcome.

Takeaway 4: Analysis of the frequency of selection of extreme endpoints indicated a slight but insignificant left-side bias of 0.2%. Adding this result to the findings from the literature slightly reduces the estimate for a left-side bias to 0.5%.

WHAT ABOUT A TOP-FIRST BIAS?

As shown in Figure 13.8, if we take an item with a horizontal format (left to right) and rotate it, the most common vertical format has the lowest number at the top (corresponding to the lowest number on the left) and the highest number at the bottom (corresponding to the highest number on the right).

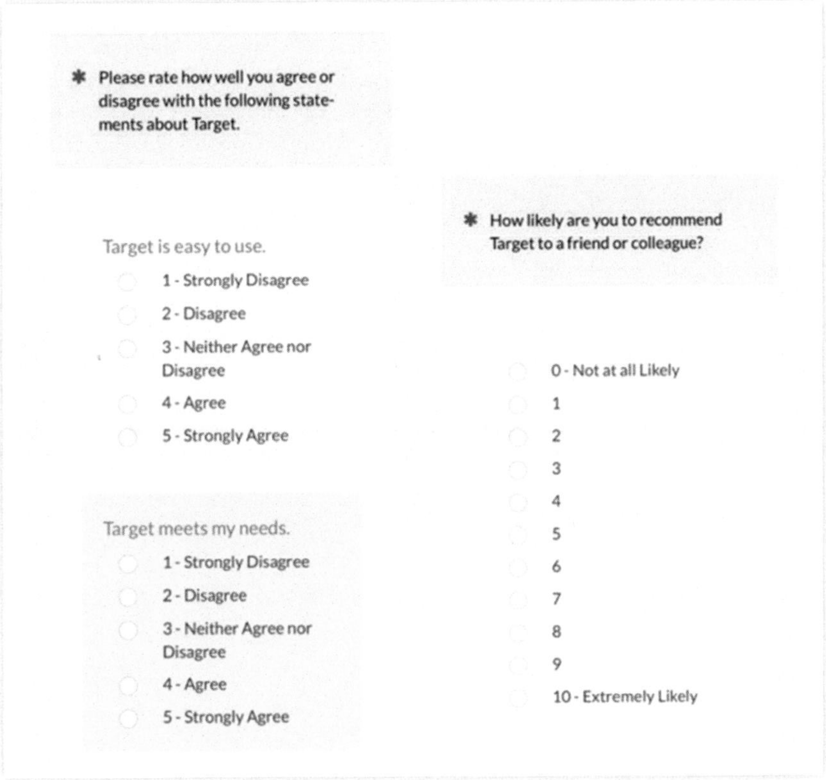

FIGURE 13.8: Examples of rating items rotated from horizontal to vertical orientations.

In Chapter 15, we review studies that compare these types of horizontal and vertical orientations, but what about manipulating which response option is at the top in a vertical orientation? Our investigation of the hypothesized left-side bias indicates that the bias, if it exists, is very small (about 0.5%). But what about the potential for a top-first bias?

There isn't much research on this topic. Callegaro et al. (2008) investigated numerous format differences for vertical five-point agreement items. In their Study 2, out of 12 relevant comparisons (six items and two endpoint-numbering schemes), there was only one significant difference. Unfortunately, the authors did not present any information about the distributions they were comparing other than the values of chi-square tests of independence, so we don't know if the effects were in the direction consistent with a top-first bias.

Stern et al. (2007) tested scale reversal for two frequency items (Travel Question and Internet Usage Question), finding a significant difference for one but not the other (between-subjects design with $n > 600$ for each item and response option order). The Travel Question had conventional response options ("Once or more a week," "Once or more a month," "Once or more a year," "About once a year," "Less than once a year"). The response options for the Internet Usage Question were less typical ("Everyday," "Nearly everyday," "A few times a week," "Once a week or less").

Even with these large sample sizes, there was no significant difference for the Travel Question. The unstandardized effect size for the mean difference was .01/4 = 0.25%, for the top box ("Once or more a week") the difference was 1.7%, and for the top-two box was 1.5% — but both results were in the opposite of the direction expected with a top-first bias.

For the Internet Usage Question, the effect size for means was 6.7%, for the top box (Everyday) was 18.8%, and for the top-two box was 5.6%. As the authors pointed out, these results were likely influenced by the similarity of "Everyday" and "Nearly everyday." For example, if you're thinking an event happens every day or so, and the first response option you read says "Everyday," why not select it? In the reverse order, when you encounter "Nearly everyday," that might well siphon off some of the responses that otherwise would have been "Everyday." It's an interesting effect, but it might be more indicative of response patterns caused by a vague frequency quantifier that has little semantic distance from an adjacent (and less vague) frequency quantifier. The response pattern for the Travel Question is much more like what we typically see for an order manipulation than the pattern for the Internet Usage Question.

Overall, there doesn't seem to be compelling evidence of a strong top-first bias. We are curious, however, what the response patterns would be like for a study of vertical scale reversals in a UX research context (and plan to investigate it in the future).

CHAPTER SUMMARY

The focus of this chapter was to review research and recommendations for either mixing positive- and negative-tone items or using only positive tone in standardized UX questionnaires and to discuss the research for and against the hypothesis of a left-side bias when responding to rating scales.

Should you vary item tones when developing multi-item UX questionnaires? …No, we generally advise keeping a consistently positive tone. The primary rationale for alternating tone is to control hypothesized acquiescence and extreme-response biases, neither of which has been shown to influence responses to standardized UX questionnaires. However, the use of alternating tone has been associated with item misinterpretation, unintentional agreement with negative-tone statements, researchers forgetting to reverse the scoring of negative-tone items, and distortion of factor structures. We recommend avoiding these problems by using a consistently positive tone. The exception is when the goal is to measure a negative construct (e.g., clutter), but even then, respondents might unintentionally agree with these types of statements when they intend to disagree.

Is there a left-side bias? …Probably not. The idea of a left-side bias is appealing because it's consistent with how we expect respondents to scan response options, but careful examination of the literature and the results of our own studies do not support this hypothesis. If there is a left-side bias, it is inconsistent and weak enough to ignore in practice.

Table 13.5 summarizes the studies associated with the estimated effect sizes for the two scale manipulations discussed in this chapter.

Topic/Studies	n	Study Description	Scales	Effect Size	Takeaway	Design Notes
Item Tone (SUS)	1179[a]	SUS ratings of various products across two studies	SUS (101-pt)	0.8%	Standard SUS scores slightly higher than positive version	Mix of between and within subjects
Left-side Bias	2227[b]	Multiple studies in which respondents provided ratings on scales with standard and reversed polarity	TAM (7-pt), SEQ (7-pt), Various other items (5-pt)	0.5%	Slight tendency for respondents to select the leftmost option	Within subjects, counterbalanced

TABLE 13.5: Summary of effect size estimates for Chapter 13 presented in descending order of effect size. These unstandardized effect sizes are mean differences divided by the range of the scale. * = statistically significant. Respondents are from panels unless otherwise indicated. The sources for this table are:

a: Sauro & Lewis (2011), n = 213; Kortum et al. (2021), n = 966

b: Mathews (1927), n = 314; Friedman et al. (1994), n = 208; Lewis (2019), n = 546; Weng & Cheng (2000),
   n = 858; Lewis & Sauro (2022, May 17), n = 301

CHAPTER 14:
AGREEMENT, END POINTS, AND CULTURAL DIFFERENCES

In this chapter, we review the research literature and our data on three topics: acquiescence bias, the effect of endpoint formats (style and intensity), and cultural/regional differences in response behaviors. We'll address the following questions:

- Are agreement items in UX research affected by an acquiescence bias?
- Does varying the intensity of endpoints affect response behaviors?
- Do UX researchers need to be aware of cultural effects on responses to rating scales?

ARE AGREEMENT ITEMS PRONE TO ACQUIESCENCE?

It is common in user experience (UX) research to include questionnaire items with an agreement format (statements with which respondents indicate a level of agreement, also known as Likert-type items). This includes commonly used standardized usability questionnaires like the System Usability Scale (SUS) and the Computer System Usability Questionnaire (CSUQ; see Appendix B).

A potential weakness of agreement items is the possibility they may be affected by acquiescence bias. As we covered in Chapter 13 in the context of item tone, acquiescence bias is the purported tendency of respondents to be more agreeable than they would otherwise be when providing ratings (Billiet & McClendon, 1998). An alternative approach to constructing items is to use item-specific rating scales (Menold & Bogner, 2016). For example, consider the items shown in Table 14.1, which shows three agreement items (adapted from Lewis et al., 2015) and content-matched item-specific items.

Label	Agreement	Item-specific
Meets requirements	This website's capabilities meet my requirements <Strongly Disagree–Strongly Agree>.	This website's capabilities <never meet my requirements–always meet my requirements>.
Ease of use	This website is easy to use <Strongly Disagree–Strongly Agree>.	This website was <very difficult to use–very easy to use>.
Ease of navigation	This website is easy to navigate <Strongly Disagree–Strongly Agree>.	This website was <very difficult to navigate–very easy to navigate>.

TABLE 14.1: Examples of three agreement items and item-specific items with matched content.

The items in the item-specific column of the table have content matched to the agreement versions, but with specific rather than generic agreement endpoints. In their review of rating scale designs, Menold and Bogner (2016) concluded, "Empirical findings suggest that it is better to use item-specific scales and to avoid agree/disagree scales as they elicit higher rates of agreement than item-specific ratings scales" (p. 8). But is this necessarily the case in the context of UX research?

This question matters because an advantage of using agreement over item-specific items is that they are more compact in their presentation and may be easier for participants to complete due to using consistent endpoint anchoring. Also, there are times when it might be easy to express an attribute using the agreement format, but it would not be easy to create an item-specific format.

Agreement vs. Item-Specific Study Overview

In a study conducted by Lewis (2018a), 248 participants (members of a panel made up of IBM employees) rated their recent experience using auto-insurance websites with one of two surveys that differed only in item format (agreement vs. item-specific endpoints). After balancing the independent groups to have equal mean ratings of overall experience, the final sample had 100 cases for each item format for a total sample size of 200.

Figure 14.1 shows the means of 11 comparisons made between metrics using agreement versus item-specific formats (all seven-point scales). Nine (82%) had no significant differences. The remaining two differences were statistically significant ($p < .05$), but in the opposite direction of the expected result if it were true that agreement items are more likely than item-specific to induce an acquiescence bias. Combining the "ease of use" and "does what I need" items to get UMUX-LITE scores, the mean for the agreement version was 79.75, and for the item-specific version was 79.25, a difference of just half a point. Thus, it appears, at least in the context of UX research and for these types of items, that researchers can use agreement items (or item-specific items) without fear of undue influence of acquiescence.

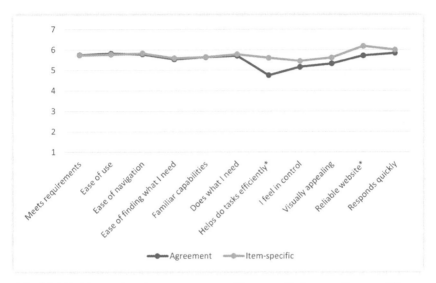

FIGURE 14.1: Mean ratings from agreement and item-specific formats (* = $p < .05$).

A Check for Acquiescence from a Large SUS Database

In an unpublished analysis, we checked for acquiescence using data from a large collection of completed SUS questionnaires. We started with 18,853 questionnaires, then removed 500 that had been straightlined. Because the SUS is made up of items that alternate between positive and negative tone, we focused on the two items of opposing tone that have the strongest correlation—Item 3 ("I thought the system was easy to use") and Item 8 ("I found the system very awkward to use") ($r = -.64$). This means that it should be unlikely for respondents to select the maximum rating of 5 for both items unless there is a strong acquiescence bias. Out of 18,353 questionnaires, there were only 93 instances (0.5%) in which respondents selected 5 for both items, providing additional evidence against the hypothesis that acquiescence plays a strong role in UX rating behaviors. (This is the same unpublished study we described in Chapter 13 as a possible estimate of the frequency of respondents mistakenly selecting 5 as indicating a positive experience regardless of the tone of the item).

DO MORE EXTREME ENDPOINTS AFFECT RATINGS?

One question that comes up frequently in our practice is what the effects are of using more intense labels on the endpoints (e.g., "Extremely" vs. "Very"). For example, the Single Ease Question (SEQ) uses "Very Easy" as its top-box anchor whereas the Likelihood-to-Recommend (LTR) item used to compute the NPS uses "Extremely Likely" as its top-box response (Figure 14.2).

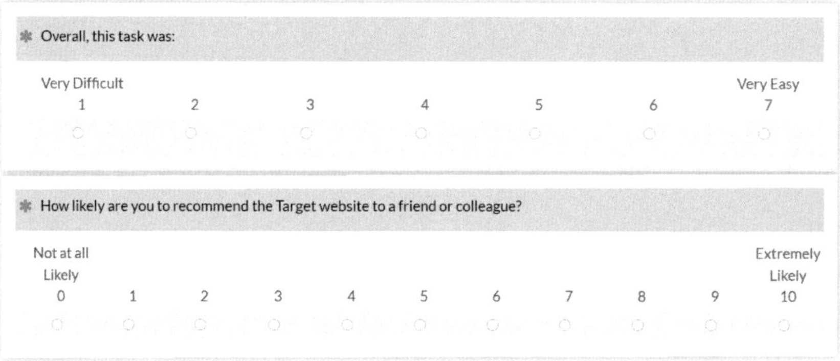

FIGURE 14.2: The SEQ (top) uses "Very" and the LTR (bottom) uses "Extremely."

And general satisfaction items with varying numbers of points sometimes use "Extremely" and sometimes "Very." What does this do to responses?

Research on Endpoint Labels

In Chapter 12 we summarized the literature on the impact of labeling points. There was, however, no research we could find on the specific effects of varying the wording of endpoint labels from "Extremely" to "Very."

Sauro (2010, Sep 21) examined the effects of changing the wording of the original SUS items by making them more extreme, either more positive or more negative.

For example, the first item in the ten-item SUS questionnaire (when asked about a website experience) is "I think that I would like to use this website frequently."

The extremely positive version of this statement used in that study was "I think that this is one of my all-time favorite websites." The extreme negative statement tested was "I think I never want to use the website again."

The results of that study showed that people were more likely to **disagree with extremely positive and negative statements**. The effect was quite large (about a 25% impact on SUS scores). And interestingly, the effect was a bit larger for the extreme-positive items, suggesting that people were more likely to disagree with extremely positive statements than negative statements.

In that study, we drastically changed the item wording but kept the response options the same (1 = Strongly Disagree to 5 = Strongly Agree). What happens when you keep the question the same and only adjust the endpoint labels from "Very" to "Extremely"? We conducted a study to find out.

Very vs. Extremely Study Overview

In October 2019, we asked 213 U.S.-based online panel participants to respond to two versions of a fully labeled five-point satisfaction item (Sauro, 2019, Dec 11). Participants who reported having purchased from at least one of four retailers (IKEA, The Home Depot, Lowes, Target) were then asked two versions of the same satisfaction items (presented in randomized order) for each retailer they selected.

The first version of the satisfaction item was scaled from "Very Dissatisfied" to "Very Satisfied" (Figure 14.3) and the second version was scaled from "Extremely Dissatisfied" to "Extremely Satisfied" (Figure 14.4). The labels for the second through fourth response options were the same, so the versions differed only in the intensity of their endpoints.

✳ Overall, how satisfied are you with your experience(s) involving Target?				
Very Dissatisfied 1	Somewhat Dissatisfied 2	Neither Satisfied nor Dissatisfied 3	Somewhat Satisfied 4	Very Satisfied 5

FIGURE 14.3: The "Very" version of the five-point satisfaction scale.

✳ Overall, how satisfied are you with your experience(s) involving Target?				
Extremely Dissatisfied 1	Somewhat Dissatisfied 2	Neither Satisfied nor Dissatisfied 3	Somewhat Satisfied 4	Extremely Satisfied 5

FIGURE 14.4: The "Extremely" version of the five-point satisfaction scale.

The satisfaction items were part of a larger survey, and the two variants were randomized to appear either at the beginning of the survey or at the end. Between the two satisfaction questions were other unrelated questions regarding attitudes toward design elements and other measures of brand attitude and intent to recommend. Roughly half of the participants saw the "Very" question first and the other half the "Extremely" variant first.

STUDY SUMMARY AND DISCUSSION

The results of our study with 213 participants responding to a "Very" vs "Extremely" version of a five-point satisfaction revealed:

Using "Extremely" instead of "Very" decreased mean scores slightly but not significantly

Our results showed only small and not statistically significant differences when changing the endpoint labels from "Very" to "Extremely." When "Extremely" was used, mean responses were slightly lower in two of the four brands we measured and about equal for the other brands. Across the four brands, the difference was just .01 (.3% of the range of the five-point scale).

"Extremely" slightly (but not significantly) reduced top-box scores

The difference was slightly larger when examining changes in top-box scores only. Fewer respondents selected the top-box satisfaction response when "Extremely" was present. Again, this difference was modest (1.4%) and not statistically significant.

Table 14.2 shows that when the "Extremely" version was shown rather than "Very," 16 out of the 520 responses changed from 5 to 4 (a 3.1% reduction in top-box scores). This was offset by 9 responses (1.7%) moving from 4 to 5 — a net difference of 1.4% more for the "Extremely" version.

Going from "Very" to "Extremely"	Total	%
4 to 5	9	1.7%
5 to 4	16	3.1%

TABLE 14.2: Shift to and from top-box responses across four brands from "Very" to "Extremely" versions of the satisfaction item.

People are less likely to agree to extremely worded item stems but seem less affected by extremely worded endpoints

Both this study and the earlier study on extreme SUS items are consistent with the general principle that the more difficult it is to agree with a question or response, the fewer who will agree to it (Thurstone, 1928). This is also the idea behind the SUPR-Qm (Sauro & Zarolia, 2017), which uses Item Response Theory (Boone, 2016) and intentionally includes items that are difficult for respondents to agree with to better differentiate between attitudes.

This study had limited scope

We tested only one type of scale, a five-point satisfaction item that was fully labeled and numbered. It's unclear whether these small differences will increase or attenuate if we also fluctuate the number of points to, say, seven or eleven or if we change the type of questions and the actual labels used (for example, in the LTR item used in the NPS). These are all good topics for future research.

CULTURAL/REGIONAL EFFECTS ON RESPONSES TO RATING SCALES

Numbers are universally understood across cultures, geography, and languages. But when those numbers are applied to sentiments (for example, satisfaction, agreement, or intention), do people respond universally, or does a 4 on a five-point scale elicit different reactions based on culture or geography?

Many international organizations use similar sets of measures (such as satisfaction or the Net Promoter Score) to compare countries and regions. If cultural differences do have a strong impact on scores, it can be difficult to disentangle the effects of meaningful differences across regions (e.g., lower product satisfaction) from cultural differences. This is a form of measurement error.

Published Research on Cultural/Regional Differences

Many published papers have identified effects of culture and geography. For example, Zax and Takahashi (1967) found cultural and gender differences between U.S. and Japanese respondents in response patterns of seven-point semantic differential ratings of characteristics of Rorschach inkblots.

They found that **U.S. respondents were 41% more likely to select the extreme responses compared to Japanese respondents** (19.2% vs. 13.6% respectively). Conversely, Japanese respondents selected the neutral response 33% more often (23.2% vs. 17.4%).

The preference for extreme responses has also been seen in other Western countries. For example, Dolnicar and Grün (2007) found that Australian respondents selected extreme responses more than Asian respondents (Chinese, Indonesian, Indian, and Malaysian) across multiple studies.

Hui and Triandis (1989) reported that Hispanic-American navy recruits who rated characteristics of supervisors were more than twice as likely as non-Hispanic recruits to select an extreme response when a five-point scale was used (but not on a ten-point scale).

Re-analyzing data from European surveys on cooking, cleaning, and shaving (five-point scales), van Herk et al. (2004) found that people in southern Europe (Italy, Spain, and Greece) had stronger acquiescence and extreme-response tendencies than northern European respondents (UK, Germany, and France). These findings were somewhat surprising because extreme responding is usually associated with individualistic cultures (UK, Germany, France) rather than more collectivist cultures (Italy, Spain, Greece), but Harzing (2006) replicated the results.

Niikura (1999) studied responses of white-collar workers to a questionnaire on modes of expression in the workplace, finding that U.S. respondents reported a more assertive style than Japanese, Malaysian, and Filipino respondents. This research did not, however, provide any analysis of extreme or neutral response styles to the questionnaire's items.

Yang et al. (2010) summarized the response-style effects by culture but concluded that the exact impact of culture on responses may be hard to predict, as it's affected by variables such as the question content and respondent motivation.

Yu and Yang (2015) conducted an international comparison using Gallup's Customer Engagement metric known as CE11 across dozens of countries for both B2B and B2C brands. The CE11's eleven five-point items provide a measure of brand affinity and include items such as satisfaction and Likelihood-to-Recommend (LTR). In their study (see their Table 2), they showed how the CE11's global mean score differed by country despite ostensibly measuring the same things. The range was almost a full point (a high of 4.35 in the U.S. for B2C down to 3.43 in Hong Kong for Cantonese B2C). Other notable lower-scoring countries included 3.59 B2C in Japan, 3.81 in B2B France, and 3.88 in B2C Germany. They established patterns of mean differences in responses for different cultures but did not provide data about tendencies toward neutral or extreme responding.

Cultural Scale Differences Study

We decided to conduct our own study to see whether we could replicate the effects found in Zak and Takahashi and Yang et al. using two commonly used scales in UX research: the eleven-point LTR item and the seven-point SEQ, examining means and neutral/extreme responses (Sauro, 2020, Feb 5).

In September 2019, we asked 215 online panel participants, 61 from the U.S., 51 from Japan, 53 from Germany, and 50 from France, to respond to three item types (six items total):

1. Likelihood-to-Recommend their mobile carrier and last restaurant visited using an eleven-point scale.

2. Satisfaction with their mobile phone carrier and the last restaurant they visited using a seven-point scale.

3. The ease/difficulty of answering two standardized math questions using the seven-point SEQ.

We selected mobile phone carriers and restaurants as products and experiences that were common in all countries tested. For the ease question, we wanted to use a task comparable across cultures that could be universally understood and calibrated for difficulty. We selected two math items from the Wonderlic pre-hiring assessment.

The questions were drafted in English for the United States and translated for participants in other countries (Japanese, German, and French). We selected these countries based on the findings of Yu and Yang (2015), which showed that these countries had large differences in CE11 scores compared to U.S. respondents.

STUDY SUMMARY AND DISCUSSION

The final sample size of 213 included a mix of gender and age for each country with some variation. Roughly half the sample were men (45% men; 55% women). Of the women, 41% were from Japan, 52% France, 62% Germany, and 66% U.S.

Age was less evenly distributed. Most respondents (72%) were 18–44 across all countries, ranging from 47% in Japan, 70% in France, 74% in Germany, and 93% in the U.S.

There are relatively large statistical differences for similar experiences
We observed statistical differences in mean scores across all six questions examined (satisfaction, LTR, and ease). The size of the difference between U.S. respondents and Japanese respondents was most pronounced, with differences of 10%–15%. These differences are much larger than other differences observed in our other scale studies (e.g., from labeling every point, adding colors, or including neutral labels). Figure 14.5 shows the results from the SEQ for the two problems from the Wonderlic test.

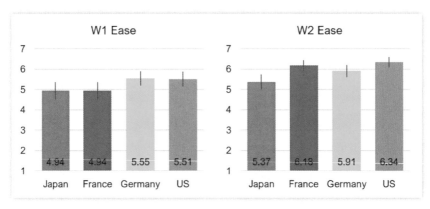

FIGURE 14.5: Mean ease ratings for the Wonderlic items.

Japanese respondents avoided the extreme positive and preferred neutral
Corroborating other research (e.g., Zax and Takahashi, 1967), our study also found that lower mean scores for Japanese respondents were driven by fewer top-box (most favorable) responses, preferring the neutral option (Figure 14.6). The effect was quite large, with U.S. respondents being twice as likely as Japanese respondents to select the top box.

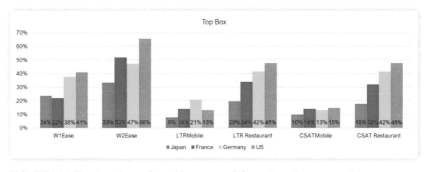

FIGURE 14.6: Top-box (most favorable response) for each scale compared by country.

Figure 14.7 shows the distribution of neutral responses by country. Japanese participants selected the neutral response at the highest rate relative to the other countries, on average selecting neutral 20% of the time (ranging from 16% to 24%). Japanese participants were on average 2.4 times more likely to select the neutral response (between 1.1x and 4x) compared to U.S. respondents.

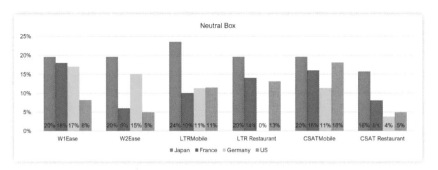

FIGURE 14.7: Neutral box response for each scale compared by country.

Germany chose the neutral option the least in the satisfaction item and interestingly didn't choose the neutral option at all for the restaurant LTR. French respondents' use of neutral options didn't differ systematically compared to the U.S. and German respondents.

German ratings were similar to the U.S.
Germany had mean scores similar to those of the U.S. and had similar response patterns (top-box and neutral response selection).

French ratings were slightly lower than the U.S.
French respondents had slightly lower means (on four of the six items) and selected the top-box score at a lower rate than U.S. respondents. This corroborates the findings by Yu and Yang (2015).

The differences may be lost in translation
Some of the differences in scores may be due to translation issues. Certain concepts don't translate well, or there are disagreements (or errors) in translation. The translated versions are available in the original article (Sauro, 2020, Feb 5)

Cultural norms may affect response patterns
One possible reason for the systematic differences in response styles from Japanese respondents is different cultural norms. For example, in many Asian cultures it is more important to be modest, so responding cautiously and toward the middle of a scale (rather than the extremes) may be an expression of this modesty (see this discussion in Zak and Takahashi, 1967).

Differences in education and experience could be mitigating factors
While we didn't find significant effects from age or gender, other variables could be confounding our results. We didn't collect data about education or other levels of experience that may explain some of the cultural differences. Future studies can more closely examine and control for education and experience as confounding effects.

Use caution when comparing responses internationally
If you are making cross-cultural comparisons (such as comparing product scores), especially between the U.S. and Japan, our study and the published research suggest that scores can be significantly affected by regional/cultural effects. While the evidence is strong that Japanese scores will be lower and could be adjusted to equalize with U.S. scores, future research is needed to see how much of a bump is needed. Our study found that increasing Japanese respondent scores by roughly 10% may be a conservative approach to compensate for the 8%–15% lower scores obtained for Japanese compared to U.S. respondents.

CHAPTER SUMMARY

The focus of this chapter was the effect of endpoint formats (style and intensity) and cultural/regional differences on response behaviors.

Are agreement items in UX research affected by an acquiescence bias? …Probably not. The hypothesis of an acquiescence bias is appealing because it's widely believed that people participating in research studies tend to want to please the researchers. That might be the case in some research domains, especially when researchers are interacting with study participants or respondents might enjoy some benefit from being agreeable. However, our investigations of agreement vs. item-specific endpoints and percentage selection of extreme agreement with positive- and negative-tone items from the SUS found only a small (less than half a percent) effect consistent with acquiescence. If there is an acquiescence bias for agreement items in UX research, it seems inconsistent and weak enough to ignore.

Does varying the intensity of endpoints affect response behaviors? …Not much, if at all. It is possible to influence response behavior through the manipulation of the intensity of the wording of item stems, but our manipulation of "very" versus "extremely" as modifiers of the endpoints of UX agreement scales had little effect on responses to a customer satisfaction item (slightly higher for "very" but only by 0.3% of the scale range).

Do UX researchers need to be aware of cultural effects on responses to rating scales? …Definitely! Our overall estimate of the effect of culture on responses to various rating scales is 12%, one of the largest effects we've seen. In that study, the main takeaway was that respondents from Japan were less likely than others to choose extreme responses.

Table 14.3 summarizes the studies associated with the estimated effect sizes for the two scale manipulations discussed in this chapter.

Topic/Studies	n	Study Description	Scales	Effect Size	Takeaway	Design Notes
Cultural Effect*	215[a]	Respondents from four countries rated mobile carriers, restaurants, and math questions	LTR (11-pt), Sat (7-pt), SEQ (7-pt)	12.0%	Respondents from Japan less likely to select upper extreme responses	Between Subjects for countries, Within Subjects for rating formats
Agreement Acquiescence	18766[b]	Three studies estimating acquiescence in different ways	SUS (5-pt), UMUX-LITE (7-pt)	0.3%	Slightly higher means for positive-tone agreement items	Mix of between and within subjects
Extremely v Very	213[c]	Recent retail purchase	CSAT (5-pt)	0.3%	Slightly higher means for "Very"	Within Subjects

TABLE 14.3: Summary of effect size estimates for Chapter 14 presented in descending order of effect size. These unstandardized effect sizes are mean differences divided by the range of the scale. * = statistically significant. Respondents are from panels unless otherwise indicated. The sources for this table are:

  a: Sauro (2020, Feb 5), $n = 215$

  b: Sauro & Lewis (2011), $n = 213$; Lewis (2018), $n = 200$; Lewis & Sauro (2023, unpublished), $n = 18353$

  c: Sauro (2019, Dec 11), $n = 21$

CHAPTER 15: PRESENTATION EFFECTS ON RATING SCALES

This chapter covers how the way survey items are presented may or may not impact results. We'll first review the common practice of presenting items in a grid. Grids allow for a compact presentation style, but do they encourage people to "straight-line" through a survey or have other undesirable effects?

We'll then compare the impacts of requiring participants to answer questions separately compared to together in a "select-all-that-apply" format. Next, we'll review how the placement of questions, early in a survey or before or after other questions, could impact responses. Last, we'll look into how presenting response options in vertical format (usually on mobile) versus a horizontal format could impact responses.

We'll address the following questions:

- Is it OK to present rating scale items in grids?
- Which is better—select-all-that-apply or yes/no questions?
- Is it better to put general before specific questions?
- Does it matter much if rating scales have a horizontal or vertical orientation?

GRIDS VERSUS STAND-ALONE ITEMS

The linear numeric scale is one of the most used response options (see Chapter 10). Examples of linear numeric scales include the Single Ease Question (SEQ) and the Likelihood-to-Recommend item (LTR, used to compute Net Promoter Scores). See Appendix B for examples of both.

When asking a lot of linear numeric questions, you can save space by combining into a multiple rating matrix, or "grid," such as the one shown in Figure 15.1.

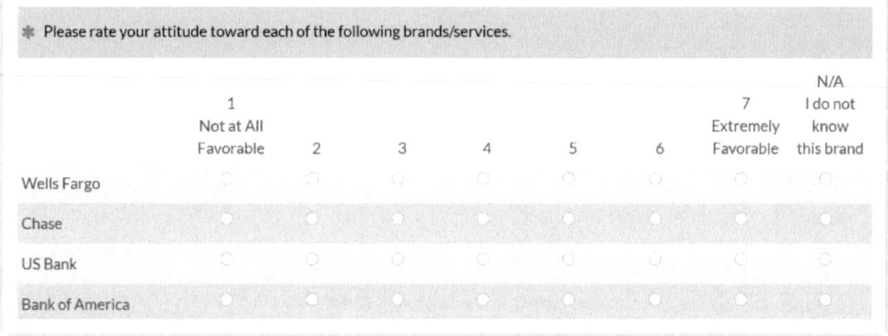
* Please rate your attitude toward each of the following brands/services.

	1 Not at All Favorable	2	3	4	5	6	7 Extremely Favorable	N/A I do not know this brand
Wells Fargo	○	○	○	○	○	○	○	○
Chase	○	○	○	○	○	○	○	○
US Bank	○	○	○	○	○	○	○	○
Bank of America	○	○	○	○	○	○	○	○

FIGURE 15.1: Example of a grid that combines four linear numeric scales.

Although using a grid allows for a more compact presentation, **does combining the items into a grid of rating scales versus asking them individually affect responses?** We reviewed the published literature to find out.

Published Literature on Grids vs. One at a Time

As is often the case with other questions on survey items and response options, it can be difficult to find general rules. A good place to start is the published literature to see what's already been researched.

When it comes to the use of survey grids, a lot has already been done. The focus of research has been on differences in reliability, straightlining (participants answering many questions with the same response options), the response/drop-out rate, and the impact of mobile screens. Here's a summary of several articles:

Couper et al. (2001), in a study of 1,602 students, found increased correlations between items (**higher reliability**) when placed in a grid versus alone, and they also found that grid responses were completed slightly faster.

Tourangeau et al. (2004) had 2,568 participants from an online panel answer eight questions about diet and eating habits with three different presentation styles: all on the same page in a grid, two pages (one grid per page), or one at a time on separate pages.

Internal reliability was highest when items were presented altogether in a grid (alpha = .62) and lowest when on separate pages (alpha = .51). However, when presented separately, the items loaded higher on their expected factors. There was also **more straightlining in grids**. Participants took **about 50% longer** to complete the questions when presented separately. The authors suspected a "near means related" (p. 370) heuristic (items close to each other ask about similar things) may cause respondents to respond similarly when items are presented on the same screen.

Yan (2005) also found an increase in **internal reliability** when presenting items in a grid versus on separate pages to 2,587 online panel participants.

Even the U.S. Census Bureau (Chestnut, 2008) tested the old-school paper-and-pencil forms and found that demographic information presented separately versus in a grid resulted in slightly **higher (1.5%) response rates**.

Toepoel et al. (2009) measured arousal-seeking tendencies from 2,565 Dutch respondents. They found that **reliability was slightly higher** when the 40 items were presented on one grid on a screen compared to separately or broken up across ten screens. However, they also found this treatment resulted in higher **nonresponse** when placed in a grid.

Thorndike et al. (2009) found that 710 Swedish respondents preferred the one-at-a-time format over a grid when asking quality-of-life questions even though it **took more time to complete**.

Bell et al. (2001) found **no difference in reliabilities** for a grid compared to one at a time and a slightly faster completion time for the grid, with 4,876 respondents.

Iglesias et al. (2001) found that older UK respondents (older than age 70) missed or skipped significantly more items (27% vs. 9%) when items were arrayed in a "stem and leaf" grid versus one at a time. They also found slightly **better reliability** when items were displayed separately.

Callegaro et al. (2009) had 2,500 U.S. panel participants answer nine items (some required reverse scoring) about mental health in one of five randomly assigned conditions ranging from displayed all in one grid to one per page. They found the one-per-page presentation had slightly **higher internal reliability** compared to the grid, but it took more than **50% longer to complete**.

Grandmont et al. (2010) also found that seven-point Likert items, when presented in a grid, generated higher drop-out rates. Even though respondents took longer to take the one-at-a-time version compared to a grid (19 vs. 15 minutes), there was no difference in how long respondents thought the surveys took (both 15 minutes). Interestingly, they found **straightlining was about the same** for both the grid and one per page but was at its highest when the grid was split across multiple pages. Respondents appeared to consciously attempt to look like they were not straightlining when completing a big grid.

Respondents reported **disliking long grids the most**. This study also asked respondents how they would want to rate 25 product characteristics. Their responses seem to support the idea that "near means related" but also don't want all items in one grid:

> "State up front that there will be 25 questions, then divide them into thematic groups, no more than 3–5 per screen."
>
> "Don't just throw a list of 25 characteristics up on the same page" (p. 5954).

Mavletova et al., (2017) also reported higher measurement error (including **straightlining**) and lower concurrent validity from grids when testing on mobile screens from a Russian panel.

Liu and Cernat (2016) examined responses from 5,644 SurveyMonkey panel participants and found **higher straightlining** in grids but similar response times (for a short, less-than-two-minute survey). They also found **higher nonresponses** for grid formats with seven or fewer response options compared to one-at-a-time presentations (especially for mobile respondents). They also found that grids with 9 or 11 response options led to substantial differences compared to item-by-item questions and posit that as the number of columns increases in a grid, the data quality may deteriorate.

Chrzan et al. (2012) and Mockovak (2018) conducted studies comparing horizontal, vertical, and grid presentations of rating scales. A comparison of results for horizontal grid versus individual horizontal items found no significant differences, but the means were slightly higher for grids (effect size of 1.5% of scale range for Chrzan et al. and 2.7% for Mockovak).

SUMMARY OF PUBLISHED LITERATURE ON GRID STUDIES

We've summarized the findings across these studies in Table 15.1 (having inferred some conclusions):

	Grid	Alone	No Difference
More Straightlining	4		1
Increases Reliability/Variance Explained	4	4	1
Scores/Distributions Differ	1		3
Higher Nonresponse	6		
Loading on Expected Factor/ Higher Validity		3	
Preference		4	2
Takes Longer		5	2
Higher Mean Ratings	2		

TABLE 15.1: Summary of studies comparing grid vs. stand-alone displays showing the number of studies that share a finding (e.g., six studies found grid displays increased nonresponse rates).

While some results are mixed as other factors moderate the effects, **we can conclude that grids seem to increase nonresponses and probably increase straightlining**. When items are presented alone, they tend to take longer to complete (although participants may not notice as much), and they better match the intended factor structure, but there isn't much difference in scores. Not all grids are created equal, as some studies explored, with massive grids (many rows and many columns) being the least preferred and potentially affecting response quality.

Three Grid Studies with UX Surveys

To add to the data on grids with a focus on UX data, in February 2019 we conducted three studies (Sauro, 2019, Mar 20). In the first study, 399 U.S.-based online panel participants were asked how likely they would be to recommend ten common brands. Participants were randomly assigned to respond to a grid with the ten brands shown together in a fixed order, or the brands were shown one at a time in a random order (see Figure 15.2).

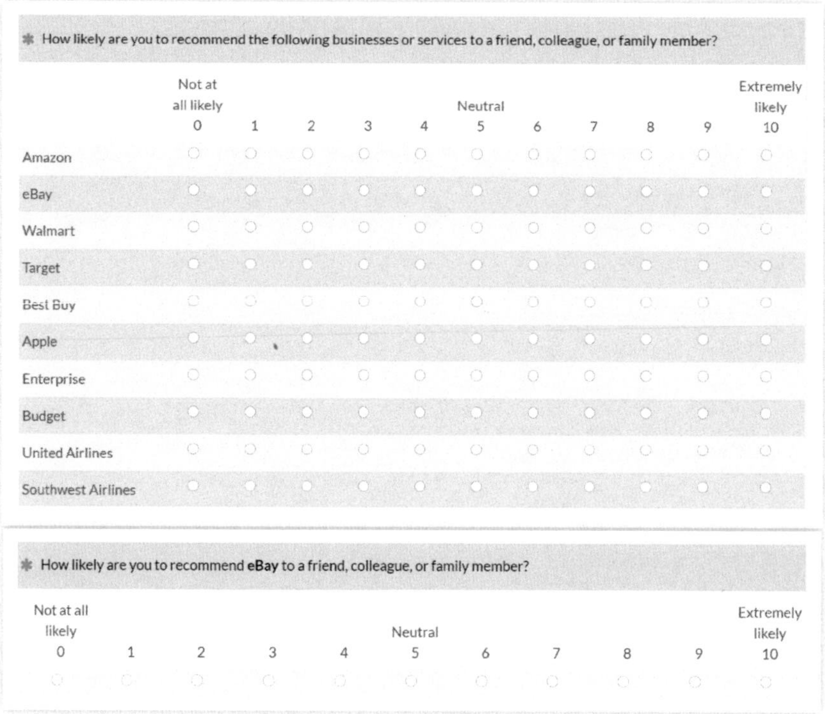

FIGURE 15.2: Differences in LTR scale presentations: grid (top) or separate pages (bottom).

After the LTR items, we also asked participants how many purchases they made with each of the brands in 2018 so we could investigate differences between customers and noncustomers. Respondents were required to answer all LTR items, so we didn't measure nonresponses in this study.

In the second study, 612 U.S.-based panel participants who reported using one of six common software products (e.g., Google GSuite, Microsoft Office) were asked to respond to the ten-item System Usability Scale (SUS). Participants were randomly assigned the SUS in a grid or the SUS with one item per page over ten pages.

In the third study, a separate set of 319 U.S.-based panel participants who reported using Facebook at least once in the previous six months answered the SUS and were randomly assigned to a grid or a one-by-one presentation.

An important aspect of the SUS is that half of its ten items are positively phrased (e.g., "I thought the system was easy to use") versus negative (e.g., "I thought there was too much inconsistency in this system"). This alternating tone leads some participants to mistakenly agree to items with which they intended to disagree (see Chapter 13). However, in the scoring of the SUS, items are reverse coded to generate a scaled score from 0 to 100, which allows us to see the effects on reliability and the overall score.

STUDY & LITERATURE SUMMARIES

An analysis of the literature and our own two studies on the effects of displaying questions in a grid versus on separate pages found:

Presenting items in a grid slightly lowers the score

Compared to presenting items separately on a page, we found the mean LTR scores were *slightly* lower on grids (Figure 15.3). On average, the effect was small (2% to 3% difference). Eight out of ten brands had higher mean scores when they were presented on separate pages for the LTR. The effect was even smaller for the SUS, with a difference of 1%.

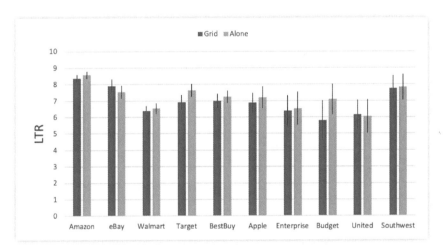

FIGURE 15.3: Difference in mean LTR scores when brands were presented in a grid versus alone (customers only).

For the Facebook study, we found similar results, albeit a bit more pronounced with the larger sample size. The mean SUS score for Facebook was 4.7 points higher (72.1 vs. 67.4, p = .02) when presented alone versus in a grid (see Figure 15.4).

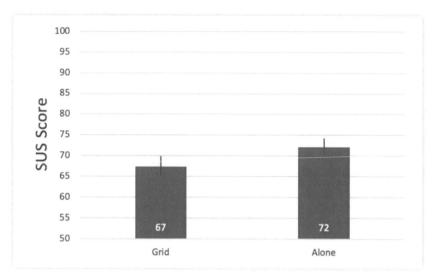

FIGURE 15.4: SUS scores were slightly lower for Facebook when presented in a grid (*n* = 160) compared to questions displayed on separate pages (*n* = 159).

Noncustomers were more affected than customers
For respondents who had purchased from the brand, the effects were even smaller, dropping the scores by only 2%. The consumer software sample were frequent users whose scores were barely different (only 1%), suggesting whatever influence the grid may have (e.g., near means related) is small.

Grids may increase nonresponses
If you don't require all responses, expect more participants to skip or miss an item in a grid (especially grids with more items). The higher number of nonresponses is likely from participants missing lines, especially in grids that contain many rows or columns.

Grids take less time to complete but often increase straightlining
Participants take less time to answer grids than when questions are on separate pages. In our analysis of SUS data, it took more than twice as long to complete the same ten items when presented on separate pages (41 vs. 92 seconds). This is an expected result, as it takes time for servers and web browsers to display new pages. But the faster time may also come from nonattentive respondents providing the same response (straightlining).

Reliability is slightly increased in grids (but maybe artificially)
In a few published studies, the internal consistency reliability increased when items were presented in a grid. The same happened in our two studies using the SUS. In Study 2, the reliability of the SUS was slightly higher when presented in a grid

(Cronbach alpha = .86 in a grid vs. .83 alone). In Study 3, the SUS reliability was also slightly higher when presented in a grid (Cronbach alpha = .89 in a grid vs. .84 when alone).

This higher reliability may be a consequence of increased straightlining (selecting the same response) and, therefore, may be an artificial increase in the correlation between items. However, this wasn't universally seen across studies, and even in studies where this was observed, the differences in reliability were small.

Near means related
One possible hypothesis for the effects on scores in grids is that participants rely on a heuristic that items placed near each other are related, and consequently, they rate such items similarly. In fact, when asked in one study, respondents seem to prefer items to be grouped but not all placed on the same page (presumably in a grid).

Should you use grids? Probably (but not large ones)
The published literature and our studies found that large grids are strongly disliked by participants and may increase dropout. Participants prefer it when items are grouped in smaller grids. It's unclear how big is too big (maybe no more than 5 or 10 items), but these smaller grids may offer a good balance of being faster to complete, easier to display, and not loathed by respondents.

YES/NO VERSUS SELECT-ALL-THAT-APPLY

In Chapter 3, we covered the details around finding the right participants (screening) and understanding the characteristics of the participants' attitudes and prior behavior. These characteristics may be about prior experiences (e.g., products purchased, stores visited) or important product features (e.g., top tasks). But will something as simple as how you present these questions affect people's responses?

Surveys often present lists of options in which respondents use checkboxes to indicate which options apply to the question being asked (Figure 15.5). A common term for this format is "Check all that apply" (CATA) or "Select-all-that-apply" (SATA).

> ✴ Which of the following websites have you visited on a desktop or laptop computer in the past 12 months? Select all that apply.
>
> ☐ Amazon
> ☐ Walmart
> ☐ Target
> ☐ Walgreens
> ☐ CVS
> ☐ Wayfair
> ☐ None of the Above

FIGURE 15.5: Example of a SATA item.

Sudman and Bradburn (1982) hypothesized that requiring respondents to take an action for each option should result in a higher selection rate than the SATA format. They reasoned that failure to check an option could be due to causes other than the option's not being applicable. For example, respondents might unintentionally skip over the item or intentionally stop reviewing items before reaching the end of the list to get through the survey faster. Based on this rational analysis, they advised against using the SATA format and recommended using a forced-choice grid (such as the one in Figure 15.6).

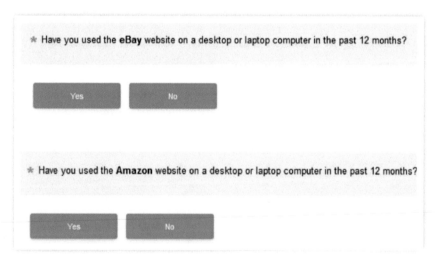

FIGURE 15.6: Example of a forced-choice yes/no item item.

In addition to a forced-choice grid, it is also possible to present forced-choice items as a series of yes/no items (Figure 15.7).

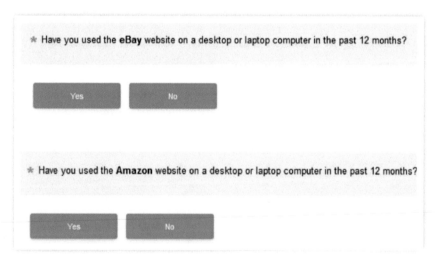

FIGURE 15.7: Example of a forced-choice yes/no item series.

It seems plausible that the forced-choice formats should produce higher rates of selection, but such reasoning doesn't provide insight regarding the magnitude of the difference or whether the forced-choice format matters (grid vs. series).

Estimating these effects requires empirical investigation. Although many papers report the use of SATA (e.g., Ares et al., 2010; Parente et al., 2011), our focus is on the few published studies that have compared SATA versus forced choice, as reviewed in the following sections.

Summary of Published Literature

In this section, we'll review the published literate comparing SATA versus forced choice.

NATIONAL EDUCATION LONGITUDINAL STUDY OF 1988

In 1994, Rasinski et al. published the first experiment that compared SATA and forced choice using data collected in the National Education Longitudinal Study of 1988 (National Center for Education Statistics, 1988). They had 2,210 high school students complete different versions of a paper-and-pencil survey about their experiences during high school. The primary independent variable of interest was the format (SATA vs. forced choice).

The experimental manipulation was applied to three items with 4, 12, and 20 response options (a total of 36). Across the three items, the mean number of selections with the SATA format was 4.04; with the forced-choice format, the mean was 4.6. One way to standardize these findings is to convert the mean number of selections to percentages by dividing them by the total number of 36 possible selections. With this manipulation, the mean of 4.04 becomes 11.2%, and 4.6 becomes 12.8%, a difference of 1.6%.

UNDERGRADUATE EXPERIENCE AT WASHINGTON STATE UNIVERSITY

Smyth et al. (2006) manipulated SATA and forced choice in three surveys of the undergraduate experience at Washington State University. In the first survey, 1,800 respondents answered three items with a total of 36 response options; in the second survey, 3,004 respondents answered six items with a total of 77 response options; and in the third survey, 3,045 respondents answered one item with 15 response options.

Across this series of surveys, there were 128 choices, with a mean selection rate of 3.6 for the SATA format and 4.5 for the forced-choice format, with statistically significant differences for all three surveys. Dividing these means by 128, the percentage of SATA selection was 2.8%, and the percentage of forced-choice selection was 3.5%, a difference of 0.7%.

In 2008, Smyth et al. conducted a similar online survey comparing SATA and a forced-choice grid with a total of 64 choices across six items. They also collected forced-choice data with telephone surveys, but since it isn't possible to collect SATA over the phone, we focus on the online results. The total number of choices across the items was 64. For the online survey ($n = 1082$), the average number of options selected from the forced-choice grid was 4.72 and from SATA was 4.17 (a significant difference in means) — respectively, percentage selections of 7.4% and 6.5%, a difference of 0.9%.

The online survey content and target population of Smyth et al. (2006) and Smyth et al. (2008) were similar to Rasinski et al. (1994), as was the magnitude of the overall difference, suggesting statistically but not practically significant differences.

NATCEN SOCIAL RESEARCH OMNIBUS SURVEY

As part of a survey conducted in 2014 by NatCen Social Research, Nicolaas et al. (2015) replicated and extended the Smyth et al. (2008) research to include computer-assisted face-to-face data collection in addition to online and telephone data collection. Because face-to-face data collection can mimic SATA using showcards, Nicolaas et al. combined their comparison of SATA with forced choice over online and face-to-face sessions. A key difference in the Nicolaas et al. online study was the use of a series of yes/no questions rather than the yes/no grid used by Smyth et al. (2008).

Across 16 choices (with n varying from 452 to 474 due to some item nonresponse), the average difference in percentages between forced choice and SATA selections was 24%, markedly different from the percentages reported in the Rasinsky et al. (1994) or the Smyth et al. (2006, 2008) studies. Given the methodological differences, this could be due to the combination of online with face-to-face data or the use of a series of yes/no questions rather than a yes/no grid.

PEW RESEARCH AMERICAN TRENDS PANEL

In 2018, Pew Research used its American Trends Panel to investigate selection rates for SATA and forced-choice versions of 12 items (Lau & Kennedy, 2019, May 9). Respondents were U.S. adults ($n = 4,581$) and were asked whether they or someone in their family had experienced different undesirable events (e.g., home break-in or denied health insurance). Their method clearly specified that the forced-choice format was a series of yes/no questions (not a grid).

They reported the selection rates for each item and format. The overall mean difference between the percentage of affirmative responses in the yes/no series condition minus the percentage of selections in the SATA condition was 7.3% (95% confidence interval at the item level from 4.6% to 10.0%).

An alternative to comparing percentage selection is to assess differences in the rank order of items (Callegaro, Murakami, et al., 2015). The rank order was similar for the two formats, with a mean absolute rank difference of 0.6.

Insights from Previous Research

Consistent with the hypothesis of Sudman and Bradburn (1982), these four lines of empirical research found statistically significant differences in selection rates from SATA and forced-choice formats. In all four cases, the percentage of forced-choice selection was greater than the percentage of SATA selection.

The research, however, differs in the estimated magnitudes of the difference, as shown in Table 15.2. The range is from less than 1% to 24%.

Study	Difference
Rasinski et al. (1994)	1.6%
Smyth et al. (2006)	0.8%
Smyth et al. (2008)	0.9%
Nicolaas et al. (2015)	24.0%
Lau & Kennedy/PEW (2019, May 9)	7.3%

TABLE 15.2: Differences in selection rates for SATA and forced-choice formats from five studies.

One could argue that differences of 1–2% would rarely be practically significant, but that's a more difficult argument to make for a difference of 24% or even 7.3%. So, why might the results of Nicolaas et al. and Lau and Kennedy be so different from Rasinsky et al. and Smyth et al.?

One possibility is the difference in the forced-choice format. The literature we reviewed has been inconsistent in two ways. First, some researchers have not specified whether they used a forced-choice grid as originally recommended by Sudman and Bradburn (1982) or a series of yes/no questions. Second, some have documented the use of forced-choice grids, while others have documented the use of forced-choice series. We did not turn up any previous research that directly compared selection rates for forced-choice grids versus a forced-choice series.

SATA vs. Forced Choice Study Overview

To better understand the impact of SATA vs. forced choice in the context of a UX research survey, we conducted our own study (Lewis & Sauro, 2021a).

From March through April 2021, we conducted two surveys using 461 U.S.-based panel participants (n = 201 for Survey 1 and n = 260 for Survey 2). Participants were asked whether they had visited any of six mass-merchant websites (e.g., Amazon, Walmart, Target) or seller marketplaces (e.g., Etsy, Craigslist).

They were randomly assigned to answer either a SATA or a forced-choice grid in Survey 1. In Survey 2, they were shown either a SATA or a forced-choice one-at-a-time question. Both studies used a Greco-Latin square experimental design that varied the presentation order of both the type of website (mass-merchant and seller marketplace) and question type (SATA or forced choice).

STUDY RESULTS

The key results from this research were:

There was virtually no difference between SATA and force-choice grid selection rates

In Survey 1, the percentage of respondents who picked one of the websites (the selection rate) was almost identical between the two formats, with 54.06% for

SATA and 54.11% for the forced-choice grid ($t(200)$ = .024, p = .98), a difference of just 0.05%.

There was more of a difference between SATA and force-choice series selection rates

However, there was a greater difference in Survey 2, which used the forced-choice series. The selection percentages in Survey 2 were 55.4% for SATA and 58.5% for the forced-choice series of yes/no questions. However, the 3.1% difference still wasn't statistically significant ($t(259)$ = 1.6, p = .11).

Participants strongly preferred SATA

In both surveys, most participants who had a preference overwhelmingly preferred the SATA option compared to the forced-choice grid (72% vs. 13%) and the forced-choice one-at-a-time series (62% vs. 17%).

STUDY RECOMMENDATION: WE RECOMMEND SATA

There isn't much empirical research on differences in selection rates for response options presented in SATA and forced-choice question formats. The data generally support the hypothesis of Sudman and Bradburn (1982) that selection rates would be greater with forced-choice formats. In some published research, the magnitudes of the reported differences were small (1.6% in Rasinski et al., 1994; 0.8% in Smyth et al., 2006; 0.05% in our Survey 1). Lau and Kennedy (2019, May 9) and Nicolaas et al. (2015) reported larger differences (respectively, 7.3% and 24%), and we found a difference of 3.1% in our Survey 2.

Based on their findings, Lau and Kennedy wrote, "Pew Research Center has adopted a policy of using a forced-choice format instead of a SATA list in its online surveys whenever possible" (2019, May 9, p. 4). Should UX researchers adopt a similar policy?

We argue the decision to use forced choice in UX surveys would be premature for the following five reasons:

UX is less emotionally charged

First, the context of much UX research is qualitatively different from the social and political research conducted by the Pew Research Center. People may be much more emotionally invested in the content of social and political research (e.g., victimization, attitudes toward political parties) than in most UX research (e.g., product usage).

Grids, which are common, weren't assessed in Lau and Kennedy's study

Second, Lau and Kennedy (2019, May 9) compared SATA with a series of forced-choice questions rather than presenting them in grids structured like the commonly used SATA grids (see Figures 15.5 and 15.6). When we used a forced-choice grid in Survey 1, we found a near-zero difference between selection rates for SATA and forced choice. When we ran the same experiment in Survey 2 using a forced-choice series instead of a grid, our estimated difference in the selection rates was 3.1%.

This was not statistically significant, so we shouldn't make too much of it, but it is interesting that the studies that had observed differences greater than 2% are known to have compared SATA with forced-choice series.

It isn't clear which format produces more valid (accurate) results
Third, although Lau and Kennedy (2019, May 9) present a rational argument that their forced-choice selection rates should be closer to reality than SATA selection rates, some counterarguments reduce our confidence in that assertion. For example, Callegaro, et al. (2015) suggested that requiring a Yes or No response could, through an acquiescence bias, inflate selection rates. Without conclusive validation studies, which would be very difficult to conduct, it isn't possible to determine which selection rate is closer to reality.

SATA and forced choice produce comparable results
Fourth, the rank order of selection rates collected with SATA track very closely with those collected using forced-choice formats.

People strongly prefer SATA
Fifth, respondents in both of our surveys indicated an overwhelming preference for SATA over forced choice, likely due to the relative ease of scanning a list and clicking as needed in a single vertical column versus forcing a selection for each item regardless of its applicability. Given the goal of keeping drop-out rates as low as possible when collecting survey data, this is not a trivial concern.

For these reasons, we recommend that UX researchers and practitioners use SATA rather than forced choice unless there is a compelling reason to do otherwise (e.g., a need to compare new results with previous research that used forced choice). When deciding which format to use, researchers should not assume that SATA and forced-choice formats will produce identical selection rates. On the other hand, they very likely will produce similar rank order patterns.

Future research on this topic should focus on investigating the relative influence of different variables on the difference in selection rates for SATA and forced-choice questions, including forced-choice format (e.g., grid vs. series) and research context (e.g., UX vs. education vs. social policy/politics).

QUESTION ORDER EFFECTS

Consider a survey that asks respondents to rate their level of agreement with the following statements:

"Public officials don't care much about what the general public thinks."

"Voting is the only way ordinary people can have a say in government."

If the order in which those items were presented was switched, would it affect how you responded?

While most UX and customer research doesn't involve sensitive topics, does the order in which items are presented in common metrics like the Net Promoter Score matter? To investigate this, we first reviewed the published literature on order effects in surveys.

Published Literature on Order Effects

There is a well-documented order effect in surveys. That is, the order in which questions or items are presented in a survey can influence how people respond.

The causes of the order effect include being primed by earlier items and a desire for respondents to be consistent (or appear consistent) in responses and avoid cognitive dissonance.

In the seminal book Questions and Answers in Attitude Surveys by Schuman and Presser (1996), they reviewed several studies (including one using the examples above) and concluded that the order effect is "not pervasive…but there are enough instances to show that they are not rare either" (p. 74).

The published literature on order effects indicates that it's not always clear how results will differ when the order is changed and whether there always is an effect. The effect depends at least on the topic being addressed, with sensitive topics being more susceptible to the influence of earlier items. Tourangeau and Rasinski (1988) describe the order effect as being "difficult to predict and sometimes difficult to replicate" (p. 299).

GENERAL VS. SPECIFIC ORDER EFFECT

One manifestation of the order effect is the general–specific order effect. That is, asking a general question (how satisfied are you overall with life?) before or after a specific question (how satisfied are you with your marriage? …with your job?) can affect both the correlation between items and the mean responses.

For example, Kaplan et al. (2013) analyzed the general satisfaction of military recruiters in one study ($n = 7,432$) and job satisfaction in another ($n = 88$), reversing the order of general and specific items. They found slightly lower mean scores and higher correlations when the **general items came before specific items** (e.g., general: "All in all, I am satisfied with my job" and specific: "Rating the number of hours I work"). For the large sample analysis of military recruiters, the effect size was 1% of the range of the 5-point scale used in that research (general first: 3.11; general second: 3.15, d = .04). In their second study (smaller convenience sample), the effect size was larger (general first: 3.73; general second: 4.02, d = .29, 7.2% of scale range).

They recommended putting general items first to get the most unbiased estimates of means, standard deviations, and correlations between the scales.

In another study, Auh et al. (2003) examined people's satisfaction with their hair care provider ($n = 191$). They also found slightly lower (around 6%) mean scores **when general satisfaction and loyalty items were first**. However, in contrast, they found explanatory power was the same or higher when the attribute items (e.g., "My hair care provider cuts my hair evenly") came before the general ones (e.g., "Overall satisfaction").

The authors suggest being consistent and, in some domains—for example, when asking about computers or expensive household appliances—asking specific attributes first, then overall questions second (which may be more natural for respondents). These two studies from the literature show some similarities (there is a general–specific order effect) but don't show the same patterns.

Van de Walle and Van Ryzin (2011) conducted a split ballot experiment (n = 3,592) in which they found a significant difference in ratings of a general satisfaction questionnaire depending on whether it appeared before or after a series of specific items (3.7% of the scale range) but in the opposite direction of the effect reported by Kaplan et al. (2013) and Auh et al. (2003).

Thau et al. (2020) reported differences in magnitudes of satisfaction ratings such that asking about overall satisfaction before specific service ratings lowered ratings of overall user satisfaction (3.8% of the scale range). Regardless of order, correlations between specific ratings and overall satisfaction were relatively stable.

ORDER EFFECTS ON ITEM-BY-ITEM AND GRID FORMATS

In a study of the effect of a priming question (a question that brings certain beliefs, values, or attitudes to mind) on related questions that follow, Stefkovics and Kmetty (2022) found a significant order effect when items were presented one at a time, but no order effect when items were presented in grids. The effect size, however, was small—accounting for about 1% of the explained variation in their regression model (n = 778).

INFLUENCE OF CULTURE ON ORDER EFFECTS

In a study that replicated order effects due to the norm of evenhandedness and perceptual contrast from a U.S. sample and extended the research to 11 other countries (e.g., Canada, Germany, Japan, UK), Stark et al. (2020) generally found expected cultural effects on responses to questions contrasting opinions about political contributions by labor unions versus businesses and suitability of legal abortions in the cases of family planning versus cases of serious genetic defects.

Order Effects in UX/CX

There isn't much research specifically examining order effects in UX or CX. For example, Lewis (2019b) examined the effects of order on usability attitudes and **didn't find an order** effect when alternating the SUS, UMUX, or CSUQ.

For the Net Promoter Score, there is at least one report that if you ask the "would recommend" question used to compute the NPS early in a survey, the score will be higher than if you ask it later in the survey, but no data are given on the size of the effect (Ramshaw, n.d.).

For the SUPR-Q, which incorporates the LTR item, Heffernan (2018, Mar 28) found that Net Promoter Scores dropped if it was asked after the other seven SUPR-Q items. It's unclear, though, whether this effect was a result of the presentation format (one at a time) or from high attrition on their web survey.

Studies on Order Effects

To look for evidence of an order effect, we conducted two studies (Sauro, 2019, Jan 9). Study 1 was conducted in November 2018 using U.S.-based online panel participants (n = 2,674). Respondents were asked how likely they would be to recommend a recently purchased product to another friend or colleague (the LTR item). The LTR item was presented either early in the survey (after about 40 questions) or later in the survey (after 72 questions).

Study 2 was conducted between October and November 2018 using 501 U.S.-based panel participants. Participants in the study were asked to reflect on their experience on brokerage websites or restaurant websites using the SUPR-Q (Appendix B). The SUPR-Q contains seven five-point items plus the eleven-point LTR item. Participants were asked the LTR item before the seven SUPR-Q items or after. All eight items were presented on the same page, but their order on the page was swapped for roughly half the respondents across the 12 websites (see Figure 15.8). Full details are available in Sauro, 2019, Jan 9.

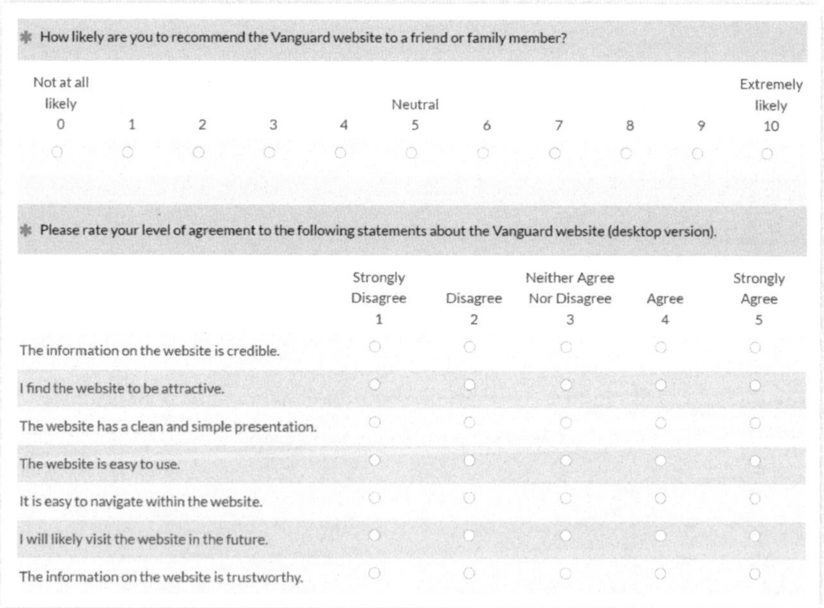

FIGURE 15.8: Showing the LTR before other SUPR-Q items slightly increased explanatory power but the same means compared to showing the LTR after the SUPR-Q items.

STUDY SUMMARY AND TAKEAWAYS

The key takeaways from this research are:

There is little evidence of an order effect on means or distributions
LTR means (and the distribution of scores) were virtually identical whether they were placed early in the survey or late in Study 1 (See Table 15.3).

LTR	Early	Later
0	1%	1%
1	0%	0%
2	0%	0%
3	0%	0%
4	0%	1%
5	3%	3%
6	3%	2%
7	9%	7%
8	15%	16%
9	16%	17%

TABLE 15.3: Differences in respondents selecting each LTR option depending on when it was presented (early vs. late) in a survey.

We found in Study 2 that placing the LTR item before the more specific seven SUPR-Q attitude items on 12 websites also didn't affect the mean scores.

There's a possible difference in explanatory power

We found that having the LTR before the SUPR-Q items increased the explanatory power (adjusted R^2) by about seven percentage points. This was consistent with Kaplan et al. (2013) but conflicted with Auh et al, (2003). The SUPR-Q items aren't as specific an attribute as pricing or features, so this may explain some of the differences, but future research with another data set would be needed for confirmation.

Order effects are real, not rare, but hard to predict

This analysis is consistent with other research that has found that order effects exist, but it's unclear when they will happen and how large the effect will be. There are many ways the LTR item can vary (e.g., being alone vs. with other items on a page), so more data are needed. In the interim, be careful about assuming how changing the item order will affect scores without data on the specific items collected from the same type of participants in a similar context.

Context is a mitigating effect

The published literature shows that the topic, context, and order manipulations may all create different types of order effects. In our first study, about 40 items preceded the first presentation of the LTR and there were more before the second placement. It could be that an order effect is attenuated because of the large number of questions, or it may be masked by other questions. It could also be that people's attitude toward recommending is less susceptible to order effects. All of these are good topics for future research.

HORIZONTAL VERSUS VERTICAL RATING SCALES

With more and more people taking surveys on mobile devices, the effect of display orientation on rating behavior has become important to understand. In Chapter 13, we discussed the effects of scale reversals in investigations of the left-side bias for horizontal formats and the top-first bias for vertical formats (neither of which has compelling empirical support). In this chapter, we review experiments that compare horizontal and vertical formats.

The most common orientation on computer monitors is horizontal (Figure 15.9). Due to screen size constraints, the most common orientation for mobile is vertical (Figure 15.10), especially when there are more than just a few response options.

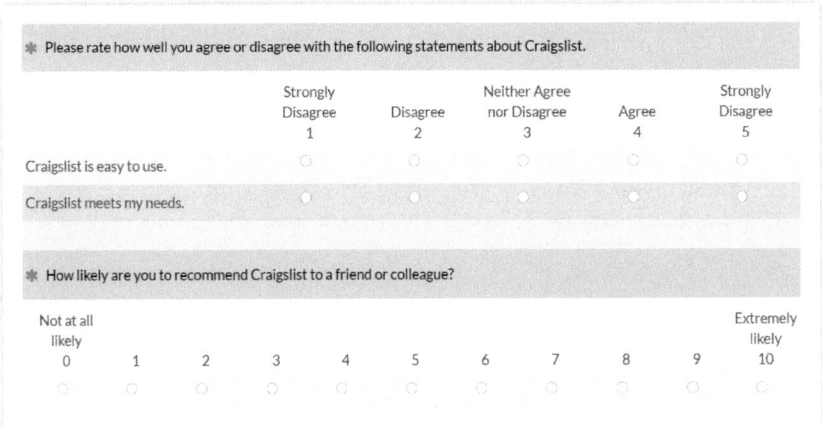

FIGURE 15.9: Scale orientation on a computer monitor for the five-point UX-Lite and the eleven-point LTR items (created with MUiQ).

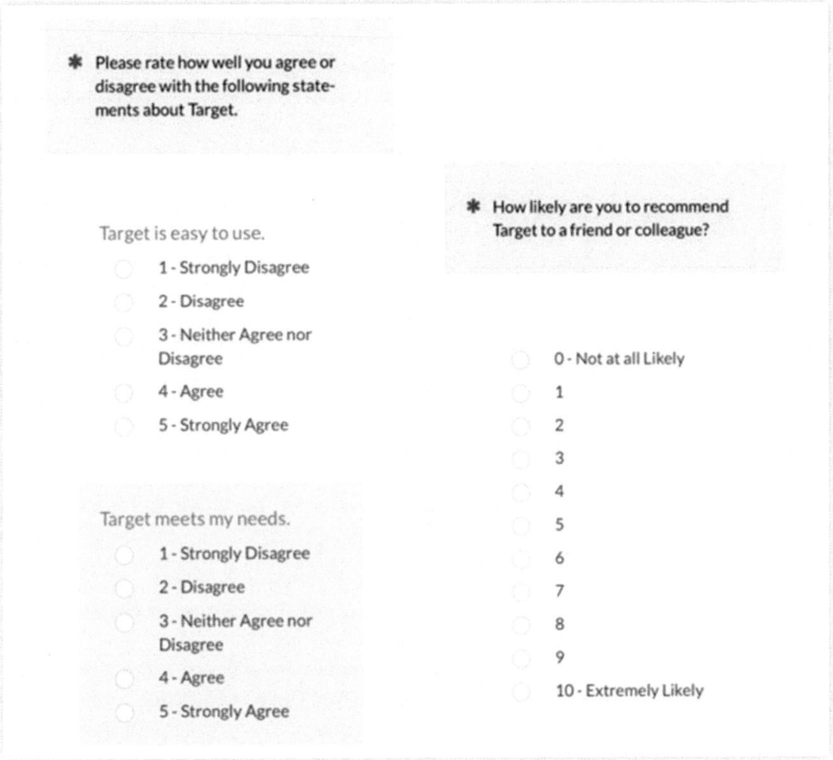

FIGURE 15.10: Scale orientation on a mobile phone for the five-point UX-Lite and the eleven-point LTR items (created with MUiQ).

If scale orientation significantly affects rating behavior, then the common practice of switching orientation to better suit mobile devices is problematic.

In this section, we briefly review the literature we found comparing horizontal and vertical orientations and present our own findings.

Previous Studies Suggest a Minor and Inconsistent Impact

The available empirical literature on scale orientation suggests that, surprisingly, this attribute might not have much effect on ratings.

Friedman and Friedman (1994) had two independent groups of respondents rate the status of six different occupations with five-point scales. One group used scales with a horizontal orientation (n = 104), and the other used scales with a vertical orientation (n = 103). There was no significant difference for three of the occupations. The difference was significant for the three other occupations, but the **direction of the effect was not consistent**, with the vertical scale producing higher ratings for two occupations and lower ratings for the third. Averaging across all six items, the mean difference was .03 (0.7% of the range of a 1–5-point scale).

At an annual conference of the American Association for Public Opinion Research, Chrzan et al. (2012) presented a paper that included a comparison of scale orientations. Of the 1,505 respondents in their research, 40% completed the survey on desktop and 60% on mobile.

Their experimental design allowed the comparison of vertical and horizontal orientations on both computer displays and mobile devices. Additionally, items were organized either in grids or presented separately. They found the highest completion rates with horizontal grids, faster completion times with grids, and longer completion times for mobile.

They found **no significant differences in ratings between PC and mobile groups**, and "no differences based on whether respondents received horizontal or vertical scales or whether their nine attributes appear as a grid or as nine individual rating scale questions" (p. 19). Overall, ratings with vertical scales were slightly higher than those with horizontal scales (1.5% of the scale range).

More recently, Mockovak (2018) compared scale orientation and grids in online data collection of six items (horizontal n = 193; vertical n = 229). He used Mechanical Turk as the source for respondents and was not able to track whether respondents were completing their assigned survey on a computer or mobile device. He found **no significant difference in orientation on ratings for five of the six items**; for one item, the mean was significantly higher for the horizontal orientation (overall ratings with horizontal scales were about 2.7% higher than with vertical scales). The analyses also included an examination of data quality (e.g., reliability, straightlining, item nonresponse, and factor structure). He concluded, "In summary, the question formats studied did not consistently affect the results or associated measures of data quality for the questions in this study" (p. 1).

Study on Horizontal Desktop vs. Vertical Mobile

As in our other experiments assessing rating scale effects, we included scales of different lengths (UX-Lite with five-point scales, LTR with an eleven-point scale) with which participants assessed multiple experiences with horizontal desktop and vertical mobile rating scales (Lewis & Sauro, 2021, Nov 9).

STUDY OVERVIEW

We set up a Greco-Latin experimental design for a within-subjects comparison of UX-Lite and LTR ratings of one of each type of online shopping website: mass merchants (Amazon, Walmart, Target, Walgreens, CVS, Wayfair) and seller marketplaces (Craigslist, eBay, Etsy, Facebook Marketplace).

Specifically, 212 participants from a U.S. panel agency rated the shopping environments in late January 2021. There were 103 participants who completed the survey on a mobile phone and 109 who completed the survey on a desktop computer. Across the experiment, this design controlled for the "nuisance" variables of Type of Website and Order of Presentation, allowing us to focus on the between-subjects independent variable of Orientation (Horizontal: Desktop vs. Vertical: Mobile—as shown in Figures 15.9 and 15.10).

One aspect of the experimental design that could be considered a weakness is the confounding between the desktop/mobile platforms and the horizontal/vertical orientations. On the other hand, from a pragmatic perspective, these combinations of platform and orientation match what researchers commonly do, either by design or by the automatic detection of mobile devices by the survey software.

If comparisons of these two experimental conditions indicate different rating behavior, then an appropriate follow-up experiment would be to construct a full factorial design to disentangle the confounding variables. If results indicate no statistically or practically significant differences, then that finding would be of value to researchers even with the confounding.

STUDY SUMMARY AND DISCUSSION

Although one might expect scale orientation to have a large effect on rating behaviors, that does not appear to be the case; at least, any effects are inconsistent when looking at published literature and our own data.

No effects on overall scores

We found no significant difference in means for either metric (UX-Lite: $p = .58$; LTR: $p = .43$). We also found no significant differences in top-box or top-two-box scores (p-values from .13 to .86).

There were possible differences in distributions

There were no significant differences in the overall Net Promoter Scores based on orientation ($p = .53$). We did find three potentially significant differences for some of the pair-wise combinations (Ease 3, LTR 4, and LTR 9), but no apparent difference for the other 20 possible comparisons. These differences could be noise or a small effect that future research might establish, but the available distributional data do not indicate strong, consistent effects on rating behavior due to scale orientation. Figure 15.11 shows the distribution for the eleven-point LTR item along with top-box and top-two-box computations.

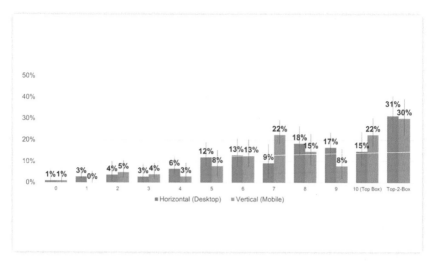

FIGURE 15.11: Response distributions of the LTR item for horizontal (desktop) and vertical (mobile) orientations (with 95% adjusted-Wald binary confidence intervals).

Device with orientation could be a confounding factor
The experimental design we used was an incomplete factorial design because only desktop-using respondents saw the horizontal orientation, and only mobile-using respondents saw the vertical orientation. The shortcoming of this design is that we can't differentiate the effects of device type from orientation. These are, however, the most common combinations used in online surveys, so it is important to know whether they promote significantly different rating behaviors.

Large effects were ruled out (but there still might be small effects)
Our sample size of 212, while not small, was not sufficiently large to produce precise enough measurements to justify practical acceptance of the null hypothesis (Lewis & Sauro, 2021, Jun 15). In other words, we can't definitively say there is no effect of orientation.

For example, even though the mean UX-Lite difference was small (1.5 points), the 95% confidence interval around that difference ranged from –3.9 to 7.0. Given this finding, a difference of 0 is plausible (therefore no statistically significant difference), but so is a difference as large as 7 points.

Considering these results and those from our literature review, we find no compelling evidence to support the hypothesis that there is a large difference in rating behavior due to scale orientation. It would, however, be premature to claim that there is no difference due to orientation. Our data suggest that if there is a real difference, it is probably relatively small, especially when comparing means.

CHAPTER SUMMARY

The focus of this chapter was on research studying various presentation effects on survey items—placing rating scales in grids as opposed to individual items, collecting frequency information with select-all-that-apply formats versus yes/no formats in grids or individually, question order effects (especially the order of general vs. specific items), and effects of scale orientation (horizontal vs. vertical).

Is it OK to present rating scale items in grids? ...Yes, as long as there aren't too many items in one grid. Much of the literature on rating scale grids is mixed regarding respondent preferences and measurement quality. The key findings are that respondents prefer grids as long as there aren't too many items in one grid and, across multiple studies comparing means collected in grids or individual items, the overall effect size is just under 1% with slightly higher means for items in grids.

Which is better—select-all-that-apply or yes/no questions? ...We generally recommend select-all-that-apply. There doesn't seem to be any difference in the frequency of selection from SATA and yes/no grids (our estimate of the effect size was just a tenth of a percent), and respondents greatly prefer SATA over yes/no grids. We recommend against asking a series of yes/no questions, for which the percentage of Yes responses is about 3% higher than SATA selections because there's no way to know which number is the "real" one. If the higher percentage of Yes responses is due to forcing a response to each item, then why is the percentage lower in yes/no grids? It's possible that forcing a response and having a long list of individual items lead people to just start clicking Yes to finish the survey.

Is it better to put general before specific questions? ...Yes, most of the time. We've estimated that general satisfaction ratings are about 2% higher after participants have responded to specific questions compared to before for most types of surveys, and about half a percent higher in UX research. Aside from measurement considerations, if there will be an open-ended component with the general rating, asking the general question first means that the open-ended text won't be influenced by the content of the specific questions. If planning to compare results with surveys in which the general question follows the specific questions, it's best to keep that constant.

Does it matter much if rating scales have a horizontal or vertical orientation? ...Not much. Our best estimate is that scores are about 2.1% higher for the vertical orientation. This effect size won't be statistically significant unless sample sizes are quite large, and even then, a difference this small will usually not be practically significant.

Table 15.4 summarizes the studies associated with the estimated effect sizes for the five scale manipulations discussed in this chapter.

Topic/Studies	n	Study Description
SATA v Y/N Series	260[a]	Selection frequencies for massv merchants/ seller market sites visited in past year
Horizontal v Vertical	2346[b]	Multiple studies in which scale orientation was manipulated
Question Order	16363[c]	Multiple studies in which a general satisfaction question is answered before or after a series of more specific items
Grids	2938[d]	Multiple studies in which respondents provided ratings as individual questions or in grids
SATA v Y/N Grid	201[e]	Selection frequencies for mass merchants/ seller market sites visited in past year

TABLE 15.4: Summary of effect size estimates for Chapter 15 presented in descending order of effect size. These unstandardized effect sizes are mean differences divided by the range of the scale. * = statistically significant. Respondents are from panels unless otherwise indicated. The sources for this table are:

a: Lewis & Sauro (2022, Jan 4), $n = 260$

b: Friedman & Friedman (1995), $n = 207$; Chrzan et al. (2012), $n = 1505$; Mockovak (2018), $n = 422$; Lewis & Sauro (2021, Nov 9), $n = 212$

c: Auh et al. (2003), $n = 191$; Van de Walle & Van Ryzin (2011), $n = 3592$; Kaplan et al. (2013), $n = 7510$; Lewis (2019b), $n = 1437$; Sauro (2019, Jan 9), $n = 3175$; Thau et al. (2020), $n = 458$

d: Chrzan et al. (2012), $n = 1505$; Mockovak (2018), $n = 422$; Sauro (2019, Mar 20), $n = 1011$

e: Lewis & Sauro (2022, Jan 4), $n = 201$

Scales	Effect Size	Takeaway	Design Notes
SATA, Y/N Series	3.1%	Slightly higher selection rate for Yes/No series of questions	Within Subjects, Greco-Latin counterbalancing
UX-Lite (5-pt), LTR (11-pt), Various (5-pt)	2.1%	Slightly higher for vertical	Within Subjects, Greco-Latin counterbalancing
LTR (11-pt), Sat (5-pt), Sat (7-pt), Sat (11-pt)	2.0%	General satisfaction ratings slightly higher after responding to specific items (UX-only effect is 0.5%)	Mixed between/within subjects
LTR (11-pt), SUS (101-pt), Various items (7- and 5-pt)	0.9%	Slightly higher means for items in grids	Between subjects
SATA, Y/N Grid	0.1%	Slightly higher selection rate for yes/no grid	Within Subjects, Greco-Latin counterbalancing

CHAPTER 16:
RESPONSE OPTION VISUAL FORMATS

This chapter is devoted to more presentation variations on rating scales, including adding color to scales, using face emojis or stars instead of numbers, and starting scales with negative numbers. We'll address the following questions:

- Is it a good idea to add colors to rating scales?
- How about using face emojis in place of numbers?
- What about stars instead of numbers?
- Is it better to start rating scales with negative numbers?
- Are sliders better than radio buttons?

ADDING COLOR TO RESPONSE OPTIONS

In Chapter 11, we reviewed the literature on the number of scale points. In general, more points provide more reliability and validity. But we did find some evidence that short scales are perceived as easier than long scales (when participants were forced to choose).

One alternative some survey designers use to help make longer multipoint scales easier is to break up them into colors. An example from an auto-dealership survey is shown in Figure 16.1.

FIGURE 16.1: Example of an eleven-point scale colored to correspond with NPS-style "net" scoring.

Figure 16.1 shows an eleven-point satisfaction item, but based on the colors, it's likely the raw responses get scored using the same "net" scoring scheme as the Net Promoter Score (NPS). Under this scheme, the top two boxes are considered satisfied (like promoters), the 7s and 8s are neutral, and anything 6 and below are dissatisfied (akin to detractors).

The colors used here also signal to the respondent which responses are considered good (green), which are bad (red), and which are somewhere in the middle (yellow). This may help respondents more easily respond to the scale, but what does it do to their responses?

Research on Scale Colors

Some online articles recommend against using colored scales. For example, Joe Hopper (2019, Apr 24) recommends not coloring scales, such as the item used in the NPS, because it will bias the respondents (but he does not provide data to support his recommendation). An Insightrix article (Brownell, 2022, Jul 25) suggests respondents may perceive colored scales as severe, inducing them to give more moderate ratings (without providing any data to support the claim).

In academic literature, a study by Tourangeau et al. (2009) offers some guidance. The authors argue that respondents use a number of heuristics (mental shortcuts) when responding to scales. To see how changing the color and hue of colors (dark to light) affects responses, they conducted two experiments.

The authors randomly assigned around 2,500 U.S.-based online panel participants to one of eight scale conditions that varied in color, hue, labels, and numbers. Two of the conditions are shown in Figure 16.2. This setup allowed the authors to investigate interaction effects between color and other scale factors. Participants answered questions about general attitudes and lifestyles using items with favor/oppose and frequency label anchors.

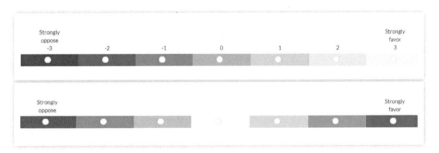

FIGURE 16.2: Adaptations of color scale variations used in Tourangeau et al. (2009), recreated with MUiQ.

They found the shading of the response options had a small but statistically significant effect. When the endpoints of the scale were shaded in different hues, the responses tended to shift toward the high end of the scale (usually between .1 and .2 points on a seven-point scale, an effect size of about 2.5% of the range of the scale).

Interestingly, they found that this small effect disappeared when the points were fully labeled, and it was generally only detectable when the scores were aggregated across items (the differences were not statistically significant at the individual item level). They found no difference in response times from changes in hue and color. In short, they found a small effect, but it was obfuscated by the larger effects of labeling. Combining data from all their data indicated a slight tendency for higher means when response options are color-coded (0.4% of the range of the scale).

To better understand how color may affect the commonly used eleven-point Likelihood-to-Recommend (LTR) and satisfaction scales, we conducted two of our own studies (Sauro, 2019, Oct 23).

Study Overview on Colors

We conducted two studies in September 2019 using online U.S.-based panel participants. In Study 1, 229 participants rated their intention to recommend using the eleven-point LTR item and their satisfaction using an eleven-point satisfaction item for a selected list of nine retailers and airlines they reported having recently purchased from (Amazon, Target, Walmart, Home Depot, Lowes, United Airlines, Southwest, Delta, IKEA).

Participants were randomly assigned to one of three scale variants as shown in Figure 16.3. Eighty responded to the standard no-color variant (16.3a); 70 to a gradient version (16.3b), and 79 to a three-color version (16.3c).

FIGURE 16.3A: A standard no-color variant of the LTR item.

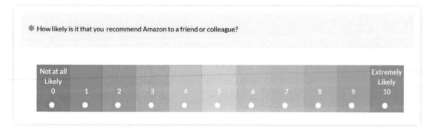

FIGURE 16.3B: A gradient variant of the LTR item.

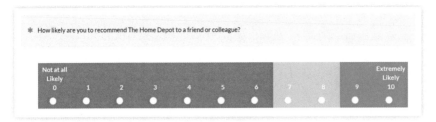

FIGURE 16.3C: A three-color variant of the LTR item.

In Study 2, 184 participants were presented with two variants of the same eleven-point scales used in Study 1 — **the three-color and no-color versions**. As in Study 1, participants reflected on their attitude toward a subset of the brands they had purchased from (Target, Lowes, Home Depot, and IKEA).

Because Study 2 was a within-subjects study, participants saw both versions of the LTR item and both versions of the satisfaction item in the same study. These questions were part of a larger survey, and the two variants were randomized to be shown either at the beginning of the survey or at the end.

SUMMARY AND TAKEAWAYS

Across two studies with 413 participants manipulating the color of the eleven-point response scale, we found the following:

Color increases scores modestly

Adding color to an eleven-point scale had a small effect in both studies, but the differences were rarely statistically significant. This modest difference was surprising given the visually salient difference of adding color. Even in our within-subjects study that controlled for variation between people, differences in scores were between 1% and 2% of the scale range.

Figure 16.4 shows the differences between brands for the LTR item. The difference (using a paired t-test) was statistically significant for Target ($p = .04$) and Home Depot ($p < .01$).

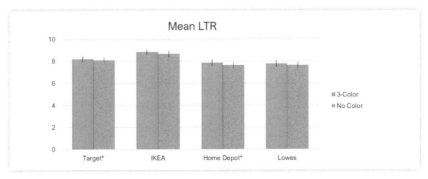

FIGURE 16.4: Differences in mean LTR scores between the three-color and no-color versions. Target and Home Depot differences were statistically significant ($p < .05$).

Figure 16.5 shows the differences between brands for the eleven-point satisfaction item. Again, the three-color version had slightly higher means (between 1% and 2%). The difference (using a paired *t*-test) was statistically significant only for Target (*p* = .03).

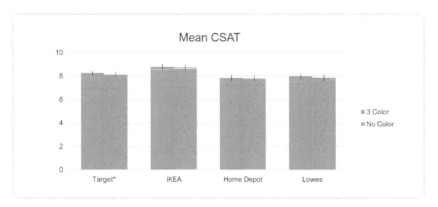

FIGURE 16.5: Differences in mean satisfaction scores between the three-color and no-color versions. The Target differences were statistically significant (*p* < .05).

The largest differences were observed when aggregating across people and brands, but even then, the differences were still modest, at around 3%. We saw larger differences between showing or not showing the neutral label (see Chapter 12), consistent with the research by Tourangeau et al. (2009) that found that labeling had a larger effect than colors.

The difference is due to a negative-to-positive shift
To better understand what is causing the shift in mean scores when colors are used, we looked at the number of participants who changed categories when the three-color scale was used for the LTR item.

In total, we had 518 responses from 184 participants across the four brands and two scale variants. Table 16.1 shows that there is shifting between all categories (we'd expect some movement just from chance), but the largest movement is from negative to positive: detractors to passives (17) and from passives to promoters (15). This is offset with around half as many moving from passive to detractor, but it's still enough to see a modest upward shift in scores. A similar pattern was seen with the satisfaction scale.

From	To	NPS Number	NPS %	CSAT Number	CSAT %
Detractor	Passive	17	3.3%	13	2.5%
Passive	Promoter	15	2.9%	13	2.5%
Promoter	Passive	8	1.5%	6	1.2%
Passive	Detractor	9	1.7%	3	0.6%

TABLE 16.1: Shift of the 518 responses across four brands from no-color to the three-color version. In general, there was a slight shift to more positive responses, somewhat offset by some shifts to more negative responses.

Colors may act as a heuristic.
Some earlier research suggests that participants look for clues on how to respond to scales (e.g., numbers, labels, and the presentation order) and color acts as another heuristic (a mental shortcut) on what points mean (e.g., red is bad, green is good).

The gradient and three-color variations had similar patterns.
In study 1, we tested two color variations (the three-color and gradient) and found that both generated similar results and had slightly higher means than the no-color group. This suggests the gradient of color, which doesn't necessarily reveal the net-scoring scheme, acts similarly.

USING FACE EMOJIS

Instead of labels and numbers, some researchers use facial expressions to convey sentiments. After all, human facial expressions are, for the most part, universally understood (Ekman, 1970). Using facial expressions might remove the need for translation, assuming different cultures interpret the faces similarly (Gao & VanderLaan, 2020).

What Are Face Emoji Scales?
Emojis are simple representations of facial expressions, and we expect people who answer questionnaires to understand emotions represented by faces, simple as they are (Jaeger et al., 2018).

Figures 16.6 and 16.7 show examples of five-option numeric and non-numeric face emoji versions of the UMUX-Lite.

FIGURE 16.6: Example of a linear numeric version of the UMUX-Lite (created with MUiQ).

FIGURE 16.7: Example of a face emoji scale version of the UMUX-Lite with expressions created through manipulations of the mouth and eyes (created with MUiQ).

Literature on Face Emojis

There has been quite a bit of research conducted with face emoji scales, especially in consumer research. For example, the K-State emoji scale (seven response options arranged from negative-to-positive valence) has been used to obtain emotional responses to products, especially with children (Deubler et al., 2019).

Alismail and Zhang (2018) conducted a qualitative study of reactions to emoji scales similar to the one shown in Figure 16.7. Participants indicated that emoji scales were easy to understand and engaging, but emojis were sometimes prone to multiple interpretations, suggesting they were not as universally understood as human facial expressions.

It isn't clear from the existing research whether it would be advantageous for UX researchers to use face emojis for response options in agreement scales (Figure 16.7) rather than the standard numbering scheme (Figure 16.6). To learn more, we (Lewis & Sauro, 2020, Sep 9) ran an experiment to see whether these format differences affected measurements made with a short standardized UX questionnaire, the UMUX-Lite.

Face Emojis vs. Numbers Experiment

In August 2020, 240 U.S.-based panel participants rated a variety of streaming entertainment services: Netflix, AT&T TV Now, Amazon Prime Video, Hulu, YouTube TV, or Disney+.

The study used a Greco-Latin square design with three independent variables:

- Item Format (linear numeric, face emojis—see Figures 16.6 and 16.7)

- Rating Context (rating of most recent experience with the service; rating of the overall experience with the service)

- Order of Presentation (numeric/recent then emojis/overall; numeric/overall then emojis/recent; emojis/recent then numeric/overall; emojis/overall then numeric/recent)

Participants were randomly assigned to one of the four orders formed by the crossing of Item Format, Rating Context, and Order of Presentation. Across the experiment, this controls for the "nuisance" variables of Rating Context and Order of Presentation.

STUDY SUMMARY AND TAKEAWAYS

The emoji versus number study found:

There were no significant differences in means or distributions

In this experiment, we found no significant differences or interactions between mean UMUX-Lite ratings collected with standard linear numeric scales and face emoji scales.

We also saw no significant differences in the distributions of responses to the different versions of the Ease and Usefulness items, even though we presented the face emojis without numbers. Figure 16.8 shows the distribution of the ease item for numbers and emojis.

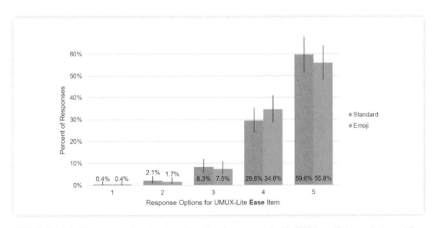

FIGURE 16.8: Response distributions for the Ease item (with 90% confidence intervals).

Emojis seem practically interchangeable with numbers

These results support the use of either format, standard or emoji, in UX research. Because there doesn't appear to be any particular advantage in using face emoji scales, UX researchers should feel comfortable with standard linear numeric rating scales.

USING STARS INSTEAD OF NUMBERS

Another alternative to numbers is star ratings. Star rating systems are quite prevalent (rating a purchase on Amazon.com, a dining experience on Yelp, or a mobile app in the App or Play Store). Does the familiarity of stars offer a better rating system than traditional numbered scales?

What Are Star Scales?

Figures 16.9 and 16.10 show examples of numeric- and star-scale versions of the UMUX-Lite (both types of scales have five response options).

FIGURE 16.9: Example of a linear numeric version of the UMUX-Lite (created with MUiQ).

FIGURE 16.10: Example of a star-scale version of the UMUX-Lite (created with MUiQ).

Star scales can have endpoints labeled or bare and, if the context is clear (as it is on Amazon and movie rating sites), often appear without any accompanying statement (e.g., "Please rate your satisfaction with this product"). People generally understand that a rating with more stars reflects a more positive sentiment or attitude.

Other than some substantial literature on using star ratings in recommender systems ("Recommender system," n.d.), there is little available about their measurement properties—and, as far as we know, no published comparison with concurrently collected linear numeric data (Figure 16.9).

Stars vs. Numbers Experiment

Between May and June 2020, 155 participants from a U.S.-based panel were asked to rate their experience with streaming entertainment services such as Netflix, HBO Now, Amazon Prime Video, Hulu, and Disney+ (Lewis & Sauro, 2020, Jul 22).

The study used a Greco-Latin square design with three independent variables:

- Item Format (linear numeric, stars—see Figures 16.9 and 16.10)

- Rating Context (rating of most recent experience with the service; rating of the overall experience with the service)

- Order of Presentation (numeric/recent then stars/overall; numeric/overall then stars/recent; stars/recent then numeric/overall; stars/overall then numeric/recent)

Participants were randomly assigned to one of the four orders formed by the crossing of Item Format, Rating Context, and Order of Presentation. Across the experiment, this controls for the "nuisance" variables of Rating Context and Order of Presentation.

STUDY SUMMARY AND TAKEAWAYS

The stars versus number study found:

Small differences in means

We found a small but statistically significant difference of 1.3 points in mean UMUX-Lite scores between the overall ratings of stars and numbers ($F(1, 151) = 4.7, p = .03$), with star means slightly higher than numbers (Figure 16.11).

There is no external benchmark for determining which of the means is "correct," but a 95% confidence interval around the difference shows that all plausible differences are relatively small (no more than 2.6 points) given the 101-point range of the UMUX-Lite.

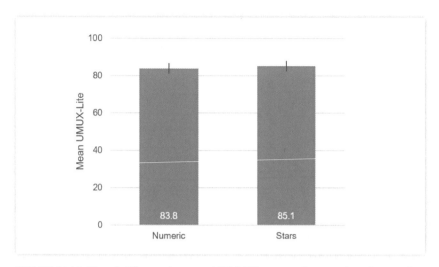

FIGURE 16.11: Overall difference between UMUX-Lite means for numeric and star scales.

Significant order effect

We also found a significant interaction effect between item format and presentation order. Star means were higher when stars were presented after numbers but not when they were presented before numbers ($F_{(1, 151)} = 5.1, p = .025$).

As shown in Figure 16.12, the means for the numeric scales were very close (a difference of about 1.5 points) despite changing presentation order. For the star scales, however, there was a greater difference (about 4.5 points). The larger mean for star scales happened when stars were presented after numeric scales. All other main effects and interactions were not statistically significant.

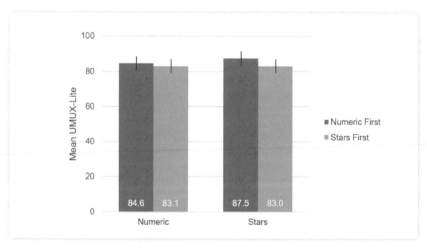

FIGURE 16.12: Item format (numeric vs. stars) by presentation order (numeric first or stars first) interaction.

Stars appear to be roughly equivalent to numbers

The significant interaction between item format and presentation order indicated a potential issue with star scales. Star means were higher when stars were presented after numbers but not when they were presented before numbers.

Taken together, these results support the use of either format in UX research, but practitioners should avoid mixing them in the same study.

USING NEGATIVE NUMBERS IN RATING SCALES

One of the most common formats to collect attitudes is the linear numeric scale with endpoint labels and numbered response options starting with 1 on the left and 5 on the right. This format is popular for standardized UX questionnaires, including the System Usability Scale (SUS), the SUPR-Q, and the UX-Lite (Appendix B).

A slightly less common approach is to assign the center response option as 0, with negative numbers on the left and positive numbers to the right. There is no standard name for this format, so we refer to it as a negative-to-positive (Neg2Pos) scale. Figures 16.13 and 16.14 show examples of the five-option standard linear numeric and Neg2Pos versions of the UMUX-Lite.

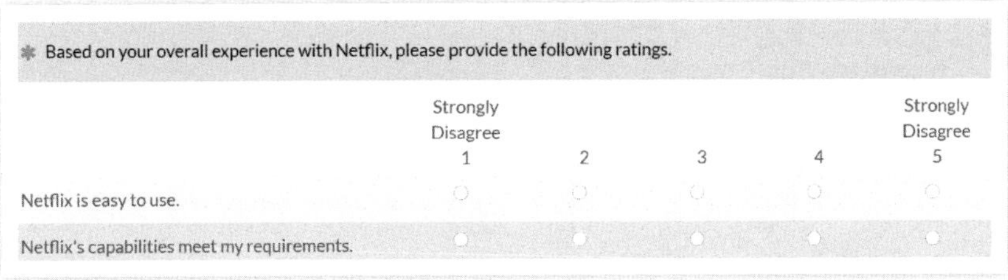

FIGURE 16.13: Example of a standard linear numeric version of the UMUX-Lite (created with MUiQ).

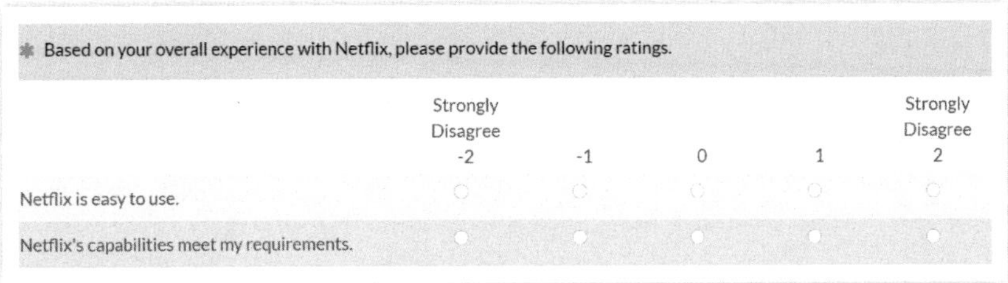

FIGURE 16.14: Example of the UMUX-Lite using a five-point Neg2Pos scale (created with MUiQ).

Published Literature on Neg2Pos Scales

The literature comparing Neg2Pos scales with standard linear numeric scales is sparse and mixed. In a recent review of item formats, DeCastellarnau (2018) cited just two relevant research papers: one reported differences in response distributions between standard and Neg2Pos scales, and the other reported no differences.

In the first paper cited (Schwarz et al., 1991), respondents in face-to-face interviews were asked to rate how successful they had been in life so far, using an eleven-point scale represented as a ladder with "not at all successful" at the bottom and "extremely successful" at the top (Figure 16.15). Each scale step also had a number assigned to it, with half of the 1,032 respondents seeing 0 to 10 and the other half seeing –5 to +5. The response distributions were significantly different; 34% selected from the bottom half of the ladder with the first version (0 to 5), but only 13% chose from the bottom half of the ladder with the second version (–5 to 0). This led to a significant difference in means, with 6.4 for the first version and 7.3 for the second. (If converted to 0–100-point scales, that would be a mean difference of 9 points.)

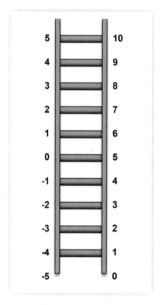

FIGURE 16.15: MacArthur ladder scale showing standard and Neg2Pos response options.

In the second paper cited by DeCastellarnau, Reips (2000) studied various context effects in web surveys (n = 292). Respondents provided ratings to the question, "Overall, how satisfied are you with the quality of your connection to the Internet?" (p. 100). None of the experimental manipulations—scale type, reading directionality, cursor entry position, question order, or type of numerical labeling—had significant effects on the resulting measurements.

These experiments had widely different outcomes, but they also had widely different contexts. In Schwarz et al. (1991), respondents chose their response option in a face-to-face setting where the question had to do with their feelings of success in life. In Reips (2000), respondents completed a short web survey about satisfaction with their Internet connection. It's plausible that in the first context, respondents were reluctant to assign their life success a negative number, and in the second context, respondents were perfectly willing to assign negative numbers to their satisfaction with their Internet connection.

Based on this limited amount of research, we would expect UX ratings with both numeric formats to produce similar results. To check, we (Lewis & Sauro, 2020, Sep 16) experimented to see whether these format differences affected measurements made with a short standardized UX questionnaire, the UMUX-Lite.

Standard Versus Neg2Pos Numeric Scales Experiment

In August 2020, 256 participants U.S.-based panel participants rated their experience on one of several popular streaming services: Netflix, AT&T TV Now, Amazon Prime Video, Hulu, YouTube TV, or Disney+.

The study used a Greco-Latin square design with three independent variables:

- Item Format (standard numeric, Neg2Pos — see Figures 16.13 and 16.14)

- Rating Context (rating of most recent experience with the service; rating of the overall experience with the service)

- Order of Presentation (standard/recent then Neg2Pos/overall; standard/overall then Neg2Pos/recent; Neg2Pos/recent then standard/overall; Neg2Pos/overall then standard/recent)

Participants were randomly assigned to one of the four orders formed by the crossing of Item Format, Rating Context, and Order of Presentation. Across the experiment, this controls for the "nuisance" variables of Rating Context and Order of Presentation.

STUDY SUMMARY AND TAKEAWAYS

The study varying negative numbers with positive numbers found:

No differences in means

In this experiment, we found no significant differences or interactions between mean UMUX-Lite ratings collected with standard linear numeric scales (1 to 5) and Neg2Pos (−2 to +2) scales.

The overall observed difference (0.7) was consistent with the differences we found in similar experiments comparing linear numeric with slider scales (0.6), star scales (1.3), and face emoji scales (0.5), all discussed in this chapter. This difference is quite small relative to the full range of the UMUX-Lite (0 to 100 points).

No distribution differences

There were also no significant differences detected in the response's distributions. Figure 16.16 shows the response distributions for the Usefulness item.

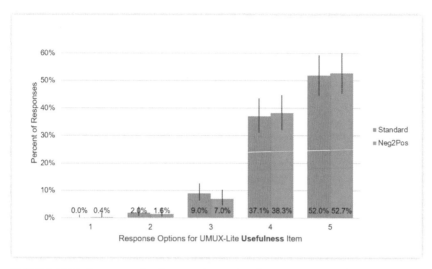

FIGURE 16.16: Response distributions for the Usefulness item (with 90% confidence intervals).

USING SLIDERS INSTEAD OF RADIO BUTTONS

Survey platforms don't just make the collection of surveys quicker, they also allow for more ways of collecting data, including real-time logic branching and different visual displays such as slider scales.

Figures 16.17 and 16.18 show examples of a numeric and a slider version of the UMUX-Lite.

FIGURE 16.17: Example of a numeric version of the UMUX-Lite (created with MUiQ).

FIGURE 16.18: Example of a slider version of the UMUX-Lite (created with MUiQ).

Due to their design, sliders require more physical space than numeric scales. Within the category of slider scales, there are different formats (DeCastellarnau, 2018). For example, some sliders display a limited number of response options (e.g., five), so the only difference with a standard numeric scale is the user interface used to select the response option (click for numeric; drag-and-drop for slider). More often, sliders cover a wide range of response options (e.g., as shown in Figure 16.18, from 0 to 100). Some sliders require dragging the slider control to the desired position with a mouse, touchscreen, or other pointing device—an interface design that is difficult for some users (e.g., Chyung et al., 2018).

Other slider designs allow, in addition to sliding, simply clicking on the desired position and then fine tuning as required with any combination of dragging and clicking (which is the case for sliders in MUiQ). These types of sliders are also known as visual analog scales (VAS; Lewis & Erdinç, 2017) due to their similarity to old pencil-and-paper VAS, on which users marked a position on a line to indicate the magnitude of an attitude or sentiment, typically a 10 cm line with the marked position measured by hand to produce a 0–100 rating.

Published Literature on Sliders

As is usually the case when discussing scale formats, the literature is inconsistent regarding the advantages of sliders over numeric scales. Some researchers favor sliders based on hypothesized advantages in respondent engagement and psychometrics (Medallia, n.d.), but data-based findings are mixed. For example:

SLIDERS CAN BE MORE SENSITIVE

Joyce et al. (1975) found the VAS to be more sensitive than a four-point numeric pain scale. Sauro and Dumas (2009) found the SMEQ (Subjective Mental Effort Questionnaire), a 150-point VAS-like scale, was slightly more sensitive than the seven-point Single Ease Question (SEQ).

SLIDERS TAKE LONGER

Several researchers have reported better results for numeric scales than VAS regarding completion time (Couper et al., 2006; Rausch & Zehetleitner, 2014), completion rates (Couper et al., 2006; Davey et al., 2007), and respondent preference (van Laerhoven et al., 2004; van Schaik & Ling, 2007).

SOME PEOPLE HAVE DIFFICULTY USING SLIDERS

Respondents, especially in clinical settings, sometimes have more trouble physically completing VAS than numeric scales (Bolognese et al., 2003; Briggs & Closs, 1999; Jensen et al., 1986).

NONRESPONSE RATES ARE HIGHER WITH SLIDERS

Toepoel and Funke (2018) found more nonresponses with sliders than radio buttons and reported poorer performance with slider bars that required dragging and dropping than with more VAS-like sliders.

SLIDERS AND NUMERIC SCALES HAVE COMPARABLE PSYCHOMETRIC PROPERTIES

Across several studies comparing VAS with numeric scales having from 4 to 20 response options, there was no significant or practical difference in psychometric properties between the two (Bolognese et al., 2003; Couper et al., 2006; Davey et al., 2007; Larroy, 2002; Lee et al., 2009; Lewis & Erdinç, 2017; Rausch & Zehetleitner, 2014; van Laerhoven et al., 2004; van Schaik & Ling, 2007).

Sensitivity Advantage of Sliders

Sauro and Dumas (2009) published a CHI paper that compared the popular SEQ with a specific type of visual analog/slider scale, the Subjective Mental Effort Questionnaire (SMEQ). Twenty-six participants attempted five tasks on two enterprise expense reporting applications. Each task was attempted three times on both systems (in counterbalanced order using a Greco-Latin design). Assessment of the two applications with the System Usability Scale (SUS) indicated a significant difference in their overall perceived usability (80 vs. 52).

Figure 16.19 shows the version of the SMEQ used in this experiment. Unlike typical sliders, which usually measure responses from 0 to 100, the SMEQ has a range from 0 to 150 and nine labels between the endpoints to guide the placement of the slider. The placement of these labels is not arbitrary and was a major focus of the research that developed the SMEQ (Zijlstra & van Doorn, 1985).

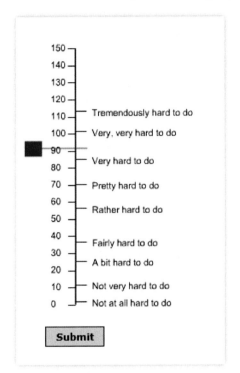

FIGURE 16.19: A digital version of the Subjective Mental Effort Questionnaire (SMEQ).

For the full sample of 26 users, after-task ratings were statistically significant on four out of five tasks for both the SEQ and the SMEQ.

To determine whether the SMEQ would be able to differentiate more than the SEQ at smaller sample sizes (i.e., if it's more sensitive), we conducted a Monte-Carlo resampling exercise.

We took a thousand random samples with replacement at sample sizes of 3, 5, 8, 10, 12, 15, 17, 19, and 20, and compared the means for the two products using a paired t-test. We counted the number of means that could differentiate between expense reporting applications at $p < .05$. The more sensitive a questionnaire type is, the more readily it can detect significant differences between products with smaller sample sizes (Figure 16.20).

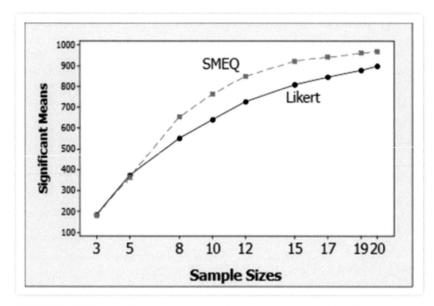

FIGURE 16.20: Monte-Carlo resampling results showing the sensitivity of three rating methods at various sample sizes (from Sauro & Dumas, 2009). The Likert format was the SEQ.

Starting with a sample size of 8, the SMEQ was more sensitive, better differentiating between the apps, identifying more samples than the SEQ as statistically significant (out of a thousand), with the advantage ranging from 8–14% depending on the sample size.

However, the SMEQ also had different (and calibrated) labels (Figure 16.19) and a range of 0 to 150, so this advantage might not generalize to standard sliders with just endpoint labeling and a range from 0 to 100. We needed more data.

Sliders vs. Numbers Experiment

We (Lewis & Sauro, 2020, Jul 15; Sauro & Lewis, 2020, Nov 10) conducted a two-part study between May and June 2020 in which 180 U.S.-based panel participants used two versions of the UX-Lite to rate their experience with a streaming entertainment service.

Part 1 of the study used a Greco-Latin square design with three independent variables:

- Item Format (linear numeric; VAS slider—see Figures 16.17 and 16.18)

- Rating Context (rating of most recent experience with the service; rating of the overall experience with the service)

- Order of Presentation (numeric/recent then slider/overall; numeric/overall then slider/recent; slider/recent then numeric/overall; slider/overall then numeric/recent)

Participants were randomly assigned to one of the four orders formed by the crossing of Item Format, Rating Context, and Order of Presentation. Across the experiment, this controls for the "nuisance" variables of Rating Context and Order of Presentation.

In Part 2 of the study, we examined the ability of sliders versus numbers to differentiate between different streaming services at various subsample sizes.

We performed a resampling exercise similar to the one we did with the SMEQ to see if standard sliders detected the statistical differences between Netflix and the other brands at smaller sample sizes. To work with larger sample sizes, we split all the data we had between Netflix (n = 73) and Not Netflix (n = 107) services, allowing exploration of sample sizes up to n = 35 (less than half the smaller sample to avoid depletion artifacts). The Not Netflix sample included Hulu and Amazon Prime data, plus smaller sets of data collected for Disney+ and HBO Now. For the full sets of data, the means for Not Netflix were 80.5 for numeric scales and 81.4 for sliders (a sliders–numeric difference of .09), both significantly different from the Netflix ratings of 88.9 for numeric scales and 89.2 for sliders (a sliders–numeric difference of .03).

STUDY SUMMARY AND TAKEAWAYS

The slider versus number study found:

There were no significant differences in means between sliders and numbers
We found almost identical overall mean scores for numeric (83.9) and sliders (84.5) showing no statistically significant difference in aggregate (a difference of .06).

Figure 16.21 shows the resulting UMUX-Lite scores for all three services and both item formats. Similar to the aggregate mean differences, there were no statistically significant differences between the slider and number formats at the full sample sizes within each brand. Netflix (n = 73) received significantly higher ratings than Hulu (n = 40) and Amazon Prime (n = 38).

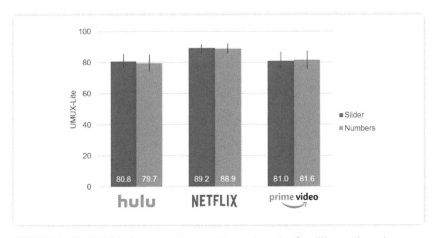

FIGURE 16.21: UMUX-Lite scores by entertainment service for sliders and numbers.

Sliders were more sensitive at larger sample sizes

We found that standard sliders did have a moderate sensitivity advantage, corroborating our earlier findings with the 2009 SMEQ study. The differences were detectable once the sample sizes were ten or more (presumably, the point at which the analyses had enough power to start discriminating between the services). At n = 10, the advantage was about 2%, increasing to about 8% at the maximum n for resampling.

Figure 16.22 shows the sensitivity advantage for sliders versus numbers when comparing Netflix to Hulu+ Prime Video.

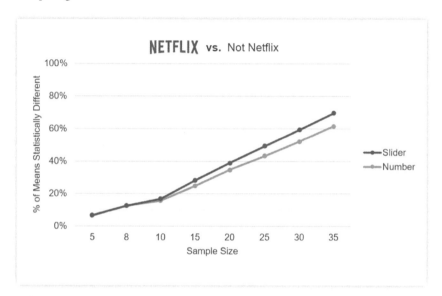

FIGURE 16.22: Percent of ten thousand differences that were statistically significant (*p* <.05) between Netflix and Not Netflix at sample sizes between 5 and 35.

SLIDERS ON MOBILE

Our previous research focused on comparing sliders with five-point numeric rating scales presented on desktop displays. Estimates of the percentage of respondents who use mobile devices to complete surveys are as high as 57% (Toepoel & Funke, 2018), so it is important to understand how differences in the display and manipulation of scales affect rating behavior.

In this section, we describe research in which respondents used sliders and numeric scales to complete a short survey on either a desktop or mobile device.

Slider Versus Numeric Mobile Study

We (Lewis & Sauro, 2021, Nov 30, Dec 14) conducted an experiment in which 212 respondents (U.S. panel agency, late January 2021) used radio buttons and sliders to rate online shopping websites (Amazon, Walmart, Target, Walgreens, CVS, Wayfair) and seller marketplaces (Craigslist, eBay, Etsy, Facebook Marketplace) with the UX-Lite (two five-point items) and a single eleven-point LTR item.About half (109) of the respondents completed the survey on a desktop computer, and the other half (103) used a mobile device. All respondents chose ratings using both numeric scales and sliders. The order of presentation and assignment of scale type to website type was randomized in accordance with a Greco-Latin experimental design.

DESIGN OF THE NUMERIC AND SLIDER SCALES

Figures 16.23 and 16.24 show numeric and slider examples of the five-point UX-Lite and eleven-point LTR on a desktop web browser. Figures 16.25 and 16.26 show how these scales appeared on mobile devices.

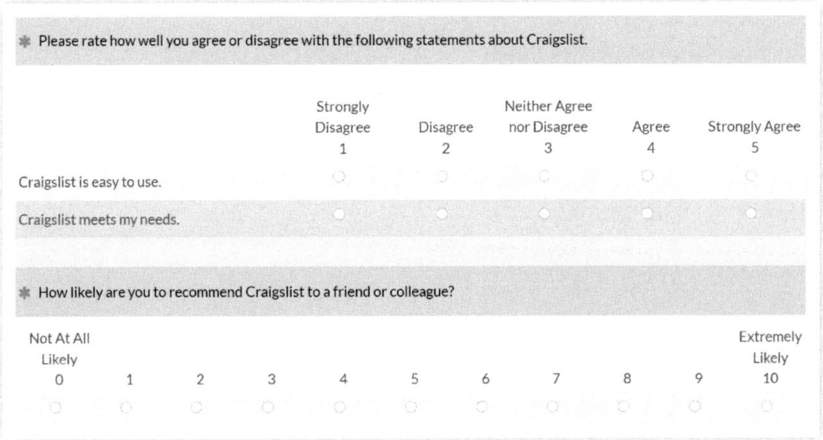

FIGURE 16.23: Example of numeric versions of the UX-Lite and LTR on a desktop web browser (created with MUiQ).

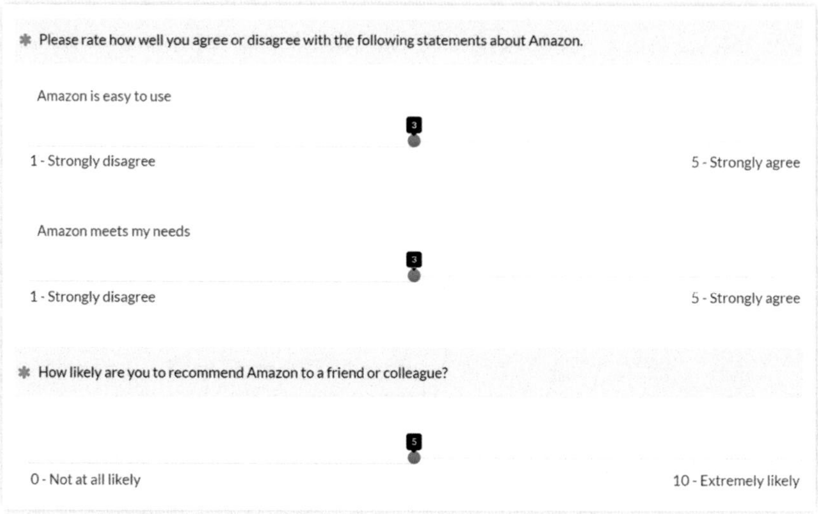

FIGURE 16.24: Example of slider versions of the UX-Lite and LTR on a desktop web browser (created with MUiQ).

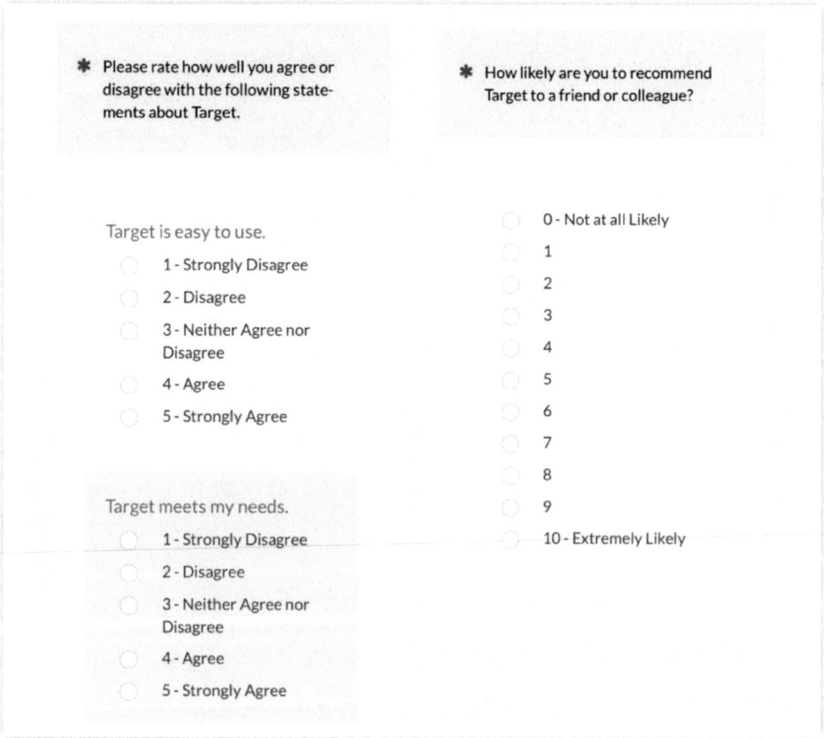

FIGURE 16.25: Example of numeric versions of the UX-Lite and LTR on a mobile screen (created with MUiQ).

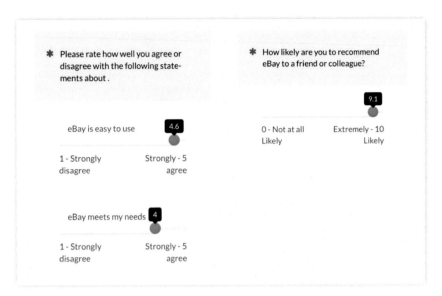

FIGURE 16.26: Example of slider versions of the UX-Lite and LTR on a mobile screen (created with MUiQ).

It isn't possible to test every potential variant of rating scales in a single experiment. For the current experiment, we explored variations in orientation, screen real estate, scale formats (radio buttons vs. sliders), and scale lengths (1–5 and 0–10) across two device formats (desktop and mobile). The slider sensitivity was 0.1, with the selected value appearing in a tooltip as shown in Figures 16.24 and 16.26. The slider's initial position was in the center of the scale, but it had no value until the user manipulated it.

SLIDER STUDY SUMMARY AND TAKEAWAYS

The main takeaway from the slider on mobile versus desktop experiment is that there do not appear to be large differences in rating behaviors for radio button numeric scales versus sliders for either five- or eleven-point scales, nor does the desktop versus mobile variable have a large impact.

There were no significant differences in means

Despite the different form factors between sliders and radio buttons, we found no statistical differences in mean scores when using either the two five-point rating scale items in the UX-Lite or the eleven-point LTR. There were no significant main effects or interactions, with observed differences of less than two points on the UX-Lite's 0–100-point scale (after converting from five points) and less than a tenth of a point on the LTR's 0–10-point scale. Our results were consistent with those reported by Funke et al., (2011), who, in a fully crossed experimental design with horizontal and vertical numeric scales and sliders, found no significant effects of orientation.

It's possible (but not proven) there were small effects on response distributions

Figures 16.27 and 16.28 show the distributions for the UX-Lite Ease item and the LTR item. None of the top-box or top-two-box analyses of UX-Lite response distributions as a function of scale format were statistically significant, but two approached significance (top box for the Ease item and top-two-box for the Usefulness item). Analysis of the LTR response distributions for the NPS categories of Detractors, Passives, and Promoters found no significant differences (*p-values ranged from .25 to .82*).

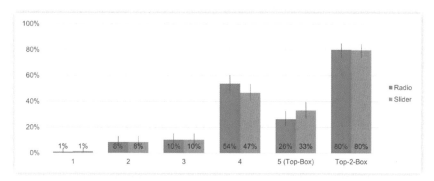

FIGURE 16.27: Distributions for UX-Lite Ease item for numeric and slider formats.

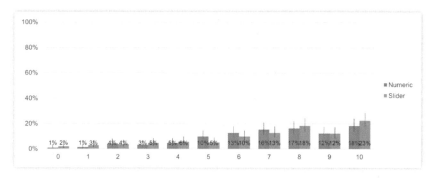

FIGURE 16.28: Distributions for the LTR item for numeric and slider formats.

The main takeaway from these results is that, for these item designs, thewot appear to be great differences in rating behaviors for radio button numeric scales versus sliders or desktop versus mobile variables. If the differences were large, our experiment would have been powerful enough to detect them. On the other hand, it is too early to claim that the differences, if they exist, are so small as to have no practical significance, especially for researchers interested in the results of top-box or top-two-box scoring.

Sliders took 37% longer to complete
Respondents were faster with radio button numeric scales than with sliders, and they were faster on desktops than on mobile devices. It took respondents about **37% longer** to complete ratings with the sliders than with the radio buttons, and it took **18% longer** to complete ratings on mobile devices than on desktop computers (both differences were statistically significant).

Radio buttons were preferred two to one
Regardless of device, respondents overwhelmingly preferred the radio button numeric scales to the sliders, primarily citing differences in their ease of use.

The bottom line is that there is little to gain by using sliders to collect ratings in online surveys but much to lose concerning the respondent experience due to increased completion time and difficulty of use relative to radio button numeric scales.

On the other hand, careful design of sliders to avoid their current pain points might (or might not) increase their acceptability to a larger proportion of respondents. That will be a topic for future research.

Study limitations
One study can't cover all aspects of this topic. We used only two instances of a five-point scale, the UX-Lite's two items, and the eleven-point LTR item. The study sample size was large enough ($n = 212$) to have the power to detect medium to large differences, but there may be small, real differences due to scale format or device. It is not, however, plausible that these manipulations have large effects. On the other hand, our analyses of completion times and user preference found large and statistically significant differences favoring the use of radio buttons over sliders.

Click Testing: A Promising Alternative to Sliders
We have been experimenting with tracking the precise location of clicks as a promising alternative to sliders. For example, Figure 16.29 shows an image of a SMEQ scale on which a participant has clicked the desired rating (between 60 and 70). The MUiQ test platform records the location of the click, which can then be converted into the appropriate score to a high level of precision.

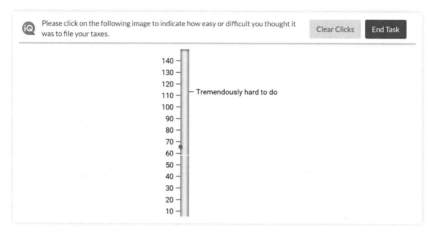

FIGURE 16.29: Example of click location on a SMEQ scale (created in MUiQ).

With this approach, scales can be represented in many ways without complex coding. From the user's perspective, relative to slider use, there is no need to grab and drag a slider to the desired location—just click. Our initial analyses of this method (Sauro & Lewis, 2023, Dec 19) indicate that, like sliders, it might lead to more sensitive measurement (e.g., lower standard deviation) than a multipoint item like the SEQ, consistent with the original research on this topic by Sauro and Dumas (2009). We have not directly compared sliders with the click method, but this is on our research list.

CHAPTER SUMMARY

The focus of this chapter was research on presentation variations of rating scales, including adding color to rating scales, using face emojis or stars instead of numbers, using scales that start with negative numbers, and using sliders in place of radio buttons.

Is it a good idea to add colors to rating scales? … We generally recommend against it. We estimate that adding color to rating scales raises means by about 1%, so adding colors doesn't seem to have much effect on the resulting measurements. Even so, adding colors to rating scales makes their preparation more complicated and can look like an attempt to manipulate respondent rating behavior.

How about using face emojis in place of numbers? …It doesn't seem to make much difference. We estimate that using face emojis in place of numbers affected means by less than one percent. Researchers who want to use emojis can certainly do so, but there seems to be no particular advantage in doing so and this makes preparation of the rating scales more difficult.

What about stars instead of numbers? …You can use stars, but don't mix them with numbers. We found an interesting interaction in our study of stars versus numbers. When stars were presented first, there was virtually no difference in mean ratings, but when stars were presented second, the means were inflated. The take-away here is the same as the use of color or emojis in scales—you can do it, but there doesn't seem to be any advantage to doing so. Researchers should be particularly cautious using stars unless they can do so throughout the entire survey.

Is it better to start rating scales with negative numbers? …You can, but it doesn't affect measurements. We estimate that starting scales with negative numbers slightly raises the resulting means, but by less than one percent.

Are sliders better than radio buttons? …In some ways, but not enough to over-come their issues. The main advantage of sliders is they provide more response options than radio button scales, which increases their sensitivity. On the other hand, our estimate of the difference in means for these methods is less than 1%, so in most cases, the additional screen space required for sliders and the difficulty some respondents have in physically manipulating slider controls argues against their routine use in surveys.

Table 16.2 summarizes the studies associated with the estimated effect sizes for the five scale manipulations discussed in this chapter.

Topic/Studies	n	Study Description	Scales	Effect Size	Takeaway	Design Notes
Stars	155[a]	Ratings of streaming entertainment services	UX-Lite (5-pt)	1.3%	Slightly higher means for stars	Within Subjects, Greco-Latin counterbalancing
Color	5717[b]	Multiple studies with constant or varied rating scale coloring	LTR (11-pt), Various (7-pt)	1.0%	Slightly higher means for scales with color	Mixed between/within subjects
Sliders	392[c]	Ratings of various websites across two studies	UX-Lite (5-pt), LTR (11-pt)	0.8%	Slightly higher means for sliders relative to radio buttons	Within Subjects, Greco-Latin counterbalancing
Negative Numbers	256[d]	Ratings of streaming entertainment services	UX-Lite (5-pt)	0.7%	Slightly higher means for scales with negative numbers	Within Subjects, Greco-Latin counterbalancing
Emojis	240[e]	Ratings of streaming entertainment services	UX-Lite (5-pt)	0.5%	Slightly lower means for face emojis	Within Subjects, Greco-Latin counterbalancing

TABLE 16.2: Summary of effect size estimates for Chapter 16 presented in descending order of effect size. These unstandardized effect sizes are mean differences divided by the range of the scale. * = statistically significant. Respondents are from panels unless otherwise indicated.

a: Lewis & Sauro (2020, Jul 22), n = 155; b: Sauro (2019, Oct 3), n = 413; Tourangeau et al. (2007), n = 5717; c: Lewis & Sauro (2020, Jul 15, Nov 10), n = 180; Lewis & Sauro (2021, Nov 30, Dec 14), n = 212 d: Lewis & Sauro (2020, Sep 16), n = 256; e: Lewis & Sauro (2020, Sep 9), n = 240

PART 4:
Data Collection & Analysis

CHAPTER 17:
SAMPLE SIZE CALCULATIONS

For researchers, one of the most perplexing aspects of conducting surveys is knowing the right sample size to set as a goal. Consequently, it's one of the most common questions we are asked. If sample costs are low, researchers will often just aim for a "large" sample size like 1,000 and figure that will fend off potential critics who may question the sample size. This can lead to the incorrect assumption that you always need a sample comparable to one for a national poll for your findings to be reliable and valid. Conversely, researchers may settle on a small number like 30 that may be reasonable to address one research question but is ultimately insufficient to detect important differences or provide enough precision in other surveys.

Although there is confusion and even some controversy around finding the right sample size for a survey, there are, fortunately, some generally scientific and straightforward approaches that we'll review. We'll address these broad questions:

- What do you need to know to compute a sample size estimate?
- How do you compute a sample size for a "simple" stand-alone survey?
- What sample size do you need to compare a score to a benchmark?
- What sample size do you need to compare two means or percentages?
- Does the sample size depend on the population size?

HOW TO KNOW WHAT SAMPLE SIZE FORMULA TO USE

To determine what sample size you need, you'll need to determine what type of analyses you intend to conduct. For sample size planning, there are two main ways: stand-alone versus comparison analyses. Comparison analyses have two subtypes: comparing to a benchmark and comparing means.

1. Stand-alone analysis (confidence interval): Using survey responses to make inferences about the total population using confidence intervals.

2. Comparative analysis: Comparing survey responses to another sample or benchmark.

    i. Comparing to a benchmark (benchmark test): Comparing responses from one group to a fixed value, such as an industry benchmark (e.g., are attitudes toward usability above the average score of 68 on the SUS?).

    ii. Comparing to another sample (difference of two means): Either to another group of respondents in the same survey or to another survey.

a) Between: Comparing responses from different participants (e.g., responses from older versus younger respondents).

b) Within: Comparing responses from the same participants (e.g., brand attitude responses for Amazon versus Walmart from the same recent shoppers).

Figure 17.1 shows all three types of sample size computations and how they build on each other. The figure also shows what all three have in common: an estimate of the standard deviation, the required precision, and the required confidence level.

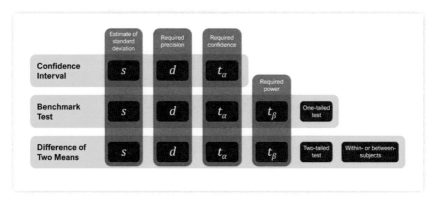

FIGURE 17.1: Drivers of sample size estimation for various types of analyses.

 TIP:

Surveys often include a mix of items (including discrete-binary and rating scales) that will be analyzed using confidence intervals for stand-alone analysis and those that will be compared. Because comparisons of discrete-binary data require larger sample sizes, this is often used as the sample size requirement for the entire survey.

You can use the sample size tables in this chapter to obtain conservative sample size recommendations for these estimation and comparison scenarios. These tables provide good approximations for many surveys and are what we typically use when scoping survey projects for clients when there is a focus on the analysis of discrete-binary data. We'll now review them in more detail (and for even more background, see Chapter 6 of *Quantifying the User Experience*, 2nd Edition, Sauro & Lewis, 2016).

SAMPLE SIZE FOR CONFIDENCE INTERVALS (NO COMPARISONS)

When conducting a stand-alone survey (or analyzing one question in a survey), you are essentially using a sample of participants to make inferences about a larger, unmeasured population. As such, the sample size you need is a function of how precise you want your estimate to be. The precision is quantified using the margin of error, so the confidence interval is twice the margin of error (see Chapter 20).

There are four things to consider when computing the sample size for confidence intervals in a stand-alone analysis—the type of metric and the first three elements depicted in the infographic in Figure 17.1:

- **The metric:** Surveys include a mix of discrete-binary (yes/no, selected/didn't select) and more continuous measures (rating scale questions or numeric input). Discrete-binary measures have less fidelity than continuous measures (it's all Yes or No, nothing in between) and so require a larger sample size to achieve the same level of precision. That is why, unless selection-type questions will not be part of the study (or a very minor part), we usually recommend using a binary rate as the metric for determining the appropriate sample size. The subsequent tables in this chapter compare binary metrics with rating scales for surveys where rating scales are the focus of analysis.

- **Estimate of the standard deviation (variability):** The more variable the thing you are measuring, the larger the sample size you need. For example, if people generally rate an experience high on a seven-point scale, or they are all likely to recommend, then each sample will have relatively consistent results. In contrast, if there is a mix of high and low responses on a seven-point scale or a mix of promoters and detractors, you have high variability, and each sample will be less consistent. In our experience, most practitioners don't have an estimate of the variability, especially when they're using a new measure. In such cases, we recommend using the highest reasonable level of variability (a conservative approach). For binary metrics that can take values from 0 to 100%, variance is maximized at the center of the distribution (50%). The point of maximum variance is not mathematically determined for rating scales, but analysis of our historical data indicates that reasonable values for typical standard deviations range from 20% to 28% of the maximum possible range of the scale.

- **Precision:** Of course, you'd like to have no uncertainty in your estimate (perfect precision), but that would require including every possible person in the target population. It's a waste of money and time. Like in polls, instead of surveying everyone, you survey enough to get a reasonable level of precision to address your study goals. To know how precise you need to be, answer a "precise enough" question (or have your stakeholders answer the question). For example, if we know 50% of participants agree to repurchase, but that figure could fluctuate by 20% (so it could be as high as 70% or as low as 30%), is that precise enough? How about 50% ± 10%, so the actual intended repurchase rate could fluctuate between 40% and 60%? The more precision you need, the larger the sample size, but there is a rapidly diminishing return as you increase the number of participants. To cut your margin of error in half, you need to approximately quadruple the sample size. The sample size tables show this relationship.

- **Level of confidence:** The outcome of your survey results will include a mean/percentage with a corresponding confidence interval (Appendix A). The result will be statements like, "We are 95% confident that between 60% and 70% of current subscribers use a mobile device to access their streaming service." The 95% in that statement is the confidence level. The more confident you need to be, the higher the confidence level and, therefore, the larger the sample size needed to maintain the same level of precision. The confidence level in industrial research is typically 90% or 95%, but it can be adjusted up or down (usually no lower than 80% and no higher than 99%).

 TIP:

If you do an Internet search for "sample sizes for surveys," our sample size computations for confidence intervals should be close to the results you find. But be careful when you read articles that provide a number like "at least 100," as these are, at best, crude estimates that are sometimes right and just as often are wrong.

Table 17.1 shows the sample size needed for the specified level of precision for either 90% or 95% confidence intervals. This table makes two assumptions. The first is that the information in the table uses the binary metric (e.g., yes/no or a selection), and the second is that the metric is at the highest level of variability (which occurs when the binary metric is equal to 50%). This level of variability is the most conservative assumption, but being conservative is generally recommended in the absence of other data because doing so guarantees an adequate sample size. This assumption greatly simplifies calculations. To use the table, perform the following steps:

1. Start with the desired margin of error on the left column (for example, 10%).

2. Find the sample size needed based on the level of confidence in the second (90% confidence level) or third columns (95% confidence level). For 90% confidence, the sample size needed is 65.

3. Interpret the estimate. To be 90% confident that an observed percentage of 50% won't fluctuate by more than 10%, you should plan on a sample size of 65.

Margin of error (+/-)	90% Confidence sample size	95% Confidence sample size
24%	10	13
20%	15	21
17%	21	30
15%	28	39
14%	32	46
13%	38	53
12%	45	63
11%	54	76
10%	65	93
9%	81	115
8%	103	147
7%	136	193
6%	186	263
5%	268	381
4%	421	597
3%	749	1,064

TABLE 17.1: Sample sizes for stand-alone analyses for 90% and 95% levels of confidence (assuming a binary metric equal to 50%).

Practice Using the Table

Here are three more examples. Remember, focus on the level of precision (the desired margin of error) and pick the confidence level (default to 90% unless stakes are high or conventions dictate otherwise—e.g., scientific publications usually require 95%)

- You want to be 95% confident that the margin of error will be no more than 5%. What sample size should you plan for? **381**

- If you anticipate receiving responses from only 20 participants, what level of precision can you expect at 90% confidence? **± 17%**

- What sample size should you plan for to have a margin of error of no greater than 15% (90% confidence)? **28**

Sample Size Using Rating Scale Data

While Table 17.1 above is simple in its calculations and requires the researcher to focus only on the margin of error and confidence level, the price for this simplicity is a conservative estimate (resulting in a large sample size).

The reason for this unfavorable property of binary data is that it is a relatively coarse measure (it's a 1 or 0, Yes or No, purchase or didn't purchase). That coarseness means you need a larger sample size than when using more continuous measures like rating scales or time for the same level of precision (or power when making comparisons).

There are two ways to reduce the sample size. The first is to move away from using .50 for the standard deviation. For example, if you know that the percentage you plan to measure is extremely unlikely to exceed 10% or fall below 90%, then you can use sample size formulas or calculators to reduce the estimated sample size (see *Quantifying the User Experience*, Sauro & Lewis, 2016, for computations).

The second is to focus on rating scales instead of binary data. Rating scales typically have more fidelity as a metric, and they consequently require a smaller sample size for the same level of precision as a binary metric.

However, computing sample sizes for rating scales presents a challenge: you need some estimate of the rating scale standard deviation to compute a sample size.

Two ways to estimate standard deviations for rating scales are to use approximations (e.g., divide the maximum scale range by a constant such as 4 or 5) and historical data. Of these two approaches, we recommend using historical data to ensure your standard deviations are reasonable for estimating sample size.

A prior survey with similar questions and the same number of response options will usually provide a good estimate of the standard deviation for future research with those items. We reviewed aggregated rating scale data from over 100,000 responses for hundreds of five, seven and eleven-point rating scales (Sauro & Lewis, 2023, Jan 31). The average standard deviation across over 4,000 scale instances was about 25% of the maximum range of the rating scale (e.g., 1 for a five-point scale, 1.5 for a seven-point scale, 2.5 for an eleven-point scale).

From our analysis of individual five, seven, and eleven-point items, we found a good estimate of a less-than-average standard deviation (25th percentile) is about 20% of the range (e.g., 0.8 points for a five-point scale). We also found 20% of the maximum range to be a good average estimate for most multi-item UX question-naires (Sauro & Lewis, 2023, Mar 14), based on analysis of the SUPR-Q, SUS, CSUQ, UMUX, UMUX-Lite, and UX-Lite.

A more conservative estimate is to use the 75th percentile of item variability from our research, which tends to be around 28% of the range of the scale (e.g., 1.12 on a five-point scale). All else being equal, sample size requirements based on these estimates (from 20%–28%) will be substantially lower than estimates based on the standard deviation of binomial metrics (which is 50% of the range of the scale when $p = .5$).

CONVERTING RATING SCALES TO 0–100-POINT SCALES

To use a single table for looking up sample sizes for standard five, seven, and eleven-point scales, we need to first convert raw scale values to 0–100 points. This will also make comparing the sample sizes for binary data easier (as it ranges from 0 to 100%).

To convert raw values, use the formulas:

- five-point (1 to 5): $y = (x - 1)(100 / 4)$—i.e., subtract 1 from the five-point rating, then multiply by 25

- seven-point (1 to 7): $y = (x - 1)(100 / 6)$—i.e., subtract 1 from the seven-point rating, then multiply by 16.67

- eleven-point (0 to 10): $y = x(10$—i.e., just multiply the eleven-point rating by 10

After this conversion, the maximum range for a rating scale is 100, so the estimated standard deviations based on a percentage of the maximum range become, respectively, 20, 25, and 28 points.

Table 17.2 shows the sample sizes needed for a desired margin of error at 95% confidence using the low (20%), medium (25%), and high (28%) estimates for rating scale standard deviations.

The first column in Table 17.2 shows the desired margin of error (percentages for binary metrics, points for rating scales interpolated to 0–100 points). The second column of the table shows the sample size needed when using a binary estimate at maximum variance/standard deviation for adjusted-Wald binomial confidence intervals (Sauro & Lewis, 2005). These are the same values used in Table 17.1 above for 95% confidence.

The third through fifth columns show the estimated sample sizes for a 0–100-point rating scale for three estimates of its standard deviation. For most planning, setting the standard deviation to 25 is the best choice. When there is any concern that the unknown standard deviation will probably be higher than average, set it to 28. When estimating sample sizes for multi-item questionnaires, it's best to set the standard deviation to 20.

Margin of Error (+/−)	Binary Metric, s = 50%	0–100-Point Rating Scale, s = 20	0–100-Point Rating Scale, s = 25	0–100-Point Rating Scale, s = 28
24(%)	13	6	7	8
20(%)	21	7	9	11
17(%)	30	8	11	13
15(%)	39	10	14	16
14(%)	46	11	15	18
13(%)	53	12	17	21
12(%)	63	14	20	24
11(%)	76	16	23	28
10(%)	93	18	27	33
9(%)	115	22	33	40
8(%)	147	27	40	50
7(%)	193	34	52	64
6(%)	263	46	70	87
5(%)	381	64	99	123
4(%)	597	99	153	191
3(%)	1064	174	270	338
2(%)	2398	387	603	756
1(%)	9600	1540	2404	3015

TABLE 17.2: Sample size estimates for binary and rating scale data for 95% confidence.

For example, to obtain a margin of error of ±20 points with 95% confidence, start in the column in Table 17.2 labeled Margin of Error (+/–) and move down to the row starting 20(%). The column labeled "Binary Metric, s = 50%" is the sample size needed for a binary metric with that margin of error which, assuming maximum variance, would be 21. Using the standard deviation estimates for rating scales would reduce the sample size to 7, 9, or 11 for a low (20% of range), medium (25% of range), or high (28% of range) estimated standard deviation. At this level of precision, the rating scale standard deviations cut the sample size estimate roughly in half!

The savings are even greater for smaller margins of error. For example, at a margin of error of ±2 points, you'd need 2,398 participants using a binary metric. You would need just a quarter of that (603) using the typical rating scale's standard deviation of 25% of the maximum range.

Table 17.3 shows the sample sizes needed for 90% confidence, a level commonly used in industrial research (Lewis & Sauro, 2021, Sep 28). Due to the lower level of confidence, all sample sizes in Table 17.3 are smaller than their corresponding entries in Table 17.2, but the ratios of rating scale over binary metric sample sizes are similar (e.g., when s = 25, that ratio is 5 / 10 = .50 for a margin of error of 24(%), and when the margin of error is 1(%), the ratio is 1693 / 6762 = .25).

Margin of Error (+/−)	Binary Metric, s = 50%	0–100-Point Rating Scale, s = 20	0–100-Point Rating Scale, s = 25	0–100-Point Rating Scale, s = 28
24(%)	10	4	5	6
20(%)	15	5	7	8
17(%)	21	6	8	10
15(%)	28	7	10	12
14(%)	32	8	11	13

(continued on pg. 269)

Margin of Error (+/−)	Binary Metric, s = 50%	0–100-Point Rating Scale, s = 20	0–100-Point Rating Scale, s = 25	0–100-Point Rating Scale, s = 28
13(%)	38	9	12	15
12(%)	45	10	14	17
11(%)	54	11	16	20
10(%)	65	13	19	24
9(%)	81	16	23	29
8(%)	103	19	29	36
7(%)	136	24	37	46
6(%)	186	32	49	61
5(%)	268	46	70	87
4(%)	421	70	108	135
3(%)	749	123	190	238
2(%)	1689	273	425	533
1(%)	6762	1085	1693	2123

TABLE 17.3: Sample size estimates for binary and rating scale data for 90% confidence.

For example, to achieve a margin of error of ±10 points with 90% confidence, plan on a sample size of 19 for the typical standard deviation of 25, and 13 or 24 for lower (20) and higher (28) estimates of standard deviation. The three sample sizes for the various rating scale standard deviations are, respectively, 20%, 29%, and 37% of the sample needed for a binary metric ($n = 65$).

NOTE: We expect our sample size estimates to be very accurate when item means are close to the midpoint and reasonably accurate until means get close to an endpoint. Because the standard deviations for binary metrics and rating scales approach 0 as means approach a scale endpoint, the actual sample size requirements for extreme means will be smaller than those in the tables. This isn't a problem when the cost of additional samples is small, but when that cost is high, consider running a pilot study to get an estimate of the actual standard deviation rather than using the tables.

MAPPING MARGINS OF ERROR FOR 0–100-POINT SCALES TO FIVE, SEVEN, AND ELEVEN-POINT SCALES

Interpolation of rating scales to 0–100 points greatly simplifies the comparison of binary and rating scale sample size requirements and generalizes its application to any number of scale points from 5 to 11. Otherwise, we'd need separate tables for each different multipoint scale. Note that we currently advise against extrapolating much beyond eleven-point scales when using these tables because we haven't specifically measured standard deviations for rating scales with more than eleven response options. If you must extrapolate, based on our research and review of the literature, consider using 25% of the maximum range for individual rating scale items and 20% of the maximum range for multi-item questionnaires (Sauro & Lewis, 2023, Apr 25).

If you or your stakeholders are used to thinking in terms of the original scales, it can be tricky to work backward from the 0–100-point scale. To help with this, Table 17.4 shows the magnitudes of a subset of possible margins of error rescaled to five, seven, and eleven points.

0–100-pt Scale	Five-pt Scale	Seven-pt Scale	Eleven-pt Scale
50	2.00	3.00	5.00
40	1.60	2.40	4.00
30	1.20	1.80	3.00
24	0.96	1.44	2.40
20	0.80	1.20	2.00
17	0.68	1.02	1.70

(continued on pg. 271)

0–100-pt Scale	Five-pt Scale	Seven-pt Scale	Eleven-pt Scale
15	0.60	0.90	1.50
14	0.56	0.84	1.40
13	0.52	0.78	1.30
12	0.48	0.72	1.20
11	0.44	0.66	1.10
10	0.40	0.60	1.00
9	0.36	0.54	0.90
8	0.32	0.48	0.80
7	0.28	0.42	0.70
6	0.24	0.36	0.60
5	0.20	0.30	0.50
4	0.16	0.24	0.40
3	0.12	0.18	0.30
2	0.08	0.12	0.20
1	0.04	0.06	0.10

TABLE 17.4: Equivalent margins of error for 0–100-point scales along with five, seven, and eleven-point scales.

The entries in Table 17.4 were calculated by dividing the margin of error for 0–100-point scales by 100 and then multiplying that by the maximum range of the multipoint scale. The maximum range of a five-point scale using the typical response options of 1 to 5 is 4 (5 − 1 = 4), for a seven-point scale is 6 (7 − 1 = 6), and for an eleven-point scale is 10 (10 − 0 = 10).

For example, if you want a margin of error for a five-point scale that is equivalent to ±10 on the 0–100-point scale, you'd use ±0.4. For a seven-point scale, the equivalent margin of error is ±0.6, and for an eleven-point scale, it is ±1.0. Then, using the typical estimate of the standard deviation for a rating scale from Tables 17.2 and 17.3 (s = 25), for 95% confidence, you'd need a sample size of 27 or, for 90% confidence, a sample size of 19.

SAMPLE SIZE FOR COMPARING AGAINST A BENCHMARK

The second method for computing sample sizes involves comparing against a benchmark (second row in Figure 17.1). When conducting a survey to assess attitudes toward a product, service, or brand, it's common to compare scores from standardized questionnaires like the SUS or NPS to an industry benchmark (e.g., 68 or 50%). When researchers want to measure other attitudes and intentions, they will often ask respondents to complete homegrown multipoint items and set target benchmarks (e.g., at least a 4 on a five-point scale).

For example, some organizations we've worked with set a goal of having their internal systems achieve a SUS score of at least 80 compared to other similar systems with publicly available data (which would put their system in the top 10%). In other cases, a company might want to show that a particular product has an intended renewal rate of at least 50%.

Refer again to Figure 17.1. When computing the sample size for comparing a mean or proportion to a benchmark, you need to know five things. The first four are the same elements required to compute the sample size for a confidence interval that we covered earlier.

1. The metric of analysis: binary or rating scale (single item or average of multiple items)
2. An estimate of the standard deviation
3. The required level of precision (using points or percentages)
4. The level of confidence (typically 90% or 95%)

Sample size estimation for comparing a mean or proportion against a set benchmark requires two additional considerations:

5. The power of the test (typically 80%)
6. The distribution of the rejection region (one-tailed for benchmark tests)

Quick Recap of Power and Tails (Rejection Regions)

The power of a test refers to its capability to detect a specified minimum difference between means (i.e., to control the likelihood of a Type II error). The number of tails refers to the distribution of the rejection region for the statistical test. In the vast majority of cases, comparisons of two rating scale means should use a two-tailed test. However, when comparing a mean to a benchmark, we use a one-tailed test because we almost always care only if the mean beats a certain threshold (e.g., above a 4 on a positive-tone five-point item, below a 2 on a negative-tone five-point item). For more details on these topics, see Chapter 6 in *Quantifying the User Experience* (Sauro & Lewis, 2016) and Lewis and Sauro (2022, Mar 1).

Sample Size Tables for Comparing Percentages with Benchmarks

Table 17.5 shows the sample sizes needed for comparing an observed percentage against a benchmark percentage. This table uses a 90% confidence level and 80% power level to derive the needed sample sizes for three common binary benchmark thresholds: 50%, 75%, and 90%.

To use the table, perform the following steps:

1. Start with the benchmark you want to achieve; for example, at least 50% of all customers intend to renew their software license.

2. Select a percentage to target from your sample data to determine the needed sample size. For example, if 55% of the sample of survey participants intend to renew (a 5% difference from the benchmark of 50%), you would need a sample size of 450 to exceed the 50% benchmark with at least 90% confidence. If 85% of the participants intended to renew when you wanted to significantly exceed the benchmark of 75%, you should plan on a sample size of 72.

Sample Percentage	Benchmark Percentage		
	50%	75%	90%
	Sample size needed		
99%	3	7	23
95%	4	13	122
90%	6	28	
85%	8	72	
80%	11	314	
75%	17		
70%	27		
65%	49		
60%	112		
55%	450		

TABLE 17.5: Sample sizes needed for comparing an observed percentage to a benchmark percentage.

The closer your sample estimate to the benchmark percent, the greater the sample size must be to claim you have exceeded the benchmark. Another way to look at this is to ask (1) What is the benchmark? and (2) What is the required level of precision? The more precision required (e.g., the closer the sample result is to the target), the larger the required sample size. If your target is 75% and the precision requirement is 5%, then you need to look at the intersection of a sample percentage of 80% (75 + 5) and a benchmark of 75%, which is $n = 314$. If your target is 75% and can accept a precision of 20%, then look at the intersection of 95% sample completion and 75% benchmark, which is $n = 13$.

Sample Sizes for Comparing Means with Benchmarks

If you are using rating scales (standardized questionnaires, multiple or single items) and comparing means to a benchmark (e.g., seeing whether a mean of a five-point scale is greater than 4), you'll need to use different calculations to compute the needed sample sizes.

STANDARDIZING RATINGS TO A 0–100-POINT SCALE

As was done in the confidence interval section, you will need to convert five, seven, and eleven-point scales to 0–100-point scales using Table 17.4. For example, a mean difference of 20 points on a 0–100-point scale is equivalent to a difference of 0.8 on a five-point scale (endpoints from 1 to 5), 1.2 on a seven-point scale (endpoints from 1 to 7), or 2.0 on an eleven-point scale (endpoints from 0 to 10).

Comparing a Rating Scale Mean with a Specified Benchmark

Table 17.6 shows the sample size estimates for tests against a set benchmark for various effect sizes (minimally detectable differences between the mean and the benchmark, percentage points for binary metrics, scale points for rating scales), four magnitudes of standard deviations ($s = 50\%$, used for binary variables; $s = 20$, suitable for multi-item questionnaires; $s = 25$, suitable for individual multipoint rating items; $s = 28$, suitable for individual multipoint rating items that are suspected to be more variable than the typical item), 95% confidence (i.e., setting the Type I error to .05), and 80% confidence (i.e., setting the Type II error to .20). The only difference in Table 17.7 is that confidence is 90% (i.e., Type I error set to .10), a common criterion for industrial research.

Effect Size	Binary Metric, $s = 50\%$	0–100-Point Rating Scale, $s = 20$	0–100-Point Rating Scale, $s = 25$	0–100-Point Rating Scale, $s = 28$
50(%)	3	2	2	3
40(%)	8	2	4	5
30(%)	15	5	6	7
20(%)	37	8	12	14
15(%)	67	13	19	24
12(%)	106	19	29	36
10(%)	153	27	41	50
9(%)	189	33	50	62
8(%)	240	41	62	78
7(%)	314	52	81	101
6(%)	428	71	109	137
5(%)	617	101	157	196
4(%)	964	157	244	305
3(%)	1716	277	431	541
2(%)	3863	620	968	1214
1(%)	15455	2475	3866	4849

TABLE 17.6: Sample size estimates for benchmark tests with 95% confidence and 80% power.

Effect Size	Binary Metric, $s = 50\%$	0–100-Point Rating Scale, $s = 20$	0–100-Point Rating Scale, $s = 25$	0–100-Point Rating Scale, $s = 28$
50(%)	2	2	2	2
40(%)	6	2	3	3
30(%)	11	4	5	5
20(%)	27	6	9	10
15(%)	49	10	14	17
12(%)	77	14	21	26
10(%)	112	20	30	37
9(%)	138	24	36	45
8(%)	175	30	46	57
7(%)	229	38	59	74
6(%)	312	52	80	100
5(%)	450	74	114	143
4(%)	703	114	178	223
3(%)	1251	202	315	394
2(%)	2816	452	706	885
1(%)	11269	1805	2819	3536

TABLE 17.7: Sample size estimates for benchmark tests with 90% confidence and 80% power.

For example, to detect a difference of 20 points between a mean and a benchmark with 95% confidence, start in the column in Table 17.6 labeled Effect Size and move down to the row starting 20(%). The column labeled "Binary Metric, $s = 50\%$" is the sample size needed for a binary metric with that margin of error which, assuming maximum variance, would be 37. Using the typical standard deviation estimate for rating scales (25% of the range) would reduce the sample size to 12. At this level of precision, the sample size for rating scales saves the expense of 25 participants and is about a third of the sample size for binary metrics!

Continuing this example, suppose you've set a benchmark to 60 points on a 0–100-point scale, and after you've collected data from 12 participants, the mean from the sample is 80 with a standard deviation of 25. The p-value from a t-test should be lower than .05 because the observed mean is exactly 20 points greater than the benchmark with a sample size for 95% confidence and 80% power. For these data, the observed mean is significantly greater than the benchmark ($t(11) = 2.77$, $p = .018$), so this result is evidence of having significantly exceeded the benchmark. Note, however, that if the observed mean had been 70—just ten points higher than the benchmark—then the result would not have been significant ($t(11) = 1.38$, $p = .19$). Keeping everything else the same, to achieve significance with a ten-point difference would require a sample size of 41.

The savings for rating scales relative to binary metrics are even greater for smaller margins of error. For example, at a margin of error of ±2 points with 95% confidence, you'd need 3,863 participants using a binary metric, but just a quarter of that (968) using the typical rating scale's standard deviation of 25% of the maximum range (saving the cost of 2,895 participants).

A FEW MORE EXAMPLES

The tables speed up finding sample sizes, but they still require working with several values. Here are a few more examples.

Single eleven-point item

Suppose you've created a new eleven-point (0–10) item to measure the likelihood that a customer will defect (stop using your product and start using a competitor), such that the higher the rating, the more likely the customer will defect. You want to test whether the mean of a sample of your current customers will be significantly higher than the midpoint of 5, and you want a sample size large enough to detect this as significant when the difference is as small as one point on the eleven-point scale. Because the cost of each sample is low, you decide to use the 75th percentile standard deviation from our historical data (28% of the range of the scale) and test with 95% confidence and 80% power.

Start with Table 17.4 to see what effect size to use in Table 17.6. A difference of 1 on an eleven-point scale corresponds to a difference of 10 on a 0–100-point scale. The entry in Table 17.6 (95% confidence) for s = 28 and an effect size of ten indicates the sample size (n) should be 50. In summary:

- *Type of scale:* eleven-point item
- *Confidence:* 95%
- *Power:* 80%

- *Standard deviation:* 28%
- *Effect size:* 1 point on an eleven-point scale (10 points on a 0–100-point scale)
- *Sample size:* 50

Single five-point item

For a new five-point (1–5) item that measures the clarity of product filter designs on a commercial website, assume you want to know the sample size requirement assuming a typical standard deviation (25% of the range of the scale) with 90% confidence, 80% power, and an effect size of 1/5 of a point (.20) on the five-point scale.

Start with Table 17.4 to see what effect size to use in Table 17.7 (90% confidence). For a five-point scale, a difference of .20 corresponds to 5 on a 0–100-point scale. The sample size in Table 17.7 for s = 25 and an effect size of 5 is n = 114. In summary:

- *Type of scale:* five-point item
- *Confidence:* 90%
- *Power:* 80%
- *Standard deviation:* 25%
- *Effect size:* .20 points on a five-point scale (5 points on a 0–100-point scale)
- *Sample size:* 114

Multi-item questionnaire

You have three new seven-point items that measure different aspects of website attractiveness, and you plan to report scores for this questionnaire based on averaging the three ratings and then interpolating the values to a 0–100-point scale for easier interpretation. You set the benchmark for an adequate level of attractiveness to 70 and want to know the sample size requirement for 90% confidence and 80% power using the typical standard deviation for multi-item questionnaires (20% of the scale range) that will indicate statistical significance when the mean is at least 7 points higher than the benchmark.

Because the scale in this example ranges from 0 to 100, you can start directly in Table 17.7 (90% confidence). The sample size for an effect size of 7 when s = 20 is n = 38. In summary:

- *Type of scale:* Multi-item questionnaire
- *Confidence:* 90%
- *Power:* 80%
- *Standard deviation:* 20%
- *Effect size:* 7 points on a 0–100-point scale
- *Sample size:* 38

SAMPLE SIZE FOR COMPARISONS (WITHIN AND BETWEEN SUBJECTS)

Returning to the graphic in Figure 17.1, when computing the sample size for comparing a mean or proportion, you need to know six things. The first four are the same elements required to compute the sample size for a confidence interval that we covered earlier:

1. The metric of analysis: binary or rating scale (single item or average of multiple items)
2. An estimate of the rating scale standard deviation
3. The required level of precision (using points or percentages)
4. The level of confidence (typically 90% or 95%)

The next two are the same as when comparing to a benchmark:

5. The power of the test (typically 80%)
6. The distribution of the rejection region (one-tailed for benchmark tests, two-tailed for comparing means)

Sample size estimation for comparing means and proportions has one additional consideration:

7. Within- vs. between-subjects approach: Within- (same people in each sample) or between-subjects study (different people in each sample)

DO YOU HAVE ENOUGH POWER?

A common problem in survey analysis is having insufficient power to detect differences. It's a waste of money and effort to conduct a survey knowing you have little ability to differentiate real differences from random noise. Ensure you have enough statistical power before conducting your survey by using the tables and by reviewing Appendix A on how to interpret statistical significancestatistical significance.

Table 17.8 shows the sample sizes needed for the specified level of precision for within or between subjects. This table makes three assumptions: The first is that your analysis is on a binary metric for both samples (e.g., percent agreeing). Second, the binary metrics will be at the highest level of variability ($p = .5$) for between-subjects estimates, and for within-subjects estimates, the effect size is centered around the conservative reasonable estimate of .28 for the mean discordant proportion (Lewis & Sauro, 2023, Oct 24). These are conservative assumptions that are generally recommended in the absence of other data. Third, the tables use a 90% confidence level and an 80% statistical power level.

A table greatly simplifies the lookup process. To use the table, perform the following steps:

1. Start with the difference you want to detect between samples from the first column, for example, 10%.

2. Find the sample size needed based on whether it is a within-subjects sample (second column) or a between-subjects sample (third column).

3. Interpret to be able to find a 10% difference (if one exists) as statistically significant between completion rates. Plan on a sample size of 436 for a within-subjects approach and a sample size of 614 for a between-subjects approach (307 for each interface).

Difference to detect 90% confidence and 80% power	Sample size within subjects	Sample size between subjects (each group)
50%	17	11
40%	21	17
30%	37	32
20%	84	75
12%	238	213
10%	343	307
9%	425	380
8%	538	481
7%	704	629
6%	959	857
5%	1382	1,234
4%	2161	1,930
3%	3844	3,433

(continued on pg. 281)

Difference to detect 90% confidence and 80% power	Sample size within subjects	Sample size between subjects (each group)
2%	8653	7,726
1%	34619	30,911

TABLE 17.8: Sample sizes for surveys for within- and between-subjects comparisons using 90% confidence and 80% power. Within-subjects estimates center the effect size around the conservative reasonable estimate of .28 for the mean discordant proportion. Between-subjects estimates assume maximum binary variance ($p = .50$) and need to be multiplied by the number of groups being compared.

Practice Using the Table.

Here are three more examples to practice with this table. Remember, focus on the level of precision (the desired margin of error) and pick the confidence level (default to 90% unless stakes are high or conventions dictate otherwise, e.g., scientific publication usually requires 95% confidence in reported outcomes).

- What sample size would you need to detect a 5% difference in participants' favorability rates (favorable/unfavorable) toward two airlines, with the same respondents providing favorability ratings toward both airlines? **1382**

- What is the size of difference (in percentage points) that you can hope to detect if you only anticipate being able to sample 50 small business owners on their attitude toward two new insurance offerings? **~30% difference for within subjects**

- If you want to compare the intent-to-repurchase rate in the next 30 days among users of four products (all different people for each product), how many should you plan on testing to detect an 8% difference? **481 × 4 = 1,924**

Sample Size for Comparing Rating Scale Means

We can use the same estimates of the standard deviation discussed in the confidence interval section to compute sample sizes when comparing rating scale means.

STANDARDIZING RATINGS TO A 0–100-POINT SCALE

As was done in the confidence interval section (Table 17.4), you will need to convert five, seven, and eleven-point scales to 0–100-point scales. For example, a mean difference of 20 points on a 0–100-point scale is equivalent to a difference of 0.8 on a five-point scale (endpoints from 1 to 5), 1.2 on a seven-point scale (endpoints from 1 to 7), or 2.0 on an eleven-point scale (endpoints from 0 to 10).

COMPARING TWO WITHIN-SUBJECTS MEANS

Table 17.9 shows the sample size estimates for within-subjects t-tests for various effect sizes (minimally detectable differences between the means, percentage points for a McNemar test of discordant proportions, scale points for rating scales), four magnitudes of standard deviations (s = 50%, used for binary variables; s = 20, suitable for multi-item questionnaires; s = 25, suitable for individual multipoint rating items; s = 28, suitable for individual multipoint rating items that are suspected to be more variable than the typical item), 95% confidence (i.e., setting the Type I error to .05), and 80% confidence (i.e., setting the Type II error to .20). The only difference in Table 17.10 is that confidence is 90% (i.e., Type I error set to .10), a common criterion for industrial research.

Unlike most binomial sample size estimation processes, sample sizes for the McNemar test are affected by the sum of the discordant proportions that the test compares (for more information see Lewis & Sauro, 2023, Oct 24). The binary sample sizes in Tables 17.9 and 17.10 use our conservative estimate for discordant proportions (75th percentile value of .28, for which s varies from 56–75%) for the binary metric sample sizes.

Unlike the McNemar test, which is relatively insensitive and therefore needs large sample sizes to reliably detect even large effect sizes, the t-test for comparison of within-subjects means is very sensitive, so the sample sizes for rating scales **are from 11–19% of those for within-subjects binary metrics.**

Effect Size	Binary Metric, s = 56–75%	0–100-Point Rating Scale, s = 20	0–100-Point Rating Scale, s = 25	0–100-Point Rating Scale, s = 28
50(%)	22	2	3	4
40(%)	27	3	5	6
30(%)	47	5	8	9
20(%)	107	10	15	18
15(%)	192	16	24	30
12(%)	302	24	36	45
10(%)	436	34	51	64
9(%)	539	41	63	78
8(%)	683	51	79	99

(continued on pg. 283)

Effect Size	Binary Metric, s = 56–75%	0–100-Point Rating Scale, s = 20	0–100-Point Rating Scale, s = 25	0–100-Point Rating Scale, s = 28
7(%)	893	67	103	128
6(%)	1217	90	139	173
5(%)	1754	128	199	249
4(%)	2743	199	309	387
3(%)	4880	351	548	686
2(%)	10985	787	1229	1541
1(%)	43950	3142	4908	6156

TABLE 17.9: Sample size estimates for within-subjects comparison with **95%** confidence and 80% power (binary metric is for differences in discordant proportions assessed with a McNemar test, centering the effect size around the conservative reasonable estimate of .28 for the mean discordant proportion so s varies from 56–75% for effect sizes from 50% to 1%).

Effect Size	Binary Metric, s = 56–75%	0–100-Point Rating Scale, s = 20	0–100-Point Rating Scale, s = 25	0–100-Point Rating Scale, s = 28
50(%)	17	2	2	3
40(%)	21	2	4	5
30(%)	37	5	6	7
20(%)	84	8	12	14
15(%)	151	13	19	24
12(%)	238	19	29	36
10(%)	343	27	41	50
9(%)	425	33	50	62
8(%)	538	41	62	78

(continued on pg. 284)

Effect Size	Binary Metric, s = 56–75%	0–100-Point Rating Scale, s = 20	0–100-Point Rating Scale, s = 25	0–100-Point Rating Scale, s = 28
7(%)	704	52	81	101
6(%)	959	71	109	137
5(%)	1382	101	157	196
4(%)	2161	157	244	305
3(%)	3844	277	431	541
2(%)	8653	620	968	1214
1(%)	34619	2475	3866	4849

TABLE 17.10: Sample size estimates for within-subjects comparison with **90%** confidence and 80% power (binary metric is for differences in discordant proportions assessed with a McNemar test, centering the effect size around the conservative reasonable estimate of .28 for the mean discordant proportion so s varies from 56–75% for effect sizes from 50% to 1%).

For example, to detect a difference of ten points between two within-subjects means with 95% confidence, start in the column in Table 17.9 labeled Effect Size and move down to the row starting with 10(%). The column labeled "Binary Metric" is the sample size needed for a binary metric with that margin of error which, assuming a relatively large but reasonable variance, would be 436. Using the typical standard deviation estimate for rating scales (25% of the range) would reduce the sample size to 51. The sample size for rating scales saves the expense of 385 participants and is about 12% of the sample size for binary metrics!

COMPARING TWO BETWEEN-SUBJECTS MEANS

All other things being equal, between-subjects comparisons require a much larger sample size than within-subjects comparisons due to the combination of dealing with two standard deviations (assumed to be equal to keep the formula simple) and because the formula produces the sample size for one group, needing to double that number when comparing two groups (and tripling it if there will be three independent groups, and so on).

Returning to the previous example (detection of a difference of ten points with 95% confidence), in Table 17.9, the sample size needed to detect a within-subjects difference of ten points for a rating scale with the typical standard deviation ($s = 25$) is 51. For a comparable between-subjects comparison (Table 17.11), the sample size for one group is 100, so the total sample size for two groups is 200 — roughly four times the within-subjects sample size but only about a quarter of the sample size needed compared to that required for a binary metric (for 90% confidence see Table 17.12). Given this, you might wonder why anyone would use a between-subjects design, but the within/between decision is more complicated than just a comparison of sample sizes.

Effect Size	Binary Metric, s = 50%	0–100-Point Rating Scale, s = 20	0–100-Point Rating Scale, s = 25	0–100-Point Rating Scale, s = 28
50(%)	13	4	6	7
40(%)	22	6	8	9
30(%)	41	9	13	15
20(%)	95	17	26	32
15(%)	171	30	45	56
12(%)	270	45	70	87
10(%)	390	64	100	125
9(%)	482	79	123	154
8(%)	610	100	155	194
7(%)	798	130	202	253
6(%)	1087	176	274	343
5(%)	1567	253	394	494
4(%)	2450	394	615	771
3(%)	4358	699	1092	1369
2(%)	9808	1571	2454	3078
1(%)	39241	6281	9813	12309

TABLE 17.11: Sample size estimates for between-subjects comparisons with **95%** confidence and 80% power. Tabled values are for one group of participants, so for a study with two groups, you need to double the values (and for three groups, triple the values).

Effect Size	Binary Metric, s = 50%	0–100-Point Rating Scale, s = 20	0–100-Point Rating Scale, s = 25	0–100-Point Rating Scale, s = 28
50(%)	10	4	5	5
40(%)	17	5	6	8
30(%)	32	7	10	12
20(%)	75	14	21	26
15(%)	135	23	36	45
12(%)	213	36	55	69
10(%)	307	51	79	98
9(%)	380	62	97	121
8(%)	481	79	122	153
7(%)	629	102	159	199
6(%)	857	139	216	271
5(%)	1234	199	311	389
4(%)	1930	311	484	607
3(%)	3433	551	860	1079
2(%)	7726	1238	1933	2425
1(%)	30911	4947	7730	9696

TABLE 17.12: Sample size estimates for between-subjects comparisons with **90%** confidence and 80% power. Tabled values are for one group of participants, so for a study with two groups, you need to double the values (and for three groups, triple the values).

A FEW MORE EXAMPLES

Single eleven-point item

Suppose you've created a new eleven-point (0–10) item to measure the likelihood that a customer will defect (stop using your product and start using a competitor) such that the higher the rating, the more likely the customer will defect. You want to test whether there is a difference in the ratings of customers who have been with you for more than a year versus those who have been with you for less than six months (two independent groups). You want a sample size large enough to detect a difference as small as 1 on the eleven-point scale. Because the cost of each sample is small, you decide to use the 75th percentile standard deviation from our historical data (28% of the range of the scale) and test with 95% confidence and 80% power.

Start with Table 17.4 to see what effect size to use in Table 17.11 (95% confidence, between subjects). A difference of 1 on an eleven-point scale corresponds to a difference of 10 on a 0–100-point scale. The entry in Table 17.11 for s = 28 and an effect size of ten indicates the sample size (*n*) for each group should be 125 (total of 250 for two groups). In summary:

- *Type of scale:* eleven-point item
- *Experimental design:* Between subjects
- *Confidence:* 95%
- *Power:* 80%
- *Standard deviation:* 28% of scale range
- *Effect size:* 1 point on an eleven-point scale (10 points on a 0–100-point scale)
- *Sample size:* 125 per group for a two-group total of 250

Single five-point item

For a new five-point (1–5) item that measures the clarity of filter designs on a commercial website, assume you want to know the sample size requirement for comparing participants' ratings of two websites that were presented in counterbalanced order to each participant (within subjects), assuming a typical standard deviation (25% of the range of the scale) with 90% confidence, 80% power, and an effect size of 1/5 of a point (.20) on the five-point scale.

Start with Table 17.4 to see what effect size to use in Table 17.10 (90% confidence, within subjects). For a five-point scale, a difference of .20 corresponds to 5 points on a 0–100-point scale. The sample size in Table 17.10 for *s* = 25 and an effect size of 5 is *n* = 157. In summary:

- *Type of scale:* five-point item
- *Experimental design:* Within subjects
- *Confidence:* 90%
- *Power:* 80%
- *Standard deviation:* 25% of scale range
- *Effect size:* .20 points on a five-point scale (5 points on a 0–100-point scale)
- Sample size: 157

Multi-item questionnaire

What if you have three new seven-point items that measure different aspects of website attractiveness, and you plan to report scores for this questionnaire based on averaging the three ratings and then interpolating the values to a 0–100-point scale for easier interpretation? You want to know the sample size requirement for 90% confidence and 80% power using the typical standard deviation for multi-item questionnaires (20% of the scale range) that will indicate statistical significance when the difference in means is at least 7 points. You are comparing two prototype websites, and each participant will see only one website (between subjects).

Because the scale in this example ranges from 0 to 100, you can start directly in Table 17.12 (90% confidence, between subjects). The sample size for an effect size of 7 when $s = 20$ is $n = 102$ for one group, so the sample size for two groups is 204. In summary:

- *Type of scale:* Multi-item questionnaire
- *Experimental design:* Between subjects
- *Confidence:* 90%
- *Power:* 80%
- *Standard deviation:* 20% of scale range
- *Effect size:* 7 points on a 0–100-point scale
- *Sample size:* 102 per group for a two-group total of 204

FINITE POPULATION CORRECTIONS

The sample size tables so far assume the population size is large enough that the recommended sample sizes won't be a substantial percentage of the population.

When the sample size used to compute estimates around a population is relatively large (and meaningfully "depletes" the population), you can use a statistical technique called the finite population correction (FPC), which accounts for the influence of larger sample sizes relative to the population size. For example, you may be sampling IT decision-makers at Fortune 500 companies, fMRI technicians, or Chick-fil-A franchise owners, where there are a limited number of people in the population.

When it's appropriate, applying the FPC reduces the width of confidence intervals, increases statistical power, and reduces needed sample sizes. It does this by reducing the standard error used in the calculations. The larger the proportion of your sample size in relation to the finite population, the more benefit there is. The benefit becomes noticeable when the sample size is at least 10% of the population.

To apply the correction to a finite population, you need only the sample size (n) and the population size (N). See Sauro and Lewis (2023, Jan 3) for more on the formulas used.

 TIP:

The FPC tends to have a more meaningful impact on your calculations once the sample size gets above 10% of the population. For anything less, the correction has a minimal effect.

Table 17.13 shows how large the correction is for different population sizes from 100 to 10,000 based on the sample size. For example, for populations that are on the large size but still not massive (e.g., 10,000), the correction is relatively insignificant until you get to a sample size of 1,000, which is 10% of the total population. At 10% of the population, you reduce the standard error by about 5%.

For small populations (e.g., 100), you get an impact right away, as even a small sample size of 10 represents 10% of the population.

Sample Size	Pop = 10,000	Pop = 1,000	Pop = 500	Pop = 100
10	99.95%	99.5%	99.1%	95.3%
25	99.9%	98.8%	97.6%	87.0%
50	99.8%	97.5%	95.0%	71.1%
75	99.6%	96.2%	92.3%	50.3%
100	99.5%	94.9%	89.5%	
250	98.7%	86.6%	70.8%	
500	97.5%	70.7%		
1,000	94.9%			

TABLE 17.13: Effect of FPC on the magnitude of standard errors for various sample sizes and population sizes.

The impact of the correction formula can be seen in Table 17.14, which shows the unadjusted sample sizes for generating a 95% confidence interval on binary data (from Table 17.1) with the uncorrected and correct sample sizes at population sizes of 500 and 100.

Margin of Error (+/−)	Uncorrected Sample Size	Corrected Sample Size (N = 500)	Corrected Sample Size (N = 100)
24%	13	13	12
20%	21	21	18
17%	30	29	23
15%	39	38	28
14%	46	44	32
13%	53	50	35
12%	63	59	39
11%	76	71	43

(continued on pg. 290)

Margin of Error (+/−)	Uncorrected Sample Size	Corrected Sample Size (N = 500)	Corrected Sample Size (N = 100)
10%	93	85	48
9%	115	103	54
8%	147	128	60
7%	193	162	66
6%	263	208	73
5%	381	276	79
4%	597	374	86

TABLE 17.14: Sample size needed for margins of error at a 95% confidence level for uncorrected and corrected sample sizes for the adjusted-Wald confidence interval assuming a proportion of .5 and population sizes of 500 and 100.

For example, the sample size needed to obtain a 5% margin of error on a 95% confidence interval is 381 (uncorrected), but if the population is 500, you need only 276 to reach that level of precision, and if $N = 100$ you only need 79. This example shows that when a population is small ($N = 100$) and a substantial amount of the population is being sampled (79%!), there's still enough uncertainty that the margin of error will be +/− 5%.

Note that this is the level of uncertainty when binomial variance is maximized (when $p = .5$). When you expect p to be somewhere in the range of .3 to .7, guidance from aids like Table 17.14 works well in practice (Cochran, 1977, p. 76–77). If, however, you expect p to have a more extreme value (say, $p < .1$ or $> .9$), it is better to estimate the sample size with the formula or use an inverse sampling strategy.

For more details on the FPC formula applied to sample sizes (and confidence intervals), see Sauro and Lewis (2023, Jan 3).

 TIP:

> **Don't define your population too narrowly.** We've found some researchers may define their population too narrowly (e.g., only existing nurses who use a product) but then want to generalize their findings to a broader audience (e.g., all future nurses who will use the product). This could lead to errors in the use of FPC if the actual population is much larger than the defined population (i.e., the correction will actually be a miscorrection).

CHAPTER SUMMARY AND TAKEAWAYS

This chapter discusses how to compute sample size estimates for surveys.

What do you need to know to compute a sample size estimate? ...At a minimum, you need the type of analysis, the type of metric, the confidence level, an estimate of variability, and the required precision.

Three types of analysis are:

- *Stand-alone:* Estimating population means or percentages with confidence intervals.

- *Comparison with a benchmark:* Assessing statistical significance of differences between estimated means or percentages with fixed benchmarks (e.g., is an estimated SUS score greater than the typical average of 68).

- *Comparison of two samples:* Assessing the statistical significance of differences between two estimated means or percentages.

The two types of metric most often collected in surveys are:

- *Discrete-binary:* These measurements can only take two values, usually scored as 0 and 1 (e.g., no/yes, failed/succeeded, rejected/chose from a select-all-that-apply list).

- *Continuous:* In practice, continuous measures are those that can take multiple ordered values (e.g., multipoint rating scales).

Confidence levels are related to statistical significance. For example, if you plan to use $p < .05$ as the significance criterion, the associated confidence level is 95%. Another commonly used criterion in industrial research is $p < .10$, for which the associated confidence level is 90%.

Variability is most commonly measured with the standard deviation. When there is no historical data to use for an estimate of the standard deviation, we recommend using the following for sample size estimation:

- *Discrete-binary data:* The maximum possible value of 0.5 (50%).

- *Rating scale data:* Use 20% of the range of the scale for multi-item UX questionnaires (e.g., SUS), 25% of the range of the scale for single rating scale items, or, to be a little more cautious, use 28% (values based on analysis of our historical data).

Precision refers to the tolerable amount of fluctuation in an estimate. For confidence intervals, this is the margin of error (the plus-or-minus part of the interval). For comparisons, this is the critical difference (the smallest difference that you want to be able to determine as statistically significant).

OK, do I need to know anything else for stand-alone estimation? ...No. With these five items, you can compute the sample size estimate by hand, put the values into a sample size calculator, or use our tables. The appropriate tables to use are 17.1 for discrete-binary data, 17.2 for rating scale data (95% confidence), and 17.3 for rating scale data (90% confidence). For rating scale data, you might also need to consult Table 17.4 for equivalent margins of error between 0–100-point scales and five, seven, and eleven-point scales.

What about comparing against a benchmark? ...Once you move from estimation to comparison, you need to account for power and the rejection region.

Power for sample size estimation is usually set to 80%. This corresponds to controlling the Type II error (likelihood of deciding a result is not significant when there really is an effect) to .20.

Rejection regions for benchmark tests are usually one-tailed because you care only about the significance of the test if you beat the benchmark.

We've accounted for these additional considerations in the tables we prepared for this chapter (Table 17.6 for 95% confidence and 80% power; Table 17.7 for 90% confidence and 80% power—both assume one-tailed testing.)

What about comparing two means or percentages? ...Power stays the same as for benchmark comparison, the rejection region changes to two-tailed, and it matters whether the comparison is within or between subjects.

Rejection regions for tests of two means or percentages are usually two-tailed because you care about significance no matter which mean/percentage is higher.

Within- and between-subjects experimental designs differ depending on whether the data being compared were collected from the same people (within subjects) or different people (between subjects). In general, sample size requirements are lower for within-subjects comparisons.

The tables you need for these sample size estimates (all with 80% confidence and two-tailed rejection regions) are 17.8 (to compare within- and between-subjects estimates for 90% confidence), 17.9, and 17.10 (discrete-binary and rating scale estimates for, respectively, 95% and 90% confidence for within-subjects comparisons), and 17.11 and 17.12 (discrete-binary and rating scale estimates for, respectively, 95% and 90% confidence for between-subjects comparisons).

Does the right sample size depend on the size of the population? ...The size of the population usually doesn't matter. The exception to this is the rare situation when the sample size is a substantial proportion of the population (e.g., when studying CTOs of Fortune 500 companies). When this is the case, you can apply the finite population correction (FPC), as illustrated in Tables 17.13 and 17.14.

CHAPTER 18:
PLANNING AND LOGISTICS

In this chapter, we'll address many of the *how*, *how long*, and *how much* questions that arise when you have decided to conduct a survey after many of the details in Part 1 have been settled—typical timelines, types of unmoderated platforms, and costs. We'll address the following questions:

- Do I need a commercial survey platform for my research?
- How much does it cost to find and pay participants?
- What needs to happen before you collect data?
- What to do when a survey doesn't fill?

COMMERCIAL SURVEY PLATFORMS

The following lists the main features to consider when conducting surveys. This is useful as a checklist when selecting an unmoderated commercial platform:

- **Enough question types:** You should expect the usual suspects (single, multi-select, and grids), but be sure other useful items aren't absent (e.g., pick some, most/least grids). Make sure you can configure item labels and numbers (e.g., sometimes rating scales don't start with 1).

- **Question screen-outs:** You need the ability to find participants' answers to specific demographic questions, such as their prior experience, brand, income, or age, to ensure you're targeting the right type of participants for your study (especially important when using online panels).

- **Branching and logic:** When different segments of a company's population (e.g., customers vs. financial advisors) are included in the same survey, you'll want to display only relevant questions to each kind of participant by branching or adding conditionals to keep studies smooth and short for each segment.

- **Piping:** It's handy to be able to pass responses from one question to subsequent ones, such as the name of a product or company.

- **Randomization:** You'll often want to randomize the order of presentation of response options in an item, items within a grid, items on a page, and sometimes even the pages themselves.

- **Quotas on questions:** To manage the right balance of participants (e.g., 50% experienced and 50% prospects), you need to have question-level quotas (a simple feature surprisingly absent from many platforms).

NOTE: We conduct many UX-based surveys at MeasuringU and want to have all the capabilities and flexibility we need in survey platforms, so we built the MeasuringU Intelligent Questioning (MUiQ) platform. The MUiQ platform provides all the key features required to conduct a survey and allows you to combine surveys with advanced UX-based items like task-based questions, click tests, and card sorts.

In addition to MUiQ, there are other survey platforms for which your organization may have an existing license. A few of the more common ones include:

- **Qualtrics:** Extensive survey feature set but tends to be expensive.

- **SurveyMonkey:** Basic surveys (no logic or branching in the free versions) with limited item sets are often free.

- **QuestionPro:** Rich features for less than the cost of Qualtrics, and it includes advanced features like MaxDiff and Choice-Based Conjoint.

- **Alchemer (formerly SurveyGizmo):** Like QuestionPro, Alchemer offers a rich set of features for less than the cost of Qualtrics and has some advanced features.

- **Google Forms:** A (currently) free Google service for basic surveys.

PARTICIPANT AND RECRUITING COSTS

The cost of finding and paying people to participate in your survey can range from trivial to substantial, depending on how hard it is to find the participants, how much you need to pay (the honorarium), and how many you need. Typical survey participant costs range from under $500 for a small-sample general consumer study to $50,000+ for a large, international, specialized sample.

Survey Recruitment Costs

For surveys that need dozens to thousands of participants, you'll need to consider many sources, often starting with an online panel.

ONLINE PANELS

There are dozens of companies that provide participants willing to take online surveys. The cost per participant will range from between $1 and $10 for a general consumer profile in the U.S. (higher for targeted groups, e.g., income > $75K) and go up substantially from $40 to $100 for a member of a difficult-to-find group (called low incidence rate or low IR), such as a financial advisor, physician, IT decision maker, or small business owner. Many participant panels also have a minimum project amount (usually > $1,000), and they may charge a project management or setup fee.

International studies also cost more and have limited availability. Get multiple quotes, as costs will vary especially for hard-to-find profiles. For example, we conducted an international survey of Android users in the U.S., Thailand, the Philippines, and Egypt. The price ranges we received for these countries differed by an order of magnitude; some quotes we received for the same country ranged from $25 to $75 per participant (see Chapter 3 for more on using online panels).

 TIP:

> Some survey platforms like MUiQ, Qualtrics, and SurveyMonkey have online panels integrated into their platform, making it easy to access a large target population without having to set up a relationship with a panel yourself.

INTERNAL LISTS

Using customer lists can be less expensive than online panels, but you are, by definition, using only existing customers who have opted in to be contacted (hopefully!). This means they'll likely be less objective for surveys that compare multiple brands. You'll need to be careful about depleting this sample, too—you don't want to over-survey your customers. You can pay participants directly using digital gift cards (typically $20 to $50 for online studies) or set up a lottery, for example, to give away iPads (be sure to consult with your legal team when planning a lottery).

ADVERTISING

You can post ads to Facebook, LinkedIn, or Google Ads to recruit participants. You'll have to pay per click and either pay each participant or pay for the cost of a raffle or giveaway.

BULK MAIL COSTS

If you are looking to email your customers directly, you'll need to have a bulk mail provider do the mailing or your email address and even your domain will be blacklisted by Internet service providers (ISPs). Bulk email providers like Decipher (now part of FocusVision), Mailchimp, and Alida have relationships with ISPs so your messages aren't marked as spam (and they will ensure you aren't a spammer, too!). The cost varies depending on the size of the list, but we often spend $1,500 to $3,000 mailing 5,000 to 50,000 customers to ask for their participation. There is usually a project management cost, a cost per email address, and a cost per delivered email. Please do us all a favor and make sure you aren't indiscriminately emailing a survey to people who never opted in.

Professional Services Costs

When outsourcing your survey, the biggest cost will be paying other professionals (ideally, those with quantitative survey experience) to assist. This typically includes survey design, data collection, and analysis.

The design phase involves writing the survey script and working through details of question wording and response options. For collecting the data, you need to manage online panels. For the analysis portion, you will need to prepare your data for presentation (see Chapter 19), run the appropriate statistical analyses (see Chapters 20 and 21), and then interpret the findings for the stakeholders. Costs for each phase can range from $10K to $20K+.

DATA COLLECTION: PRETESTING AND SOFT LAUNCHING TO PREPARE FOR THE FULL LAUNCH

With your participant source identified, it's time to start collecting data. Before you go into the full launch, you'll want to properly pretest and soft launch your survey to limit the number of issues and to ensure participants can effectively complete the study. The following section highlights things to consider before fully launching your study.

Prepare for Data Collection

Many things can go wrong when preparing a survey. Use the following suggestions to pretest your survey.

CHECK SURVEY TIMING

Have some internal participants go through the survey to generate a realistic estimate of how long it will take the typical participant to complete it, and then let the survey participants know the expected completion time on the welcome page of the survey. If there is a change, update the welcome screen with the new times. For example, if it takes 10 minutes for someone familiar with the survey to read and respond to every question, it may take a typical participant between 15 and 20 minutes to complete. Continually revisit the advertised time if you see the median study time is longer or shorter than your initial estimate.

VERIFY THE LOGIC AND BRANCHING

Logic and branching are the terms used to describe which participants see which question. For example, financial advisors may "branch" to a set of questions about their clients that wouldn't be relevant to general consumers. Some questions may appear only if other questions are answered in a certain way. For example, if participants indicate they are familiar with a brand, you might ask them to rate their satisfaction with that brand. Go through all the pathways participants can take to make sure your logic and branching work as expected. The more conditions and branches there are, the more time this will take.

ENSURE FOR RANDOMIZATION

For certain questions, randomization is essential to spread the unwanted effects of learning and fatigue across tasks and competitors evenly. You should take the survey enough times to see that your randomization scheme is working as intended (and be sure to delete the test data before launch).

EVALUATE REQUIRED QUESTIONS

If you need participants to respond to a question, ensure they can't proceed without answering. Although you don't want to burden participants, skipped questions can complicate analysis. There are some approaches to working with missing data, but the best approach is to avoid missing data altogether. During pretesting, you might "unrequire" questions to make it easy to go through and check other aspects of the study. Be sure you make them required again by making this one of your later steps.

TEST WITH THINK-ALOUD PARTICIPANTS

Consider having a small sample of participants "think aloud" as they complete the survey to identify misunderstandings of questions or response options. You can conduct the think aloud live over a Zoom meeting with a target participant, or you can use an unmoderated think-aloud service (also part of MUiQ) where participants can record their screens and voices while they think aloud. For high-stakes surveys that reach a broad population, this step is essential (for more on usability testing your survey, see Geisen & Bergstrom, 2017).

PREPARE TO LAUNCH—SOFTLY!

Instead of fully launching your survey at the outset, recruit around 10% of your intended number of participants (e.g., 15 out of 150) to test the survey. This is often referred to as a "soft" launch, like the soft opening of a restaurant to help work out any kinks in the system. Instead of checking recipes and service, you check your data, study timing, logic, and branching with actual participants to ensure you're properly collecting the data from the right people. Pay particular attention to any open-ended questions where participants might indicate potential problems. Make corrections before proceeding to the full launch.

What Happens When a Survey Doesn't Fill?

Who wants to plan a huge party only to have no one show up? You may launch your survey in anticipation of combing through hundreds of responses to find after serval days that only a handful of participants have completed the survey (a researcher's nightmare!). Unlike an auction on eBay where all the bids come in at the last minute, the opposite is generally true for surveys using online panels or direct email recruiting: you'll usually see the bulk of your sample in the first few days, then the remaining trickle in. The reason is people usually receive an email invitation and respond quickly. The more time goes by, the more buried the email is in people's inboxes.

Here are some common causes of lack of participant engagement and what to do about them.

REDUCE THE SURVEY LENGTH

We have found that the length of a study is one of the biggest factors behind study dropout (Sauro, 2015, Mar 17). If you can't find a way to cut questions, consider assigning a subset of questions or tasks to each participant so that your study length isn't too onerous. See Chapter 3 for information about how long it takes to complete a typical online survey. If yours is on the high end (more than 20 minutes long), this may be your problem.

ADD MORE LOGIC OR BRANCHING

Does everyone need to answer every question or attempt every task? Look for ways to reduce the burden by removing some questions and directing participants to relevant (and away from irrelevant) questions and tasks.

INCREASE OR CHANGE THE INCENTIVE

If you can't reduce the study length or burden, try increasing the incentive to attract more participants. If you're using one, your panel can guide you on the right amount to offer. If you are offering sweepstakes, you may need to consider direct payment or increase participants' odds of winning.

ASSESS AND/OR REMOVE REQUIRED QUESTIONS

While you don't want to have missing data in your analysis, be sure the required questions really need to be answered. In particular, look at open-ended questions that require participants to type a lot (especially on mobile devices). Remove required questions if possible, though we recommend doing this after reducing study length because length has a bigger impact than the number of required questions.

CHANGE PANELS

If you are using an online panel, consider looking to other companies. For specialized participants, and especially for different countries, some panels just have more participants than others.

USE DIFFERENT RECRUITING METHODS

It could be that your participant profile is difficult to fill for online panels and needs to be adjusted. You may need to look into using your customer list or posting ads to find qualified participants.

SEND A REMINDER

If you are conducting recruitment, send a reminder email. If working with a panel, they also should be able to remind participants the study is still open. Participants often assume a study has been filled if a few days have passed, so a simple reminder may be all you need to fill your survey.

CHAPTER SUMMARY AND TAKEAWAYS

This chapter covered many of the *how, how much*, and *how long* questions that come up when planning a survey.

Do I need a commercial survey platform for my research? ...Probably. The kinds of research you can conduct with free versions of survey platforms are very limited. If you're a professional UX researcher, you probably need the capabilities of a commercial survey platform (e.g., a wide variety of question types, branching logic, piping, randomization, and question-level quotas). When Jim worked at IBM, he paid out of his own pocket for a SurveyGizmo (now Alchemer) license because his consulting department didn't have UX tools in its budget. Jeff has invested millions of dollars over many years to develop the MUiQ platform for unmoderated UX research (which can be licensed from MeasuringU®). Professional researchers need professional tools.

How much does it cost to find and pay participants? ...These costs range from trivial to substantial. Potential participant sources include online panels, internal lists, advertising, and bulk mail providers. Typical survey participant costs range from under $500 for a small-sample general consumer study to $50,000+ for a large international specialized sample.

OK, I've got my platform, identified participants, and designed the survey, so I'm ready to collect data—right? ...No, first you need to pretest. Many things can go wrong when preparing a survey. Be sure to:

- Check survey timing.
- Verify logic and branching.
- Ensure randomization is working properly.
- Evaluate required questions.
- Test with think-aloud participants.

Once pretesting is done, what's next? ...Conduct a soft launch. Test the survey with about 10% of the planned sample size to check if everything works as expected. Inspect responses to open-ended questions for indication of any problems.

What can you do when a survey doesn't fill? ...There are several strategies. You can:

- Reduce the survey length.
- Add more logic or branching so that participants only see relevant questions.
- Engage more online panels.
- If possible, relax the participant profile requirements.
- Send reminders.

CHAPTER 19:
PREPARING FOR SURVEY ANALYSIS

This chapter discusses steps and methods for identifying poor-quality responses, what to do with missing data, and analytical platforms. Spending time upfront removing poor-quality responses and handling missing data saves a lot of time and headaches from having to rerun your analyses. We'll cover the following questions:

- What should I do to prepare for analysis?
- How should I approach "cleaning" data?
- What do I do about missing data?
- What tools can I use for analysis?

Before getting into the analysis of your data, you're going to need to clean it. Cleaning doesn't involve a disinfectant, and it doesn't mean removing responses that aren't favorable.

CLEANING DATA

In our experience, around 10% of participants (often ranging from 1% to 20%) "cheat" in surveys, and their data need to be tossed out or "cleaned." These participants are usually a combination of cheaters, speeders, respondents misrepresenting themselves, or people just not putting forth effort—all of which threaten the validity of the survey's findings. We see this with both internal customer lists and paid panels.

 TIP:

> To clean your data, you can export it to Excel or Google Sheets. Some platforms may also allow you to exclude or filter participants online but be sure you can see the timings and responses by participant.

There's no simple rule for excluding participants in a survey. Instead, we use a combination of the following methods to flag poor-quality respondents, progressing from the obvious to the obscure indicators. This process helps ensure we're obtaining high-quality results and valid findings from our surveys.

Most Obvious and Easiest Detection Methods

You'll want to start with the easiest methods to eliminate poor-quality responses. These methods help you remove the most obvious poor-quality responses. Notice that if one response falls into just one category, you don't automatically throw it out; however, if a response falls into two or more categories (flagged with simple or advanced methods), you should think twice about including it.

POOR VERBATIM RESPONSES

Multiple verbatim responses that consist of gibberish ("asdf ksjfh") or terse, repetitive words ("good" or "idk") can indicate when a respondent is not taking the survey seriously and may be speeding through rather than answering thoughtfully. Examining answers to open-ended questions is one of the easiest ways to identify poor-quality respondents, so do this first before moving to other methods.

While multiple poor responses are usually grounds for removal, a single gibberish or nonsense response is not necessarily a big problem, provided the other verbatim responses are answered thoughtfully. In some cases, we've found that these types of responses can be caused by requiring otherwise high-quality respondents to answer questions they are unable to answer meaningfully.

IRRELEVANT RESPONSES

Occasionally, people provide responses that are not gibberish but still do not match the question asked. These could be lines that were copied and pasted from other places (e.g., a related website), or even the question itself could have been copied and pasted into the answer. At first glance, these responses look legitimate (because they are long and contain common words you'd expect in a thoughtful response), but on close examination, there may be indications of participants gaming the study. Unfortunately, there are even cases of automated "bots" providing random yet plausible responses to open-ended questions—a problem that also happens in scientific research. As with poor responses, multiple nonsense responses are a bigger concern than a single suspicious response.

CHEATER QUESTIONS

If you include a "cheater question" in your survey (e.g., "Select 3 for this response") and the participant answers it wrong, that is cause for additional examination. One wrong answer can simply be a mistake, so use caution when deciding to include or exclude participants based on this criterion. We've found that removing those who incorrectly answered a single cheater question may exclude too many otherwise reliable participants (those who made mistakes when responding or were perhaps only distracted).

SPEEDERS

A participant who completes a survey too quickly is a cause for concern. For example, if a participant takes two minutes to finish a 50-question survey, it is highly unlikely that he or she is providing genuine, thoughtful responses. It's more common for participants to speed through questions or some pages than through the entire study. Here are two suggestions when deciding how fast is too fast: First, be sure not to be too strict in defining your too-fast threshold; we have been quite surprised by how quickly some people can answer survey questions. Second, where possible, look at the speed of individual pages or questions as opposed to the time it takes to complete the entire study. We've found that these more granular measures of time are sensitive to detecting speeders.

While flagging speeding participants for removal seems like an easy first step, earlier research and our data show that it's not necessarily a good indicator of poor- and high-quality responses by itself. The same goes for very slow participants: taking a very long time may just mean the participant got distracted while taking the survey and does not necessarily indicate a poor-quality response. The good news is that even if you don't detect and remove all speeders, we've found little difference between speeder and non-speeder data.

Less Obvious and More Difficult Detection Methods

Like hackers who learn to evade anti-spam detectors or speeding motorists who know where the speed traps are, some panel participants have found increasingly more sophisticated ways to game the system and receive their honorarium without conscientiously responding. This is especially concerning when a small number of participants may disproportionally account for participation across multiple panels.

INCONSISTENT RESPONSES

Some questions in a study tap into a similar concept but can be phrased with a positive or a negative tone. The SUS is a good example of a questionnaire that alternates tone. It doesn't make much sense for a participant to strongly agree with the statement "The website is easy to use" and strongly agree with the statement "I found the website very cumbersome to use." This indicates an inconsistent response.

Be careful when using this technique. We've found that people can make a legit-imate effort to complete a study but still forget to disagree with negatively toned statements when they have agreed with the positive statements. If you're using this approach, consider evaluating multiple inconsistent responses.

MISSING DATA

When compensating participants, we'll often make many, if not all, questions in our studies mandatory. When questions are not required, and participants neglect to answer many of them, this nonresponse is another symptom of poor-quality responses. Just as concerning with nonresponse though, is how your data might be biased if participants are systematically not responding to some questions. Consider examining whether the missing data are random or more systematically biased.

PATTERN DETECTION

Participants who respond using conspicuous patterns such as straightlining (all 5s or all 3s) or alternating from 5s to 1s on rating scales also indicate a bot or a disingenuous respondent. But again, be careful—if participants had a good experience on a website, it's not unsurprising for them to rate the experience as exceptional on, say, 8 of 10 items. There's more cause for concern if you see straightlining or patterns for 20 or 30 questions in a row.

DISQUALIFYING QUESTIONS

For many studies, we look for participants with particular characteristics. If a participant is admitted into a survey by answering a screening question a certain way, but then reveals in the open-ended answers she is not qualified, she is excluded (e.g., a participant needs to have a particular credit card, but in an open-ended question reveals that she doesn't have any credit cards). This can also be done with a cheater question if, for example, participants state they are familiar with fictitious brands or have bought products that don't exist.

 TIP:

If, after all this, you discover bad data after analysis and reporting, you should investigate the problem and acknowledge any problems, assess the magnitude of the issue, determine whether removing the data changes the conclusions or actions, identify the source of the problem, and resolve it.

DEALING WITH MISSING OR INCOMPLETE DATA

Despite the best planning, you'll inevitably have to deal with missing data in your surveys. Missing data typically come from participants not answering questions (either intentionally or unintentionally).

The first step in addressing missing data is identifying the type of missing data. There are three types of missing data (Sauro, 2015, Jun 2):

- **Missing completely at random:** There is no pattern in the missing data for any variable. This is the least problematic type of missing data.

- **Missing at random:** There is a pattern in the missing data but not for your primary dependent variables such as Likelihood-to-Recommend or SUS scores.

- **Missing not at random:** There is a pattern in the missing data that affects your primary dependent variables. For example, it could be that lower-income participants would be less likely to respond to a survey and thus affect your conclusions about income and the Likelihood-to-Recommend. Missing not at random is your worst-case scenario. Proceed with caution.

Missing data are like a medical concern: ignoring the problem doesn't make it go away. Ideally, your data are missing at random, and one of these approaches will help you make the most of the data you have. Here is a list of solutions to help you manage missing data:

- **Listwise deletion:** Delete all data from any participant with missing values. If your sample is large enough, then you can likely drop data without a substantial loss of statistical power. Be sure that the values are missing at random and that you are not inadvertently removing a class of participants.

- **Recover the values:** You can sometimes contact the participants and ask them to fill out the missing values. For in-person studies, we've found it helpful to have an additional check for missing values before the participant leaves.

- **Imputation:** Imputation is replacing missing values with substitute values. The following methods use some form of imputation:

  - *Educated guessing:* It sounds arbitrary, and it isn't a preferred course of action, but you can often infer a missing value. For related questions, for example like those often presented in a matrix like in Figure 19.1, if the participant responds with all 4s, assume that the missing value is a 4.

❋ Please rate your level of agreement to the following statements about the Chipotle website.

	Strongly Disagree 1	2	3	4	Strongly Agree 5
The Chipotle website has a clean and simple presentation.	○	○	○	○	○
The Chipotle website is easy to use.	○	○	○	○	○
I find the Chipotle website to be attractive.	○	○	○	○	○
The Chipotle website is trustworthy.	○	○	○	○	○
It is easy to navigate within the Chipotle website.	○	○	○	○	○
The Chipotle website's features meet my needs.	○	○	○	○	○
The information on the Chipotle website is credible.	○	○	○	○	○
I will likely return to the Chipotle website in the future.	○	○	○	○	○

FIGURE 19.1: Example of participant responses with a missing value. The participant would likely have selected a 4 for the missing value.

  - *Average imputation:* Use the average value of the responses from the other participants to fill in the missing value. If the average of the 30 responses to the question is 4.1, use 4.1 as the imputed value. This choice is not always recommended because it can artificially reduce the variability of your data, but in some cases, it makes sense.

- *Common-point imputation:* For a rating scale, this involves using the middle point or the most-chosen value. For example, on a five-point scale, substitute a 3, the midpoint, or a 4, the most common value (in many cases). This is a bit more structured than guessing, but it's still among the riskier options. Use caution unless you have a good reason and data to support using the common-point value.

- *Regression substitution:* You can use multiple regression analysis to estimate a missing value. We use this technique to deal with missing SUS scores. Regression substitution predicts the missing value from the other values. In the case of missing SUS data, we had enough data to create stable regression equations and predict the missing values automatically in the calculator.

- *Multiple imputation:* The most sophisticated and currently most popular approach is to take the regression idea further and take advantage of correlations between responses. With multiple imputation, software creates plausible values based on the correlations for the missing data and then averages the simulated datasets by incorporating random errors in your predictions. It is one of how computers continue to change the statistical landscape. Most statistical packages like SPSS come with a multiple-imputation feature.

 TIP:

You may need to revisit this list after your initial round of analysis to see how results may or may not change when addressing missing data.

PREPARING FOR ANALYSIS

With the data gathered, it's time to conduct analyses to understand the user experience. To analyze the data, you can use the following common platforms.

Research/survey platforms web apps: Most commercial survey platforms (including MUiQ, SurveyMonkey, and Qualtrics) contain their own core graphing and data summarization tools. These are typically only sufficient for providing basic descriptive statistics around your demographics, and they have less support for statistical comparisons or providing confidence intervals. If you're using them, be sure you can filter out any participants you removed. We intentionally included built-in confidence intervals, cross tabbing, and statistical tests with p-values in MUiQ to streamline the analysis phase (see Figure 19.2).

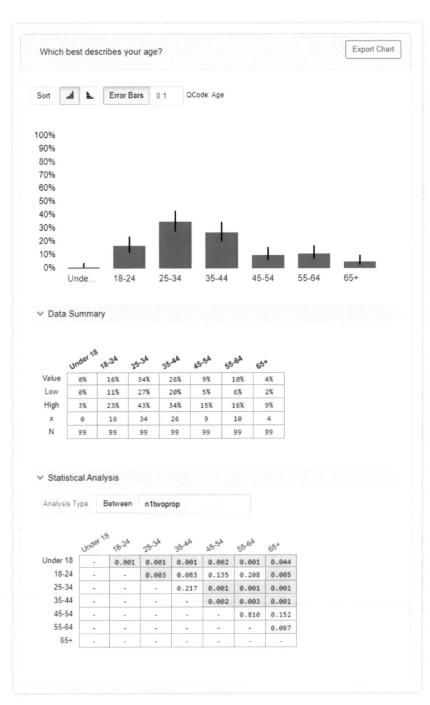

FIGURE 19.2: Example of MUiQ statistical output.

Microsoft Excel: Excel is our go-to program for summarizing study-level and task-level metrics. It's not great for conducting advanced analyses like regression or ANOVA, but for 90% of graphs and analyses, Excel does the trick. To learn some essential Excel skills, see Sauro (2016, Jun 21: Part 1 and Jun 28: Part 2).

Usability Statistics Package (Expanded): We created a statistics package using Excel that does just about everything you'd need to do to apply statistics to survey data (and just about any UX data). We also wrote a companion book to *Quantifying the User Experience* (Sauro & Lewis, 2016) that shows you step-by-step instructions on how to conduct the most frequent analyses, appropriately called Excel & R Companion to the *2nd Edition of Quantifying the User Experience* (Lewis & Sauro, 2016). Both are available online (Excel Statistics Package and the PDF book).

SPSS: Many graduate students in the behavioral sciences are familiar with the Statistical Package for the Social Sciences (SPSS) software. The software has since expanded into other markets and has everything you need to conduct basic and advanced statistical analyses. The major drawback is it comes with a huge price tag. We've also found its graphs cumbersome to create.

R: The free R statistical package is an alternative to SPSS that many graduate programs are adopting. It's open source and has lots of free add-on packages that can accomplish more than even SPSS can. The major drawback is that it is command-line based, so you'll need to get comfortable with its syntax. The free RStudio helps with some of the core commands, but there is still a bit of a learning curve with R. We have published a set of common and unique R functions (Lewis & Sauro, 2016).

Minitab: Minitab is a statistical package that is less expensive than SPSS and has more of an engineering focus compared to SPSS's behavioral science focus.

CHAPTER SUMMARY

This chapter covered steps and methods for identifying poor-quality responses, what to do with missing data, and analytical platforms.

I've collected data, so I'm ready for analysis — right? …No, first you should clean the data. We estimate that about 10% of survey respondents are problematic (cheating, speeding, misrepresenting, not engaged).

How should I start the cleaning process? …Start with the easiest methods. There are several indicators of potentially problematic data. Don't automatically exclude data with one indicator, but if there are two or more, examine all the participant's responses and decide whether to include it. The easier methods include:

- Look for poor-quality verbatim responses (e.g., "asdf jkl," "idk").

- Look for irrelevant responses (e.g., text pasted from a convenient location like survey instructions or questions).

- Check for incorrect responses to cheater questions (e.g., a response of 2 to an item directing respondents to select 3).

- Check survey completion times for obvious speeders (total survey and ideally by page).

I've completed the easy checks, so what else can I do to get clean data? ...The less obvious methods require closer inspection of the data. These methods include:

- Check for inconsistent responses (e.g., strong agreement to a statement that a website is easy to use and strong agreement to a statement that a website is hard to use).

- Check for excessive amounts of straightlining (e.g., all 5s) or systematic alternation (e.g., from 1 to 5 to 1 to 5...) across a series of rating items.

- Check for disqualifying responses to questions (e.g., survey responses that are different from screening responses, an indication of familiarity with fictitious brands).

- Check for missing data.

I have some missing data, so what should I do? ...First, identify the type of missing data, then manage it. The three types of missing data are missing completely at random, missing at random, and missing not at random. These differ depending on whether there are patterns in the missing data and if the patterns affect primary dependent variables. To manage missing data, you can:

- Delete all data from any participant with missing data, but only if your sample size is large enough to do this without substantial loss of statistical power.

- Ask participants to provide the missing data, but you can only do this if you can communicate with them after they submit their survey responses.

- Use imputation to replace missing values with substitute data, using methods that range from educated guessing to advanced statistical approaches like regression or multiple imputation.

Now that I have a clean and complete set of data, what tools can I use for analysis? ...There are a variety of analytical tools that vary in price and functionality. Some of the common analytical platforms are:

- Built-in graphing and data summarization tools provided in commercial survey platforms are convenient but typically have limited capability for inferential statistics (e.g., confidence intervals or t-tests—a limitation for which MUiQ is a notable exception).

- Excel is the go-to program for summarizing findings, but it is not adequate for advanced analyses (e.g., multiple regression).

- The MeasuringU Usability Statistics Package (Expanded) is an Excel package that has sheets for most of the statistical analyses that UX researchers conduct, including specialized methods for discrete-binary data that are not available in other packages. Due to the limitations of Excel, however, it cannot perform advanced methods like multiple regression, factor analysis, cluster analysis, or discriminant analysis.

- SPSS is a highly advanced package for statistical analysis, often used in the behavioral sciences, but there is a hefty license fee for full functionality, and graphing with SPSS can be cumbersome.

- Minitab is a statistical package with an engineering focus that is less expensive than SPSS.

- R is a free, open-source statistical package with many free add-ons, but it comes with a steep learning curve.

CHAPTER 20:
SINGLE-ITEM (UNIVARIATE) ANALYSIS

It can be daunting when you're faced with the task of analyzing thousands of responses to dozens or hundreds of questions. A good place to start is to revisit the research questions that provided the impetus for the survey (see Chapter 1). Then address the "main effect" of each research question (e.g., are people likely to purchase a new product?) and proceed to interaction or secondary effects (e.g., are experienced users more likely to purchase a new product?). We'll refer to two surveys that measured people's experiences and attitudes with airline and travel aggregator websites (e.g., Airlines: United Airlines, British Airways; Travel: Kayak, Orbitz). For more information about the airline websites survey, see Sauro et al. (2022, Jul 26), and for the travel aggregator websites survey, see Sauro et al. (2022, Aug 30).

To address each research question, consider whether your analysis will need one, two, or three or more items, how to display the results (table or graph), and finally where, if at all, your findings will appear in a report.

A single item in a survey can contain a small amount of information (e.g., age or gender, a mean on a rating scale) or a lot, such as in a pick-some item with more than a hundred choices. But it is also possible for a single item to measure a main effect (e.g., UX-Lite rating of perceived ease of use). We'll start with analyzing measurement items (closed-ended questions) and then address discovery (open-ended questions).

As covered in the decision tree for measurement items (see Chapter 10), start the analysis by determining if the item is categorical (e.g., education, gender) or noncategorical (e.g., a satisfaction rating scale). We'll answer the following core questions:

- What are good ways to analyze data from single survey items?
- How should I analyze discrete-binary data from single items?
- How do I analyze data from rating scales or ranking?
- Should I compute modes or medians for rating scales?
- Which are better: means or box scores?
- How do you analyze data from allocation question types?

CATEGORICAL

Categorical data are collected as the number of respondents selecting one or more response options, and it is typically presented as a percentage of the total cleaned sample. Categorical data can be mutually exclusive (respondents can select *only* one option, e.g., age) or not mutually exclusive (respondents can select more than one response option, e.g., clothing websites visited in the past six months).

It can be easier to interpret percentages than raw numbers, especially if the sample sizes are not round numbers (e.g., 133 vs. 100, 978 vs. 1000). Categorical percentages are often called frequency distributions, as you can see how frequently responses are distributed across the options.

 TIP:

Be sure to use data *after* cleaning to generate the percentages. For example, if the initial survey contained 370 responses and you removed 20, the denominator for your overall percentages should be 350.

Mutually Exclusive

Examples of frequency distributions for mutually exclusive items of income and age are shown in Tables 20.1 and 20.2.

Income Category	%
$0–$24k	16%
$25k–$49k	18%
$50k–$74k	22%
$75k–$99k	19%
$100k+	25%

TABLE 20.1: Income distribution from a survey on airline website usage (*n* = 350).

Age	Value
Under 18	0%
18–24	18%
25–34	40%
35–44	22%
45–54	11%
55–64	6%
65+	3%

TABLE 20.2: Age distribution from a survey on airline website usage (*n* = 350).

Frequency distributions can help identify high or low percentages across categories. Table 20.1 shows that a substantial percentage of respondents had household incomes higher than $100k (86 / 350 = 25%). The higher income is somewhat expected because, for participants to qualify for the survey, they must have visited or purchased on an airline website in the last few months. Also, many respondents were frequent users, suggesting they take multiple flights in a year (reasonably associated with higher incomes).

TIP:

In some cases, ordered categorical data (e.g., age, income) can be converted to means (e.g., average age, median income) if it needs to be analyzed quantitatively (e.g., as a continuous variable in a regression equation). One approach is to take the midpoint or upper or lower bound of a category (e.g., 45–54 becomes 50). Keep in mind this introduces additional error and should be used only as an approximation.

TIP:

In mutually exclusive frequency distributions, double check that your percentages add up to 100%. If they don't, it could be a simple rounding error, a calculation error (e.g., double counting), or missing data you need to explain. One of the first things stakeholders will do is inspect the percentages. If they don't add up to 100%, you'd better have an explanation ready.

Non–Mutually Exclusive

Categorical data can extend beyond characterization and screening questions and help answer primary research questions. Figure 20.1 shows the percentages of respondents in the airline survey reporting if they would be willing to pay an extra fee for different types of seats (along with 90% confidence intervals). Figure 20.2 shows the primary reasons respondents reported visiting the airline website. In both figures, the percentages can add up to over 100% because respondents could select more than one response option (the item was not mutually exclusive).

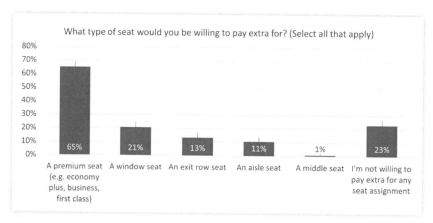

FIGURE 20.1: Graph of respondents reporting what type of seat they would pay for, if any (select-all-that-apply). Black lines are 90% confidence intervals.

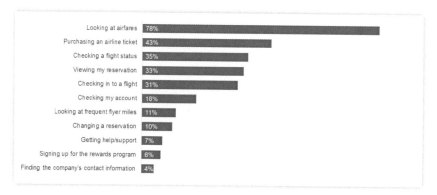

FIGURE 20.2: Primary reasons participants reported visiting the airline website (select-all-that-apply).

Frequency Data

How frequently something was reported is also a common type of data collected in surveys, both for screening and characterizing respondents. It's often one of the key variables used for weighting and calibrating responses to known external criteria in sampling (see Chapter 21). There is a natural order to frequency data, and that order (usually from low to high or high to low) should be indicated in the results.

Some of the most consequential concepts that impact UX metrics are what people do (prior experience with a product and/or domain) which we often feature early and prominently in our survey results. Prior experience can be presented using a frequency distribution as shown in Table 20.3.

Frequency of Visits to Air Canada Website	% of Respondents
Daily	0%
Few Times a Week	4%
Few Times a Month	18%
Few Times a Year	58%
Once in the last 12 Months	20%

TABLE 20.3: Frequency of reported visits to Air Canada's website (from the survey of airline website usage).

Table 20.4 shows an example of frequency data for participants across multiple airlines from the airline survey. The most common frequency (mode) is highlighted in green and shows comparable prior experience by airline.

	Daily	Few Times a Week	Few Times a Month	Few Times a Year	Once in the Last 12 Months
Air Canada	0%	4%	18%	58%	20%
Air France	0%	2%	14%	56%	28%
Alaska Air	0%	4%	16%	60%	20%
American Airlines	2%	4%	22%	60%	12%
British Airways	2%	4%	18%	58%	18%
Delta	0%	2%	10%	64%	24%
Frontier	0%	2%	14%	50%	34%

(continued on pg. 315)

	Daily	Few Times a Week	Few Times a Month	Few Times a Year	Once in the Last 12 Months
Luftansa	2%	2%	16%	56%	24%
Ryan Air	2%	2%	20%	62%	14%
Southwest	0%	0%	14%	60%	26%
United	0%	4%	12%	56%	28%

TABLE 20.4: Reported usage of airline websites with the modal frequency in green.

Confidence Intervals for Categorical Data

These survey results (like in most applied surveys) sample only a small portion of the population (see Chapter 4 on sampling). The percentages from the categories will fluctuate each time we sample, and each sample we take differs by some small amount from the population value.

Confidence intervals provide the most plausible range for the unknown population. We recommend adding confidence intervals to most categorical questions that are used to generalize about the overall population. See Appendix A for more on selecting the level of confidence.

For percentages of binary data, we recommend using the adjusted-Wald confidence interval. It provides accurate confidence intervals for small sample sizes ($n < 10$) and large sample sizes ($n > 10,000+$). For more information on the adjusted-Wald confidence interval and its derivation, see Chapter 3 in *Quantifying the User Experience* (Sauro & Lewis, 2016).

 TIP:

We typically do not put confidence intervals around demographic questions or items that just describe the sample (especially when data are collected from a nonprobability panel). These percentages show how the sample was characterized, and we don't typically use those to generalize about the composition of the population. Of course, if we want to estimate the population characteristics from a probability sample (such as age, gender, or income), we can include confidence intervals around those. Keep in mind that confidence intervals from a probability sample characterize the population of interest, while those from a nonprobability sample characterize the panel used for the survey

TIP:

Be careful when communicating confidence intervals. A 95% confidence interval doesn't tell you the probability a population percentage falls within a range (that would be a probability interval). It's more like saying we are 95% confident in the method of computing confidence intervals, but not for any given interval. Any given interval we compute from sample data may or may not contain the population average. Even though 95% of samples will contain the population average, we just don't know when a specific interval is one of the 5% that doesn't.

ADDING ERROR BARS TO GRAPHS IN EXCEL

Most researchers I've worked with have some experience with Excel and can generally figure out how to create and customize graphs and tables. Adding error bars to Excel graphs, however, seems to give most people trouble. It's not something they do often, if ever, and it's not the most intuitive process. For more on Excel, see our articles on essential Excel skills for researchers (Sauro, 2016, Jun 21: Part 1 and Jun 28: Part 2).

NOT CATEGORICAL: RATING, RANKING, AND ALLOCATION

Noncategorical data include the rating scales and ranking questions often used to address the main research questions of a survey (e.g., agreement data, intent to purchase, attitude toward usage). There are several different ways to analyze these types of data.

Rating Scale

Multipoint rating scale data can be analyzed as averages, frequency distributions, and box scores. Throughout this book (especially Part 3), we've shown several examples of how both means and frequency distributions (from which box scores are derived) address slightly different questions, so both have a role in survey analysis.

MEASURING THE AVERAGE: MEANS AND MEDIANS

What is the average satisfaction rating? Did the average satisfaction score change? "Average" is a generic term for a more technical term — *central tendency*. The mean is the most common, but not the only, measure of the central tendency, and it is a good place to start when analyzing rating scale data like the linear numeric scale in Figure 20.3.

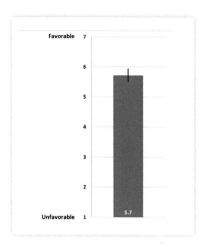

FIGURE 20.3: Mean brand favorability of Kayak.

The mean of Kayak can be made more meaningful when compared to other travel brands (Figure 20.4).

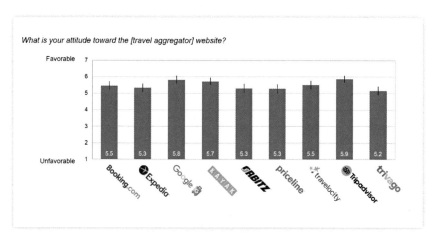

FIGURE 20.4: Means for the travel websites' brand attitude (with 90% confidence intervals).

Figure 20.5 shows the mean likelihood of continued use of the websites.

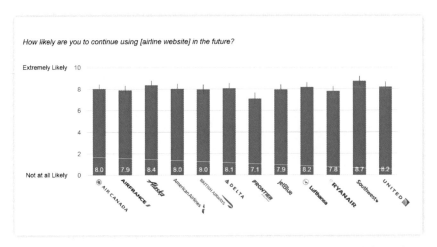

FIGURE 20.5: Means for likelihood to continue using airline websites (with 90% confidence intervals).

Confidence interval around the mean

When presenting means, we recommend including confidence intervals (usually 90% or 95% confidence). For example, Figures 20.4 and 20.5 show the means with 90% confidence intervals. For rating scale data, we recommend using the *t*-confidence interval because it works well for both small and large sample sizes (from fewer than 10 to more than 10,000). For details on computing *t*-confidence intervals, see Chapter 3 in *Quantifying the User Experience*.

Adding numbers to agreement labels

If your response options didn't include numbers (e.g., non-numbered verbal labels like "Strongly Disagree" to "Strongly Agree" or unlabeled radio buttons), you can still compute means and confidence intervals. Just assign numbers (e.g., 1 to 5) to the response options, then compute the average rating. Be warned: there are some who disagree (often passionately) with taking the mean of rating scale data and adding numbers to labels and Likert-type data—a topic we'll discuss next.

CAN YOU TAKE THE MEAN OF ORDINAL DATA?

In a recent correspondence, a client commented that they were surprised that we suggested using means to analyze rating scale data, as this type of response option doesn't lend itself to taking averages. We're used to encountering this concern. So, can you take the mean of ordinal data?

Our answer is yes, of course you can. But it depends on who you ask! (See Chapter 9 in *Quantifying the User Experience*.)

Figure 20.6 shows an example where we assign numbers to an agreement scale and take the mean. An item in a survey asked 62 participants to rate their agreement to a five-point version of the Single Ease Question (SEQ) on the Budget rental car website.

The website is easy to use:

✳ The website is easy to use.				
Strongly Disagree	Disagree	Neutral	Agree	Strongly Disagree
1	2	3	4	5

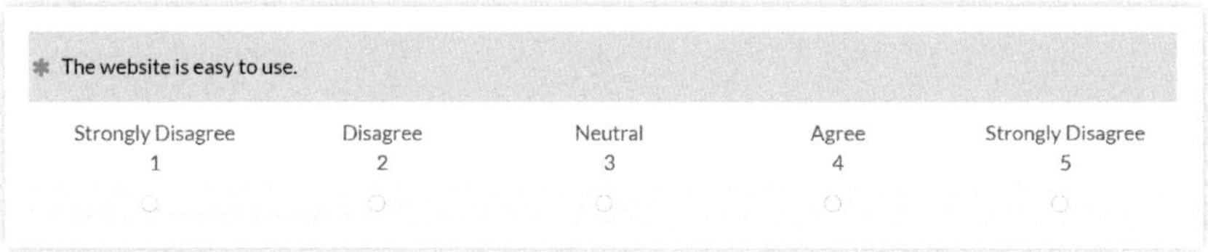

FIGURE 20.6: Five-point version of the SEQ.

Table 20.5 shows the frequency distribution of raw responses for the 62 participants (with corresponding values):

Coded Value	Response Option	# Responding
5	Strongly Agree	26
4	Agree	22
3	Neutral	7
2	Disagree	5
1	Strongly Disagree	2

TABLE 20.5: Frequency distribution of 62 SEQ ratings of a task on the Budget website.

If we assign numbers from 1 to 5 for each category label (Strongly Disagree = 1, Strongly Agree = 5), we create an ordered set of categories called *ordinal data*. If we then take the average of the 62 coded responses, the result is 4.05, or about 4. Is such an operation permissible? And what exactly does a 4 mean in this context?

The cautious approach
Some people (in industry and academia) would say not only is it not allowed, but also the result is meaningless. For example, the author of a statistics guide for students (Kostoulas, 2013, Feb 13) says it means nothing: "To put it in the simplest terms possible: Ordinal data cannot yield mean values."

The guide goes on to recommend the "right" way to analyze multipoint scale data: "A safer way forward, if you are interested in finding what the 'average' or 'typical' response is, is to look at the median response."

The term *ordinal*, as used in the field of measurement, comes from the work of S.S. Stevens, who in 1946 delineated four levels of measurement:

- **Nominal:** Numbers that are simply labels, such as the numbering of football players or product model numbers.

- **Ordinal:** Numbers that have an order, but where the differences between numbers do not necessarily correspond to the differences in the underlying attribute, such as levels on multipoint rating scales or rank order of products based on percentage of market share.

- **Interval:** Numbers that are not only ordinal but for which equal differences in the numbers correspond to equal differences in the underlying attribute, such as Fahrenheit or Celsius temperature scales.

- **Ratio:** Numbers that are not only interval but for which there is a true 0 point, so equal ratios in the numbers correspond to equal ratios in the underlying attribute, such as time intervals or monetary amounts.

While the categorization seems uncontroversial, Stevens went so far as to say that the level of measurement dictates what you can do with the numbers. He said you can only take the mean and standard deviation of data if it's at least the interval level. But not everyone agreed with him then (Lord, 1953), nor do they now (Sauro & Lewis, 2016, Chapter 9).

Differing perspectives

Most people assume that when numbers are involved, there's a clear right or wrong answer. What many people don't realize is that this question is more like asking someone if the government should more strongly regulate trade and less like does 2 + 2 = 4. The answer to a political question will, of course, depend on who you ask! The answer is influenced by that person's particular world views.

As much as the media depicts science as some sort of book of facts—unchanging and written with consensus—the truth is that science in general and measurement in particular are in flux, with people differing on theory, the interpretation of facts, and sometimes on the very facts themselves.

Like an ideological spectrum from liberal to conservative, there is also a statistical spectrum from liberal to conservative. People who tend to be more liberal in statistics and measurement tend to relax rules and theory when it serves useful purposes (a pragmatic style) but not to the point of doing everything possible to squeeze significance out of the data. In contrast, those who are more conservative tend to be more rigid with theories and rules and are reluctant to bend them, even if relaxing the "rules" generates useful results. Knowing where your professor or the author of a book or website falls on that spectrum will help you understand why they recommend or prohibit certain operations.

Different approaches, similar conclusions

Even the progenitor of this rigid thinking, Stevens himself, acknowledged that taking the mean of ordinal data will often lead to fruitful results. The good news for practitioners who are less concerned with theory and just want to do the "right" thing is that, in most cases, the differing approaches lead to similar conclusions.

For example, we can use the mode (one of the "approved" measures of central tendency) for summarizing Likert-type data. In Table 20.6, the most common response (the mode) is Neutral, with 17 (27%) participants picking it. This is about as informative as knowing the mean response is 4. And it so happens the median is also 4. But if you think using the median instead of the mean or mode is a panacea, that cure is often worse than the purported problem (Lewis, 1993).

Whether you take the mean, median, or mode, you still have a similar challenge with interpretation. The challenge to the researcher is less in how to summarize raw responses and more in how you derive meaning from the numbers. To make any measure meaningful, we must compare it to something.

Compared to what?

For example, we can compare the responses from the same participants who rented a car on the Enterprise website (Table 20.6).

Coded Value	Response Option	# Responding
5	Strongly Agree	7
4	Agree	16
3	Neutral	17
2	Disagree	13
1	Strongly Disagree	9

TABLE 20.6: Frequency distribution of 62 SEQ ratings of a task on the Enterprise website.

Assigning numbers to the categories, we get a mean of 2.98, or about 3. Some would say this 3 is also meaningless. But now we know that mean is a full point below the Budget mean of 4. This difference is also visible in the bar chart of the frequency distributions for both websites in Figure 20.7. See Chapter 21 for guidance on statistically comparing means and categorical data.

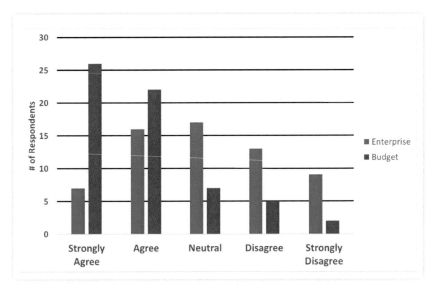

FIGURE 20.7: Frequency distribution on a Likert-type item asking the participant's experience with Budget and Enterprise rental car websites.

A few things to keep in mind when averaging ordinal data

When working with items that have multipoint response options, especially the five-point Likert variety, keep a few things in mind:

- Some people will object to your taking the mean of this type of data and will more often than not tell you that what you're doing is wrong, meaningless, impermissible, or even "illegal!"

- Whether someone tells you it's permissible to average ordinal data depends on their view of measurement theory—and not all people agree (despite most people being fine with averaging ranks, which are also ordinal).

- Despite disagreement on the permissibility of operations on ordinal data, doing so is usually helpful in making decisions in user research—something even the most rigid thinker would have a hard time disputing.

- You'll often reach similar conclusions regardless of whether you use mode, median, or mean.

- The mean and standard deviation, however, have the advantage of often revealing statistical differences at smaller sample sizes—which is one of the reasons we recommend the approach.

- While some people have an issue with computing the mean of a single ordinal item, far fewer take issue with averaging multiple Likert-type items, such as those in the SUS or SUPR-Q, as it offers a more continuous and interval-like measure.

- Be careful with the interpretation of ordinal data. Using the mean of ordinal data is fine; just be careful not to make interval or ratio statements about your data—even researchers who take a relaxed view of averaging ordinal data would disagree with that practice. While we can say that the mean rating is consistently higher on Budget, we can't say that participants find the Budget website one unit easier than Enterprise—that's an interval statement. And we certainly can't say Budget is 27% more usable than Enterprise—that's a ratio statement.

Should you use the median?

The mean is a good measure of central tendency when the distribution of responses is reasonably symmetrical. When the data aren't symmetrical, a few large values can pull the mean away from the center. For example, in a survey that collects salary information for an industry (e.g., the UXPA salary survey), it's advisable to take the median (or perform a log transformation) when describing the "average" salary, as a few very high salaries can pull the mean up.

Rating scale data tend to NOT be symmetrical, which can be seen in the frequency distributions above for Enterprise and Budget and below in Figure 20.8 for attitudes toward Kayak.

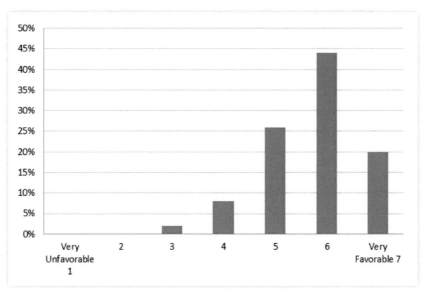

FIGURE 20.8: Frequency distribution of responses to a brand favorability question toward the website kayak.com collected in the summer of 2022.

In nonsymmetrical distributions, the median can be a better measure of the center. Consequently, some analysts advocate using the median rather than the mean for measuring the central tendency of rating scale data.

However, there are some important differences between discrete rating scales and more continuous variables like time or money. First, the maximum and minimum possible values of rating scales are limited, so even when a rating scale distribution is skewed, the influence of extreme scores on the mean is limited, unlike time or money where a few very extreme values can substantially influence the mean.

Second, rating scales can take only specific values over a limited range, while variables like time and money can take an essentially infinite number of values. So, the median of a five-point rating scale can only be one of nine discrete values (1, 1.5, 2, 2.5, 3, 3.5, 4, 4.5, or 5), but the mean of a rating scale becomes more and more continuous as the sample size increases, making it a much more sensitive measure of the central tendency of rating scales. See the sidebar for a story about the real-world consequences of these properties of rating scales and the evidence favoring the use of the mean rather than the median for these types of analyses.

FOR RATING SCALES, MEAN DIFFERENCES ARE MORE INFORMATIVE THAN MEDIAN DIFFERENCES

In the late 1980s, Jim was involved in a high-profile project at IBM in which he compared performance and satisfaction across a set of common tasks for three competitive office application suites (Lewis et al., 1990). As he tells the story:

Based on what I had learned in my college statistics classes about Stevens' levels of measurement, I pronounced that the multipoint rating scale data we were dealing with did not meet the assumptions required to take the mean of the data for the rating scales because they were ordinal rather than interval or ratio, so we should present their central tendencies using medians rather than means. I also advised against the use of t-tests for individual comparisons of the rating scale results, promoting instead its nonparametric analog, the Mann–Whitney U-test.

The folks who started running the statistics and putting the presentation together (which would have been given to a group that included high-level IBM executives) called me in a panic after they started following my advice. In the analyses, there were cases where the medians were identical, but the U-test detected a statistically significant difference. It turns out that the U-test is sensitive not only to central tendency, but also to the shape of the distribution, and in these cases the distributions had opposite skew but overlapping medians. As a follow-up, I systematically investigated the relationship among mean and median differences for multipoint scales and the observed significance levels of t- and U-tests conducted on the same

(continued on pg. 325)

> *data, all taken from our fairly large-scale usability test. It turned out that the mean difference correlated more than the median difference with the observed significance levels (both parametric and nonparametric) for discrete multipoint scale data.*
>
> *Consequently, I no longer promote the concepts of Stevens' levels of measurement with regard to permissible statistical analysis, although I believe this distinction is critical when interpreting and applying results. It appears that t-tests have sufficient robustness for most usability work—especially when you can create a set of difference scores to use for the analysis.*

For details, see Lewis (1993).

FREQUENCY DISTRIBUTIONS

Frequency distributions show the number and percentages of respondents who selected each response option. The frequency distribution also allows the researcher to easily visualize the most frequently selected option (mode) and the top-box and top-two-box percentages. In the frequency distribution of the brand favorability of kayak.com (Figure 20.8), the most common selection (the mode) was a 6, with 44% of respondents.

Top-box score

The percentage of selection of the most favorable response option is often called the *top-box score*. The term stems from the origins of paper-administered surveys, which had rating scales displayed as a series of boxes (illustrated in Figure 20.9).

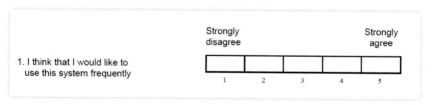

FIGURE 20.9: Illustration of "boxes" from the original paper version of the System Usability Scale (Brooke, 1996).

Table 20.7 shows the top-box scores from respondents' answers to a set of seven-point rating scales about their experience on an airline website toward some common features (*1 Very Poor—7 Excellent*). It is presented using the "heat map" option in Excel, which presents lower scores as red and higher scores as green (see Chapter 22 for how to display information).

Airline	Choosing a seat	Checking in to your flight	Using miles or points to book a ticket	Making a flight reservation	Finding airline contact information	Changing a reservation
Air Canada	19%	34%	13%	32%	15%	13%
Air France	21%	35%	8%	35%	25%	19%
Alaska Air	33%	40%	19%	44%	27%	15%
American Air	42%	48%	21%	44%	35%	21%
BritishAirways	19%	23%	12%	27%	12%	12%
Delta	27%	45%	27%	41%	29%	12%
Frontier	20%	39%	11%	33%	20%	13%
JetBlue	31%	39%	20%	31%	29%	24%
Lufthansa	23%	34%	4%	30%	28%	15%
Ryan Air	14%	16%	2%	20%	4%	6%
Southwest	29%	60%	29%	60%	48%	50%
United	38%	44%	21%	44%	25%	21%

TABLE 20.7: Top-box scores for a set of UX ratings of airline websites.

Top-two-box score

Extending the idea of the top-box score is the top-two-box score. As the name suggests, it includes the first and second most favorable response (e.g., 6s and 7s for seven-point scales). Table 20.8 shows the top-two-box scores for the same rating scales shown in Table 20.7. The most obvious difference here is that, not too surprisingly, the top-two-box percentages are larger than the top-box percentages.

Airline	Choosing a seat	Checking in to your flight	Using miles or points to book a ticket	Making a flight reservation	Finding airline contact information	Changing a reservation
Air Canada	49%	66%	23%	72%	45%	36%
Air France	54%	71%	23%	67%	48%	29%
Alaska Air	79%	79%	40%	79%	50%	46%
American Air	69%	81%	35%	77%	63%	40%
BritishAirways	54%	75%	29%	79%	44%	25%
Delta	61%	71%	45%	69%	45%	24%
Frontier	35%	54%	24%	67%	48%	20%
JetBlue	47%	65%	29%	59%	43%	41%
Lufthansa	51%	74%	15%	70%	40%	32%
Ryan Air	33%	51%	6%	57%	24%	16%
Southwest	48%	79%	40%	83%	71%	63%
United	69%	73%	40%	73%	48%	42%

TABLE 20.8: Top-two-box scores for a set of UX ratings of airline websites.

Bottom-box score

The bottom box is the least favorable response, and a bottom-box score is the percentage of responses choosing the bottom box. For example, Figure 20.8 above shows that there are no "Very Unfavorable" responses for Kayak, so its bottom-box score is 0%.

Table 20.9 shows the percentage of responses choosing a Very Poor 1 for the same airlines shown in Tables 20.7 and 20.8. In this case, the heat mapping is reversed, so lower scores are better (fewer bad responses) and displayed green. Top-box and bottom-box scoring are correlated (participants can't select both the least and most favorable response options for the same question), so there are similar patterns in Tables 20.7, 20.8, and 20.9. However, this approach highlights the poorly perceived experience of changing a reservation on Ryan Air (10% bottom box), whereas other low-scoring top-box attitudes (e.g., using miles, finding airline contact information) had few or no bottom-box responses.

Airline	Choosing a seat	Checking in to your flight	Using miles or points to book a ticket	Making a flight reservation	Finding airline contact information	Changing a reservation
Air Canada	2%	0%	0%	0%	0%	0%
Air France	0%	0%	2%	2%	2%	2%
Alaska Air	0%	0%	0%	0%	2%	0%
American Air	0%	0%	4%	4%	2%	2%
BritishAirways	0%	0%	4%	0%	2%	0%
Delta	2%	2%	2%	2%	6%	4%
Frontier	2%	0%	2%	0%	2%	7%
JetBlue	0%	2%	2%	0%	2%	2%
Lufthansa	0%	0%	0%	0%	2%	0%
Ryan Air	0%	0%	6%	0%	4%	10%
Southwest	2%	0%	0%	0%	0%	0%
United	4%	0%	4%	0%	0%	6%

TABLE 20.9: Bottom-box scores for a set of UX ratings of airline websites.

Net Scoring

There is usually a strong need to provide a single number for analyzing or communicating the attitude toward an item, hence the use of the mean, top-box, top-two-box, or bottom-box scores. However, there is information contained in the bottom box that isn't necessarily reflected in the top box (and vice versa). One way to pack more information into a single score is to use *net scoring*. Net scoring involves subtracting bottom-box from top-box percentages (using any specified number of top and bottom boxes).

Three examples of net scoring are the Net Promoter Score (NPS), the Microsoft Net Satisfaction (NSAT), and Forrester's Customer Experience Index (CxPi).

- **Net Promoter Score:** Top-two minus bottom-seven-box scores for one eleven-point item.

- **MSFT NSAT:** Top-box minus bottom-box scores for one four-point item.

- **Forrester's CxPi:** Average of top-two minus bottom-two-box scores over three five-point items.

Table 20.10 shows the net scoring (top box minus bottom box) for the same airline data presented for top, top-two, and bottom-box scoring.

	Choosing a seat	Checking in to your flight	Using miles or points to book a ticket	Making a flight reservation	Finding airline contact information	Changing a reservation
Air Canada	17%	34%	13%	32%	15%	13%
Air France	21%	35%	6%	33%	23%	17%
Alaska Air	33%	40%	19%	44%	25%	15%
American Air	42%	48%	17%	40%	33%	19%
BritishAirways	19%	23%	8%	27%	10%	12%
Delta	24%	43%	24%	39%	22%	8%
Frontier	17%	39%	9%	33%	17%	7%
JetBlue	31%	37%	18%	31%	27%	22%
Lufthansa	23%	34%	4%	30%	26%	15%
Ryan Air	14%	16%	-4%	20%	0%	-4%
Southwest	27%	60%	29%	60%	48%	50%
United	33%	44%	17%	44%	25%	15%

TABLE 20.10: Net box scores for a set of UX ratings of airline websites.

MEAN OR BOX SCORE?

A common criticism of box scores relative to means is that box scores lose information because, unlike the mean, box scores are based on a fraction of the available responses. As we have shown (especially in the chapters in Part 3), there are times when we see differences in the mean score of a rating scale but not in top-box scores. In other cases, however, there's no significant mean difference, but there is a significant difference in measures of extreme responses (e.g., top-box scores). There are also times when their statistical outcomes are the same. Both means and top-box scores can be helpful in UX research because they answer different questions. There is some evidence that the percentage of extreme responders (top or bottom box) tends to be a better predictor of future behavior than the mean, while the mean does a better job of characterizing changes in central tendency that might not be detected at the extremes (Sauro, 2018, May 2).

TOP BOX, TOP-TWO BOX, BOTTOM BOX, OR NET BOX?

Participants can have a very positive attitude, a tepid attitude, or a very negative attitude. Because measurements of extreme responses (bottom box and top box) tend to be better predictors of future behavior than average or more tepid respondents, we prefer top-box to top-two-box measurements. The top-two-box score includes responses from more respondents, but the downside is that the additional respondents have a less extreme attitude.

The decision to measure bottom- rather than top-box scores depends on which seems to offer the best opportunity to discriminate between the products being rated. For certain questions, there may be few if any respondents who select the bottom (or top box). For example, in the airline survey examples, there were few bottom-box responses for "Choosing a seat," offering little ability to discriminate between airlines.

TIP:

If you have generally favorable responses to an item, the top box will likely offer better differentiation than the bottom box (and vice versa)

It's a bit harder to provide guidance for net-box scores. An advantage of net box is it uses information about both negative and positive extreme responses, so you don't need to worry about whether top box or bottom box is more discriminating on a case-by-case basis. A disadvantage of net box is that it is an uncommon type of metric—a trinomial. Unlike a binomial, which takes only two values (usually 0 and 1), a trinomial can take three values (–1 when a response is in the bottom box(es), +1 when a response is in the top box(es), and 0 for all other boxes). Our experience in working out statistical methods appropriate for trinomials indicates that the variability of trinomials is usually higher than for binomial metrics, so for a given sample size, the trinomial will be less precise, or alternatively, for a given precision, the sample size for trinomials will need to be larger than for binomial metrics (Lewis & Sauro, 2021, Aug 17).

SCALING TO 100

Researchers often want to compare the results from different point scales (e.g., 5 to 7 or 7 to 11). Alternatively, a researcher may want to scale raw values into a more executive-friendly range from 0 to 100. When the original scale starts at 1 (e.g., 1 to 5), first subtract 1 from its ratings, and then stretch it to 100 by multiplying it by 100 divided by the maximum value of the new scale (which will be the maximum value of the original scale minus 1). Table 20.11 shows the conversion for five, seven, and eleven-point scales (Lewis & Sauro, 2020, Jul 8).

5-point	1		2		3		4		5	
101-point	0.0		25.0		50.0		75.0		100.0	
7-point	1	2	3	4	5	6	7			
101-point	0.00	16.67	33.33	50.00	66.67	83.33	100.00			
11-point	0	1	2	3	4	5	6	7	8	9	10
101-point	0.0	10.0	20.0	30.0	40.0	50.0	60.0	70.0	80.0	90.0	100.0

TABLE 20.11: Conversions of five, seven, and eleven-point scales to 0–100-point scales.

SPECIAL ITEM SCORING

Certain items, especially standardized questionnaires with multiple items, have their own scoring methods (e.g., the SUS, SUPR-Q, and UX-Lite). See Appendix B for details on scoring some of the more common questionnaires used in UX and CX surveys.

Ranking

There are two common ways to analyze ranking data: the mean of the ranks or the frequency distribution of the item rank order. Ranking data can be displayed with 1 as the highest or lowest rank. We've found that having the most important item ranked the lowest can be confusing for some stakeholders (1st place is better than 3rd place), so by default, we invert the scale of our ranking graphs as shown in Figure 20.10 with 1.0 (first place) at the top.

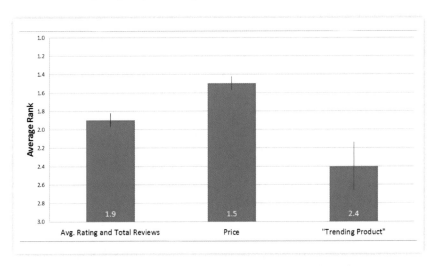

FIGURE 20.10: Mean ranking from respondents who selected the items in a survey about the importance of product details on a retail website. Participants picked and ranked their top three features (out of 20 possible features). Sample sizes are 346, 270, and 20 respectively.

Adding to the complexity of rank questions, ranking analysis needs to account for how participants were asked to rank. They can be asked to rank all items (e.g., force rank three features), or they can be asked to rank only a subset (e.g., pick and rank the top 3 of 20 features). As we covered in Chapter 5, the pick-some feature reduces the burden on the respondent but adds complexity for the researcher who needs to decide whether to analyze and report ranks, percentages, or both.

Figure 20.10 shows the mean ranks (as an inverted scale) for three items that came from a survey with 549 participants regarding the features of an e-commerce website. Figure 20.11 is a graph from the same ranking data that shows the percentage of respondents who selected the three displayed items as the most important (out of 20 possible choices). The number of respondents varied by item from 346, 270, and 20 respectively, which impacts the width of the error bars, but the differences in sample sizes aren't readily apparent. Finally, Figure 20.12 shows the percentage of ALL participants in the survey who gave these three items a rank of 1 (most important).

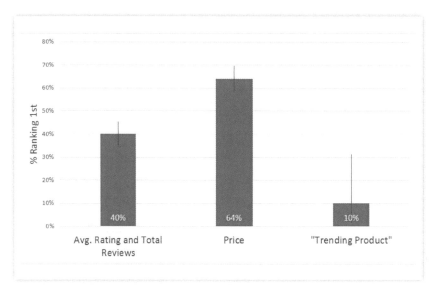

FIGURE 20.11: Of the percentage of respondents who selected the item, the percentage who ranked it 1st. Sample sizes are 346, 270, and 20 respectively.

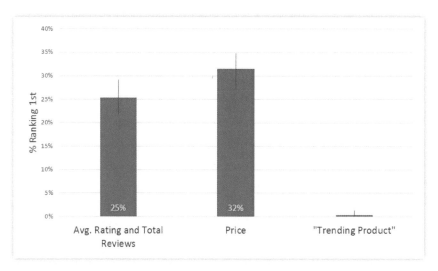

FIGURE 20.12: Percentage of all 549 respondents in the survey who selected the item as 1st.

All three figures differ in their details but reveal the same rank ordering of these three features (price is most important and "Trending Product" is least). In this case, Figure 20.12 may best represent the differences in one graph. If respondents had to rank all items, then Figure 20.11 would look exactly like Figure 20.12, and the confidence intervals in Figure 20.10 will all be the same width.

Another example of ranking comes from a survey given to participants after they were asked to use three different computer mouse designs of varying shapes with one, two, or three buttons (Lewis & Alfonso, 1989).

Figure 20.13 shows the mean rank order of the participants' preference for each type of mouse, and Figure 20.14 uses the same data to show the percentages of first-place selections. In both graphs, Design 2 is the clear winner (little to no overlap of its confidence intervals with those of the other designs).

The graphs illustrate the similarity of rank means with rating means and the percentage of first-place ranks with top-box scores. In Figure 20.13, the rank means capture a potential difference between Designs 1 and 3 that is obscured in the percentage of first-place ranks in Figure 20.14. On the other hand, the extreme responses graphed in Figure 20.14 provide a sharper illustration of the superiority of Design 2. The two approaches answer different research questions, and both can be of value to UX researchers (some decisions can be both/and rather than either/or).

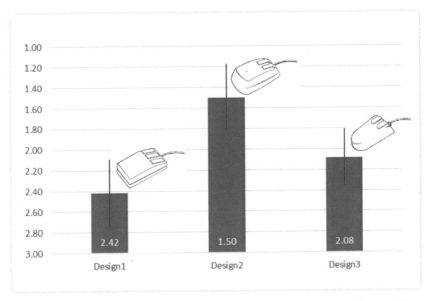

FIGURE 20.13: Mean preference ranks for three mouse designs (Lewis & Alfonso, 1989, $n = 24$).

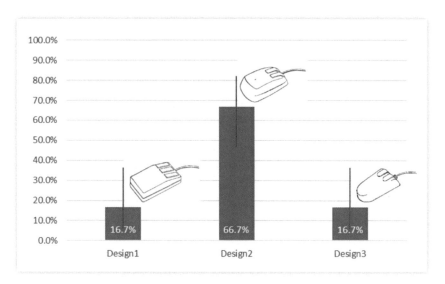

FIGURE 20.14: First-place percentages for three mouse designs (Lewis & Alfonso, 1989, *n* = 24).

Allocation

Allocation data can be presented by averaging the values (e.g., points, dollars) of the responses for each item. For example, in a survey of TV and video streaming behavior, 487 respondents were asked to indicate the composition of their TV-watching time. Respondents needed to allocate 100 percentage points across four categories. Figure 20.15 shows the mean percent allocation by category type with 95% confidence intervals.

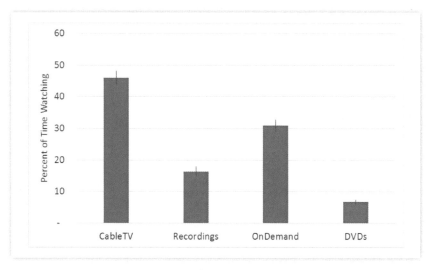

FIGURE 20.15: Bar graph showing allocation of time watching video across four sources.

Because this allocation amount adds up to 100%, it may also be helpful to display the results as a pie graph to better show each content type's share of the whole (Figure 20.16). The sample size was large enough that all differences were statistically significant, but when that isn't the case, a bar graph may be needed to show the margin of error from the sample data.

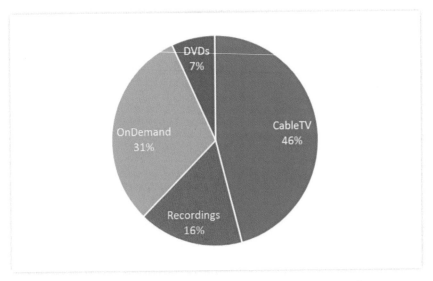

FIGURE 20.16: Pie chart showing allocation of time watching video across four sources.

OPEN-ENDED QUESTIONS

The items covered so far addressed the analysis of the Measurement branch of the survey item decision tree covered in Chapter 10. The other branch, Discovery, includes only open-ended response options. Despite being only one leaf in the decision tree, most surveys contain at least some form of open-ended response option, from asking the respondents for a single word to asking for a lengthy explanation (see Chapter 10 for more on when to use open-ended questions).

Among other reasons, open-ended comments provide insight into the "why" behind closed-ended rating scale data such as the Likelihood-to-Recommend (LTR) score. An open-ended question immediately following the closed-ended LTR question can provide reasons for low scores.

You can evaluate responses systematically by sorting and coding them. However, even a quick reading of a subset of what participants are saying will give you some idea about what's driving high or low scores.

For example, respondents to a survey we conducted on business software (Sauro & Lewis, 2022, Sep 20) reflected on their experience with common B2B software programs and provided their rating of LTR (which drives the Net Promoter Score). We asked participants to briefly explain their ratings, which can be particularly helpful for understanding low-scoring responses. One respondent gave a Learning Management System (LMS) software program a score of 5 on an eleven-point scale (a detractor) and said:

> *"Although [name of software] allows you to connect with students on a more personal level than email...it still has a large amount of issues present. The layout of [name of software] is horrid, and users should have an option to collapse the menu found on the left-hand side of the screen. Although it's an adequate LMS program, it isn't better than [another LMS software]."*

There's a lot of great feedback packed into that one comment. It doesn't mean the product developers should immediately start updating the software, but it does mean it's likely worthy of further investigation.

Open-ended items can also be systematically analyzed. Raw comments from respondents can be sorted into common themes and then analyzed as percentages. Table 20.12 shows an example from the travel websites survey where participants were asked to describe one thing they particularly dislike about the Expedia travel website.

Issue	%	Example Quote
Prices fluctuate/ Not the best deals	24%	"I feel like I don't always get the best deals."
Unappealing design/ Too cluttered	21%	"The webpage has a lot of blank/white space. It's almost too bright in my opinion."
Site crashes or is slow to load	17%	"It's 'laggy' and glitchy and irritating to try to use finding flights."
Difficult to navigate	14%	"I think the user interface is a little confusing to navigate. There's so much information thrown at you on a single page that it takes a few moments to read each bit when you're at the search process."
Difficulty related to third-party booking	10%	"If you ever have an issue during your trip, dealing with them is a nightmare. It's ALWAYS someone else's fault."
Missing preferred airlines or hotels	7%	"Sometimes the search results are not particularly what I'm looking for."
Filters not sufficient for needs	7%	"Sometimes it's difficult to find hotels within a particular range of a city."

TABLE 20.12: Open-ended analysis of one thing participants disliked about the Expedia website.

For more detailed steps on sorting and coding verbatim comments, see Sauro (2017, Aug 16).

CHAPTER SUMMARY

This chapter covered methods for analyzing univariate (single-item) metrics.

What are good ways to analyze data from single items? …It depends on whether you're analyzing discrete-binary or continuous data. Data collected with categorical items that are select-one or select-all-that-apply are discrete-binary (e.g., income range, age range, frequency of use), as are data from analysis of text from open-ended items. Types of items that produce more continuous data include rating, ranking, and allocation.

How should I analyze discrete-binary data from single items? …Compute percentages and confidence intervals. Percentages are easier to interpret than raw numbers and are easy to compute—just make sure that you're dividing your counts by the correct denominator. Confidence intervals show the inherent uncertainty in estimated percentages. You don't need to compute confidence intervals for every percentage (e.g., demographic items that just describe the sample), but they can be very useful when the result will drive a decision. If you would make the same decision for the lower and upper limits of the interval, then you can more confidently make that decision. If the decision would be different for the upper and lower limits, then making any decision based on that data would be risky.

How about more continuous data from rating scales or ranking? …Compute means, percentages, and confidence intervals. Although, strictly speaking, rating and ranking data are not continuous in the same way as time or temperature, as the sample size increases, the distribution of their means becomes more and more continuous, and consequently, statistical methods for continuous data work better (but avoid making interval or ratio claims about the results). In addition to means, you can compute percentages (e.g., top-box scores, net box scores, percentage of first-place ranks). For both means and percentages, you can compute confidence intervals to show the plausible range around those point estimates.

Why don't you recommend computing modes or medians for rating scales? … You can compute them, but they aren't as useful as means or percentages. The mode is the most frequently selected rating, and the median is the value at the center of a distribution (the 50th percentile). The mode is rarely used in UX research because few decisions can be made based on the mode. The median is a good measure of central tendency when at least one endpoint of the distribution is unlimited (e.g., time, money), and it is the preferred measure of central tendency when distributions aren't symmetrical. It doesn't work as well for rating scales because their minimum and maximum values are limited, and their medians (unlike their means) can only take a small number of values even when sample sizes are large.

Which is better to compute for rating scales — means or box scores? ...They measure different aspects of the data, so it often makes sense to compute both. The percentage of extreme responders (top box and bottom box) tend to be better predictors of future behavior than the mean, while the mean does a better job of characterizing changes in central tendency that might not be detected at the extremes. So why not compute and track them both?

How should allocation data be analyzed? ...Compute means and confidence intervals. Allocation items can ask respondents to allocate points, dollars, or time, but most often are framed as allocating percentages of these variables. This is different from the percentages that are computed from discrete-binary data, so their central tendency can be assessed with means and confidence intervals around those means.

CHAPTER 21:
TWO-ITEM (BIVARIATE) AND THREE+ ITEM ANALYSIS

A two-item analysis may address both primary and second-order effects of research questions. Are new users more likely to recommend? Are customers over 50 more likely to open a new account? Is there a relationship between income and product satisfaction? Two-item analyses are useful for making comparisons (looking at differences) or examining relationships (correlation and regression). We'll cover the following questions:

- What do I need to know to compare two responses?
- How do you compare responses to a benchmark?
- What is the best way to analyze preference data?
- What is the difference between cross-tabbing and collapsing variables?
- How do you adjust for prior experience?
- How do you compute relationships instead of differences between responses?
- Are there statistical methods for analyzing more than two variables?

MAKING COMPARISONS (DIFFERENCES)

Comparing survey responses largely involves subtracting means or percentages (occasionally medians) of two response options. As with individual items, we usually want to generalize these differences. We go beyond confidence intervals and use statistical tests to tell us if the differences in the sample are large enough to suggest they're beyond what we'd expect from chance alone—in short, if the difference is statistically significant (see Appendix A for more about statistical significance).

The actual statistical test to use depends on two things:

- The type of data: continuous or discrete-binary
- If the data were collected within or between subjects

Fortunately, most survey comparisons can be done using only two statistical tests for between-subjects comparisons and two different but related tests for within-subjects comparisons.

Between subjects means that the responses we are comparing are from different respondents, for example, looking for differences in mean satisfaction or top-box percentages from respondents aged 65+ compared to those under 25. The two recommended statistical tests are:

- Two-sample *t*-test: Rating scale data and other continuous values (e.g., numeric input).
- $N-1$ two-proportion test: Percentages (e.g., percent selecting or box scores).

Within-Subjects means that the responses we are comparing are from the *same* respondents. For example, looking for differences between Product A and Product B in mean satisfaction or top-box percentages. The two recommended statistical tests are:

- Paired *t*-test: Rating scale data and other continuous values (e.g., numeric input).
- McNemar exact test: Percentages (e.g., percent selecting or box scores).

You'll want to use software to conduct the statistical calculations. The exact procedure for setting up these comparisons will differ depending on your stats package. For the formulas and background, see Chapter 5 in *Quantifying the User Experience*, 2nd Edition (Sauro & Lewis, 2016) and the detailed step-by-step instructions for using R or Excel in the *Excel & R Companion to the 2nd Edition of Quantifying the User Experience* (Lewis & Sauro, 2016).

USING CONFIDENCE INTERVALS FOR COMPARISON

You can use the overlap in confidence intervals as a quick way to check for statistical significance. For example, if 95% intervals do not overlap, then you can be at least 95% confident there is a difference (i.e., $p < .05$). If there is a large overlap, then the difference is probably not significant (at the $p < .05$ level). Intervals can overlap when the difference is statistically significant, so when there is a modest overlap, it's best to conduct the appropriate test of significance to find the p-value. The three graphs in Figure 21.1 illustrate this.

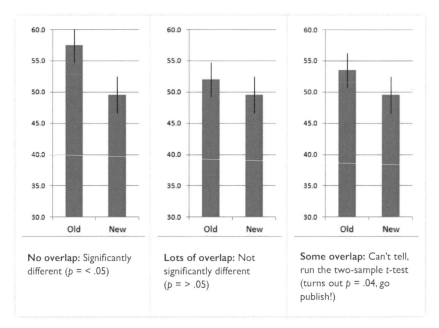

| No overlap: Significantly different (p = < .05) | Lots of overlap: Not significantly different (p = > .05) | Some overlap: Can't tell, run the two-sample t-test (turns out p = .04, go publish!) |

FIGURE 21.1: Using the overlap (or non-overlap) in the confidence intervals to determine statistical significance.

Between-Subjects Comparisons

The two-sample t-test and the $N–1$ two-proportion test are the statistical tests used when comparing different participants in different groups.

THE TWO-SAMPLE T-TEST

The two-sample t-test uses the means, standard deviations, and sample sizes from two independent samples.

For example, using data obtained from an airline website survey, we can compare the attitude current customers had toward the changing reservations on the website between British Airways and Ryan Air. Respondents provided their agreement (1 = strongly disagree and 5= strongly agree) to the item "I can easily change my reservation on the website." Table 21.1 shows the descriptive statistics (mean, standard deviation, and sample size) for both airlines.

	British Airways	Ryan Air
Mean	3.51	2.96
SD	0.81	1.07
n	55	50

TABLE 21.1: Descriptive statistics for ratings of both airlines' ease of changing reservations online.

The means and 95% confidence intervals are shown in Figure 21.2.

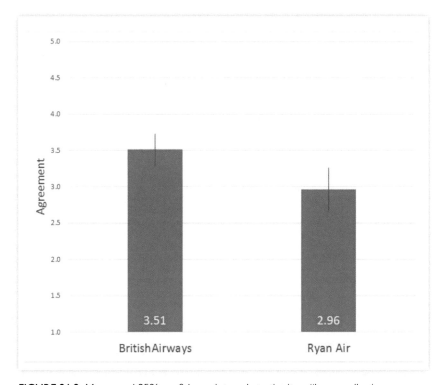

FIGURE 21.2: Means and 95% confidence intervals to the item "I can easily change my reservation on the website" for British Airways and Ryan Air.

Ryan Air has a lower mean (2.96) than British Airways (3.51), a bit more than half a point (.55). The two-sample t-test provides a p-value of .004, which is below the traditional significance level of $p < .05$, indicating that this difference is statistically significant — the British Airways experience of changing reservations on the website is better than Ryan Air's. Figure 21.3 shows the two-sample t-test output from SPSS.

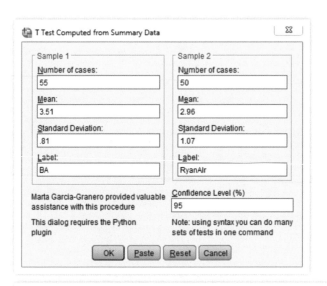

Summary T-Test

Summary Data

	N	Mean	Std. Deviation	Std. Error Mean
BA	55.000	3.510	.810	.109
RyanAlr	50.000	2.960	1.070	.151

Independent Samples Test

	Mean Difference	Std. Error Difference	t	df	Sig. (2-tailed)
Equal variances assumed	.550	.184	2.986	103.000	.004
Equal variances not assumed	.550	.187	2.947	90.954	.004

Hartley test for equal variance: $F = 1.745$, Sig. $= 0.0224$

95.0% Confidence Intervals for Difference

	Lower Limit	Upper Limit
Asymptotic (equal variance)	.189	.911
Asymptotic (unequal variance)	.184	.916
Exact (equal variance)	.185	.915
Exact (unequal variance)	.179	.921

FIGURE 21.3: Two-sample t-test output from SPSS (From Analyze > Compare Means > Summary Independent Samples t-test Menu in SPSS 23).

THE N-1 TWO-PROPORTION TEST

The recommended statistical procedure for comparing two between-subjects percentages/proportions is the $N-1$ two-proportion test. It's a derivation of the chi-square test that works well for small and large samples (it used $N-1$ degrees of freedom, which is where it gets its clumsy name). While it's not a default test in SPSS, Minitab, or R, it is available as part of the MeasuringU Usability Statistics Package (Expanded) and available free online at https://measuringu.com/calculators/ab-cal/.

Figure 21.4 shows the frequency distribution of raw responses for the same item "I can easily change my reservation" for the British Airways and Ryan Air websites.

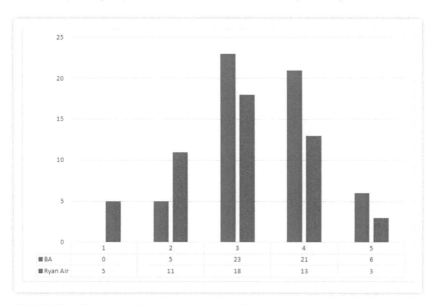

FIGURE 21.4: Frequency distribution to the item "I can easily change my reservation on the website" for British Airways (BA) and Ryan Air.

Figure 21.5 shows the output from MeasuringU's online calculator, indicating the difference in top-box proportions (6/55 for BA and 3/50 for Ryan Air) is not statistically significant ($p = .37$).

	Successes	Total	%
Group 1	6	55	10.91
Group 2	3	50	6

Compute

Two Tailed p-value: **0.371774** One Tailed p-value: **0.185887**

FIGURE 21.5: Output from the *N*–1 two-proportion test (aka A/B test calculator) from https://measuringu.com/calculators/ab-cal/.

The frequency distribution in Figure 21.4 shows more separation in the bottom-box responses between airlines. Figure 21.6 shows the output from the MeasuringU Usability Statistics Package (Expanded) and confirms that this difference is statistically significant (*p* = .01677) using the traditional significance level of *p* < .05. Respondents were significantly more likely to give Ryan Air the lowest possible rating.

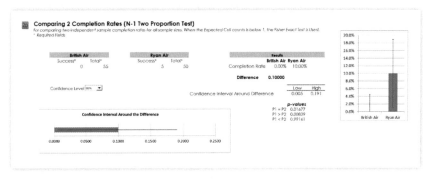

FIGURE 21.6: Output of the *N*–1 two-proportion test from the MeasuringU Usability Statistics Package (Expanded).

Within-Subjects Comparisons

The paired *t*-test and the McNemar exact test are the statistical tests used when comparing the same participants in both groups.

PAIRED T-TEST

The paired *t*-test compares rating scale data when the participants provide both ratings. In the airline survey, the same participants answered multiple questions about their experience on one airline's website. While the comparisons across airlines were between subjects (different people), the analyses within airlines include both between- and within-subjects comparisons. For example, we can compare the same respondents' attitudes toward different aspects of the Ryan Air website experience. Figure 21.7 shows the mean for four items on the Ryan Air website. The mean for finding cheap airfare was lower (3.74) than checking in for a flight (4.1), suggesting the former is a harder experience.

 TIP:

> As mentioned in the section on confidence intervals, when two intervals don't overlap, you can be sure the means are significantly different. When they do overlap, the means might or might not be significantly different—you won't know until you conduct a significance test. This is true for both between- and within-subjects comparisons. When comparisons are within subjects, however, confidence intervals around two means can have a very large overlap but still be significantly different because there is no between-group variation in the test (i.e., participants act as their own controls).

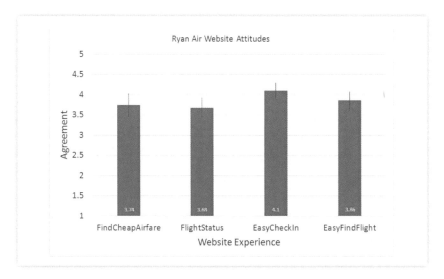

FIGURE 21.7: Means and 95% confidence intervals for four items on the Ryan Air website experience. The same participants answered each item (within subjects).

TIP:

You need access to the raw data for within-subjects comparisons. Be sure your data are set up "paired" so the same participant's data are on the same row.

Figure 21.8 shows the output of a paired *t*-test from SPSS and shows that the difference in mean attitudes for these two items is statistically significant (*p* = .04).

➡ **T-Test**

Paired Samples Statistics

		Mean	N	Std. Deviation	Std. Error Mean
Pair 1	FindCheapAirfare	3.7400	50	1.02639	.14515
	EasyCheckIn	4.1000	50	.67763	.09583

Paired Samples Correlations

		N	Correlation	Sig.
Pair 1	FindCheapAirfare & EasyCheckIn	50	.038	.793

Paired Samples Test

		Paired Differences					t	df	Sig. (2-tailed)
		Mean	Std. Deviation	Std. Error Mean	95% Confidence Interval of the Difference Lower	Upper			
Pair 1	FindCheapAirfare - EasyCheckIn	-.36000	1.20814	.17086	-.70335	-.01665	-2.107	49	.040

FIGURE 21.8: Paired t-test output from SPSS (From Analyze > Compare Means > Paired Samples t-test menu in SPSS 23).

MCNEMAR EXACT TEST

The McNemar exact test is the analog to the *N*–1 two-proportion test for within-subjects proportions/percentages. Again, be sure your data are aligned so each row has the same participant's data. Using the same two items we used in the previous mean comparison, we can compare top-two-box scores, which were 64% for finding cheap airfare and 86% for the ease of online check-in.

Figure 21.9 below shows the output from the MeasuringU Usability Statistics Package (Expanded), with the responses lined up by respondent and showing the difference is statistically significant (*p* = .022).

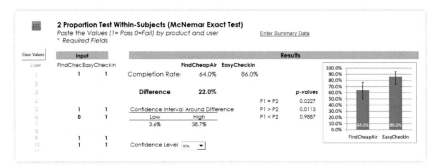

FIGURE 21.9: McNemar exact test.

Additional Two-Way Comparisons

MEANS OVER TIME
To compare rating scale data over time (longitudinally), use the same statistical tests. If the means come from the same participants at different intervals, match up the responses and use the paired *t*-test.

COMPARING DIFFERENCES IN NET SCORES
Net scoring, like in the Net Promoter Score, involves using the difference between dependent measures. If you need to conduct a statistical test on Net Promoter Scores, see Lewis and Sauro (2021, Aug 17).

COMPARING TO A BENCHMARK
One of the benefits of using existing items, especially standardized items that have historical data, is that you can compare scores from your survey to known benchmarks. This could be for rating scale means, top-box scores, net scores, or other derived scores. The benchmarks can be published in journals, on company websites, or from internal non–publicly available sources.

Comparing a mean to a benchmark
The two approaches for comparing a mean to a benchmark use the boundaries of confidence intervals or the one-sample *t*-test. You need the mean, standard deviation, and sample size.

For example, in our survey of consumer software users, we asked 35 existing users to rate the perceived usability of Adobe Photoshop with the System Usability Scale (SUS).

The mean SUS was 61, with a standard deviation of 15.2. Multiple sources have published benchmarks showing that an average SUS score is around 68 (Sauro, 2011, Feb 3). Is this mean (61) significantly below the published average SUS score (68)?

The mean and a 90% confidence interval are shown in Figure 21.10. The confidence interval ranges from 56 to 65. The upper boundary of the confidence interval is below 68, showing the average SUS score is statistically significantly below average.

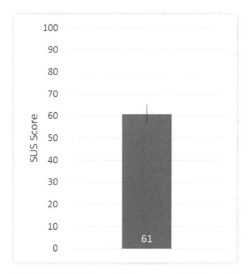

FIGURE 21.10: Mean SUS score and 90% confidence interval for Adobe Photoshop.

Figure 21.11 shows the results of a one-sample *t*-test from the MeasuringU Usability Statistics Package (Expanded). There is a *p*-value of .01, also showing an observed mean significantly lower than 68.

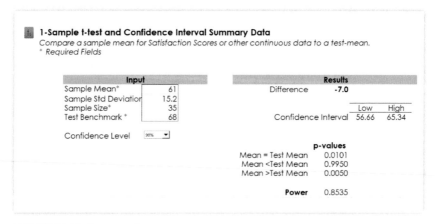

FIGURE 21.11: One-sample t-test.

Comparing a percentage to a benchmark

You can compare the percentage of respondents who agree to a benchmark percentage using an appropriate box score. You can inspect binomial confidence intervals or conduct the recommended statistical procedure, the binomial test (available in most statistics packages and on the MeasuringU website https://measuringu.com/calculators/onep/).

In the airline survey, for example, 50 participants were asked if they agree that purchasing a ticket on the Southwest website is easy. Of the 50 respondents, 46 selected a 4 or 5 (top-two-box score of 92%). Is this percentage evidence that at least 80% of respondents agree that it's easy?

Figure 21.12 shows the results using the binomial calculator and confidence intervals. The *p*-value is .0329, showing that the observed percentage is statistically different than .80. The range of the 95% confidence interval is 80.64 to 97.36. Because the lower bound is above 80%, this method also indicates statistical significance.

FIGURE 21.12: Binomial test comparing a top-box score to a benchmark percentage.

Comparing a net score to a benchmark

The same strategies — inspection of confidence intervals or hypothesis testing — can be used to compare net scores to benchmarks. The trick with net scores, however, is that taking the difference between two binomial proportions creates a trinomial metric that has unique properties. We have worked out methods for computing confidence intervals and conducting tests of significance against benchmarks for the most widely used net score, the Net Promoter Score (Lewis & Sauro, 2021, Aug 17).

ANALYZING PREFERENCE DATA

Measuring respondents' preferences is a common research question addressed with a survey through direct questions (e.g., which airline do you prefer?) or through concepts (which homepage design do you prefer?).

Preference data are typically analyzed as part of a within-subjects analysis (same participants experiencing multiple websites) or rating multiple brands. For example, in Chapter 13, we described an experiment in which we asked respondents their preference for starting the Single Ease Question with Very Easy compared to Very Difficult. In an experiment described in Chapter 11, we asked respondents if they preferred having the same number of points for each item in a survey or changing to five, seven, and eleven points.

There are a few ways to analyze preference data, including:

- Comparing the most selected choice using the one-sample binomial against random chance (5 choices = .20, 4 choices = .25, 3 choices = .333, and 2 choices = .5).

- Conducting a chi-square goodness of fit test to see whether the distribution deviates from chance. A limitation of this test is that significant p-values won't tell you whether the deviation is for the most or least selected choice. Compute confidence intervals to compare the alternatives directly. Keep in mind, it's more conservative because a confidence interval doesn't take the dependencies between choices into account.

- To compare choices directly and take dependence into account, use the McNemar exact test, as explained earlier in this chapter.

- When there are more than two choices (but not too many), consider having respondents rank them so you can compare rank averages and proportions of first choices (see the mouse design preference example in Chapter 20).

For more information on analyzing preference data, see "How to Statistically Test Preference Data" (Sauro, 2015, Jun 30).

Cross-Tabbing Variables

Cross tabbing is the process of examining more than one variable in the same table or chart. It's essentially looking at the data in a table or chart with the goal of "crossing out" similar variables, which allows you to see to what extent the variables for groups differ. It can be a simple yet powerful way to understand how segments differ. It can be done with rating scales and proportions/binary variables.

For example, Figure 21.13 shows a cross tab of the Net Promoter Score by site experience for four websites in a comparative retail website benchmark survey. Focusing on Site 4, we can see that participants with less experience (visiting 1 to 3 times) generally had lower Net Promoter Scores.

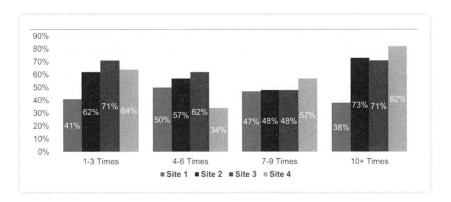

FIGURE 21.13: Cross-tabbing Net Promoter Scores by website and experience on the website (from 1–3 times to 10+ times in the last year).

Collapsing Variables

One technique to help for both cross tabbing and a better understanding of patterns in your data is to collapse variables. *Collapsing* variables is just another way of saying *combining* variables, often into two groups (which is called *dichotomizing*), so you can more easily cross tab and run statistical comparisons between the lower and higher ends of an independent variable. While it's good to have a lot of fidelity in a set of response options, collapsing variables is a good option for analyzing certain aspects of data. For example, Table 21.2 shows the distribution of prior experience of 76 participants on the Marriott or Best Western websites (Sauro, 2018).

	Marriott		Best Western	
0 Times	15	20%	36	47%
1–3 Times	41	54%	33	43%
4–6 Times	16	21%	5	7%
7–9 Times	2	3%	2	3%
10+ Times	2	3%	0	0%

TABLE 21.2: Distribution of prior experience with the Marriott and Best Western websites.

You can collapse these levels into no experience and at least some experience as shown in Table 21.3.

	Marriott		Best Western	
No experience	15	20%	36	47%
At least some experience	61	80%	40	53%

TABLE 21.3: Collapsed categories of prior experience with the Marriott and Best Western websites.

This new collapsed variable can be used in cross tabs and other analyses. For example, Figure 21.14 shows the newly dichotomized experience variable (No Experience vs. Some Experience) with respondents' stated likelihood to revisit the website after using it.

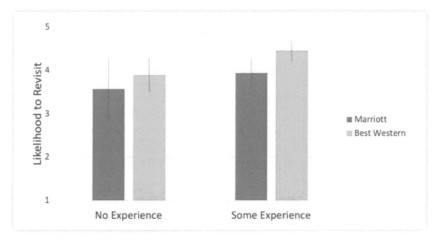

FIGURE 21.14: Stated likelihood to revisit the website by dichotomized prior experience for the Marriott and Best Western websites.

This cross-tabbing analysis allows us to see that although prior experience affects the likelihood to revisit a website (as we'd expect), participants for the Best Western website who have some experience had statistically higher scores than participants with the same level of experience for the Marriott website.

 TIP:

When collapsing variables, you'll need to set the breakpoints to yield a reasonably balanced group—you typically don't want 95% of your responses categorized as having a high experience and 5% with a low experience.

Controlling for Prior Experience

We covered the importance of measuring prior experience with products, companies, and domains in Chapter 3. Prior experience has a strong influence on attitudes measured in surveys. In general, the more experience respondents have had, the more positive their attitudes toward a product, brand, or service will be. For example, you may be comparing the intention of respondents to use an online streaming service (e.g., Netflix, Hulu, or HBO Max). However, if your sample contains a large percentage of current Netflix users, then it's likely attitudinal measures will tend to favor Netflix.

One way to control for prior experience in surveys is to match the experience level of the sample with the expected experience level of the population in the recruiting process (see Chapter 4). If you believe, for example, that 60% of website visitors use the site weekly and the other 40% use it less often, you can recruit participants to match that composition. You can then compute confidence intervals and run statistical comparisons (between, say, two design alternatives) and draw conclusions as to which design is preferred or perceived as more usable.

However, you can't weight your sample to match the population if you have trouble finding enough people for each group. This is especially the case when surveying attitudes about a new product or concept for which there are few or no existing users. You want to be able to filter out the effects of experience. One way to mitigate and control for the effects of prior experience on outcome measures is to conduct a weighted *t*-test.

ABOUT THE WEIGHTED T-TEST

A relatively simple method for handling weighted data is the aptly named weighted *t*-test. This is a variation of the *t*-test described earlier. The *t*-test works for large and small sample sizes and uneven group sizes, and it's resilient to non-normal data. (We cover it extensively in Chapter 5 of *Quantifying the User Experience*.) While the *t*-test is a workhorse of statistical analysis, it considers only one variable when determining statistical significance. This means that you can't compare participants' attitudes on two websites and factor in their prior experience (say, low experience and high experience).

However, the weighted version of the *t*-test does factor in a second variable. It adjusts the means and standard deviations based on how much to weigh each respondent. For example, participants that should account for 60% of the population have scores weighted at 60%, even if they make up only 20% of your sample. You can see the computation notes in "Weighted Comparison of Means" (Bland & Kerry, 1998).

USING THE WEIGHTED T-TEST

Here's an example of how the weighted *t*-test works. For a study of an online retail website, we wanted to see which website was statistically preferred on several dimensions, including confidence and ease. For this example, we had 857 qualified participants who were randomly assigned to Website A or Website B. We used a ten-point confidence scale.

The mean, standard deviation, and sample size for both groups for the confidence question are shown in Table 21.4.

	Mean	SD	N
Website A	8.58	1.74	429
Website B	8.37	1.92	428

TABLE 21.4: Unweighted mean confidence scores for two websites (on ten-point scales).

Even though Website A had a nominally higher mean score (8.58 vs. 8.37), a standard t-test indicated a marginally significant difference (p = 0.095).

However, we know that prior experience has a major impact on attitudes toward interfaces, and packed within both samples are four groups of participants, each with progressively more experience with the website.

Not only did the sample contain a heterogeneous subgroup of experience, but it was also not proportionally representative of the population's experience breakdown. Table 21.5 shows the breakdown of the sample in Website A and Website B compared to the makeup of the user population.

Experience Level	Website A	Website B	Population
1	2%	3%	2%
2	12%	10%	9%
3	44%	47%	39%
4	42%	41%	50%

TABLE 21.5: Experience level for the participants assigned to Website A and B compared to the population composition (1 = least experienced and 4 = most experienced).

We see the biggest difference with people with the most experience (Level 4 in the table). While this group makes up half of the population, it only composed between 41% and 42% of the sample in Websites A and B.

These groups also have differing opinions about the designs they were exposed to. Table 21.6 shows that one of the biggest differences in attitudes was for the most experienced participants (experience level 4), which rated Website A .39 points higher than B. What's more, the least experienced participants preferred Website B over A.

Experience Level	Website A	Website B	Difference	Population
1	8.42	8.67	−0.25	2%
2	8.85	8.82	0.03	9%
3	8.56	8.44	0.12	39%
4	8.53	8.14	0.39	50%

TABLE 21.6: The mean responses to a confidence question (higher is better), the difference in means by experience level (1 to 4), and the population composition of that experience level.

The weighted *t*-test creates a composite mean and standard deviation to proportionally account for the subgroup size. The updated means and standard deviations are shown in Table 21.7 with the original data.

	Weighted		Non-Weighted	
	Mean	SD	Mean	SD
Website A	8.56	1.68	8.58	1.74
Website B	8.29	1.94	8.37	1.92

TABLE 21.7: Experience level for the sample of customers assigned to Website A and B compared to the population composition.

The results of the weighted *t*-test generate a *p*-value of .03, which is statistically significant at the alpha = .05 level of significance. You won't always see differences in significance values between the weighted and unweighted approaches; it depends on how disproportionate your sample is and how much the lower-weighted groups differ from the higher-weighted groups.

With these results, we can conclude that Website A had higher ratings and that the rating difference wasn't attributable to incorrectly proportioned sample sizes. You can also use the approach for any mediating variable in a benchmark survey (such as geography, gender, or occupation), not just for prior experience.

TIP:

You should have a good reason and actual data to support using weights. Don't just weight your data to achieve statistical significance. Although some characteristics like homeownership, political party affiliation, age distributions, or annual income can be externally verified using census data, other factors like frugal value seeking, environmental consciousness, or early adoption can be harder to define and verify. Many variables in your sample will differ from the population, but few of them are likely to have a large enough effect (if any at all) to justify weighting. If you reach different conclusions between a weighted and unweighted analysis, we recommend verifying the strength of the evidence for the weights.

Measuring Relationships: Correlation and Regression

To look for relationships between two variables, you can use bivariate correlations. The Pearson correlation works for continuous rating scale data. For rank data, the nonparametric Spearman rank correlation is recommended. Both generally provide comparable results (see the sidebar on analyzing rank data).

PARAMETRIC OR NONPARAMETRIC?

We're often asked if it's better to analyze rating scale data using rank methods (e.g., Spearman correlation) than parametric methods (Pearson correlation). There are entire books written about distribution-free (nonparametric) methods, for analyzing data. For UX data, when there is a choice, we use parametric methods unless there is a clear reason not to do so (Sauro & Lewis, 2022, Jun 7). In practice, the statistical outcomes of parametric and nonparametric analyses usually lead to the same practical decisions (e.g., see Lewis, 1993).

For example, participants' attitudes toward the ease of use of the British Airways website correlated with scores on the Likelihood-to-Recommend (LTR) item. Figure 21.15 shows a scatter plot of the relationship.

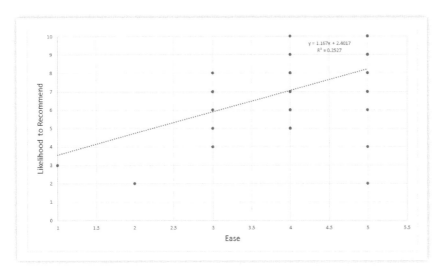

FIGURE 21.15: Scatter plot between attitudes toward website ease of use and Likelihood-To-Recommend the British Airways website (*n* = 55).

The Pearson correlation is .502, and the Spearman correlation is .463. Both are significantly different than 0 (*p* < .01). Correlations can be easily conducted in most statistical packages. Figure 21.16 shows the output from SPSS after selecting the Analyze > Correlate > Bivariate menu option (SPSS 23).

Beyond using a graph with a line, a regression equation can be used to describe the linear relationship shown in Figure 21.16 and can be used to predict values. The regression equation shown in Figure 21.15 is $y = 1.167x + 2.4017$. In the equation, y is the dependent variable (LTR), and x is the independent variable (attitude toward website ease). The response value for the ease item (1 through 5) can replace the x in the equation to predict LTR values. A 3 predicts an LTR of 5.9, a 4 predicts an LTR of 7.1, and a 5 predicts an LTR of 8.2. For more on using regression equations, see Chapter 10 of *Quantifying the User Experience*.

Correlations

[DataSet0]

Correlations

		LTR	Ease
LTR	Pearson Correlation	1	.503**
	Sig. (2-tailed)		.000
	N	55	55
Ease	Pearson Correlation	.503**	1
	Sig. (2-tailed)	.000	
	N	55	55

**. Correlation is significant at the 0.01 level (2-tailed).

```
NONPAR CORR
  /VARIABLES=LTR Ease
  /PRINT=SPEARMAN TWOTAIL NOSIG
  /MISSING=PAIRWISE.
```

➔ **Nonparametric Correlations**

Correlations

			LTR	Ease
Spearman's rho	LTR	Correlation Coefficient	1.000	.463**
		Sig. (2-tailed)	.	.000
		N	55	55
	Ease	Correlation Coefficient	.463**	1.000
		Sig. (2-tailed)	.000	.
		N	55	55

**. Correlation is significant at the 0.01 level (2-tailed).

FIGURE 21.16: SPSS output correlating LTR and ease from the Analyze > Correlate > Bivariate menu option (SPSS 23).

THREE+ (MULTIVARIATE) ITEM ANALYSIS

For many research questions, fundamental statistical techniques like confidence intervals, the statistical tests of the two-sample t-test, a paired t-test, the N–1 two-proportion test, the McNemar exact test, and simple correlation/regression will do the trick. But to answer some questions most effectively, you need to use more advanced techniques.

Five techniques that we often use in survey analyses to answer more specific research questions include multiple regression analysis, analysis of variance (ANOVA), logistic regression, factor analysis, and cluster analysis. Each of these techniques requires specialized software (e.g., SPSS, Minitab, R) and training to learn how to set up and interpret the results. But even if you aren't ready to execute these techniques yourself, you can still learn what they are, when to use them, and what to look out for. We briefly cover each technique here and suggest places where you can learn more, as it takes at least one book to cover each topic.

Multiple Regression Analysis

Multiple regression analysis extends what we covered in the correlation and regression section above. When you want to understand what combination of independent variables best predicts a single continuous outcome variable like customer satisfaction, Likelihood-to-Recommend (LTR), intent to purchase, or brand attitudes, use a multiple regression analysis. This technique also goes by the name of *key driver analysis* because you're able to determine which independent variables have the biggest impact on your dependent (outcome) variable.

You can use both continuous and discrete variables as independent (predictor) variables. For example, in our survey of travel websites, we conducted a key driver analysis to understand what features of airline websites significantly impacted LTR and by how much (Figure 21.17).

FIGURE 21.17: Example output (after graphic design) of a key driver analysis of airline websites.

We found that the ease of filtering, ease of finding the cheapest hotel, and knowing the total charge (including fees) made up the top three drivers of intent to recommend. Eight variables explained (accounted for) 50% of the variance in LTR ratings.

ANOVA

An analysis of variance (ANOVA) tells you whether the means from more than two groups have a significant difference, such as the SUPR-Q scores across five websites. The more familiar *t*-test covered earlier is a special use of ANOVA when there are only two groups to compare.

What makes ANOVA powerful is that it allows you to look at multiple variables and understand what combination results in the largest difference. This is called the *interaction effect*.

For example, you may want to know which of four websites is rated highest in overall satisfaction. That's one variable (with four levels). You can answer this research question using multiple *t*-tests or by examining confidence intervals. But if you want to understand how another variable, say, the device type (mobile vs. desktop), affects overall satisfaction and interacts with the website variable, you should use an ANOVA.

Figure 21.18 shows a significant interaction from a SUPR-Q survey of automobile insurance websites (*p* = .07). For most companies, respondents who had been customers for more than two years provided higher ratings. Liberty Mutual stands out as an exception.

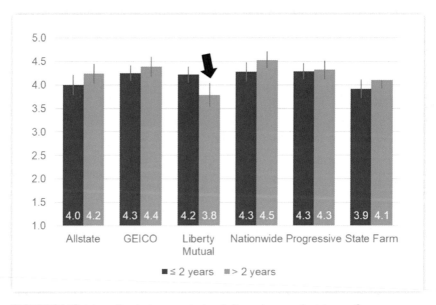

FIGURE 21.18: Interaction between rated website and respondent tenure for raw SUPR-Q scores.

Mathematically, ANOVA is a type of regression analysis with discrete independent variables. Both techniques are part of a larger body of methods called general linear modeling. See Chapter 10 in *Quantifying the User Experience* for more on ANOVA.

TIP:

> When you compare many pairs of groups, you increase the chance of finding a difference from chance alone (called alpha inflation). Plan to use a multiple-comparison technique, such as a Bonferroni correction, or our preference, the Benjamini–Hochberg procedure, to differentiate the signal from the noise. Often when you're comparing groups, you only care about comparisons with your product or website, which reduces the number of comparisons and consequently reduces alpha inflation.

Logistic Regression

Dependent variables are often discrete and not continuous. For example, you may be primarily interested in purchase rates (purchase vs. not purchase) or conversion rates (recommend or didn't recommend) — both are discrete-binary. In such cases, a regular regression analysis won't work. Instead, you need to use a different but related technique called *logistic regression analysis*, which converts the data using a logit transformation. In logistic regression, you still want to know what combination of independent variables best predicts the outcome, as in regular regression. The only difference is the outcome variable is discrete (usually binary). For example, you may want to understand how attitudes toward a brand (favorable or unfavorable) and customer tenure (new vs. existing) affect the Likelihood-to-Recommend a product.

TIP:

> While logistic regression doesn't have the same linearity assumptions as regular regression, you still need to avoid including highly correlated independent variables (multicollinearity), and you must have a large sample size and know how to interpret log-odd ratios, which is more challenging than interpreting means.

Factor Analysis

Sometimes the variables you're most interested in are those you can't directly observe or measure easily. For example, there isn't a direct measure of usability (no usability thermometer); instead, you must rely on the outcomes of good and bad experiences to quantify usability. *Factor analysis* is a technique that takes many observed correlated variables and reduces them to a few latent (hidden) variables called *factors*.

For example, we used factor analysis (Sauro & Lewis, 2009) to identify usability as a single factor from the correlated variables of task time, completion rates, errors, and perceived task difficulty.

Factor analysis is also a staple of questionnaire development, where you determine which items group together to best embody a construct. Sauro (2015) used factor analysis extensively to build the SUPR-Q (uncovering the latent variables of usability, loyalty, trust, and appearance from dozens of potential items).

 TIP:

> There are several ways to determine how many factors are in your data, so different researchers examining the same data with different methods may uncover a different number of factors. You generally need a large sample size to conduct a factor analysis, and like in many techniques, the variables should have linear relationships.

Cluster Analysis

When you want to know what items to group together, you use *cluster analysis*. Like in factor analysis, these groupings aren't directly measurable but are inferred from the data (another type of latent variable). Cluster analysis is the approach used in card sorting when you want to know how closely products, content, or functions relate from the users' perspective.

We use cluster analysis to segment customers and build personas. When we conduct segmentation studies for clients, we'll look at several variables, including demographic (income, age) and psychographic (e.g., likelihood to use a new service), to see what defines a segment.

 TIP:

> Like factor analysis, there's some subjectivity involved in determining the number of clusters. You can easily justify more granular or broader clusters based on how closely you want the items to relate.

Multivariate Techniques Summary

Simple statistical techniques can answer many questions posed to UX researchers. There are times, however, when you need more advanced techniques to best answer the question. Figure 21.19 shows how 12 analytical methods fall along two axes—focus on differences vs. structure and lower vs. higher complexity.

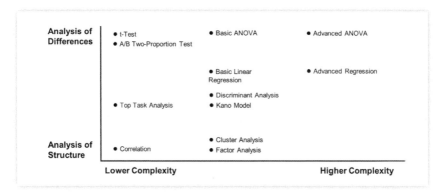

Analysis of Differences	• t-Test • A/B Two-Proportion Test	• Basic ANOVA	• Advanced ANOVA
		• Basic Linear Regression	• Advanced Regression
	• Top Task Analysis	• Discriminant Analysis • Kano Model	
Analysis of Structure	• Correlation	• Cluster Analysis • Factor Analysis	
	Lower Complexity		Higher Complexity

FIGURE 21.19: Map of analytical methods by analytical focus and level of complexity.

Table 21.8 lists six common research questions, appropriate analytical methods for those questions, and sample applications.

Question	Methods	Sample Application
	Two Proportion Test	A/B testing
Are there significant differences?	t-Test	Test two designs
	ANOVA	Test multiple designs and interactions
Are there significant similarities?	Correlation	Assess relationships (e.g., CSAT and age)
Are there significant predictors?	Linear Regression	Key driver analysis
	Cluster Analysis	Persona development
Is there latent (hidden) structure?	Factor Analysis	Develop standardized UX questionnaire
	Latent Class Analysis	Advanced persona development
Can we determine membership in classes?	Discriminant Analysis	Customer segment classification tool
	Logistic Regression	Statistical basis for feature prioritization
	Conjoint Analysis	Exhaustive feature prioritization
What are the most important features/tasks?	MaxDiff Analysis	Streamlined feature prioritization
	Kano Model	Alternative feature prioritization method
	Top Task Analysis	Identify most important tasks

TABLE 21.8: Applications of advanced analytical methods.

CHAPTER SUMMARY AND TAKEAWAY

This chapter covered advanced (but often essential) methods for analyzing two (or more) metrics.

What do I need to know to compare two metrics? ...The type of data (discrete-binary or continuous) and the experimental design (between or within subjects). For a between-subjects comparison of discrete-binary data, use the $N-1$ two-proportion test, and for continuous data, use the two-sample t-test. For within-subjects comparison of discrete-binary data, use the McNemar exact test, and for continuous data, use the paired t-test.

What about comparison with benchmarks? ...The methods are different for discrete-binary and continuous data. To compare a mean (continuous data) to a benchmark, conduct a one-tailed one-sample t-test. For discrete-binary data, conduct a binomial test.

What is the best way to analyze preference data? ...Consider a combination of analyses. There are multiple ways to analyze preference data, but at a minimum, test each preference percentage against its expected occurrence by chance (one-proportion binomial test), potentially followed by testing each preference percentage against every other preference percentage (McNemar exact tests, as long as there aren't too many preference options). That way, you can see which preference percentages are greater or lower than expected by chance and how each preference percentage compares with the others.

What's the difference between cross-tabbing and collapsing variables? ...Cross tabbing increases; collapsing decreases. Cross tabbing is a way of examining the similarities and differences between two or more variables. For example, if there are four levels of experience and four websites, there will be 16 values (4 × 4) after cross tabbing. Collapsing is a strategy for reducing measurements with many values into fewer values (e.g., taking five levels of experience and combining them so there is one level for "no experience" and a second level for "at least some experience").

My sample doesn't have the right proportions for prior experience—can I fix that? ...Yes, if you know the population proportions. You can use the population proportions as a second variable in a special version of the t-test known as the weighted t-test. This strategy also works with other individual differences like age range or educational level.

What if I'm interested in relationships instead of differences? ...Then you can perform correlation or regression analysis. Correlation is a measure of the shared (co) relationship of two variables, which can range from –1 (perfect negative correlation) to 0 (no correlation) to +1 (perfect positive correlation). For continuous data, use the Pearson correlation; for ranks, use the Spearman correlation. To model the linear relationship between two continuous variables, use simple linear regression.

Are there statistical methods for analyzing more than two variables? ...Yes, there are many multivariate analytical methods. These methods are the topics of multiple semesters of graduate statistics courses and require significant investment in training and tooling. The following methods are commonly used in UX research:

- *Multiple regression* is an extension of correlations and simple linear regression, but with two or more variables predicting the value of a continuous dependent variable. When combined with stepwise elimination or retention methods to determine which predictors are the most important, the method is sometimes referred to as key driver analysis (KDA).

- *Analysis of Variance* (ANOVA) extends the *t*-test to compare multiple means, enabling the simultaneous analysis of main effects and their interactions.

- *Logistic regression* is like multiple regression, but the dependent variable is discrete instead of continuous (e.g., using independent variables to predict whether a respondent will or won't make a purchase).

- *Factor analysis* refers to a collection of related methods for identifying how groups of variables align with hypothesized constructs (e.g., how the items of the SUS align with the hypothesized construct of usability). Factor analysis is often used in the development of standardized UX questionnaires.

- *Cluster analysis* is used to identify structure by analyzing the multivariate distance between objects of interest based on their measured characteristics. Cluster analysis is often used in UX research to analyze card sort data and to identify customer segments.

CHAPTER 22:
DISPLAYING SURVEY RESULTS

Applied surveys generate a lot of data that need to be synthesized, presented, and (usually) acted upon. Better understanding can lead to better action. But what's the best way to display the results? Well, it depends. In this book, we've tried to provide empirically supported recommendations that are based on more than conventional wisdom. While conventions aren't all bad (there are many we agree with), we've found, in some cases, that the conventional wisdom might not be too wise, supported only by a "this is how it's always been done" attitude (e.g., the practice of alternating the tone of items in a rating scale in Chapter 13).

The debate (often heated) about the "right" way to ask survey questions also extends to how to display survey data. One of the most influential authors in this field is Edward Tufte, a now–professor emeritus at Yale, who has written at least five books on displaying information, including from surveys (see *The Visual Display of Quantitative Information*, Tufte, 2001). We'll refer to Tufte's recommendations throughout this chapter.

From childhood, pictures make the books we had to read more approachable. Data visualizations can make digesting numbers *seem* easier, and they will ideally lead to more efficient and accurate decisions. But graphs and visualizations aren't without their risks. The choice of scales, graph types, and styles can all have an effect, for better or worse, on how your audience interprets the findings.

This chapter focuses on best practices (and what to watch for) that we've compiled from our experiences graphing and displaying survey data, with references and evidence-based recommendations. We use visualization examples beyond typical survey data like bar graphs and pie graphs because you're likely to encounter various visualizations in other survey reports and may consider using them yourself. We'll address the following questions:

- What is chart junk?
- Should I always start the vertical (y) axis of a graph at zero?
- Is it better to present pairs of raw scores or just the difference scores?
- Should I always avoid 3D representations?
- What is the problem with cumulative graphs?
- Are graphs always better than tables?
- Should graphs include error bars?
- What else can I do to help people interpret my graphs?
- What words should I use to describe changes in data?
- Are graphs that follow guidelines enough?

WATCH FOR CHART JUNK

Visual elements on a graph that aren't necessary to convey information, or worse, that distract from the main point, are what Tufte calls *chart junk*. Common chart junk suspects include pictures, thick gridlines, shadows, or 3D elements (see Figure 22.1).

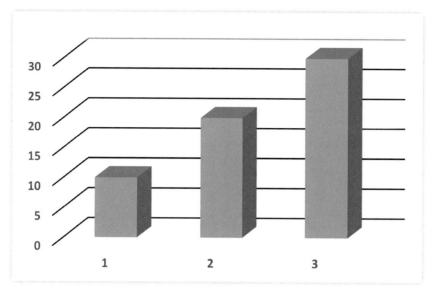

FIGURE 22.1: Example of a graph with 3D elements.

Visually, the grid lines are quite prominent (and use lots of precious ink) but are likely unimportant compared to the differences between the values.

Despite Tufte's strong condemnation of chart junk, not all graph pictures are necessarily chart junk. Tufte has a way of exaggerating to make a point, and there is some evidence that the right pictures (some would call junk) on a graph can *improve* recall and interpretation (Kosara, 2010, Apr 22; Lewis et al., 2023, Sep 12).

Don't clutter graphs with thoughtless junk, but if you can add elements that enhance the reader's experience or grab their attention, don't let fear of junk criticism stop you.

Y-SCALING

The y-scale (vertical axis) you choose can intentionally or unintentionally obscure or magnify differences in data. While you don't want to mislead or be misled, keep in mind that no graph is objective; always assume there's an agenda behind each graph (some more benign than others). The context matters, and the reader should understand the context and consequences of how the y-scale was chosen. The two graphs in Figure 22.2 illustrate the same global temperature data but have different y-scales.

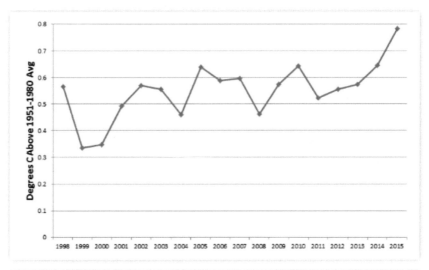

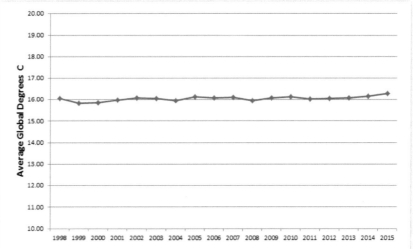

FIGURE 22.2: Two representations of the same global temperature with different y-scales.

A CX or UX survey is unlikely to display temperatures. It's more common to see things like reported spending or the amount most people are willing to spend. Figure 22.3 shows the results from an item on a consumer survey asking respondents their willingness to spend based on a series of feature tradeoffs for a consumer electronic device. The average amount was $413. They both display the same average amount, but the scaling makes one look a lot more costly than the other.

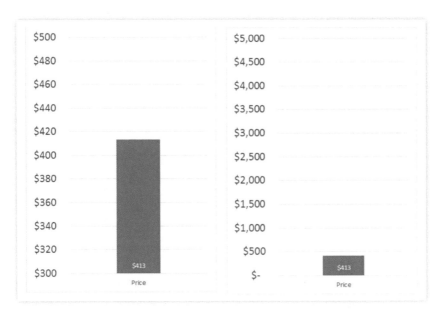

FIGURE 22.3: Two representations of the same willingness to spend results.

Neither of these representations is wrong. When deciding on appropriate upper and lower bounds of the y-axis, try to select values that are plausible for your research context.

ZERO IS NOT ALWAYS A HERO

Given the challenges with "objective" graphs, one remedy is to always "show the zero." But showing or not showing the zero alone is insufficient to declare a graph "objective" or, conversely, "deceptive."

Don't think graphs always have to start at zero. While it's a good idea to have best practices when displaying data in graphs, the "show the zero" can clearly be broken.

Figure 22.4 shows a graph of the reduction in cable subscribers from 2011 to 2015. The authors of the graph want to convey the idea that people are "cutting cords," and the visual drop from 2011 shows this. The visual reduction of the bars from 2011 to 2015 is about 68%. However, the actual reduction of subscribers is only around 3%.

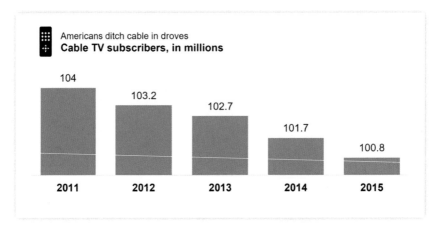

FIGURE 22.4: Drop in cable subscribers from 2011 to 2015 with a nonzero lower bound of the y-axis.

But is the representation in Figure 22.5 really a better graph because it includes the zero?

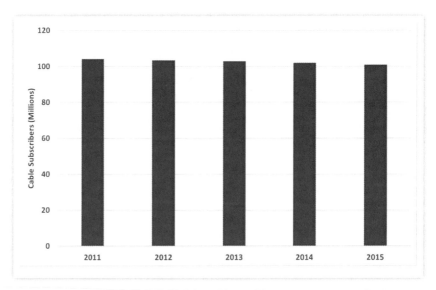

FIGURE 22.5: Drop in cable subscribers from 2011 to 2015 with a zero bound for the y-axis.

A 3% drop in subscribers is certainly not something to ignore (3.2 million subscribers leaving is likely a loss of significant revenue for cable companies), but the reduction and any sense of trend are not apparent in this new graph (Figure 22.5). But what happens if the drop is greater than 3.2 million? In 2020, the actual number of subscribers dropped even more, close to 75 million (a 25% drop) (Stoll, 2023, Mar 20). A drop of this magnitude would be evident in Figure 22.5, but could not be represented in Figure 22.4 without adjusting the lower bound of the y-axis.

CONSISTENTLY SCALE THE Y-AXIS

Whatever y-scale you decide on, be consistent when presenting multiple graphs in the same report by using the same y-scale (if possible). The two graphs in Figure 22.6 show similar SEQ results, but because the y-scale differs, it looks like the scores on the right are much lower.

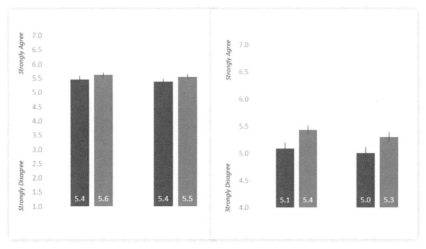

FIGURE 22.6: Two representations of the same SEQ results.

DIFFERENCE AND RAW SCORES CAN TELL DIFFERENT STORIES

Difference scores (the difference between two data points) can help clear the noise on graphs that have many data points. Difference scores draw attention to important differences that may get lost with raw scores. Figure 22.7 shows the same satisfaction scores (on an eleven-point scale) between two product versions. One panel in the figure shows the raw means and the other panel shows only the differences between versions.

Accentuated differences can suggest a difference is more impactful in the real world, even if the difference is modest. Be careful with difference scores, though; they can be harder to interpret than the original values.

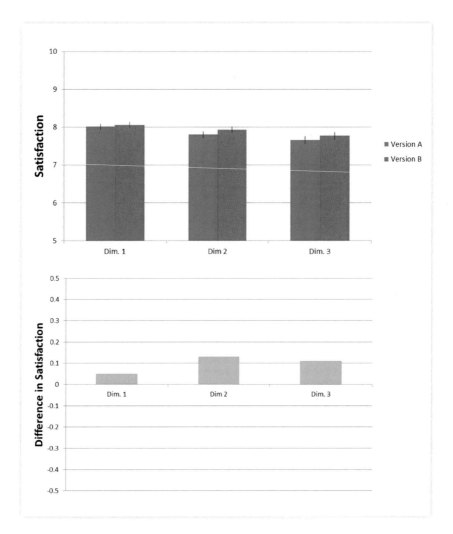

FIGURE 22.7: Two visualizations of differences with paired data points in the top panel and corresponding difference scores in the bottom panel.

BE WARY OF 3D

The volume of an object increases at a faster rate than its area. Therefore, showing 3D graphs for comparison depicts a bigger difference than a 2D representation (Figure 22.8), which could result in poor decision-making (a point suggested by Edward Tufte without strong evidence).

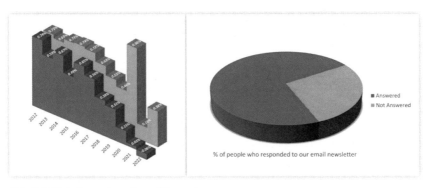

FIGURE 22.8: Examples of two 3D graphs.

Interestingly, some research has found that 3D graphs don't hurt as much as visualization gurus like Tufte suggest it does (Zacks et al., 1998). Sauro et al. (2023, Dec 12) tested how quickly participants could identify which of two bars in an Excel graph was taller for a range of differences in height. The main manipulation in this experiment was whether the graph was 2D or 3D (Figure 22.9). Overall, selection times for 3D bar graphs were slightly but statistically longer than for 2D ($t(98)$ = 2.75, p = .007). It took participants about 6% longer, which is only .08 seconds (2D: 1.38 seconds; 3D: 1.46 seconds, 95% confidence interval from .02–.13 seconds).

That difference, while consistent enough to be statistically significant, isn't necessarily perceptible (e.g., statistically significant but not practically significant), but we still recommend using 3D only when 2D doesn't fully convey the needed information.

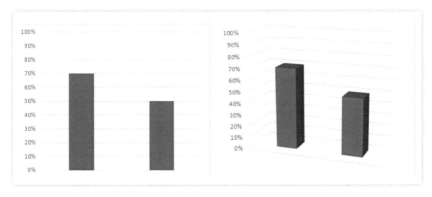

FIGURE 22.9: Examples of 2D and 3D bar charts used in Sauro et al. (2023, Dec 12).

CUMULATIVE GRAPHS ARE EASILY MISUNDERSTOOD

Cumulative graphs are used to show rates of change over time. They aren't used often as a primary way of displaying survey results. They may potentially be used in longitudinal survey data or when asking participants to recall events bound by time (e.g., products sold each day in a month, illustrated in Figure 22.10). The pandemic of 2020 brought a plethora of cumulative graphs. But we found the increased exposure didn't necessarily translate into increased comprehension.

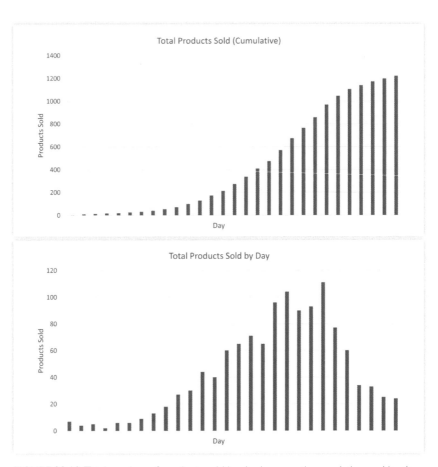

FIGURE 22.10: Total number of products sold by day in a month, cumulative, and by day.

We found people routinely misinterpret the rate of change on cumulative graphs (Sauro & Lewis, 2020, Apr 22). Across two studies, we found that respondents were between four and seven times more likely to misinterpret the rate of change on cumulative graphs compared to daily graphs (z = 10.0, $p < .001$). Cumulative graphs, by definition, can only increase (or stay flat), so they don't clearly indicate when a periodic trend turns downward. Our recommendation is to **use cumulative graphs with caution.** While the authors of these graphs may not intend readers to use cumulative graphs to interpret the rate of change, people will likely do so, and thus will likely be incorrect in their interpretation if the rate of change is decreasing.

A TABLE MIGHT BE BETTER THAN A GRAPH.

If you find yourself with too many bars on a graph, don't be afraid to display values in a table. A display of numbers in a table is often a better way to present a lot of data in a compact form. It can reduce chart junk and other subtle biases including exaggerated differences or questionable y-scales (e.g., Table 22.1).

Country	Count	%
United States of America (USA)	927	75%
France	63	5%
United Kingdom (UK)	50	4%
Canada	36	3%
Germany	20	2%
India	17	1%
Switzerland	15	1%
Singapore	12	1%
Czech Republic	12	1%
Australia	9	1%

TABLE 22.1: Example of using a table for compact representation of findings.

HEATMAPS: ADD A LITTLE "HEAT" TO THE TABLES

Adding color to tables, often referred to as *heatmaps*, provides good visual differentiation among many numbers. Table 22.2 shows the percentage of top-box (strongly agree) responses by airline for several online experiences. Table 22.3 shows the same data but with colors showing relatively low and high percentages. Heatmaps call attention to low and high areas with a lot less visual space than the same number of bar graphs.

Airline	Choosing a seat	Checking in to your flight	Using miles or points to book a ticket	Making a flight reservation	Finding airline contact information	Changing a reservation
Air Canada	19%	34%	13%	32%	15%	13%
Air France	21%	35%	8%	35%	25%	19%
Alaska Air	33%	40%	19%	44%	27%	15%
American Air	42%	48%	21%	44%	35%	21%
BritishAirways	19%	23%	12%	27%	12%	12%
Delta	27%	45%	27%	41%	29%	12%
Frontier	20%	39%	11%	33%	20%	13%
JetBlue	31%	39%	20%	31%	29%	24%
Lufthansa	23%	34%	4%	30%	28%	15%
Ryan Air	14%	16%	2%	20%	4%	6%
Southwest	29%	60%	29%	60%	48%	50%
United	38%	44%	21%	44%	25%	21%

TABLE 22.2: Example of top-box scores in a table without heatmaps.

Airline	Choosing a seat	Checking in to your flight	Using miles or points to book a ticket	Making a flight reservation	Finding airline contact information	Changing a reservation
Air Canada	19%	34%	13%	32%	15%	13%
Air France	21%	35%	8%	35%	25%	19%
Alaska Air	33%	40%	19%	44%	27%	15%
American Air	42%	48%	21%	44%	35%	21%
BritishAirways	19%	23%	12%	27%	12%	12%
Delta	27%	45%	27%	41%	29%	12%
Frontier	20%	39%	11%	33%	20%	13%
JetBlue	31%	39%	20%	31%	29%	24%
Lufthansa	23%	34%	4%	30%	28%	15%
Ryan Air	14%	16%	2%	20%	4%	6%
Southwest	29%	60%	29%	60%	48%	50%
United	38%	44%	21%	44%	25%	21%

TABLE 22.3: Example of top-box scores in a table with heatmaps.

INDICATE SAMPLING ERROR

Consider indicating sampling error by providing confidence intervals or some other indication of statistical significance when you need to help your audience differentiate likely real differences from random noise. For example, Figure 22.11 shows confidence intervals displayed as error bars. Additional options include asterisks, notes, or shaded bars (Sauro, 2016, Dec 6).

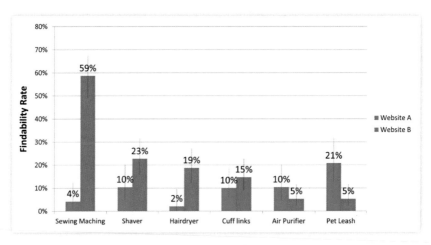

FIGURE 22.11: Sampling error indicated with confidence intervals.

Compared to What?

A recommendation Tufte made that we agree with is to answer the question "Compared to what?" That is, when it's possible, provide a comparison to improve interpretation, such as to an external benchmark, like an industry average or a best-in-class competitor, as we covered in Chapter 21.

Figure 22.12 shows task-ease (SEQ) data and includes the industry average (horizontal dashed line) and three competitor scores per task. These comparisons help make the metrics more meaningful and answer the critical question: Is this good or bad?

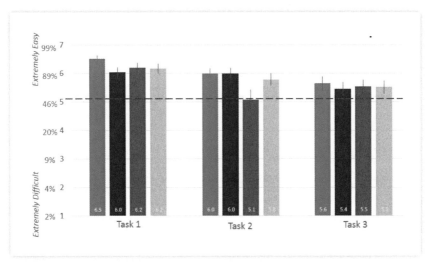

FIGURE 22.12: Example of SEQ means compared with each other and the industry average.

When making comparisons, think about what the audience will need to compare most and try to place them as close together as possible to make comparisons easier.

DESCRIBING CHANGES

To help describe changes in values, such as the same value over time (e.g., satisfaction over time), or when making comparisons to different brands (e.g., airline satisfaction), we need to use change verbs like "dropped," "increased," or "surged." Unlike mathematics, much of natural language is ambiguous, including expressions of uncertainty and change.

To help understand how people interpret the magnitude of such claims, we analyzed estimates from 454 U.S.-based respondents on 12 verbs in four contexts, using either sliders or open numeric fields (Sauro & Lewis, 2020, Dec 1), with the results shown in Figure 22.13.

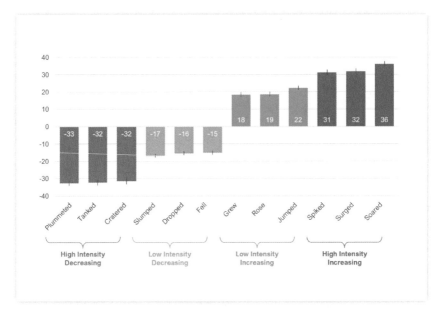

FIGURE 22.13: Interpretations of the magnitude of verbal descriptions of change.

Despite the wide range in estimates for the verbs (which we somewhat expected), it was interesting that the verbs tended to fall into four groups defined by decreasing/increasing direction and lower/higher intensity: Plummeted, Tanked, Cratered; Slumped, Dropped, Fell; Grew, Rose, Jumped; Spiked, Surged, Soared.

WHEN IN DOUBT, TEST

If you have time, test your visualizations to see if your audience's understanding and interpretation match yours (Sauro, 2017, Feb 8). Like usability testing of products, don't just ask people if they "like" the graph; use a mix of open- and closed-ended questions to assess their comprehension. You may find that some of the "rules" on good visualizations proclaimed by experts aren't supported by data — as appears to be the case with chart embellishments and 3D perspectives.

CHAPTER SUMMARY

This chapter covered practice- and research-guided practices for presenting survey results.

What is chart junk? …Any unnecessary visual elements on a graph. For example, pictures, thick gridlines, shadows, and 3D elements are sometimes identified as chart junk, a term coined by Edward Tufte. Don't clutter graphs with thoughtless junk, but keep in mind that there is some evidence that incorporating the right pictures on a graph can improve recall and interpretation.

Should I always start the vertical (y) axis of a graph at zero? … This is often the best choice, but not always. You usually won't be criticized for starting the y-axis at 0 (or whatever the lowest possible value is for the scale), but there are times when doing this obscures the visual representation of an important finding. If you start at a value other than 0, choose that starting point carefully to avoid any misleading representation. Whatever starting point you use, be consistent when presenting multiple graphs of the same type of data in the same report.

Is it better to present pairs of raw scores or just the difference scores? …It depends. The presentation of difference scores reduces the number of chart elements on a graph. This sometimes makes it easier to see the important differences, but there are also times when differences are harder to interpret than raw scores. If in doubt, create both versions, then choose the one that best conveys the finding.

Should I avoid 3D representations? …Usually. This is related to the chart junk question. We recommend using 2D representations unless a 3D representation more fully conveys the needed information (which, in our experience, is rarely the case).

What is the issue with cumulative graphs? …They don't clearly indicate downward trends. Cumulative graphs always rise, so they obscure downward trends. When trends are important to convey, choose a representation that has the proper visualization.

Are graphs always better than tables? …No. When graphs become very complex, consider displaying the results in a table. For complex tables, consider using methods like heatmaps to call attention to low and high values in the table.

Should graphs include error bars? …Yes, whenever it's important to show plausible ranges of measurement. It isn't always necessary to include error bars, but it is often a good idea. Graphing programs offer different choices for error bars. We prefer the presentation of confidence intervals (usually 90% or 95%) to help differentiate likely real differences from random effects.

What else can I do to help people interpret my graphs? …Answer the question, "Compared to what?" If there is an external benchmark you can add to a graph to show which values are above or below the benchmark, add it. When creating a graph to make comparisons, consider which comparisons are most important and place them as close together as possible.

How should I describe changes? . . . Choose appropriate words. Consider both the valence (decreasing/increasing) and intensity (low/high) of the words you use to describe changes. For example, save "plummeted" and "soared" for large changes; for small changes, use "fell" or "grew."

I've followed all these guidelines, so my graphs must be great — right? …Not necessarily. As part of the report review process, time permitting, check to see if the target audience interprets your graphs as expected with a mix of open- and close-ended questions.

APPENDIX A:

Statistical Considerations

HOW CONFIDENT DO YOU NEED TO BE?

The typical confidence level we work with is 90%. This means that over time, our methods of computing confidence intervals will contain the actual unknown completion rate or average score for 90 out of 100 samples.

The confidence level is related to the p-value obtained when conducting statistical tests. For most of our applied research, we flag a difference as "statistically significant" if its p-value is less than 0.10 (or 10%) and especially if its p-value is less than .05 (or 5%).

The confidence level and the p-value that determines the threshold for statistical significance are values we set ahead of time using what we call the *alpha level*. If we choose an alpha level of 0.05, for example, then a p-value smaller than 0.05 is considered statistically significant, and our confidence level (1−alpha) is 0.95 (95%). Although it is common practice to set alpha to 0.05, it can take any value from just above 0 (e.g., 0.00001) to just below 1 (e.g., 0.99999). The right level of confidence to use depends on the consequences of being wrong (Lewis & Sauro, 2021, Sep 28). Here are different thresholds commonly used to determine the confidence level (and p-values) in different situations; you can use these examples as a guide to what is appropriate for your situation.

Pharmaceutical confidence level—99%+: When a bad decision can lead to injury or death—say, when you're evaluating clinical trials and drug interactions—you want a high level of confidence in your intervals and a high standard for declaring statistical significance. Of course, high levels of confidence come with high costs: testing in the pharmaceutical environment often involves sample sizes in the thousands.

Publication confidence level—95%+: When your reputation is on the line, as in peer-reviewed journals and high-level political polls, a confidence level of 95% is typically required (and a corresponding p-value of less than 0.05). When you choose to break with the 0.05 norm, plan to defend your choice. And, if publication is one of your goals, it's going to be difficult to publish your research if your p-values exceed .05.

Industrial confidence level—90%+: When we are trying to understand if a product or service is providing a good (or great, or not so great, etc.) user experience, we often use a 90% confidence level. For example, when we complete an analysis for a client, we often analyze both survey data and usability benchmarks, so we need a 90% confidence level to ensure that a two-sided statement equates to 95% confidence for a one-sided statement (e.g., at least 75% of users can complete a task). In many environments, dipping below 90% takes stakeholders out of their comfort zone. In our book *Quantifying the User Experience,* 2nd Edition, see Chapter 4 for more discussion on one- and two-sided confidence intervals and Chapter 9 on associated controversies in measurement and statistics.

Exploratory confidence level—80%+: When you need only reasonable evidence—when, for example, you're looking at product prototypes, early-stage designs, or the general sentiments from customers—an 80% level of confidence is often sufficient. When your sample sizes are small, confidence intervals widen, and you rarely get statistically significant results with high confidence. Also, when you relax your alpha to 0.20, you'll be fooled more often by chance variation. However, when the consequences of being wrong are not dire, this may be an appropriate level to choose.

Casino confidence level—51+%: When there's little or no downside to being wrong, and if you must pick among poor alternatives, a 51% confidence level is at least better than flipping a coin. As they say: What happens in Vegas, stays in Vegas—and that's the case with your money too. In a casino, the longer you play, the less likely you're going home a winner. Games of chance are rigged to give the house an edge. However, if your business is on the line, we don't recommend declaring statistical significance with p-values of 0.49—unless your business happens to be high-stakes poker.

While you may want to go for high confidence in every situation to minimize the chance of being wrong, the price to pay for high confidence is large sample sizes. With high confidence and a small sample size, you increase the chances of another problem in statistics: a false negative, that is, not declaring statistical significance when there actually is a difference.

WHAT DOES STATISTICALLY SIGNIFICANT MEAN?

Statistically significant: it's a phrase that's packed with meaning—and syllables. It's hard to say and harder to understand. Yet it's one of the most common phrases heard when dealing with quantitative methods.

While the phrase "statistically significant" represents the result of a rational exercise with numbers, it has a way of evoking much emotion: bewilderment, resentment, confusion, and even arrogance (for those in the know). To help demystify this phrase, we've unpacked the following most important concepts to help you interpret p-values when making statistical comparisons.

When it's not due to chance. In principle, a statistically significant result (usually a difference) is a result that can't reasonably be attributed to chance. More technically, it means that if the null hypothesis is true (which means there really is no difference), there's a low probability of getting a result that is as large or larger than what you observed.

Statisticians can get picky about the definition of statistical significance and use confusing jargon to build a complicated definition. While it is important to be clear on what statistical significance means *technically*, it is just as important to be clear on what it means *practically*.

Consider these two factors:

- **Sampling error:** There's always a chance that the differences we observe when measuring a sample of users are just the result of random noise, chance fluctuations, or happenstance.

- **Probability:** There's never certainty. Statistics is about probability; you cannot buy 100% certainty. Statistics is about managing risk. Can we live with a 10% likelihood that our decision is wrong? A 5% likelihood? 33%? The answer depends on context: What does it cost to increase the probability of making the right choice, and what is the consequence (or potential consequence) of making the wrong choice? Most publications suggest a conventional cutoff of 5% — it's okay to be fooled by randomness 1 time out of 20. That's a reasonably high standard, and it may match your circumstances. It could just as easily be overkill, or it could expose you to far more risk than you can afford.

What it means in practice. Let's look at a scenario from a survey of 100 respondents (50 with experience using Website A and 50 experienced with Website B).

- 25 out of 50 respondents rated Website A as exceptionally useful (50% top-box score)

- 35 out of 50 different respondents rated Website B as exceptionally useful (70% top-box score)

Can we reliably attribute the 20 percentage point difference in top-box scores for the usefulness of one website over the other, or is this random noise?

How do we get statistical significance? The test we use to detect statistical differences depends on our metric type and whether we're comparing the same users (within subjects) or different users (between subjects). To compare two top-box scores, as we're doing here, we use the $N-1$ two-proportion test (between subjects). Figure A.1 shows a screenshot of the results using the MeasuringU Usability Statistics Package (Expanded) for comparing two proportions.

FIGURE A.1: Using the *N–1* two-proportion calculator to assess statistical significance.

To determine whether the observed difference is statistically significant, we look at two outputs of the statistical test.

- *p*-value: The primary output of statistical tests is the *p*-value (probability value). It indicates the probability of the observed difference if, in reality, no difference exists. In the example shown in Figure A.1, the *p*-value is 0.042, which indicates that we'd expect to see a meaningless (random) difference of 20% or more only about 42 times in 1,000. If we are comfortable with that level of chance (something we must consider before running the test), then we declare the observed difference to be statistically significant.

- **Confidence interval around difference:** A confidence interval around a difference that does not cross zero also indicates statistical significance. Using Figure A.1 as an example, the graph shows the 95% confidence interval around the difference between the proportions computed by the stats package. The observed difference was 20% (70% minus 50%), but we can expect the difference itself will fluctuate if this study is replicated. The CI around the difference tells us that it will most likely fluctuate between about .08% and 38% in favor of the second website. But because the difference is greater than 0%, we can conclude that the difference is statistically significant (not due to chance). If the interval crossed zero—if it went, for example, from –2% to 35%—we could not be 95% confident that the difference is nonzero, or even that it favors the second website.

What it doesn't mean. *Statistical significance* does not mean *practical significance.* The word "significance" in everyday usage connotes consequence and noteworthiness. Just because you get a low *p*-value and conclude a difference is statistically significant (unlikely to have happened by chance), this doesn't mean the difference will automatically be important. It's an unfortunate consequence of the words Sir Ronald Fisher selected when describing this method of statistical testing. One way to connect statistical to practical significance is to compute confidence intervals around the observed difference. If the lower limit is meaningful to you, given your understanding of your research context, then the result has practical significance (Lewis & Sauro, 2021, Jun 15).

APPENDIX B:

Commonly Used Questionnaires and Questions

This appendix provides the wording and response formats for commonly used questionnaires in UX and CX survey research.

SYSTEM USABILITY SCALE (SUS)

Measures: Perceived System Usability

Year Created: 1986

Number of Items: 10

Response Options: 5

Description: Participants rate ten items to assess the perceived usability of a system (e.g., a product or a website) either at the end of a usability study or in a retrospective survey.

The following are the SUS's ten items along with its five-point response options (Figure B.1).

1. I think that I would like to use this system frequently.
2. I found the system unnecessarily complex.
3. I thought the system was easy to use.
4. I think that I would need the support of a technical person to be able to use this system.
5. I found the various functions in this system were well integrated.
6. I thought there was too much inconsistency in this system.
7. I would imagine that most people would learn to use this system very quickly.
8. I found the system very cumbersome to use.
9. I felt very confident using the system.
10. I needed to learn a lot of things before I could get going with this system.

Strongly Disagree 1	2	3	4	Strongly Agree 5
○	○	○	○	○

FIGURE B.1: SUS response format.

Scoring:

- For odd items, subtract one from the user responses.

- For even-numbered items, subtract the user responses from 5.

- This scales all values from 0 to 4 (with 4 being the most positive response).

- Add up the converted responses for each user and multiply that total by 2.5. This converts the range of possible values from 0 to 100 instead of from 0 to 40.

Another less intuitive method (but more efficient when programming) is to use this formula:

- SUS = 2.5(20 + SUM(SUS01,SUS03,SUS05,SUS07,SUS09) – SUM(SUS02,SUS04,SUS06,SUS08,SUS10))

Benchmark Data: The average SUS score is 68, with percentile ranks derived from a large database of products.

Based on the percentile ranks, SUS means can be interpreted with a letter grade from A+ to F, as shown in Table B.1

SUS score range	Grade	Percentile range
84.1–100	A+	96–100
80.8–84.0	A	90–95
78.9–80.7	A–	85–89
77.2–78.8	B+	80–84
74.1–77.1	B	70–79
72.6–74.0	B–	65–69
71.1–72.5	C+	60–64
65.0–71.0	C	41–59
62.7–64.9	C–	35–40
51.7–62.6	D	15–34
0.0–51.6	F	0–14

TABLE B.1: SUS score to grade and percentile range.

More Details:

- *A Practical Guide to the System Usability Scale: Background, Benchmarks & Best Practices* (Sauro, 2011)

- *Quantifying the User Experience: Practical Statistics for User Research*, 2nd Edition (Sauro & Lewis, 2016).

- "The System Usability Scale: Past, Present, and Future" (Lewis, 2018b)

COMPUTER SYSTEM USABILITY QUESTIONNAIRE (CSUQ) VERSION 3

Measures: Overall: Perceived Usability; Subscales: System Usefulness, Information Quality, Interface Quality

Year Created: 1995

Number of Items: 16

Response Options: 7

Description: Participants rate their perception of ease toward a product or interface experience overall and for three subscales (System Usefulness, Information Quality, and Interface Quality). As shown in Figure B.2, lower ratings indicate a better user experience (Lewis, 1995). The CSUQ is the survey version of the Post-Study System Usability Questionnaire (PSSUQ).

Example:

✱ Please indicate your level of agreement with the following statements.	Strongly Agree 1	2	3	4	5	6	Strongly Disagree 7	N/A
Overall, I am satisfied with how easy it is to use this system.	○	○	○	○	○	○	○	○
It is simple to use this system.	○	○	○	○	○	○	○	○
I am able to complete my work quickly using this system.	○	○	○	○	○	○	○	○
I feel comfortable using this system.	○	○	○	○	○	○	○	○
It is easy to learn to use this system.	○	○	○	○	○	○	○	○
I believe I became productive quickly using this system.	○	○	○	○	○	○	○	○
The system gives error messages that clearly tell me how to fix problems.	○	○	○	○	○	○	○	○
Whenever I make a mistake using the system, I recover easily and quickly.	○	○	○	○	○	○	○	○
The information provided with the system is clear.	○	○	○	○	○	○	○	○
It is easy to find the information I need.	○	○	○	○	○	○	○	○
The information provided with this system is effective in helping me complete my work.	○	○	○	○	○	○	○	○
The organization of information on system screens is clear.	○	○	○	○	○	○	○	○
The interface of this system is pleasant.	○	○	○	○	○	○	○	○
I like using the interface of this system.	○	○	○	○	○	○	○	○
This system has all of the functions and capabilities I expect it to have.	○	○	○	○	○	○	○	○
Overall, I am satisfied with this system.	○	○	○	○	○	○	○	○

FIGURE B.2: The current version of the CSUQ.

Scoring:

- Overall: Mean of responses for items 1 to 16
- System Usefulness: Mean of responses for items 1 to 6
- Information Quality: Mean of responses for items 7 to 12
- Interface Quality: Mean of responses for items 13 to 15

Benchmark Data: Seven analyses of correspondence between concurrently collected SUS and overall CSUQ scores found, on average, the CSUQ scores (after converting to a 0–100-point scale) were just 1.6 points higher than the SUS. This means that until there is a larger CSUQ database to use for its own benchmarks, UX researchers can convert overall CSUQ scores to a 101-point scale like the SUS, then use the SUS benchmarks, especially the curved grading scale, for interpretation. After all, after converting scores to grade point averages (from 0 for F to 4 for A+), the mean difference between CSUQ and SUS was just 0.1 on the GPA scale. To convert CSUQ scores from their raw form to a 0–100-point scale, use this formula:

- $CSUQ100 = 100 - (CSUQ-1) \times (100 / 6)$

For example, if the CSUQ score is 1 (best possible), then CSUQ100 will be $100 - (1 - 1) \times (100 / 6) = 100 - 0 \times (100 / 6) = 100 - 0 = 100$. For a CSUQ score of 7 (worst possible), the CSUQ 100 will be $100 - (7 - 1) \times (100 / 6) = 100 - 6(100 / 6) = 100 - 100 = 0$.

More Details:

- *Using the PSSUQ and CSUQ in User Experience Research and Practice* (Lewis, 2019c)

SINGLE EASE QUESTION (SEQ)

Measures: Perceived Task Ease/Difficulty

Year Created: 2010

Number of Items: 1

Response Options: 7

Description: Participants rate the ease or difficulty of a task immediately after a usability test, or they rate a task after recalling an earlier experience (Figure B.3).

Example:

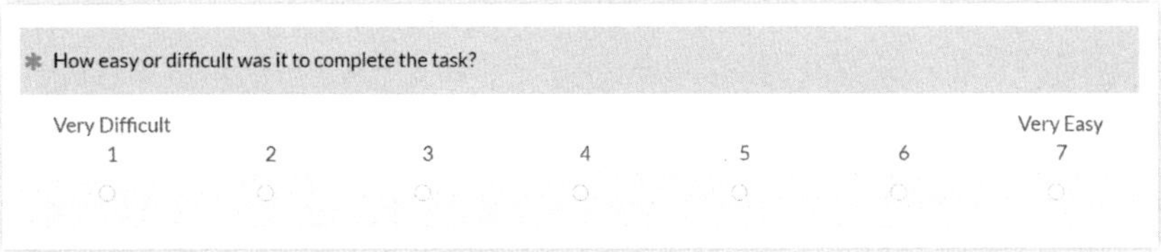

✳ How easy or difficult was it to complete the task?						
Very Difficult						Very Easy
1	2	3	4	5	6	7
○	○	○	○	○	○	○

FIGURE B.3: The current version of the SEQ.

Scoring: Scores are averaged across participants by task. Raw scores can be converted to percentile scores.

Benchmark Data: The average SEQ score is 5.5, and percentiles have been derived from a large database of tasks.

More Details:

- "10 Things to Know About the Single Ease Question" (Sauro, 2012, Oct 30)
- "Evaluation of Three SEQ Variants" (Sauro & Lewis, 2022, Sep 13)

STANDARDIZED USER EXPERIENCE PERCENTILE RANK QUESTIONNAIRE (SUPR-Q)

Measures: Overall: Perception of Website UX Quality; Subscales: Usability, Appearance, Trust, Loyalty

Year Created: 2010

Number of Items: 8

Response Options: 5/11

Description: Participants rate their experience with a website with eight items. The raw means for each subscale are combined (using half of the score of the eleven-point Likelihood-to-Recommend item). The raw score for the overall SUPR-Q is the mean of the four subscale scores (Figure B.4).

Example:

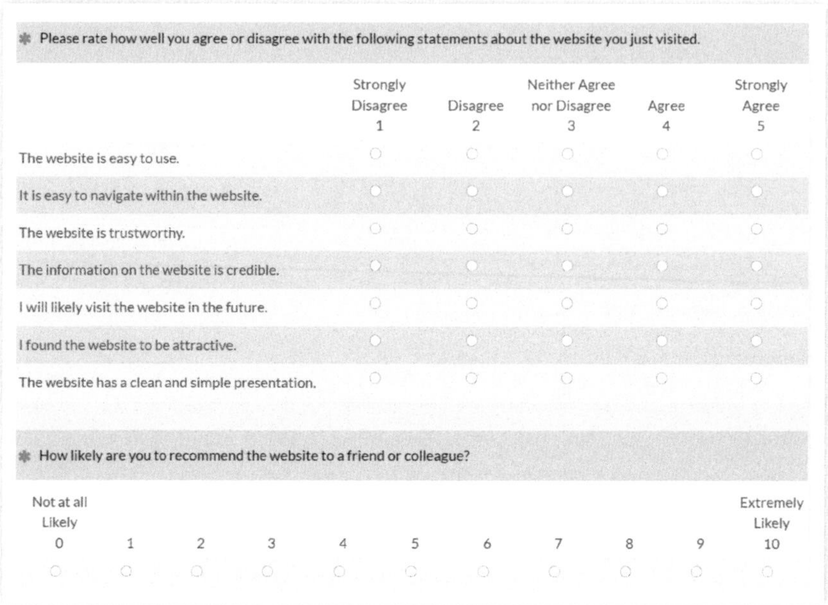

* Please rate how well you agree or disagree with the following statements about the website you just visited.

	Strongly Disagree 1	Disagree 2	Neither Agree nor Disagree 3	Agree 4	Strongly Agree 5
The website is easy to use.	○	○	○	○	○
It is easy to navigate within the website.	○	○	○	○	○
The website is trustworthy.	○	○	○	○	○
The information on the website is credible.	○	○	○	○	○
I will likely visit the website in the future.	○	○	○	○	○
I found the website to be attractive.	○	○	○	○	○
The website has a clean and simple presentation.	○	○	○	○	○

* How likely are you to recommend the website to a friend or colleague?

Not at all Likely 0	1	2	3	4	5	6	7	8	9	Extremely Likely 10
○	○	○	○	○	○	○	○	○	○	○

FIGURE B.4: The standard SUPR-Q.

Scoring: Items are averaged (taking half the Likelihood-to-Recommend item to keep its maximum value the same as the other items) with overall SUPR-Q and subscale scores ranging from 1 to 5. Raw scores can be analyzed as is or converted to normed scores for comparison against benchmarks.

- Overall: Mean of subscale scores (Usability, Appearance, Credibility, Loyalty)
- Usability: Mean of the first pair of items in Figure B.4 (easy to use, easy to navigate)
- Appearance: Mean of the second pair of items in Figure B.4 (clean and simple, attractive)
- Credibility: Mean of the third pair of items in Figure B.4 (trustworthy, credible)
- Loyalty: Mean of the last item in the Figure B.4 grid (likely return) and half the rating of Likelihood-to-Recommend

Benchmark Data: The SUPR-Q uses a proprietary database of 200+ websites with updates each quarter. Some published benchmarks are available on MeasuringU.

More Details:

- "SUPR-Q: A Comprehensive Measure of the Quality of the Website User Experience" (Sauro, 2015)

- "SUPR-Q Full License" (MeasuringU, n.d.)

NET PROMOTER SCORE

Measures: Intent to Recommend

Year Created: 2003

Number of Items: 1

Response Options: 11

Description: Participants rate their Likelihood-to-Recommend a brand, product, or experience.

Example:

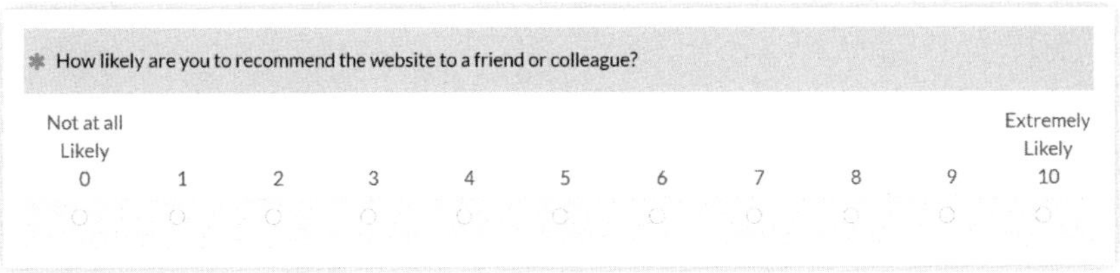

FIGURE B.5: The Likelihood-to-Recommend item used to compute the Net Promoter Score.

Scoring: Subtract the percentage of detractors (those who respond with 0–6) from the percentage of promoters (those who respond with 9 or 10) (Figure B.5).

Benchmark Data: Several organizations provide benchmarks by industry, company, and product. General guidelines are any NPS over 0 is good in the sense that there are more promoters than detractors, over 20 is favorable, over 50 is excellent, and over 80 is world class. Several times a year we publish NPS benchmarks for various industries in articles on our website (free) and in our UX reports (fee).

More Details:

- "Business Software UX and NPS Benchmarks (2022)" (Sauro & Lewis, 2022, Sep 20)

- "Consumer Software UX and NPS Benchmarks (2022)" (Sauro & Lewis, 2022, Nov 1)

- "UX and NPS Benchmarks of Ticketing Websites (2022)" (Sauro et al., 2022, Oct 17)

- "UX and NPS Benchmarks of Airline Websites (2022)" (Sauro et al., 2022, Jul 26)

Net Promoter Score® and *NPS*® are *registered trademarks* of Bain & Company, Inc., Satmetrix Systems, Inc., and Fred Reichheld.

USER-EXPERIENCE-LITE (UX-LITE)

Measures: Overall: User Experience; Subscales: Perceived Ease of Use, Perceived Usefulness

Year Created: 2021

Number of Items: 2

Response Options: 5

Description: Participants rate their perceptions of ease and usefulness toward a product or interface experience. The UX-Lite is derived from the UMUX-Lite (an earlier seven-point version with an alternate wording for the Usefulness item), which was itself derived from the UMUX (published in 2010 as an alternate form for the SUS, four seven-point items with alternating tone) (Figure B.6).

Example:

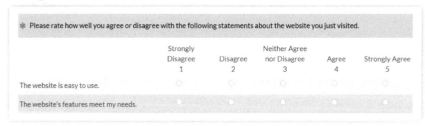

FIGURE B.6: Current version of the UX-Lite.

Scoring: Convert raw item scores to two 0–100-point scales, one for ease and one for usefulness. The UX-Lite score is the mean of the rescaled item scores.

Benchmark Data: Early benchmarks are available on MeasuringU.com in articles published in 2022 for business and consumer digital products.

More Details:

- "Business Software UX and NPS Benchmarks (2022)" (Sauro & Lewis, 2022, Sep 20)

- "Consumer Software UX and NPS Benchmarks (2022)" (Sauro & Lewis, 2022, Nov 1)
- "UX-Lite Calculator Package" (MeasuringU, n.d.)
- "Measuring Usability: From the SUS to the UMUX-Lite" (Sauro, 2017, Oct 11)
- "Measuring UX: From the UMUX-Lite to the UX-Lite" (Lewis & Sauro, 2021, Sep 15)
- "Evolution of the UX-Lite" (Lewis & Sauro, 2021, Oct 12)

MICROSOFT NET SATISFACTION (NSAT)

Measures: Satisfaction

Year Created: 2011

Number of Items: 1

Response Options: 7

Description: Participants rate their satisfaction with a product, brand, or experience (Figure B.7).

Example:

Very Satisfied	Somewhat Satisfied	Somewhat Dissatisfied	Very Dissatisfied
○	○	○	○

FIGURE B.7: The Microsoft NSAT item.

Scoring: The "net" is derived by taking the Very Satisfied percent of the total (top box) and subtracting the two dissatisfied options as a percent of the total (bottom-two boxes). The "Somewhat Satisfied" scores aren't factored in the score, only in the total responses. An unusual twist about the scoring is that Microsoft adds 100 to this net percentage to avoid negative scores.

Benchmark Data: No known reliable benchmark information.

More Details:

- "Scorecarding: How Microsoft Measures Its Own Success" (Foley, 2011, Mar 1)
- "10 Things to Know about the Microsoft NSAT Score" (Sauro, 2019, Sep 25)

PRODUCT-MARKET FIT (PMF)

Measures: How someone would feel if they could no longer use a product.

Year Created: Circa 2000

Number of Items: 1

Response Options: 4

Description: After using a product, participants rate how they'd feel if they could no longer use it (Figure B.8).

Example:

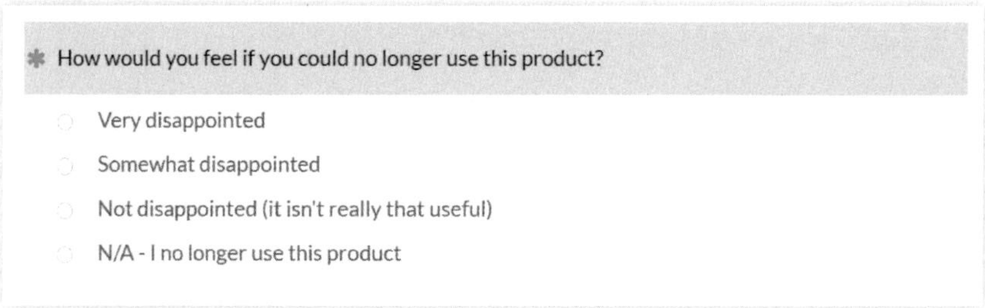

> ❋ How would you feel if you could no longer use this product?
>
> ○ Very disappointed
> ○ Somewhat disappointed
> ○ Not disappointed (it isn't really that useful)
> ○ N/A - I no longer use this product

FIGURE B.8: The Product-Market Fit item.

Scoring: The percentage of respondents who select "Very disappointed."

Benchmark Data: 40% is considered a minimum PMF score for new products. Some PMF benchmarks for established products are available on MeasuringU.com (e.g., in our 2022 business and consumer software benchmark articles and reports).

More Details:

- "What is the Product-Market Fit (PMF) Item?" (Lewis & Sauro, 2022, Mar 15)

- "Business Software UX and NPS Benchmarks (2022)" (Sauro & Lewis, 2022, Sep 20)

- "Consumer Software UX and NPS Benchmarks (2022)" (Sauro & Lewis, 2022, Nov 1)

CUSTOMER EFFORT SCORE (CES)

Measures: Perception of ease with interacting with a company.

Year Created: 2010

Number of Items: 1

Response Options: 7

Description: Customers are asked to rate the ease of interacting with a company (the previous version of the CES used a five-point scale anchored from Very Low Effort to Very High Effort) (Figure B.9).

Example:

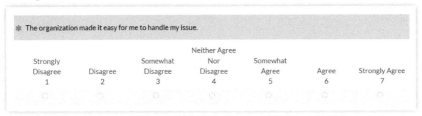

FIGURE B.9: Current version of the CES.

Scoring: Top-three-box percentage or mean.

Benchmark Data: Limited data available suggests an average score of 5.5 (like the SEQ).

More Details:

- "10 Things to Know about the Customer Effort Score" (Sauro, 2019, Nov 6)

REFERENCES

Alismail, S., & Zhang, H. (2018). The use of emoji in electronic user experience questionnaire: An exploratory case study. In *Proceedings of the 51ˢᵗ Hawaii International Conference on System Sciences* (pp. 3366–3375). Institute of Electrical and Electronics Engineers.

Alwin, D. F. (1997). Feeling thermometers versus 7-point scales: Which are better? *Sociological Methods & Research, 25*(3), 318–340.

Alwin, D. F., & Krosnick, J. A. (1991). The reliability of survey attitude measurement: The influence of question and respondent attributes. *Sociological Methods & Research, 20*(1), 139–181.

Andrews, F. M. (1984). Construct validity and error components of survey measures: A structural modeling approach. *Public Opinion Quarterly, 48*(2), 409–442.

Ares, G., Barreiro, C., Deliza, R., Giménez, A., & Gámbaro, A. (2010). Application of a check-all-that-apply question to the development of chocolate milk desserts. *Journal of Sensory Studies, 25*(1), 67–86.

Auh, S., Salisbury, L. C., & Johnson, M. D. (2003). Order effects in customer satisfaction modelling. *Journal of Marketing Management, 19*(3–4), 379–400.

Baddeley, A. (1992). What is autobiographical memory? In M. A. Conway, D. C. Rubin, H. Spinnler, & W. A. Wagenaar (Eds.), *Theoretical perspectives on autobiographical memory* (NATO ASI Series, vol. 65, pp. 13–29). Springer.

Bell, D. S., Mangione, C. M., & Kahn, C. E., Jr. (2001). Randomized testing of alternative survey formats using anonymous volunteers on the World Wide Web. *Journal of the American Medical Informatics Association, 8*(6), 616–620.

Billiet, J. B., & McClendon, M. J. (1998). On the identification of acquiescence in balanced sets of items using structural models. *Advances in Methodology, Data Analysis, and Statistics, 14*, 129–150.

Bishop, G. F. (1987). Experiments with the middle response alternative in survey questions. *Public Opinion Quarterly, 51*(2), 220–232.

Blair, I. V., Urland, G. R., & Ma, J. E. (2002). Using Internet search engines to estimate word frequency. *Behavior Research Methods, Instruments, & Computers, 34*(2), 286–290.

Bland, J. M., & Kerry, S. M. (1998). Weighted comparison of means. *BMJ, 316*(7125), 129.

Bolognese, J., Schnitzer, T. J., & Ehrich, E. W. (2003). Response relationship of VAS and Likert scales in osteoarthritis efficacy measurement. *Osteoarthritis and Cartilage, 11*(7), 499–507.

Boone, W. J., (2016). Rasch analysis for instrument development: Why, when, and how? *CBE Life Sciences Education, 15*(4), rm4, 1–7.

Boyce, A. C. (1915). *Methods for measuring teachers' efficiency.* University of Chicago Press.

Briggs, M., & Closs, S. J. (2000). A descriptive study of the use of visual analogue scales and verbal rating scales for the assessment of postoperative pain in orthopedic patients. *Journal of Pain and Symptom Management, 18*(6), 438–446.

Brooke, J. (1996). SUS: A "quick and dirty" usability scale. In P. W. Jordan, B. Thomas, B. A. Weerdmeester, & I. L. McClelland (Eds.), *Usability evaluation in industry* (pp. 189–194). Taylor & Francis.

Brooke, J. (2013). SUS: A retrospective. *Journal of Usability Studies, 8*(2), 29–40.

Brownell, B. (2022, July 25). *Do colours affect survey responses?* Insightrix. https://insightrix.com/colours-affect-survey-responses/

Burton, S., & Blair, E. (1991). Task conditions, response formulation processes, and response accuracy for behavioral frequency questions in surveys. *Public Opinion Quarterly, 55*(1), 50–79.

Callegaro, M., Baker, R. P., Bethlehem, J., Göritz, A. S., Krosnick, J. A., & Lavrakas, P. J. (Eds.) (2014) *Online panel research: A data quality perspective.* John Wiley.

Callegaro, M., Murakami, M. H., Tepman, Z., & Henderson, V. (2015). Yes–no answers versus check-all in self-administered modes: A systematic review and analyses. *International Journal of Market Research, 57*(2), 203–224.

Callegaro, M., Shand-Lubbers, J., & Dennis, J. M. (2009). Presentation of a single item versus a grid: Effects on the vitality and mental health scales of the SF-36v2 health survey. In *Proceedings of AAPOR* (pp. 5887–5897). American Statistical Association.

Callegaro, M., Wells, T., & Kruse, Y. (2008). Effects of precoding response options for five point satisfaction scales in web surveys. In *PAPOR Annual Conference* (pp. 1–22). Pacific Chapter of the American Association for Public Opinion Research.

Cechanowicz, J., Gutwin, C., Brownell, B., & Goodfellow, L. (2013). Effects of gamification on participation and data quality in a real-world market research domain. In *Proceedings of the First International Conference on Gameful Design, Research, and Applications* (pp. 58–65). Association for Computing Machinery.

CEIC Data. (n.d.) United States number of subscriber fixed line. https://www.ceicdata.com/en/indicator/united-states/number-of-subscriber-fixed-line

Cerasoli, C. P., Nicklin, J. M., & Ford, M. T. (2014). Intrinsic motivation and extrinsic incentives jointly predict performance: A 40-year meta-analysis. *Psychological Bulletin, 140*(4), 980–1008.

Chan, J. C. (1991). Response-order effects in Likert-type scales. *Educational and Psychological Measurement, 51*(3), 531–540.

Chestnut, J. (2008). *Effects of using a grid versus a sequential form on the ACS basic demographic data*. U.S. Census Bureau.

Chrzan, K., Saunders, T., & Brazil, J. (2012). Scale orientation, number of scale points and grids in mobile web surveys. Presentation at *Proceedings of AAPOR*. American Statistical Association.

Chudoba, B. (n.d.). *Does adding one more question impact survey completion rate?* SurveyMonkey. https://www.surveymonkey.com/curiosity/survey_questions_and_completion_rates/

Chyung, S. Y., Swanson, I., Roberts, K., & Hankinson, A. (2018). Evidence-based survey design: The use of continuous rating scales in surveys. *Performance Improvement, 57*(5), 38–48.

Cochran, W. G. (1977). *Sampling techniques* (3rd ed.). John Wiley.

Cole, J. S., Sarraf, S. A., & Wang, X. (2015). Does use of survey incentives degrade data quality? Paper presented at the *Association for Institutional Research Annual Forum*. Association for Institutional Research.

Commarford, P. M., Lewis, J. R., Smither, J., & Gentzler, M. D. (2008). A comparison of broad versus deep auditory menu structures. *Human Factors, 50*(1), 77–89.

Coromina, L., & Coenders, G. (2006). Reliability and validity of egocentered network data collected via web: A meta-analysis of multilevel multitrait multimethod studies. *Social Networks, 28*(3), 209–231.

Couper, M. P., Tourangeau, R., Conrad, F., & Singer, E. (2006). Evaluating the effectiveness of visual analog scales: A web experiment. *Social Science Computer Review, 24*(2), 227–245.

Couper, M. P., Traugott, M. W., & Lamias, M. J. (2001). Web survey design and administration. *Public Opinion Quarterly, 65*(2), 230–253.

Cox, E. P., III. (1980). The optimal number of response alternatives for a scale: A review. *Journal of Marketing Research, 17*(4), 407–422.

Cronbach, L. J. (1946). Response sets and test validity. *Educational and Psychological Measurement, 6*(4), 475–494.

Crystal, T. H., & House, A. S. (1990). Articulation rate and the duration of syllables and stress groups in connected speech. *Journal of the Acoustical Society of America, 88*(1), 101–112.

Dalal, D. K., & Carter, N. T. (2015). Negatively worded items negatively impact survey research. In C. E. Lance & R. J. Vandenberg (Eds.), *More statistical and methodological myths and urban legends* (pp. 112–132). Routledge/Taylor & Francis Group.

Davey, H. M., Barratt, A., Butow, P. N. Deeks, J. J. (2007). A one-item question with a Likert or visual analog scale adequately measured current anxiety. *Journal of Clinical Epidemiology, 60*(4), 356–360.

Davis, D. (1989). Perceived usefulness, perceived ease of use, and user acceptance of information technology. *MIS Quarterly, 13*(3), 319–339.

Dawes, J. (2008). Do data characteristics change according to the number of scale points used? An experiment using 5 point, 7 point, and 10 point scales. *International Journal of Market Research, 50*(1), 61–104.

DeCastellarnau A. (2018). A classification of response scale characteristics that affect data quality: A literature review. *Quality & Quantity, 52*(4), 1523–1559.

Deming, W. E. (1950). *Some theory of sampling.* Dover Publications.

Deubler, G., Swaney-Stueve, M., Jepsen, T., & Su-fern, B. P. (2019). The K-State emoji scale. *Journal of Sensory Studies, 35*(1), e12545.

Dickinson, T. L., & Zellinger, P. M. (1980). A comparison of the behaviorally anchored rating and mixed standard scale formats. *Journal of Applied Psychology, 65*(2), 147–154.

Dillman, D. A., Smyth, J. D., & Christian, L. M. (2014). *Internet, phone, mail, and mixed-mode surveys: The tailored design method* (4th ed.). John Wiley.

Dolnicar, S., and Grün, B. (2007). Cross-cultural differences in survey response patterns. *International Marketing Review, 24*(2), 127–143.

Ekman, P. (1970). Universal facial expressions of emotion. *California Mental Health Research Digest, 8*(4), 151–158.

Fessler, N. J. (2003). Experimental evidence on the links among monetary incentives, task attractiveness, and task performance. *Journal of Management Accounting Research, 15*(1), 161–176.

Finn, R. H. (1972). Effects of some variations in rating scale characteristics on the means and reliabilities of ratings. *Educational and Psychological Measurement, 32*(2), 255–265.

Finstad, K. (2006). The System Usability Scale and non-native English speakers. *Journal of Usability Studies, 1*(4), 185–188.

Finstad, K. (2010). The Usability Metric for User Experience. *Interacting with Computers, (22)*5, 323–327.

Foley, M. J. (2011, March 1). *Scorecarding: How Microsoft measures its own success.* Redmond. https://redmondmag.com/articles/2011/03/01/how-microsoft-measures-its-success.aspx

Frary, R. B. (2002). *A brief guide to questionnaire development.* Virginia Polytechnic Institute and State University.

Fricker, S., Kopp, B., Tan, L., & Tourangeau, R. (2015). A review of measurement error assessment in a U.S. household consumer expenditure survey. *Journal of Survey Statistics and Methodology, 3*(1), 67–88.

Friedman, H. H., & Amoo, T. (1999). Rating the rating scales. *Journal of Marketing Management, 9*(3), 114–123.

Friedman, H. H., Herskovitz, P. J., & Pollack, S. (1993). The biasing effects of scale-checking styles on responses to a Likert scale. In *Proceedings of the American Statistical Association Annual Conference: Survey Research Methods* (pp. 792–795). American Statistical Association.

Friedman, H. H. & Friedman, L. W. (1994). A comparison of vertical and horizontal rating scales. *Mid-Atlantic Journal of Business, 30*(1), 107–111.

Funke, F., Reips, U., & Thomas, R. K. (2011). Sliders for the smart: Type of rating scale on the web interacts with educational level. *Social Science Computer Review, 29*(2), 221–231.

Gao, B., & VanderLaan, D. P. (2020). Cultural influences on perceptions of emotions depicted in emojis. *Cyberpsychology, Behavior, and Social Networking, 23*(8), 567–570.

Garrett, M. F. (1990). Sentence processing. In D. N. Osherson & H. Lasnik (Eds.), *Language: An invitation to cognitive science,* Vol. 1, (pp. 133–175). The MIT Press.

Geisen, E., & Bergstrom, R. (2017). *Usability testing for survey research.* Morgan Kaufmann.

Ghiselli, E. E. (1939). All or none versus graded response questionnaires. *Journal of Applied Psychology, 23*(3), 405–413.

Grandmont, J., Goetzinger, L., Graff, B., & Dorbecker, K. (2010). Grappling with grids: How does question format affect data quality and respondent engagement? In *Proceedings of AAPOR* (pp. 5949–5958). American Statistical Association.

Grey Matter Research & Consulting. (2012). *More dirty little secrets of online panel research.* Grey Matter.

Groth, S. W. (2010). Honorarium or coercion: Use of incentives for participants in clinical research. *Journal of the New York State Nurses Association, 41*(1), 11–22.

Groves, R. M., Fowler, F. J. Jr., Couper, M. P., Lepkowski, J. M., Singer, E., & Tourangeau, R. (2009). *Survey methodology* (2nd ed.). John Wiley.

Gunner, J. (2021, June 2). *Should you use "can" or "may?" An explanation everyone can understand.* YourDictionary. https://grammar.yourdictionary.com/vs/can-vs-may-in-simple-terms.html

Harris, D. F. (2014) *The complete guide to writing questionnaires.* I&M Press.

Harzing, A.-W. (2006). Response styles in cross-national survey research: A 26-country study. *International Journal of Cross Cultural Management, 6*(2), 243–266.

Heffernan, K. (2018, March 28). *Understanding how the SUPR-Q impacts the NPS.* https://www.kaylaheffernan.com/blog/2018/3/28/supr-q-and-npsimpacts

Heggie, L., & Wade-Woolley, L. (2017). Reading longer words: Insights into multisyllabic word reading. *Perspectives of the ASHA Special Interest Group, 2*(1), 86–94.

Hjermstad, M. J., Fayers, P. M., Haugen, D. F., Caraceni, A., Hanks, G. W., Loge, J. H., Fainsinger, R., Aass, N., & Kaasa, S. (2011). Studies comparing numerical rating scales, verbal rating scales, and visual analogue scales for assessment of pain intensity in adults: A systematic literature review. *Journal of Pain and Symptom Management, 41*(6), 1073–1093.

Hopper, J. (2019, April 24). *Don't color-code your NPS Net Promoter Scale.* Versta Research. https://verstaresearch.com/blog/dont-color-code-your-nps-net-promoter-scale/

Hui, C. H., & Triandis, H. (1989). Effects of culture and response format on extreme response style. *Journal of Cross-Cultural Psychology, 20*(3), 296–309.

Iglesias, C. P., Birks, Y. F., & Torgerson, D. J. (2001). Improving the measurement of quality of life in older people: The York SF-12. *QJM: An International Journal of Medicine, 94*(12), 695–698.

Jacoby, J., & Matell, M. S. (1971). Three-point Likert scales are good enough. *Journal of Marketing Research, 8*(4), 495–500.

Jaeger, S. R., Xia, Y., Lee, P.-Y., Hunter, D. C., Beresford, M. K., & Ares, G. (2018). Emoji questionnaires can be used with a range of population segments: Findings relating to age, gender and frequency of emoji/emoticon use. *Food Quality and Preference, 68*, 397–410.

Jensen, M. P., Karoly, P., & Braver, S. (1986). The measurement of clinical pain intensity: A comparison of six methods. *Pain, 27*(1), 117–126.

Johnson, R. L., & Morgan, G. B. (2016). *Survey scales: A guide to development, analysis, and reporting* (Annotated ed.). The Guilford Press.

Joyce, C. R. B., Zutshi, D. W., Hrubes, V. F., & Mason, R. M. (1975). Comparison of fixed interval and visual analogue scale for rating pain. *European Journal of Clinical Pharmacology, 8*(6), 415–420.

Kaplan, S., Luchman, J. N., & Mock, L. (2013). General and specific question sequence effects in satisfaction surveys: Integrating directional and correlational effects. *Journal of Happiness Studies, 14*(5), 1443–1458.

Kieruj, N. D., & Moors, G. (2013). Response style behavior: Question format dependent or personal style? *Quality & Quantity, 47*, 193–211.

Kortum, P., Acemyan, C. Z., & Oswald, F. L. (2021). Is it time to go positive? Assessing the positively worded System Usability Scale (SUS). *Human Factors, 63*(6), 987–998.

Kosara, R. (2010, April 22). *Chart junk considered useful after all.* Eagereyes. https://eagereyes.org/criticism/chart-junk-considered-useful-after-all

Kostoulas, A. (2013, February 13). *On Likert scales, ordinal data and mean values.* Applied Linguistics & Language Teacher Education. https://achilleaskostoulas.com/2013/02/13/on-likert-scales-ordinal-data-and-mean-values/

Kouzes, J. M., & Posner, B. Z. (2003). *The Leadership Practices Inventory (LPI)* (3rd ed.). Pfeiffer.

Kraljic, T., & Brennan, S. E. (2004). Prosodic disambiguation of syntactic structure: For the speaker or for the addressee? *Cognitive Psychology, 50*, 194–231.

Krosnick, J. A., & Presser, S. (2010). Question and questionnaire design. In P. V. Marsden & J. D. Wright (Eds.), *Handbook of survey research* (2nd ed.) (pp. 263–314). Emerald Group Publishing.

Krosnick, J. A., & Berent, M. K. (1993). Comparisons of party identification and policy preferences: The impact of survey question format. *American Journal of Political Science, 37*(3), 941–964.

Krosnick, J. A., & Fabrigar, L. R. (1997). Designing rating scales for effective measurement in surveys. In L. Lyberg, P. Biemer, M. Collins, E. De Leeuw, C. Dippo, N. Schwarz, & D. Trewin (Eds.), *Survey measurement and process quality* (pp. 141–164). John Wiley.

Kühne, S., & Kroh, M. (2016). *Using personalized feedback to increase data quality and respondents' motivation in web surveys?* SOEP.

Kurbat, M. A., Shevell, S. K., & Rips, L. J. (1998). A year's memories: The calendar effect in autobiographical recall. *Memory & Cognition, 26,* 532–552.

Larroy C. (2002). Comparing visual-analog and numeric scales for assessing menstrual pain. *Behavioral Medicine, 27*(4), 179–181.

Lau, A., & Kennedy, C. (2019, May 9). *When online survey respondents only 'select some that apply'.* Pew Research. https://www.pewresearch.org/methods/2019/05/09/when-online-survey-respondents-only-select-some-that-apply/

Lau, M. Y-K. (2007). *Extreme response style: An empirical investigation of the effects of scale response format and fatigue* (Publication No. 3299156) [Doctoral dissertation, University of Notre Dame]. ProQuest Dissertations Publishing.

Laurent, A. (1972) Effects of question length on reporting behavior in the survey interview. *Journal of the American Statistical Association, 67*(338), 298–305.

Leading questions: Definitions, types, and examples. (n.d.). Formplus. Retrieved May 22, 2023, from https://www.formpl.us/blog/leading-question

Lee, J. Y., Stone, E. A., Wakabayashi, H., & Tochihara, Y. (2009). Issues in combining the categorical and visual analog scale for the assessment of perceived thermal sensation: Methodological and conceptual considerations. *Applied Ergonomics, 41*(2), 282–290.

Lehmann, D. R., & Hulbert, J. (1972). Are three-point scales always good enough? *Journal of Marketing Research, 9*(4), 444–446.

Lenzner, T., Kaczmirek, L., Lenzner, A. (2010). Cognitive burden of survey questions and response times: A psycholinguistic experiment. *Applied Cognitive Psychology, 24*(7), 1003–1020.

Lewis, J. R. (1993). Multipoint scales: Mean and median differences and observed significance levels. *International Journal Human-Computer Interaction, 5*(4), 383–392.

Lewis, J. R. (1995). IBM computer usability satisfaction questionnaires: Psychometric evaluation and instructions for use. *International Journal of Human-Computer Interaction, 7*(1), 57–78.

Lewis, J. R. (2006). Effectiveness of various automated readability measures for the competitive evaluation of user documentation. In *Proceedings of HFES 50th Annual Meeting* (pp. 624–628). Human Factors and Ergonomics Society.

Lewis, J. R. (2018a). Comparison of item formats: Agreement vs. item-specific endpoints. *Journal of Usability Studies, 14*(1), 48–60.

Lewis, J. R. (2018b). The System Usability Scale: Past, present, and future. *International Journal of Human-Computer Interaction, 34*(7), 577–590.

Lewis, J. R. (2019a). Comparison of four TAM item formats: Effect of response option labels and order. *Journal of Usability Studies, 14*(4), 224–236.

Lewis, J. R. (2019b). Measuring perceived usability: SUS, UMUX, and CSUQ ratings for four everyday products. *International Journal of Human-Computer Interaction, 35*(15), 1404–1419.

Lewis, J. R. (2019c). *Using the PSSUQ and CSUQ in user experience research and practice.* MeasuringU Press.

Lewis, J. R. (2021). Measuring user experience with 3, 5, 7, or 11 points: Does it matter? *Human Factors, 63*(6), 999–1011.

Lewis, J. R., & Alfonso, P. (1989). Developing the IBM Personal System/2 mouse: An industrial design/human factors collaboration. In *Proceedings of INTERFACE 89* (pp. 263–267). Institute of Electrical and Electronics Engineers.

Lewis, J. R., & Erdinç, O. (2017). User experience rating scales with 7, 11, or 101 points: Does it matter? *Journal of Usability Studies, 12*(2), 73–91.

Lewis, J. R., Henry, S. C., & Mack, R. L. (1990). Integrated office software benchmarks: A case study. In *Proceedings of INTERACT '90* (pp. 27–31). IFIP.

Lewis, J. R., & Sauro, J. (2009). The factor structure of the System Usability Scale. In M. Kurosu (Ed.), *Human centered design* (pp. 94–103). Springer-Verlag.

Lewis, J. R., & Sauro, J. (2016). *Excel & R companion to the 2nd edition of Quantifying the User Experience.* MeasuringU Press.

Lewis, J. R., & Sauro, J. (2017). Revisiting the factor structure of the System Usability Scale. *Journal of Usability Studies, 12*(4), 183–192.

Lewis, J. R., & Sauro, J. (2020, January 29). *Three branches of standardized UX measurement.* MeasuringU. https://measuringu.com/three-branches-ux/

Lewis, J. R., & Sauro, J. (2020, July 8). *Converting rating scales to 0–100 points.* MeasuringU. https://measuringu.com/converting-scales-to-100-points/

Lewis, J. R., & Sauro, J. (2020, July 15). *Are sliders better than numbered scales?* MeasuringU. https://measuringu.com/numbers-versus-sliders/

Lewis, J. R., & Sauro, J. (2020, July 22). *Are star ratings better than numbered scales?* MeasuringU. https://measuringu.com/numbers-versus-stars/

Lewis, J. R., & Sauro, J. (2020, August 19). *The evolution of the Mean Opinion Scale: From MOS-R to MOS-X2.* MeasuringU. https://measuringu.com/evolution-of-mos-part2/

Lewis, J. R., & Sauro, J. (2020, September 9). *Are face emoji ratings better than numbered scales?* MeasuringU. https://measuringu.com/numbers-versus-face-emojis/

Lewis, J. R., & Sauro, J. (2020, September 16). *Should you use negative numbers in rating scales?* MeasuringU. https://measuringu.com/standard-versus-neg2pos-numeric-scales/

Lewis, J. R., & Sauro, J. (2020, December 15). *From functionality to features: Making the UMUX-Lite even simpler.* https://measuringu.com/simpler-umux-lite/

Lewis, J. R., & Sauro, J. (2021a). Comparison of select-all-that-apply items with yes/no forced choice items. *Journal of Usability Studies, 17*(1), 21–30.

Lewis, J. R., & Sauro, J. (2021b). Usability and user experience: Design and evaluation. In G. Salvendy and W. Karowski (Eds.), *Handbook of human factors and ergonomics* (pp. 972–1015). John Wiley.

Lewis, J. R., & Sauro, J. (2021, June 15). *From statistical to practical significance.* MeasuringU. https://measuringu.com/from-statistical-to-practical-significance/

Lewis, J. R., & Sauro, J. (2021, August 17). *How to statistically analyze Net Promoter Scores.* MeasuringU. https://measuringu.com/statistical-analysis-nps/

Lewis, J. R., & Sauro, J. (2021, September 15). *Measuring UX: From the UMUX-Lite to the UX-Lite.* MeasuringU. https://measuringu.com/from-umux-lite-to-ux-lite/

Lewis, J. R., & Sauro, J. (2021, September 28). *For statistical significance, must* p *be < .05?* MeasuringU. https://measuringu.com/setting-alpha/

Lewis, J. R., & Sauro, J. (2021, October 12). *Evolution of the UX-Lite.* MeasuringU. https://measuringu.com/evolution-of-the-ux-lite/

Lewis, J. R., & Sauro, J. (2021, November 9). *Horizontal versus vertical rating scales.* MeasuringU. https://measuringu.com/horizontal-vs-vertical-rating-scales/

Lewis, J. R., & Sauro, J. (2021, November 30). *Sliders versus five-point numeric scales on desktop and mobile devices.* MeasuringU. https://measuringu.com/uxlite-numeric-slider-desktop-mobile/

Lewis, J. R., & Sauro, J. (2021, December 14). *Sliders versus eleven-point numeric scales on desktop and mobile devices.* MeasuringU. https://measuringu.com/ltr-numeric-slider-desktop-mobile/

Lewis, J. R., & Sauro, J. (2022, March 1). *Sample sizes for comparing SUS to a benchmark.* MeasuringU. https://measuringu.com/sample-sizes-for-SUS-benchmark-tests/

Lewis, J. R., & Sauro, J. (2022, March 15). *What is the Product-Market Fit (PMF) item?* MeasuringU. https://measuringu.com/product-market-fit-item/

Lewis, J. R., & Sauro, J. (2022, April 19). *Difficult–easy or easy–difficult: Does it matter?* MeasuringU. https://measuringu.com/reversing-seq-endpoints-means/

Lewis, J. R., & Sauro, J. (2022, May 17). *Difficult–easy or easy–difficult: Does it affect response distributions?* MeasuringU. https://measuringu.com/reversing-seq-endpoints-response-distributions/

Lewis, J. R., & Sauro, J. (2022, August 16). *Does changing the number of response options affect rating behavior?* MeasuringU. https://measuringu.com/changing-the-number-of-response-options/

Lewis, J. R., & Sauro, J. (2023, August 8). *Does removing the neutral response option affect rating behavior?* MeasuringU. https://measuringu.com/removing-the-neutral-response-option/

Lewis, J. R., & Sauro, J. (2023, October 24). *Sample sizes for comparing dependent proportions.* MeasuringU. https://measuringu.com/sample-sizes-for-the-mcnemar-test/

Lewis, J. R., Sauro, J., & Schiavone, W. (2023, September 12, 2023). *Are 3D graphs always worse than 2D graphs?* MeasuringU. https://measuringu.com/is-3d-worse-than-2d/

Lewis, J. R., Utesch, B. S., & Maher, D. E. (2013). UMUX-LITE—When there's no time for the SUS. In *Proceedings of CHI 2013* (pp. 2099–2102). Paris, France: Association for Computing Machinery.

Lewis, J. R., Utesch, B. S., & Maher, D. E. (2015). Measuring perceived usability: The SUS, UMUX-LITE, and AltUsability. *International Journal of Human-Computer Interaction, 31*(8), 496–505.

Likert, R. (1932). A technique for the measurement of attitudes. *Archives of Psychology*, *22*(140), 5-55.

The Literary Digest. (2023, April 17). In *Wikipedia*. https://en.wikipedia.org/wiki/The_Literary_Digest

Liu, M., & Cernat, A. (2016). Item-by-item versus matrix questions: A web survey experiment. *Social Science Computer Review*, *36*(6), 690–706.

Loftus, E. F. (2005). Planting misinformation in the human mind: A 30-year investigation of the malleability of memory. *Learning & Memory*, *12*(4), 361–366.

Loftus, E. F., & Fathi, D. C. (1985). Retrieving multiple autobiographical memories. *Social Cognition*, *3*(3), 280–295.

Loftus, E. F., & Marburger, W. (1983). Since the eruption of Mt. St. Helens, has anyone beaten you up? Improving the accuracy of retrospective reports with landmark events. *Memory & Cognition*, *11*(2), 114–120.

Loftus, E. F., Miller, D. G., Burns, H. J. (1978). Semantic integration of verbal information into a visual memory. *Journal of Experimental Psychology: Human Learning and Memory*. *4*(1), 19–31.

Loken, B., Pirie, P., Virnig, K., Hinkle, R. L., & Salmon, C. T. (1987). The use of 0–10 scales in telephone surveys. *Journal of the Market Research Society*, *29*, 353–362.

Lord, F. M. (1953). On the statistical treatment of football numbers. *American Psychologist*, *8*(12), 750–751.

Lozano, L. M., García-Cueto, E., & Muñiz, J. (2008). Effect of the number of response categories on the reliability and validity of rating scales. *Methodology*, *4*(2), 73–79.

Luna, K. (Host). (2019, October). How memory can be manipulated, with Elizabeth Loftus, PhD. (Number 91) [Audio podcast episode]. In *Speaking of psychology*. American Psychological Association. https://www.apa.org/news/podcasts/speaking-of-psychology/memory-manipulated

Madden, J. M., & Bourdon, R. D. (1964). Effects of variations in rating scale format on judgment. *Journal of Applied Psychology*, *48*(3), 147–151.

Mathews, C. O. (1929). The effect of the order of printed response words on an interest questionnaire. *Journal of Educational Psychology*, *20*(2), 128–134.

Mathiowetz, N. A., & Duncan, G. (1988). Out of work, out of mind: Response errors in retrospective report of unemployment. *Journal of Business and Economic Statistics*, *6*(2), 221–229.

Mavletova, A., Couper, M. P., & Lebedev, D. (2018). Grid and item-by-item formats in PC and mobile web surveys. *Social Science Computer Review*, *36*(6), 647–668.

Mcleod, S. (2023, June 15). *Theories of forgetting in psychology*. SimplyPsychology. https://www.simplypsychology.org/forgetting.html

Means, B., Swan, G. E., Jobe, J. B., Esposito, J. L. (1994). The effects of estimation strategies on the accuracy of respondents' reports of cigarette smoking. In N. Schwarz & S. Sudman (Eds.), *Autobiographical memory and the validity of retrospective reports* (pp. 107–119). Springer.

Medallia. (n.d.). Likert scales vs. slider scales in commercial market research. CheckMarket. https://www.checkmarket.com/blog/likert-scales-slider-scales/

Menold, N., & Bogner, K. (2016). Design of ratings scales in questionnaires. *GESIS Survey Guidelines*, Mannheim, Germany: GESIS — Leibniz Institute for the Social Sciences. https://doi.org/10.15465/gesis-sg_en_015

Mercer, A., Caporaso, A., Cantor, D., & Townsend, R. (2015). How much gets you how much? Monetary incentives and response rates in household surveys. *Public Opinion Quarterly, 79*(1), 105–129.

Miller, G. A. (1956). The magical number seven, plus or minus two: Some limits on our capacity for processing information. *The Psychological Review, 63*(2), 81–97.

Mockovak, W. (2018). *Horizontal vs. vertical scales vs. use of a grid in online data collection: Which is better?* U.S. Bureau of Labor Statistics.

Moors, G., Kieruj, N. D., & Vermunt, J. K. (2014). The effect of labeling and numbering of response scales on the likelihood of response bias. *Sociological Methodology, 44*(1), 369–399.

Morrison, D. G. (1972). Regressions with discrete dependent variables: The effect on R^2. *Journal of Marketing Research, 9*(3), 338–340.

National Center for Education Statistics. (1988). *National Education Longitudinal Study of 1988.* U.S. Department of Education.

Neter J., & Waksberg, J. (1964). A study of response errors in expenditures data from household interviews. *Journal of the American Statistical Association, 59*(305), 18–55.

Nicolaas, G., Campanelli, P., Hope, S., Jäckle, A., & Lynn, P. (2015). Revisiting "yes/no" versus "check all that apply": Results from a mixed modes experiment. *Survey Research Methods, 9*(3), 189–204.

Nielsen, J. (2020, November 15). *10 usability heuristics for user interface design.* Nielsen Norman Group, https://www.nngroup.com/articles/ten-usability-heuristics/

Niikura, R. (1999). Assertiveness among Japanese, Malaysian, Filipino, and U.S. white-collar workers. *Journal of Social Psychology, 139*(6), 690–699.

Nunnally, J. C. (1978). *Psychometric theory* (2nd ed.) McGraw Hill.

Overjustification effect. (2023, May 1). In *Wikipedia.* https://en.wikipedia.org/wiki/Overjustification_effect

Paap, K. R., & Roske-Hofstrand, R. J. (1986). The optimal number of menu options per panel. *Human Factors, 28*(4), 377–385.

Parente, M. E., Manzoni, A. V., & Ares, G. (2011). External preference mapping of commercial antiaging creams based on consumers' response to a check-all-that-apply question. *Journal of Sensory Studies, 26*(2), 158–166.

Payne, S. L. B. (1951/2016). *The art of asking questions: Studies in public opinion, 3* (Princeton Legacy Library, 451). Princeton University Press.

Pearson, R. W., Ross, M., & Dawes, R. M. (1992). Personal recall and the limits of retrospective questions in surveys. In J. M. Tanur (Ed.), *Questions about questions: Inquiries into the cognitive bases of surveys* (pp. 65–94). Russell Sage Foundation.

Pedersen, M. J., & Nielsen, C. V. (2016). Improving survey response rates in online panels: Effects of low-cost incentives and cost-free text appeal interventions. *Social Science Computer Review, 34*(2), 229–243.

Peterson, R. A. (2000). *Constructing effective questionnaires.* Sage Publications.

Pew Research Center. (2019, January 18). *Views of nation's economy, personal finances, job availability.* https://www.pewresearch.org/politics/2019/01/18/2-views-of-nations-economy-personal-finances-job-availability/

Porter, J. (2003, April 16). *Testing the three-click rule.* UIE. https://articles.uie.com/three_click_rule/

Presser, S., & Schuman, H. (1980). The measurement of a middle position in attitude surveys. *Public Opinion Quarterly, 44*(1), 70–85.

Preston, C. C., & Colman, A. M. (2000). Optimal number of response categories in rating scales: Reliability, validity, discriminating power, and respondent preferences. *Acta Psychologica, 104*(1), 1–15.

Ramshaw, A. (n.d.). *Net Promoter Score benchmarks: Don't waste your time on external data.* Genroe. https://www.genroe.com/blog/dont-waste-your-time-on-external-net-promoter-benchmarks/8217

Rasinski, K. A., Mingay, D., & Bradburn, N. M. (1994). Do respondents really "mark all that apply" on self-administered questions? *Public Opinion Quarterly, 58*(3), 400–408.

Rausch, M., & Zehetleitner, M., (2014). Comparison between a visual analogue scale and a four point scale as measures of conscious experience of motion. *Consciousness and Cognition, 28*, 126–140.

Rayner, K., & Raney, G. (1996). Eye movement control in visual search: Effects of word frequency. *Psychonomic Bulletin & Review, 3*(2), 245–248.

Raz, G. (Host). (2017, October 13). *Elizabeth Loftus: How can our memories be manipulated?* [Radio broadcast transcript]. NPR. https://www.npr.org/transcripts/557424726

Recommender system. (2022, December 23). In *Wikipedia.* https://en.wikipedia.org/wiki/Recommender_system

Reichheld, F. F. (2003). The one number you need to grow. *Harvard Business Review, 81*, 46–54.

Reips, U. (2000). Context effects in web-surveys. In B. Batnic, U. Reips, & M. Bosnjak (Eds.), *Online social sciences* (pp. 95–104). Hogrefe & Huber.

Reliability of memory. (n.d.) IB Psych Matters. https://ibpsychmatters.com/reliability-of-memory

Roberts, P.-J., Roberts, C., Sibbald, B., & Torgerson, D. J. (2000). The effect of a direct payment or a lottery on questionnaire response rates: A randomised controlled trial. *Journal of Epidemiology & Community Health, 54*, 71–72.

Robinson, S. B., & Leonard, K. F. (2018). *Designing quality survey questions.* Sage Publications.

Saris, W., & Gallhofer, I. N. (2004). Operationalization of social science concepts by intuition. *Quality and Quantity, 38*(3), 235–258.

Saris, W., & Gallhofer, I. N. (2007a). *Design, Evaluation, and Analysis of Questionnaires for Survey Research.* John Wiley.

Saris, W., & Gallhofer, I. N. (2007b). Estimation of the effects of measurement characteristics on the quality of survey questions. *Survey Research Methods, 1*(1), 29–43.

Sauro, J. (2010, September 14). *Survey respondents prefer the left side of a rating scale.* MeasuringU. https://measuringu.com/left-side-bias/

Sauro, J. (2010, September 21). *That's the worst website ever! Effects of extreme survey items.* MeasuringU. https://measuringu.com/extreme-items/

Sauro, J. (2011). *A practical guide to the System Usability Scale: Background, benchmarks & best practices.* MeasuringU Press.

Sauro, J. (2011, February 3). *Measuring usability with the System Usability Scale (SUS).* MeasuringU. https://measuringu.com/sus/

Sauro, J. (2012, October 30). *10 things to know about the Single Ease Question (SEQ).* MeasuringU. https://measuringu.com/seq10/

Sauro, J. (2012, December 18). *10 tips for your next survey.* MeasuringU. https://measuringu.com/survey-tips/

Sauro, J. (2013, September 10). *How to conduct a top task analysis.* MeasuringU. https://measuringu.com/top-tasks/

Sauro, J. (2014, February 11). *10 ways to get a horrible survey response rate.* MeasuringU. https://measuringu.com/horrible-responserate/

Sauro, J. (2015). SUPR-Q: A comprehensive measure of the quality of the website user experience. *Journal of Usability Studies, 10*(2), 68–86.

Sauro, J. (2015, March 17). *How hard are your surveys to take?* MeasuringU. https://measuringu.com/hard-surveys/

Sauro, J. (2015, June 30). *How to statistically test preference data.* MeasuringU. https://measuringu.com/preference-data/

Sauro, J. (2016, June 21). *Essential Excel skills for researchers: Part 1.* MeasuringU. https://measuringu.com/excel-1/

Sauro, J. (2016, June 28). *Essential Excel skills for researchers: Part 2.* MeasuringU. https://measuringu.com/excel-2/

Sauro, J. (2016, August 30). *Can you change a standardized questionnaire?* MeasuringU. https://measuringu.com/change-standardized/

Sauro, J. (2016, December 6). *6 ways to visualize statistical significance.* MeasuringU. https://measuringu.com/visualize-significance/

Sauro, J. (2017, January 17). *How accurate are estimates from online panels?* MeasuringU. https://measuringu.com/online-panels/

Sauro, J. (2017, February 1). *How accurate are UX metrics from online panels?* MeasuringU. https://measuringu.com/ux-panel-metrics/

Sauro, J. (2017, February 8). *10 best practices for graphing & displaying data*. MeasuringU. https://measuringu.com/graphing-displaying-data/

Sauro, J. (2017, March 22). *8 things to consider when using online panels*. MeasuringU. https://measuringu.com/panel-research/

Sauro, J. (2017, August 16). *How to code & analyze verbatim comments*. MeasuringU. https://measuringu.com/code-verbatim/

Sauro, J. (2017, October 11). *Measuring usability: From the SUS to the UMUX-Lite*. MeasuringU. https://measuringu.com/umux-lite/

Sauro, J. (2017, November 29). *Changing the Net Promoter Scale: How much does it matter?* MeasuringU. https://measuringu.com/nps-scale-change/

Sauro, J. (2018). *Benchmarking the user experience*. MeasuringU Press.

Sauro, J. (2018, May 2). *Are top box scores a better predictor of behavior?* MeasuringU. https://measuringu.com/top-box-behavior/

Sauro, J. (2018, June 13). *10 things to know about the SUPR-Q*. MeasuringU. https://measuringu.com/10-things-suprq/

Sauro, J. (2018, July 25). *The user experience of health insurance websites*. MeasuringU. https://measuringu.com/ux-health-insurance/

Sauro, J. (2018, November 28). *Do detractors really say bad things about a company?* MeasuringU. https://measuringu.com/detractors/

Sauro, J. (2019, January 9). *Does changing the order of the NPS item affect results?* MeasuringU. https://measuringu.com/nps-order/

Sauro, J. (2019, March 6). *Effects of labeling the neutral response in the NPS*. MeasuringU. https://measuringu.com/labeling-nps-effects/

Sauro, J. (2019, March 20). *Do survey grids affect responses?* MeasuringU. https://measuringu.com/grids-responses/

Sauro, J. (2019, April 24). *How accurate is self-reported purchase data?* MeasuringU. https://measuringu.com/self-reported-purchase/

Sauro, J. (2019, May 29). *Do promoters actually recommend more? A longitudinal analysis*. MeasuringU. https://measuringu.com/promoters-recommend/

Sauro, J. (2019, June 12). *Do attitudes predict behavior?* MeasuringU. https://measuringu.com/attitudes-behavior/

Sauro, J. (2019, April 24). *How accurate is self-reported purchase data?* MeasuringU. https://measuringu.com/self-reported-purchase/

Sauro, J. (2019, August 14). *Is a three-point scale good enough?* MeasuringU. https://measuringu.com/three-points/

Sauro, J. (2019, August 21). *Can you use a 3-point instead of an 11-point scale for the NPS?* MeasuringU. https://measuringu.com/3-point-nps/

Sauro, J. (2019, September 25). *10 things to know about the Microsoft NSAT score*. MeasuringU. https://measuringu.com/microsoft-nsat/

Sauro, J. (2019, October 23). *Does coloring response categories affect responses?* MeasuringU. https://measuringu.com/coloring-responses/

Sauro, J. (2019, November 6). *10 things to know about the Customer Effort Score.* MeasuringU. https://measuringu.com/customer-effort-score/

Sauro, J. (2019, November 13). *Will you recommend or would you recommend?* MeasuringU. https://measuringu.com/will-would/

Sauro, J. (2019, November 20). *How do you measure delight?* MeasuringU. https://measuringu.com/measure-delight/

Sauro, J. (2019, December 11). *Very vs. extremely satisfied.* MeasuringU. https://measuringu.com/very-vs-extremely/

Sauro, J. (2020, February 5). *Cultural effects on rating scales.* MeasuringU. https://measuringu.com/scales-cultural-effects/

Sauro, J., & Dumas, J. S. (2009). Comparison of three one-question, post-task usability questionnaires. In *Proceedings of the Conference in Human Factors in Computing Systems* (pp. 1599–1608). Association for Computing Machinery.

Sauro, J., & Lewis, J. R. (2005). Estimating completion rates from small samples using binomial confidence intervals: Comparisons and recommendations. In *Proceedings of Human Factors and Ergonomics Society Annual Meeting* (pp. 2100–2104). HFES.

Sauro, J., & Lewis, J. R. (2009). Correlations among prototypical usability metrics: Evidence for the construct of usability. In *Proceedings of the Conference in Human Factors in Computing Systems* (pp. 1609–1618). Association for Computing Machinery.

Sauro, J., & Lewis, J. R. (2011). When designing usability questionnaires, does it hurt to be positive? In *Proceedings of the Conference in Human Factors in Computing Systems* (pp. 2215–2223). Association for Computing Machinery.

Sauro, J., & Lewis, J. R. (2016). *Quantifying the user experience: Practical statistics for user research* (2nd ed.). Morgan Kaufmann.

Sauro, J., & Lewis, J. R. (2020, January 8). *Should all scale points be labeled?* MeasuringU. https://measuringu.com/scale-points-labeled/

Sauro, J., & Lewis, J. R. (2020, January 22). *Comparing fully vs. partially labeled five- and seven-point scales.* MeasuringU. https://measuringu.com/labeling-scales/

Sauro, J., & Lewis, J. R. (2020, April 22). *Are cumulative graphs misunderstood?* MeasuringU. https://measuringu.com/cumulative-graphs/

Sauro, J., & Lewis, J. R. (2020, June 24). *Sample size recommendations for benchmark studies.* MeasuringU. https://measuringu.com/sample-size-recommendations/

Sauro, J., & Lewis, J. R. (2020, November 10). *Are sliders more sensitive than numeric rating scales?* MeasuringU. https://measuringu.com/are-sliders-more-sensitive/

Sauro, J. & Lewis, J. R. (2020, December 1). *From soared to plummeted: Can we quantify change verbs?* MeasuringU. https://measuringu.com/change-verbs/

Sauro, J., & Lewis, J. R. (2021, January 12). *Five reasons to use open-ended questions.* MeasuringU. https://measuringu.com/open-ended-reasons/

Sauro, J., & Lewis, J. R. (2021, October 5). *Do people use all available response options?* MeasuringU. https://measuringu.com/do-people-use-all-response-options/

Sauro, J., & Lewis, J. R. (2022, June 7). *Should you use nonparametric methods to analyze UX data?* MeasuringU. https://measuringu.com/should-you-use-nonparametric/

Sauro, J., & Lewis, J. R. (2022, September 13). *Evaluation of three SEQ variants.* MeasuringU. https://measuringu.com/evaluation-of-three-seq-variants/

Sauro, J., & Lewis, J. R. (2022, September 20). *Business software UX and NPS benchmarks.* MeasuringU. https://measuringu.com/business-software-ux2022/

Sauro, J., & Lewis, J. R. (2022, November 1). *Consumer software UX and NPS benchmarks.* MeasuringU. https://measuringu.com/consumer-software-ux2022/

Sauro, J., & Lewis, J. R. (2023, January 3). *How to use the finite population correction.* MeasuringU. https://measuringu.com/finite-population-correction/

Sauro, J., & Lewis, J. R. (2023, January 31). *How variable are UX rating scales? Data from 100,000 responses.* MeasuringU. https://measuringu.com/how-variable-are-ux-rating-scales-data-from-100000-responses/

Sauro, J., & Lewis, J. R. (2023, March 14). *The variability and reliability of standardized UX scales.* MeasuringU. https://measuringu.com/reliability-and-variability-of-standardized-ux-scales/

Sauro, J., & Lewis, J. R. (2023, April 25). *How to estimate the standard deviation for rating scales.* MeasuringU. https://measuringu.com/rating-scale-standard-deviations/

Sauro, J., & Lewis, J. R. (2023, December 19). *Comparison of standard SEQ and click SMEQ sensitivity.* MeasuringU. https://measuringu.com/standard-seq-and-click-smeq-sensitivity/

Sauro, J., Lewis, J. R., & Atkins, D. (2023, December 12). *An experiment comparing 2D and 3D bar graphs* MeasuringU. https://measuringu.com/are-3d-bar-graphs-worse-than-2d/

Sauro, J., Lewis, J. R., & Metzler, G. (2022, July 26). *UX and NPS benchmarks of airline websites.* MeasuringU. https://measuringu.com/airlines-benchmark-2022/

Sauro, J., Lewis, J. R., & Short, E. (2022, May 31). *User experience salaries & calculator.* MeasuringU. https://measuringu.com/salary-survey2022/

Sauro, J., Lewis, J. R., & Short, E. (2022, July 12). *The methods UX professionals use.* MeasuringU. https://measuringu.com/ux-methods-2022/

Sauro, J., Lewis, J. R., Yazvec, M., & Nawalaniec, N. (2022, October 17). *UX and NPS benchmarks of ticketing websites.* MeasuringU. https://measuringu.com/ticketing-benchmark-2022/

Sauro, J., Metzler, G., & Lewis, J. R. (2022, August 30). *UX and NPS benchmarks of travel aggregator websites.* MeasuringU. https://measuringu.com/travel-benchmark-2022/

Sauro, J., & Zarolia, P. (2017). SUPR-Qm: A questionnaire to measure the mobile app user experience. *Journal of Usability Studies, 13*(1), 17–37.

Schaeffer, N. C., & Dykema, J. (2011). Questions for surveys: Current trends and future directions. *Public Opinion Quarterly, 75*(5), 909–961.

Schneider, D., Berent, M., Thomas, R., & Krosnick, J. (2008, June). *Measuring customer satisfaction and loyalty: Improving the 'Net-Promoter' score.* [Presentation] Annual Meeting of the American Association for Public Opinion Research. https://www.van-haaften.nl/images/documents/pdf/measuring%20customer%20satisfaction%20and%20loyalty.pdf

Schwarz, N., Knäuper, B., Hippler, H.-J., Noelle-Neumann, E., & Clark, L. (1991). Rating scales: Numeric values may change the meaning of scale labels. *Public Opinion Quarterly, 55*(4), 570–582.

Schuman, H. W., & Presser, S. (1996). *Questions & answers in attitude surveys: Experiments on question form, wording, and context.* Sage Publications.

Shannon, C. E., & Weaver, W. (1949). *The mathematical theory of communication.* University of Illinois Press.

Singer, E. (2017). The use and effects of incentives in surveys. In D. L. Vanette & J. A. Krosnick (Eds.), *The Palgrave handbook of survey research* (pp. 63–70). Palgrave Macmillan.

Singer, E., & Ye, C. (2013). The use and effects of incentives in surveys. *The Annals of the American Academy of Political and Social Science, 645*(1), 112–141.

Smyth, J. D., Christian, L. M., & Dillman, D. A. (2008). Does "Yes or No" on the telephone mean the same as "Check-All-That-Apply" on the web? *Public Opinion Quarterly, 72*(1), 103–113.

Smyth, J. D., Dillman, D. A., Christian, L. M., & Stern, M. J. (2006). Comparing check-all and forced-choice question formats in web surveys. *Public Opinion Quarterly, 70*(1), 66–77.

Stark, T. H., Silber, H., Krosnick, J. A., Blom, A. G., Aoyagi, M., Belchior, A., Bosnjak, M., Clement, S. L., John, M., Jónsdóttir, G. A., Lawson, K., Lynn, P., Martinsson, J., Shamshiri-Petersen, D., Tvinnereim, E., & Yu, R. (2020). Generalization of classic question order effects across cultures. *Sociological Methods & Research, 49*(3), 567–602.

Stefkovics, Á., & Kmetty, Z. (2022). A comparison of question order effects on item-by-item and grid formats: Visual layout matters. *Measurement Instruments for the Social Sciences, 4*, 8.

Stern, M. J., Dillman, D. A., & Smyth, J. D. (2007). Visual design, order effects, and respondent characteristics in a self-administered survey. *Survey Research Methods, 1*(3), 121–138.

Stoll, J. (2023, March 20). *Number of pay TV households in the United States from 2013 to 2027.* Statista. https://www.statista.com/statistics/251268/number-of-pay-tv-households-in-the-us/

Strunk, W, Jr., & White, E. B. (1959). *The elements of style.* Macmillan.

Sudman, S., & Bradburn, N. M. (1982). *Asking questions: A practical guide to questionnaire design.* Jossey-Bass.

SUPR-Q full license. (n.d.) MeasuringU. https://measuringu.com/product/suprq/

Thau, M., Mikkelsen, M. F., Hjortskov, M., Pedersen, M. J. (2021). Question order bias revisited: A split-ballot experiment on satisfaction with public services among experienced and professional users. *Public Administration, 99*(1), 189–204.

Thompson, C. P., Skowronski, J. J., Larsen, S. F., & Betz, A. (1996). *Autobiographical memory: Remembering what and remembering when.* Lawrence Erlbaum Associates, Inc.

Thorndike, F. P., Carlbring, P., Smyth, F. L. Magee, J. C., Gonder-Frederick, L., Ost, L.-G., & Ritterband, L. M. (2009). Web-based measurement: Effect of completing single or multiple items per webpage. *Computers in Human Behavior, 25*(2), 393–401.

Thurstone, L. L. (1928). Attitudes can be measured. *American Journal of Sociology, 33*, 529–554.

Toepoel, V., Das, M., & Van Soest, A. (2009). Design of web questionnaires: The effects of the number of items per screen. *Field Methods, 21*(2), 200–213.

Toepoel, V., & Funke, F. (2018). Sliders, visual analogue scales, or buttons: Influence of formats and scales in mobile and desktop surveys. *Mathematical Population Studies, 25*(2), 112–122.

Tourangeau, R., Couper, M. P., & Conrad, F. (2004). Spacing, position, and order: Interpretive heuristics for visual features of survey questions. *Public Opinion Quarterly, 68*(3), 368–393.

Tourangeau, R., Couper, M. P., & Conrad, F. (2009). Color labels, and interpretive heuristics for response scales. *Public Opinion Quarterly, 71*(1), 91–112.

Tourangeau, R., & Rasinski, K. A. (1988). Cognitive processes underlying context effects in attitude measurement. *Psychological Bulletin, 103*(3), 299–314.

Tourangeau, R., Rips, L. J. & Rasinski, K. (2000). *The psychology of survey response.* Cambridge University Press.

Tufte, E. (2001). *The visual display of quantitative information* (2nd ed.). Graphics Press.

UX-Lite calculator package. (n.d.) MeasuringU. https://measuringu.com/product/ux-lite-calc/

van Beuningen, J., van der Houwen, K., & Moonen, L. (2014). *Measuring well-being: An analysis of different response scales.* Statistics Netherlands.

Van de Walle, S., & Van Ryzin, G. (2011). The order of questions in a survey on citizen satisfaction with public services: Lessons from a split-ballot experiment. *Public Administration, 89*(4), 1436–1450.

van Herk, H., Poortinga, Y. H., & Verhallen, T. M. M. (2004). Response styles in rating scales: Evidence of method bias in data from six EU countries. *Journal of Cross-Cultural Psychology, 35*(3), 346–360.

van Laerhoven, H., van der Zaag-Loonen, H. J., & Derkx, B. (2004). A comparison of Likert scale and visual analogue scales as response options in children's questionnaires. *Acta Paediatrica, 93*(6), 830–835.

van Schaik, P., & Ling, J. (2007). Design parameters of rating scales for web sites. *ACM Transactions on Computer-Human Interaction, 14*(1), article 4.

Wallsten, T. S. Budescu, D. V., Zwick, R., & Kemp, S. M. (1993). Preferences and reasons for communicating probabilistic information in verbal or numerical terms. *Bulletin of the Psychonomic Society, 31*(2), 135–138.

Wedell, D. H., Parducci, A., & Lane, M. (1990). Reducing the dependence of clinical judgment on the immediate context: Effects of number of categories and type of anchors. *Journal of Personality and Social Psychology, 58*(2), 319–329.

Weijters, B., Cabooter, E., & Schillewaert, N. (2010). The effect of rating scale format on response styles: The number of response categories and response category labels. *International Journal of Research in Marketing, 27*(3), 236–247.

Weng, L.-J. (2004). Impact of the number of response categories and anchor labels on coefficient alpha and test-retest reliability. *Educational and Psychological Measurement, 64*(6), 956–972.

Weng, L.-J., & Cheng, C.-P. (2000). Effects of response order on Likert-type scales. *Educational and Psychological Measurement, 60*(6), 908–924.

Whitten, W. B., & Leonard, J. M. (1981). Directed search through autobiographical memory. *Memory & Cognition, 9*(6), 566–579.

Yan, T. (2005). *Gricean effects in self-administered surveys* (Publication No. 3201221) [Doctoral dissertation, University of Maryland]. ProQuest Dissertations Publishing.

Yang, Y., Harkness, J. A., Chin, T.-Y., & Villar, A. (2010). Response styles and culture. In J. A. Harkness, M. Braun, B. Edwards, T. P. Johnson, L. Lyberg, P. P. Mohler, B.-E. Pennell, & T. W. Smith (Eds.), *Survey methods in multinational, multiregional, and multicultural contexts* (pp. 203–223). John Wiley.

Yu, D., & Yang, Y. (2015). Measurement equivalence of a concise customer engagement metric across country, language, and customer types. *Public Opinion Quarterly, 79*(S1), 325–358.

Zacks, J., Levy, E., Tversky, B., & Schiano, D. J. (1998). Reading bar graphs: Effects of extraneous depth cues and graphical context. *Journal of Experimental Psychology: Applied, 4*(2), 119–138.

Zax, M., & Takahashi, S. (1967) Cultural influences on response style: Comparisons of Japanese and American college students. *Journal of Social Psychology, 71*(1), 3–10.

Zhang, C., Lonn, S., & Teasley, S. D. (2017). Understanding the impact of lottery incentives on web survey participation and response quality: A leverage-salience theory perspective. *Field Methods, 29*(1), 42–60.

Zijlstra, F. R. H & van Doorn, L. (1985). *The construction of a scale to measure subjective effort* [Technical Report]. Delft University of Technology.

INDEX

A

acronyms, 84, 88
active voice, 86-88
adjunct wh-questions, 72, 84, 88
advertising, 295, 299
agreement items, 109-110, 191-193, 202-203
all-positive item tone, 172
Analysis of Variance (ANOVA), 359-361, 365
assessing system usability, 9, 10
attitudes, 12, 27
attributes, 27, 38, 58, 63, 65, 66

B

bar graphs, 373, 375
behaviors, 59, 60, 63, 66, 70
benchmark, 12, 260, 272-278, 291, 338, 347-350, 355, 364, 377, 379, 385-395
    external benchmarks, 31, 43-46, 50, 144, 377, 379
between-subjects means, 279, 284, 292, 338, 340, 343
biases, 16-20, 25, 171, 173, 181, 183, 186, 189
    acquiescence bias, 19, 171-173, 181, 186, 191-193, 202
    left-side bias, 174-187, 189-190
    representative bias, 17, 20
    source bias, 17
    sponsorship bias, 18, 79
    tech literacy bias, 17
    top-first bias, 187-190

bipolar items, 111
bottom-box score, 326
branching, 293, 296, 298-299
bulk mail, 295, 299

C

categorical data, 55, 68, 101, 310, 312-316
categorical measurement, 101-104, 310-316
census, 3, 14-15
census-matching, 3, 45-46, 50
chart junk, 366-367, 378, 379
Check All that Apply (CATA), 211-217
cleaning data, 300-303
cluster analysis, 362
collapsing variables, 351, 352, 364
color scale, 231
commercial survey platforms, 293-294, 299
comparative analysis, 260, 272-291, 338-363
comparative questions, 108
Computer System Usability Questionnaire (CSUQ), 387-388
concepts, 26-27, 38, 64-65, 74, 79
confidence intervals, 261-270, 288, 291, 315-318, 336-337, 339-340, 381, 383
construct, 26-27, 64-66, 70
convenience sampling, 44, 46
coverage errors, 20-22, 25
cross-tabbing, 350-352, 364
cultural effects, 197-203, 219
Customer Effort Score (CES), 394-395

D

data collection, 296-299
decision tree, 98-99, 112
defining target participants, 26-28, 38
detractors, 120-122, 141-144, 165, 391-392
direct email, 32, 297
direct request, 55, 67, 70
disconfirmation item, 111-112
discovery, 55-56, 62, 68, 70, 99-100, 112-113, 334-335
domain experience, 27, 28, 38

E

eleven-point scale, 118-125, 133-137, 140-151, 163-169, 224-229, 265-266, 270-271, 277-278, 286-287, 329
embedded clauses, 72, 84-85, 88
emoji scale, 235-238, 256-258
endpoints, 75, 130-131, 152-163, 191-197
    agreement, 109-110, 112, 191-193, 202-203, 318-319
    extreme, 77-78, 80, 119, 130, 155, 171, 194-197
    item-specific, 191-193, 202
    labels, 127-131, 148, 152-168, 194-196
errors, 20-25
existing customers/prospects, 32

F

factor analysis, 361-362, 365
false inferences, 76, 80
faulty presuppositions, 73-74, 79
Finite Population Correction (FPC), 288-290, 292
five-point scale, 118, 127, 129, 132, 134-137, 147, 160-162, 222-223, 266, 270-271, 278, 287
forced-choice grid, 211-217
frequency distribution, 311-313, 325-329

G

gamify, 34, 39
grids, 204, 219, 226-228

H

horizontal rating scale, 187-189, 206, 222-228,

I

incentive, 34-40, 298
indirect request, 55, 67, 70
instructions, 54, 62, 87, 96
internal reliability, 123
intrinsic motivation, 34, 39
item tone (positive/negative), 170-174, 189-190

K

Key Driver Analysis (KDA), 359, 364
key tasks, 27, 38

L

labeling points (response options), 152-169, 194-196
    neutral label, 162-169
left-embedded syntax, 73, 85, 88
legal issues with compensation, 36-37, 40
Likelihood-to-Recommend (LTR) item, 109, 120, 140, 389, 391-392
Likert-type item, 109-110, 318-325
linear numeric scale, 109-111
logic branching, 293, 296-299
logistic regression, 361
logistics (planning), 29, 293-299
lotteries, 36, 40

M

MaxDiff, 106-107
McNemar exact test, 282-284, 339, 346-348
measurement, 99-115, 318-334
measurement error, 24-25
memory distortion, 91-92
Microsoft Excel, 307
Microsoft Net Satisfaction (NSAT), 327, 393
Minitab, 307, 309
missing data, 302-305, 308
modal verbs, 78-80

MUiQ, 294-295, 308
multiple panels, 30, 32, 39, 302
mutually exclusive, 102-104, 113,
    311-312

N

n-1 two-proportion test, 343-344, 363
neg2pos scales, 241-243
net box, 327-329, 336
Net Promoter Score (NPS), 391-392
neutral point, 137-147, 149-151, 162-169
noncategorical data, 105-115, 316-334
nonprobability sampling, 44-46
nonresponse error, 23, 25
number of scale points, 116-151, 270-271

O

online panel, 29-32, 38, 294-295
open-ended questions, 99-100, 113, 301,
    334-335
order effect, 217-222, 227-229

P

paired *t*-test, 339-346, 363
panel quality, 31, 39
participation rate, 33-40
passive voice, 86-88
performance item, 111
personalized feedback, 35, 40
personal landmarks, 93-96
planning surveys, 29, 293-299
poll, 3-4, 14-15
population estimates, 30, 39
Post-Study System Usability
    Questionnaire (PSSUQ), 387-38
presentation effects, 204-229
prestige bias, 18-19, 25
primacy (left-side, top-first) biases,
    174-190
probability panels, 31, 39
probability sampling, 42-43
product experience, 27-28, 38, 43
Product-Market Fit (PMF), 394
promoters, 120, 390-391
proportional matching, 43-50

Q

Questionnaire for User Interaction
    Satisfaction (QUIS), 139, 170

R

R statistical package, 307
radio buttons, 244-255
raffle, 36-37, 295
random sampling, 42-43, 45, 50
ranking question, 105, 113
rating scale, 98-99, 108-115, 204-229,
    230-258, 265-278, 281-287, 316-
    329, 339-342, 344-348, 356
    number of points, 116-151, 271-272
recall, improving, 92-96
reconstruction errors, 91, 96
recruiting costs, 294-295
reference period, 60, 63, 66, 91-96
regional effects, 197-203
requests for an answer, 55
research goals, 13, 15, 55, 63, 93
research grid, 13-15
response options, 55-56, 68-70, 75,
    98-115, 124-151, 152-169, 230-258
    adding color, 230-235, 256
    emoji, 235-238, 256
    labeling, 152-169
    number of options, 116-151, 270-271
    sliders, 128-129, 131, 148, 244-258
    stars, 238-241, 257-258
response rates, 23, 33-40, 59
retrieval failure, 90, 95
rubric scales, 153, 159, 162, 168

S

sample size, 260-292
sampling error, 22-23, 376, 382
sampling strategies, 42-50
scale point(s), 116-151, 270-271
Select-All-that-Apply (SATA), 211-217,
    227-229
self-reported behavior, 59-60
semantic adjective items, 108-109
simple random sampling, 42, 45, 50
Single Ease Question (SEQ), 388-389

sliders, 128-129, 131, 148, 244-258
snowball sampling, 44-46, 50
social desirability bias, 18-19, 25
soft launch, 37, 296-299
special item scoring, 329-334
stand-alone analysis, 260-271
stand-alone items, 204-217
Standardized User Experience Percentile
Rank Questionnaire (SUPR-Q),
389-391
standardized UX questionnaires, 5, 7-11,
15, 149, 189
Statistical Package for the Social Sciences
(SPSS), 307, 309
statistical significance, 380-383
straightlining, 205-207, 210-211, 303,
308
stratified random sampling, 42-43, 50
subgroups, 28, 38
Subjective Mental Effort Questionnaire
(SMEQ), 246-248
survey analysis preparation, 307-309
survey question, 52-87
    anatomy, 52-56
    clarify, 81-88
    misinterpretation, 71-80, 189
    types, 52-63, 98-115, 384-395
surveys, history of, 2
surveys, increasing participation, 33-40
sweepstakes, 36, 40
syntax, 72-73, 84-88
System Usability Scale (SUS), 10, 384-387

T

target respondents, 67, 70, 84
task-based question, 60-61
Technology Acceptance Model (TAM),
10, 75, 157, 174-175
    modified Technology Acceptance
    Model (mTAM), 175
ten-point scale, 127, 128, 132, 143-144,
156, 164, 198
three-point scale, 117-124, 129, 148-151
top-box scores, 325-326, 328-329, 336

top-two-box scores, 325, 328-329
two-sample t-test, 339-342

U

UMUX-Lite, 392
unfamiliar terms, 76, 80
Usability Metric for User Experience
(UMUX), 170, 392
usability statistics package, 307, 309
User-Experience-Lite (UX-Lite), 392-393
UX questionnaires, 5, 7-11, 15, 384-395

V

vague concepts, 74, 79
vague modifiers, 60, 75, 127, 130-131
vague quantifiers, 75, 79
variability, 24, 25, 49, 262-263, 266, 279,
291, 304
vertical rating scale, 222-224
visual analog scales, 245

W

website intercepts, 11, 17, 29, 32-33, 38
weighted t-test, 353-356, 364
wh-request, 55, 62, 67, 70
within-subjects, 279-284, 292, 339, 344-
347, 363

Y

Y-Scaling, 367-369

Made in the USA
Monee, IL
09 April 2024

56656725R00262